IDENTITY, GENDER AND POVERTY

New Perspectives on Caste and Tribe in Rajasthan

Maya Unnithan-Kumar

Berghahn Books
Providence • Oxford

First published in 1997 by

Berghahn Books

© Maya Unnithan-Kumar 1997

All rights reserved.
No part of this publication may be reproduced
in any form or by any means
without the written permission of Berghahn Books.

Library of Congress Cataloging-in-Publication Data

```
Unnithan-Kumar, Maya, 1961-
    Identity, gender, and poverty : new perspectives on caste and
  tribe in Rajasthan / Maya Unnithan-Kumar.
       p.    cm.
    Includes bibliographical references and index.
    ISBN 1-57181-918-5 (alk. paper)
    1. Grasia (Indic people)  2. Women, Grasia.  3. India--Scheduled
  tribes.  4. Caste--India.  I. Title.
  DS432.G7U55  1997
  305.42'089'914--dc21                                        97-15986
                                                                  CIP
```

British Library Cataloguing in Publication Data

A catalogue record for this book is available
from the British Library.

Printed in the United States on acid-free paper.

CONTENTS

Preface and Acknowledgements	vi
Note on Abbreviations, Italics, Measures etc.	xi
General Map of India: Showing Sirohi in Rajasthan	xii

Chapter 1: Introduction 1
    Identities, Communities, Boundaries
    Women, Gender and Differences
    Poverty and Identity
    Tribes in Southern Rajasthan
    The Context of 'Fieldwork'
    The Plan of the Book

Chapter 2: Historical Background: The Rajput State and Related Identities 45
    Organisation of the Rajput State
    'Writing' and Representing the Rajputs

Chapter 3: Rajputs and Girasias in Independent India: Identity Politics and Administration 69
    Rajput 'Custom' and Women
    'Tribe' in Official Classifications

Chapter 4: Being a Girasia: The Lineage and the Village 94
    The Taivar Lineage and Related Social Units
    Experiencing Age and Gender Differences

Chapter 5: Across Villages: Marriage Ideals, Practices and Strategies 121
    Processes of Marriage
    The Stated and Unstated Rules of Marriage
    Marriage Negotiation and Lineage Boundaries
    Marriage and Hierarchy in the Region

Chapter 6: Resource Management and the Divisions of Kinship and Gender 156
    The Lineage and Subsistence: Land, Water, Labour
    Food Transactions and Status
    The Market and Girasia Identity

Contents

Chapter 7: Girasia Brideprice and the Politics of Marriage Payments — 189
  Some Issues in the Study of Marriage Payments
  Girasia Brideprice
  Brideprice and Economic Transactions
  Marriage Payments and Gender Inequalities
  Marriage Payments, Shifting Economic Pressures and Identities

Chapter 8: Religion and the Experience of Kinship — 215
  Locating the Sacred
  Religion and Power in the Lineage

Chapter 9: Class, Resistance and Identity — 238
  The Anop Mandal and Peasant Resistance in Southern Rajasthan
  The Girasia 'Believers'

Chapter 10: Conclusions — 264

Appendix 1: List of Scheduled Tribes: Rajasthan — 269
  Note on Scheduled Castes/Scheduled Tribes

Appendix 2: Rural Population of Garasias and Bhils in Rajasthan by District — 270

Glossary — 271
Bibliography — 274
Index — 289

Tables/Figures/Maps

Tables:

1.1	Area and Population of Rajasthan and Sirohi	33
1.2	Distribution of Tribal Population in Sirohi	34
1.3	Distribution of Scheduled Tribe and Scheduled Castes in Sirohi	36
3.1	Apparel of Girasia Women and Some Non-Girasia Women	75
3.2	Jewellery of Girasia Women and Some Non-Girasia Women	76
4.1	Distribution of Taivar Households According to Sublineages and Geographical Location	98
4.2	Distribution of Non-Taivar Households According to Geographical Location	98
4.3	Number of Elders and Other Adults Resident in Taivar Households	100
5.1	Details of a Girasia Wedding	130
5.2	Affinal Lineages of Wives in the Taivar Village	141
6.1	Land Use in the Taivar Girasia Village	157

6.2	Quantity of Corn Produced in 1985 and 1986 for 56 Taivar Households	158
6.3	Distribution of Landholdings in the Taivar Village for 56 Taivar and 12 Non-Taivar Households	161
6.4	Distribution of Well Shares in the Taivar Village for 56 Taivar and 12 Non-Taivar Households	162
6.5	Expenditure on the Funeral of Pema's Daughter-in-Law	176
8.1	Taivar Girasia Ritual Occasions	219

Figures

4.1	The Vaijjath Hojvan (Sublineage)	98
5.1	Vaijjath-Damar Marriages (A, B)	142
6.1	Well Sharers in Beechalli *Phalli*	165
9.1	'Believers' in the Vaijjath Hojvan (Sublineage)	250

Maps

India, showing Sirohi in Rajasthan	xvi
1.1 Abu Road *Tehsil*	36

PREFACE AND ACKNOWLEDGEMENTS

*I*n India, members of a 'tribe' are generally considered to be very different from the majority of women and men who live in caste groups. It is this apparent contrast between tribal and caste lifestyles and the paucity of material on tribal groups which lay behind my desire to stay with a tribal community. I was particularly eager to spend time with women who lived in circumstances very different from my own. Growing up in urban north India, I had been struck by the distinctive attire, the *ghagra-odhani* (skirt and wrap) worn by village women in contrast to the *sari* of the urban, middle- and upper-class and caste women. I had always wanted to find out what village women talked about, how they viewed other groups and how they constructed the world around them. If village women seemed a world apart, 'tribal' women seemed even more mysterious and difficult to know. In the academic as well as non-academic material I came across, tribal women were always described in opposed terms to women in caste society. Most forcibly, tribal women were perceived to be endowed with a greater 'freedom' and to be 'valued' in terms of their contributions in the work sphere. If this was indeed the case, I wanted to know what implications this 'freedom' had for the control over productive resources which tribal women were likely to have when compared to 'traditional' Hindu wives. In 1986, with these images and ideas in my head and as part of my Ph.D work at Cambridge University, I went to stay with a group of 'tribals', the Girasia in Rajasthan.

The issue of the differences between urban, village and tribal women in northern India led me to a concern with the wider issue of identity, of the similarities and differences between members, communities, and between caste and tribe. The picture of tribes as different to caste was I found, largely constructed by those unfamiliar with the history, culture and economy of the so called tribal people. Fieldwork was to reveal that the difference was often a construct of the outsider. In fact, what became evident were the similarities in the discourse on difference, especially how both insider (member) and outsider (non-member) descriptions of community identities referred to women in their portrayal of the distinctiveness of a community. A detailed study of Girasia kinship and gender roles, relations and experiences revealed more continuity than difference with north Indian caste society. Living with the Girasia, the concerns of my research shifted from, among other issues, explaining why and how the Girasia were similar and different from the rest of caste society, to why a difference was perceived and sustained. In this sense, the research into Girasia identity came to revolve around a regional, historical discourse of power rooted in economic inequality.

In India, where the identities of social groups, especially those perceived to be on the social, cultural and economic margins of society, are linked to the dispersal of state funds, the question as to whether a community such as the Girasia is a caste or a tribe becomes not merely an academic issue but one which has major implications for the Girasia themselves. The Girasia are included in the list of Scheduled Tribes in Rajasthan but not in the neighbouring state of Gujarat. Being 'scheduled' or identified for support by the state, entitles the Girasia to receive a certain quota of the state's resources allocated to the development of tribal areas. In reality, this translates into the provision of handpumps for drinking water, health, veterinary and agricultural facilities, all necessary to help the Girasia cope with their exacting, harsh and marginally productive environment. Social and cultural identities have increasingly become linked to strategies for social and economic mobility in post-independence India. Work on community identifications, such as presented in this work, may inevitably and unintentionally become party to this process of the politics of representation. What I would stress at the outset, therefore, is that whatever the findings of the present study, the Girasia remain a poor community with every need to get state funds to help them survive the rigours of their daily existence.

There was disease and scarcity of food and fodder in the village in 1986 as a result of the successive failure of the monsoons in the two years prior to my fieldwork. When I revisited the village in 1989, I was told that up to a hundred people had died in the previous year, mainly the elderly and children, due to their inability to cope with malaria and dysentry. What was striking though, was that the hardship of their lives was never overridingly evident in the conversations or attitudes of Taivar men and women. A major impression, which the statistics on deprivation cannot convey, is the zest for life shown by those Girasia women whom I came to know. It was by the happiness and friendliness of these women that my research interests were sustained. I would especially like to thank Palvi, my 'elder sister', for teaching me the Girasia ways. Palvi bai had a unique position among the women in the village as she was one of the few daughters who had 'brought' in a resident son-in-law and lived in her 'own' (father's/brothers') village rather than live as a married wife in another village. It was Palvi's confidence, based on her being the 'eldest daughter' (for most daughters were married early into other villages), which gave her a position of authority in contrast to the subordinate roles of other married women in the village. She was among the more progressive women, and played a significant role in the

Preface

state's *anganwadi* (government childcare) activities in the village. It was due to her support that my intentions as a researcher were not misunderstood.

The Girasia were quite surprised that I had come to stay in their village, not just as a someone whose motives were not quite clear to them, but also because they saw their own place as inhospitable. The village is part of a wider area, popularly known as the *Bhakar* (rugged hilly terrain). I was told that 'before the days of the *sarkar* [national Indian government] no-one would dare enter the *Bhakar* except at the risk of death'. No-one, not even the Girasia walked unarmed and without a gun, sword or bow and arrows, especially on trips outside the village. Women were either accompanied by men carrying arms or carried axes themselves and usually travelled with one or more companions. It is possible that, for most of the period of my stay, the belief remained among some Girasia that the cotton sling bag in which I carried my notebook, camera and tape-recorder, actually contained a gun. Although the Girasias are bound by the Indian constitution as citizens of India to submit to the law and state authorities, the Girasia experienced police and related security activity only outside the *Bhakar*. Within the *Bhakar* and other Bhil and Girasia areas in the surrounding region, they continued to protect themselves. There were frequent disputes relating to landholding, adultery and brideprice payments among the Girasia groups, which could continue for several generations. The most worrying social situation for both the villagers and for me was the tense period following the murder of one of the residents who was found sleeping with another man's wife. Violence and arms were a way of life linked to the difficult economic conditions in which the Girasia lived. Periods of scarcity and drought were particularly insecure times and then, I was told, 'even Girasia stole from Girasia'. I was thus constantly uneasy and aware of being a target for thieves.

For most of the first two months I was quite scared to be in the *Bhakar*, not just because of what the few Girasia I met told me, but also by uncertain and unpredictable encounters with snakes and scorpions. With the nearest serious medical care almost twenty two kilometres away, I often felt a strong urge to pack and leave whilst I could. These fears were perhaps enhanced by a general feeling of isolation. Unlike my experience in other Indian villages, villagers in the *Bhakar* do not rush out to meet visitors. Unlike other multi-caste villages, the Girasia huts are scattered over the hills and I found it difficult to get a sense of the village as a bounded geographical and social unit. Showing a city bias against isolated habitations, I asked a woman of the village whether she felt unsafe living in houses so far apart. To this she replied, 'Living like this we see much more clearly who approaches our house as well as who visits other houses. It is the closely packed houses of the towns that scare us, because then you cannot see who comes to your house and you can be more often taken by surprise'. As a woman who had come to stay in a village, I found that there was no immediate adoption or invitation to stay with a family, as is common in other villages. Later I came to realise that it was the Girasia's own fear, both of my perceived ambiguous intentions and of their poverty. Being poor made the obligatory hospitality towards visitors difficult to sustain. I was apprehensive being a 'woman on my own' (with no father or brother at close quarters), although Vishwanathan, a young boy from my father's village in south India had accompanied me to assist in the nitty gritty of domestic work. He became an honorary younger brother and to some extent provided me with 'protection'. I thank him, especially, for all the buckets of water that he carried from the well and for his help with cooking and cleaning which without him would have been enormous tasks for the conditions in which we lived.

Praveen Purohit was one of those rare outsiders trusted by the Taivar Girasia and it was my good luck to have him help me during my stay, particularly in the initial stages in finding my way around the thirty-six square kilometres of the village and to the huts spread over the hills in the area. Purohitji's familiarity with the Girasia was based on thirteen years of work as an Ayurvedic assistant. Known locally as 'doctor-ji' he was a resident of one of the nearest multicaste villages in the area and had provided 'out of duty' medical aid (often in the form of allopathic remedies) to several Girasia families in the village. He had also studied with Phoola, the Girasia headmaster of the village primary school. Despite Purohitji's presence which allowed me to visit some Girasia families in the first days of my fieldwork, in retrospect I realise what an intrusion my very presence constituted and how odd it must have all seemed to the Girasia. Thankfully, I became more articulate in the unwritten dialect spoken by the Girasia which is a mixture of Bhili, Gujarati and Marwari, and, helped by my developing friendship with the *anganwadi* Girasia women, the major social barriers were overcome.

Apart from the opportunity to stay with another community in the country in which I grew up, the concerns of my work also introduced me to Britain and the English ways, to yet different kinds of identities and representations. I learnt of academic preoccupations and ways of writing and different contexts of isolation and togetherness. It made me think about the differences between Indian anthropologists and sociologists and British and European anthropologists, and the extent to which my growing up in Rajasthan, although not with the Girasia, could lead to an 'indigenous' view. There is perhaps something in the idea that European anthropologists who start from a secondary understanding of Indian society may hold certain views more strongly because that is all they know, whereas an Indian anthropologist may know, but not know that they know. This is not to suggest that those who are natives (or near natives) make better anthropologists but rather to query why so few Indians make good anthropologists. I think this has to do with the use of a specific kind of writing (transmitting, translating, representing and conceptualising) in English which privileges Anglo-Saxon academics as well as a certain section of upper-class Indians. I have had the opportunity to acquire an English medium education in India, and even then do not always find it easy to express myself in ways which satisfactorily, or even elegantly, convey what I mean, often making me feel disadvantaged in the process.

Preface

This work is the product of many conversations and discussions. I would especially like to thank Caroline Humphrey, who supervised my thesis, not only for her support and guidance, but especially for making me know more fully both what I knew and what I did not. Pat Caplan and Esther Goody were helpful and considerate examiners. Pat Caplan's encouraging words whenever I wrote to her have been a source of inspiration. It has been good to have had Ursula Sharma's thoughtful feedback and advice. Barbara Bodenhorn and Simon Coleman, also engaged in thesis activity, were always accessible for discussing many of the issues, especially what anthropology is all about. Various parts of the study have benefited from comments made by Ernest Gellner, Chris Bayly, Declan Quigley, Jean-Claude Galey and Vinita Damodaran. I thank them all. In India I gratefully acknowledge the help I received from N.N. Vyas at the MLV Tribal Research Institute in Udaipur, the staff of the Rajasthan University Library in Jaipur for access to the Abu Collection, the members of Gujarat Vidyapeeth particularly R.B. Lal, the officers of the Sirohi district, *tehsil, panchayat samiti* and Tribal Area Development offices and Vinod and Dudha Kumar. A special note of appreciation for Kavita Srivastava and Gerda Unnithan who have shared with me their rich experiences of women's concerns and agency in Rajasthan, and to Narayan Unnithan for helpful discussions. Since the completion of my thesis I have been at Sussex and would like to thank Hilary Standing, Ralph Grillo and Anne Whitehead for their pertinent and thought-provoking comments on my work presented in the anthropology seminars. A special thanks to Hilary Standing and Barbara Bodenhorn for their editorial input, and to Jan Brogden for help with the tables. An unrepayable debt is due to Sanjiv Kumar for his encouragement, unfailing support at home and work, and for his assistance with the computer.

For the finances which sustained me I appreciate the assistance given to me by the Ling Roth Fund (Department of Anthropology, Cambridge), the William Wyse Fund (Trinity College, Cambridge), the Radcliffe-Brown Fund (Royal Anthropological Institute), the Smuts Fund (Cambridge University), the Worts and Chadwick Funds (Cambridge University) and the Charles Wallace Fund (British Council). For initial help, the financial assistance given by George Kurien is much appreciated. I would also like to mention with thanks the Haddon Museum and Paul Sant Cassia for the grant from the Crowther Beynon fund to make a collection for the museum. This led to an interesting exploration of material artefacts of the Girasia which may otherwise not have taken place with such attention to detail.

This book is dedicated to Gerda Unnithan, Narayanan Unnithan and Sanjiv Kumar who have given so much of themselves in its production. Vikram Unnithan and little Arjun have sustained me in their belief of the unimportance of such ventures.

Preface

Notes on Abbreviations, Measures, Italics and other Matters

- Terms indicating kinship relations such as 'father', 'mother', 'brother' have been abbreviated in capitals by their first letters, except for the term 'sister', which is denoted by a Z. For example, FBDS refers to the father's brother's daughter's son, and WZH refers to the wife's sister's husband. The letters 'e' and 'y', refer to elder and younger respectively.
- I have italicised all indigenous Girasia and Indian words, both in my own work and in quotes and in references to the work of others. I have done this to introduce uniformity in the following text and to facilitate its reading.
- I have added the letter 's' after native terms when I refer to them in the plural form. In local usage, the term by itself could refer to the singular or the plural form, depending on the context.
- In the text I use the Indian rupee (abbreviated Rs.) as the monetary unit. The rate of exchange of the rupee to the pound sterling in 1986/87 was approximately thirty rupees to the pound. Apart from the rupee, the Girasia talk in terms of the *viri*, a unit equivalent to twenty rupees. For convenience, I use only the rupee as the monetary unit.
- The Girasi measure for weight is the *her* or the kilo, equivalent to one kilogram. The smallest measure for weighing grain was the *paili*. For example, four *paili* are equivalent to two and a half kilograms. I use the kilogram (or kilo; abbreviated as kg.) as the measure for weight.
- The census statistics for population and area used are based on the 1981 census documents of the Indian government. The 1991 census material only became accessible in parts in the summer of 1995. I mention the later figures in the footnotes and only if they are significantly different from the previous figures.
- Some of the material used in the book has previously appeared as articles in journals elsewhere (see bibliography).

India, showing Sirohi in Rajasthan

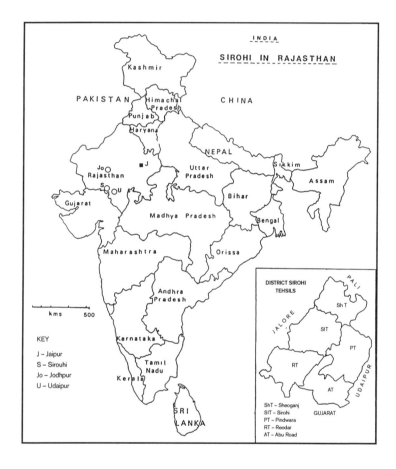

Adapted from sketches of J. Reynell (1985) and Rajasthan District Census Handbook (1981).

Chapter 1

INTRODUCTION

Most studies of the so-called tribal communities in India stress their social, economic, and political differences from communities organised on the basis of caste.[1] Drawing on the experiences of a poor community of Girasia 'tribals' in Rajasthan, northwestern India, this book questions the distinction between caste and tribe made by academics. Historical material indicates that the Girasia have been subject to processes which have marginalised them from the dominantly caste-based society of Rajasthan. Despite the Girasia claim of belonging to a Rajput caste, others regard the Girasia as tribal. Contestations and conflicts over identifications are features particularly associated with the colonial and postcolonial processes of administration in India, and lead me to suggest that the boundaries between communities such as caste and tribe are not as clear, or as impermeable, as has been imagined. Caste and tribe, I believe, are constructed and represent categories which are products of historical and contemporary social, economic and political processes. If we examine this interplay between lived social facts and imaginings, we can begin an examination of them as much more fluid than has so far been acknowledged in writings on India.

1. For example, Doshi 1971, 1978, Sinha 1962, Vyas and Mann 1978, Meherda 1985, Dave 1960, Deliege 1985, Furer-Haimendorf 1982, Fuchs 1973, Dube 1977, Majumdar 1937,1961, Vidyarthi 1986, Mandelbaum 1980, Dumont 1980, Bird 1982. Notable exceptions are Bailey 1960, Chauhan 1978, Beteille 1984, 1986, Trautman 1981.

The central concern of the present study is not so much with the categories of caste and tribe per se, but with the wider and more complex issue of identification and the processes by which communities and people choose to represent themselves, or, conversely, are powerless in the ways they are represented by others. The book is, thus, about what Girasia women and men think of themselves and others and how they, in turn, are perceived by the world around them. Caste and tribe distinctions, while they are important, are not central to everyday relations among the Girasia where processes of descent and marriage, as well as scarcity and hardship, drive identifications. The book suggests that the different perceptions of Girasia identity, the ways the Girasia construct and negotiate their identities, the ways in which they and others insist on a seeing of themselves as different, and the ways in which they want to be the same, must all be seen in the context of their poverty as well as in the strategic use of kinship and gender relations in the region. Focusing on identity allows me, on the one hand, to present the Girasia self-image in relation to more widespread concerns with representation in northern Indian society; on the other hand, it allows me to consider the more general issue of the symbolic construction, expression and use of differences and similarities between groups and people. What emerges from the study is the important role that kinship, gender and poverty play in the conceptualisation, evaluation and presentation of identifications. These are matters of interest and relevance not only to South Asianists but also to those who regard South Asian ethnography as unintelligible, caste-driven and accessible only to the initated.

The story I have to tell is a complicated one and many different 'grounds' need to be set out before I can address the arguments themselves. In this introductory chapter I discuss some of the core ideas which form the backdrop to the book. The central themes of the book are raised in three sections of this first chapter. The section on 'Identities, Communities, Boundaries' considers some recent trends in the studies on caste and related identities; I also discuss the politically orientated, academic and administrative constructions of the category of tribe in India. The section on 'Women, Gender and Differences' looks at both the symbolic and material dimensions in studies of gender representations in anthropology, with reference to studies on Indian women. In the following section, I discuss briefly the ways in which poverty is important for this work. In the rest of the chapter I describe specific details relating to my fieldwork, first locating this study in the social and geographical context of Sirohi in southern Rajasthan in the section on 'Tribes in Southern Rajasthan'.

I will then comment on the process of 'fieldwork' and my own experiences of Girasia experiences.

At the widest level, I use material on Girasia kinship, gender, economy, authority and religious beliefs and practices to talk about my understandings, at best a partial account, of what it means to be Girasia. I present Girasia preoccupations in terms of the concerns of other groups in the region, especially the Rajput and Bhil, two communities with whom the Girasia most closely identify. The Rajput are the landed, erstwhile ruling caste in Rajasthan; the Bhil are the archetypical 'tribe' who are popularly considered 'primitive' and outside the caste system. The Girasia claim to be Rajput, others see them as relatives of the Bhil. My own experiences with the Girasia indicate that, given the complexities of the politics of identities in the region, it is impossible to use 'caste' to describe some communities and 'tribe' to describe others. It has been more worthwhile to explore how these identities have been invested with meaning and used in the social, political and economic strategies of the individuals and communities concerned. Fieldwork and archival research lead me to the following conclusions. Firstly, I find that the Rajput, Bhil and Girasia communities share a centrality of territorially defined lineal kinship in their lives which leads them to experience caste in ways which are both similar to and, at the same time different from caste as we know it generally, i.e., as a set of agnatic and affinal groups dispersed over a wide territory.[2] Secondly, the shift in the meaning of caste for the Rajputs, in response to the politics of the nation state, to a more generally experienced diffuse caste identity, has further marginalised lower groups such as the Girasia and Bhil from their claims to a status based on being members of a Rajput caste. The increasingly tribal identity of the Girasia is not merely of academic concern but has implications for their existing and future control over the economic, political and symbolic resources in the region and state. Thirdly, some of the Girasia have responded to the changing political and economic circumstances by moving towards the formation of class-type solidarities which reinforce rather than negate their ties based on kinship. Fourthly, gender is an important means of representing, conceptualising and evaluating identities, both among communities as well as at various individual and group levels within them. While the perceptions of gender roles and relations seemingly

2. In a historical study of the Rajput polity in Uttar Pradesh, Fox, 1975 has made a similar observation of the different conception of caste among the Rajput as compared to other castes.

vary across the communities in the region, there are striking similarities between the structural and ideological contexts in which women and men live in Rajasthan. The conclusions outlined point to three core areas of the study: firstly, the importance of lineal kinship and descent in understanding caste and related identities; secondly, the prevalence of a greater degree of fluidity in status and authority within and between communities which allows for a negotiated social order; and, thirdly, the centrality of kinship and gender in the experience and conceptualisation of wider, kin and non kin, social relationships and in processes of identification. Although central to any study of India, the combination of these issues has not, to my knowledge, been the focus of any study in Rajasthan so far. This book contributes not only to the limited ethnographic information available on marginalised ('tribal') groups such as the Girasia, but also provides insights into the study of social processes in India, more generally.

Identities, Communities, Boundaries

'the sense of social self at the levels of both individuality and collectivity are informed by implicit or explicit contrast' (Cohen 1985, 115)

Part of my discovery as an anthropologist among the Girasia was that the very institutions and practices which embodied a Girasia identity also contained similarities which they shared with other caste and tribal groups in the region. Thus, like Cohen (1985), I find that the simultaneous presence of similarities and differences in social organisation lies at the heart of questions of identity.[3] The Girasia had a distinct identity which could not be suitably portrayed as 'tribal'. The ways in which the Girasia have come to be described as 'tribal' and their increasingly tribalised identity is related to the images which the non-Girasia project on to them, images which are informed by the notions of caste held by the dominant and powerful communities in India, specific caste groups, as well as by academics and government administrators.

3. I follow Cohen's use of the term 'community', which is predicated on the notion of the simultaneous possession of similarity and difference in that the community is a group within which members have something in common amongst themselves and who also share a similar difference to other groups. For Cohen, the use of the word community is motivated by its members' desire or need to express a distinction (1985:12). Cohen's work is important as it moves the focus away from the structure to look at the meanings of community to its members.

In 1986-87 there were approximately 60,000 Girasia living in the district of Sirohi in Rajasthan (see general map of India). Like most other locals, the Girasia were a community of poor farmers. However, unlike the local population who lived in multicaste villages, the Girasia lived in single caste villages which were most often in the hilly and relatively inaccessible parts of the district at some distance from the other castes. Unlike the members of the neighbouring multicaste villages, the Girasia were not connected to towns and trade centres through transport facilities and nor did they benefit from a flow of services and communication. The Girasia village in which I stayed had members of mainly one lineage, called the Taivar. The lineage members were subdivided into eight sublineages which were important as far as relationships within the village and lineage were concerned. While I did not see the tribe/caste distinction as a real one with regard to the Girasia, I suggest that the notion of 'inside' (those considered part of) and 'outside' (those not part of) is important in order to understand the Girasia sense of their own identity, both in the representation of one Girasia group vis-à-vis other Girasia groups and the personal senses of Girasia identity in relations internal to the group.

Identities are analytically complex to study because they are constructed and shifting, not fixed, entities, which can be negotiated, contested and reformulated as categories of representation. Furthermore, the categories caste, tribe and gender especially, are also products of imposition and dominance which at the same time have practical realities. In this sense, a study of identity becomes, above all, a study of the process and politics of social relations. I use the concept of identity and identifications rather than ethnicity to talk about the Girasia because I can then describe processes of differentiation between communities which were clearly not ethnically exclusive. Furthermore, such an approach allows me to account for what I saw as the more immediate senses of Girasia identity which were at the social and the personal levels within their community.[4] I suggest that boundaries are constructed to maintain identity not only at the level of caste and tribe, but also at the levels of sub-groups and people within them.[5]

4. Following Hall (1992), I see identity in its sociological sense as a concept which brings together the 'inside' and the 'outside', the personal and the public worlds. For Hall there is at the same time a projection of oneself into a given cultural identity and the internalisation of its meaning and values in a way which fixes identity to the subjective and objective, social and cultural positions one occupies (Hall, ibid.: 276).
5. In this I follow the anthropological approach to identity developed in the late 1960s and represented in the works of Barth 1969, Berreman 1972, Epstein 1978,

Differences or boundaries of the caste/tribe or other inside/outside levels (such as class, religion, language etc.) are essentially maintained by members because they represent their separate and distinct identities. In turn, the boundaries are most symbolised because they are the places where the distinctions/differences are the most marked.[6] Both the maintenance of distinctions and the symbolisation of them indicate the strategic use to which boundaries and identities are put. The boundary then becomes, in Cohen's words, a good model to formulate the interests of the group's members (Cohen, ibid., 107). The social and cultural boundaries become most 'visible' in the context of social interactions between groups and members, as the Girasia material in the book powerfully demonstrates. While members of a community use the same symbolic constructions of the boundary, Cohen suggests, it may mean different things to them.[7] It thus becomes important to address the way members relate to their identities, maintaining them or even changing them. So far I have talked about identities as created, maintained and changed as a self conscious process of a group and its members, but often identities may also be forced and imposed as a result of wider inequalities of power, as in the way the label of 'tribe' has become attached to the Girasia.

The preoccupation in South Asian anthropology with the concept of hierarchy as structuring relations between homogeneously acting caste units has, I suggest, drawn academic attention away from the study of how individuals or groups construct boundaries (differences) within (inside) their communities both in terms of hierarchy and in terms other than hierarchy.[8] I would suggest, contrary to the emphasis on intergroup dynamics, that it is intragroup rela-

---

Barth 1978, Cohen 1985, Tapper 1989. In their studies, identity came to be seen as formed through social interactions rather than based on the possession of essential qualities intrinsic to the groups in question. For these scholars, a focus on boundaries and interaction between social groups was a way out of the earlier emphasis on the cultural uniqueness of the groups in question.

6. The more one goes into a community or 'down the scale' of identity, the boundaries may become less objectively visible, but at the same time more symbolically constructed (Cohen, ibid.: 13).

7. According to Cohen, conceiving of the boundary in symbolic, rather than structural, terms allows an understanding of the different meanings which members give to the boundary (the individual component) while at the same time investing it with a shared meaning (the collective component).

8. According to Appadurai (1983) for example, hierarchy is only one facet of caste of which there are other, more inclusive principles and processes which are at the same time more closely connected to culturally specific moral and biological concerns. As Cohen (1985) cautions, a concentration on the structure of

tions, based on kinship and gender in the context of shiftig economic considerations, which provide the paradigm for intergroup interactions. Well known commentators on caste organisation such as Hocart, Dumont and their followers, who concentrated on structure and structural change respectively, gave us to believe that caste society, more than any other society, was one in which the boundaries between groups were well and rigidly defined. This in turn makes it difficult to account for the strategic and shifting uses to which group identities are put. Nevertheless, I regard the insights of Hocart and Dumont regarding the nature of social dominance and the centrality of notions of 'purity', respectively, to be of crucial importance to more recent studies of identity; I will discuss this in the following subsection. I see the present study as contributing to the emerging, alternative perspectives on Indian society which are concerned with the diverse and politicised constructions, individual, collective, historical and contemporary, of social identifications, including caste.[9]

The following subsection on 'Hierarchy and Fluidity in Studies on Caste' provides the background by looking at the work of some major theorists and their preoccupations with structure in earlier studies on caste, and the shift towards meaning and fluidity of identities in more recent studies on India. Even though 'tribe' has been treated as a category separate from caste in most studies, it has nevertheless been influenced by the way caste has been conceptualised. The second subsection on 'Caste and the Concept of Tribe' describes the category of tribe in India as it has been constituted in academic terms.

Hierarchy and Fluidity in Studies on Caste

There have been a vast number of studies on the institution of caste in India.[10] Yet it is only recently that the complexities in the study of caste are emerging. Members of a caste unit have, most often, been regarded as related through birth, endogamy, a hierarchy of occupations and a restricted commensality (Dumont 1980, Inden and Marriott 1974). Most theorists on caste, notably followers of Hocart, Dumont and Marriott who represent the major trends, agree on its 'organic nature' or the stratified division of labour and occupation of

---

groups, which I see in the focus on hierarchy, can only reveal the simplified common identity which the members of a group present to the outside world.
9. Among the most recent examples are Searle-Chatterjee and Sharma, 1994; Raheja and Gold, 1994.
10. Already in 1946, when Hutton published his book on caste in India, there existed over 5,000 published works on caste (1946: 1).

caste groups, but disagree on what holds the system in its state of hierarchy. More recent studies stress that it is productive also to consider the role of centrality and egalitarianism rather than solely hierarchy in defining social relations in caste communities.[11] Some authors, for example, emphasise that differences in occupations are not necessarily representative of caste differences.[12] Increasingly, it is becoming important to approach caste not just as a system of ideological classification (in terms of *varna*) or social grouping *(jati)* but in terms of the relationship between the two as experienced through the everyday religious, economic and political contexts in which women and men live. The following lines trace some of the concerns with the structure of caste that have stimulated new ways of thinking about the processes of social organisation in India.

For Hocart (1950), caste was a product of divine kingship and centred on the sacrificial nature of Hindu ritual. The king as patron and chief sacrificer (the foremost servant of god) occupied the position of supreme authority at the apex, and all the other *varna* had their occupations specified by the nature of their service to the king. For Dumont (1980; first published in 1960) on the other hand, caste was a product of the Hindu preoccupation with purity and pollution. The priests of the Brahmin *varna* had to be necessarily 'pure' (by unmixed birth and having no association with unclean occupations) in order to fulfil their occupation as servants to the gods of the Hindu pantheon. According to Dumont, a consequence of the purity of the priests was their position as the most superior caste. (In Hocart's classification of the Hindu social order, the priests were seen as assistants to the king in his role as chief sacrificer). For Dumont the graded occupations relative to the ritual purity of the Brahmin priests defined the structure of the caste system. This notion has, however, been subject to much criticism.[13] I find a combination of both the 'purity' and 'dominance' models important for this study. The ideas of Hocart are, more so than Dumont, relevant in understanding social and political processes in states such as Rajasthan which have been dom-

11. For example, Parry 1974, Barnett 1977, Daniel 1984, Raheja 1988.
12. Barnett 1977, Daniel 1984.
13. According to Fuller (1979), for example, the concepts of purity and pollution which for Dumont structured the caste hierarchy have wider meanings than those solely related to caste identity. For Fuller, 'pollution, sin and evil, disrespect towards gods and divine anger are all interconnected. They are not identical to each other but pollution does not have to do only with social status but rather with morality and the relationship between gods and men as well' (ibid.: 493; with reference to Das, 1970, and O'Flaherty, 1976).

inated by kings and chiefs (the *kshatriya varna*). Recent research supporting Hocart's position asserts that Dumont's emphasis in presenting the priest caste *(brahmin varna)* at the apex of the caste system is misplaced (Fuller, 1979)[14] and a product of colonial classification (Quigley 1989, 1994).[15] There is support for Hocart's ideas from studies in other ethnographic regions as well.[16]

Apart from Hocart and Dumont, Marriott (1976) has spearheaded a different approach to the study of caste. Marriott gave an impetus to transactionalist and culturally orientated studies on caste. For Marriott, who was influenced by Hocart, it was not purity and pollution but the maintenance of subordination through transaction which was the key to caste hierarchy. He presented caste transactions within the monist context of divisible or 'dividual' beings to avoid the duality of Western thought reflected, for example, in the work of Dumont. Through the study of transactions based on exchange relationships, Marriott has been able to present a greater fluidity between the positions of the individual and the collective, a position closer to the observed reality of complex caste interactions. Both the transactor and what is transacted unite in Marriott's theory of 'encoded substance' through which he is able to explain the various dimensions of social rank. The implications of such a perspective can

14. Fuller (1979) questions Dumont's claim of supreme status for the priest based on the notion that the priest's purity allowed him divine access. Fuller's assertion in turn casts doubt on many academic observers who use the priest/god relation as an analogy to explain the relations between high and low castes. Fuller suggests that the relationship of the priest to the divine hierarchy was like that of an unequal wife with her husband and not, as Dumont suggests, like that of a low-caste servant to his high-caste master (ibid.: 470).
15. According to Quigley, and it is perhaps by now common knowledge, the Brahmin priest because of his literary and ritual knowledge was privileged by the British colonial officials who came from a Western tradition which respected literacy. The colonial officials privileged the Kshatriya (caste of warrior clans) in a different manner because they were a ruling class with noble and martial qualities, and equally divorced from ritual responsibilities as the lords in feudal England (1989, ibid.: 17). The colonial officials reinforced the category of 'martial race' in relation to the Kshatriyas (which in turn supported the recruitment requirements of the Imperial armed forces in India). It is these insights which lead recent researchers to claim that in colonial India, the priests exchanged places with the kings at the apex of the caste hierarchy.
16. Sahlins' (1985) work on the relationship between history and anthropology in the context of Fiji, New Zealand and Hawaii, emphasises Hocart's view on the importance of primogeniture for the noble lineages in the system. Sahlins finds his own model of the hierarchic heroic society similar to that of Hocart's divine theory of kingship, especially in the stress on an internal diachrony. Sahlins criticises Dumont for ignoring this in his comparatively rigid structural analysis.

be seen in the kind of research it has stimulated, especially related to an analysis of the multidimensional aspects of caste identity and interaction, the individual and personhood. Although Marriott himself does not question the importance of occupation as a signifier of caste, those who follow him do so.[17]

Barnett (1977), for example, studying contemporary identity choice and caste ideology among the KV (a fictitious abbreviation) Tamil community in South India, observes a reduced emphasis by the KV Tamils on customary and prescribed modes of behaviour in occupational interactions. Simultaneously, according to Barnett, there has been a greater emphasis on purity by birth. He shows that the decreased importance given to codes of conduct between castes has widened the choice of identity for the KV Tamils. He refers to the added emphasis on blood purity (and birth, the 'substance' aspect of caste) as resulting in the 'substantialisation' of caste for the KV Tamils who can, for example, group themselves at the regional level, under the racial banner of 'Dravidian'. Barnett's study shows how identity is structured less by the holistic conceptions of caste and more by a specific selection of attributes (i.e., where birth becomes more important than occupation as a factor of differentiation). Kolenda (1978), too, questions the importance of occupational specialisation resulting from the Brahmanic needs of purity and pollution.[18] Processes by which selective aspects of caste have become important for identifications are noted in Rajasthan as well. On the one hand, there has been a 'substantialisation' of caste in regional politics where different Rajput clans and lineages have come together under the common banner of 'Rajput'.[19] On the other hand, there are communities such

17. For example, Barnett 1977, Daniel 1984, Raheja 1988.
18. Contemporary trends, noted by Kolenda (also see Tambiah, 1973), show a decline in ranking of the traditionally, occupationally specialised interdependent castes, by purity and pollution. She predicts a future 'beyond organic solidarity', wherein the new system would have a competitive solidarity, as fused combinations of castes compete with one another. This is in contrast to the cooperative but hierarchical organic solidarity of the traditional system'(ibid.: 4, 5). For Kolenda, the permanent features of caste are kinship and descent. Kolenda and Barnett (1977) make the important observation that the organic theory of caste is simplistic and ill-equipped to explain the complexities of caste-orientated action in India. A similar thought is echoed by Sahlins in his elaboration of the hierarchic heroic model of Hocart. For Sahlins the structure of such a heroic society can be seen as 'interjecting and cross-cutting the caste/tribe polarity based on organic society'. In other words the heroic society gives opportunity to individual endeavour outside the organically (functionally) orientated caste rules of action, and a position for achievement besides ascription.
19. Kothari, 1970, chapter 3, this volume.

as the Girasia, who remain on the margins of the recent, national, political processes and for whom birth defined genealogical units such as the *jath* [20] or lineage which are couched in terms of the 'purity' of kinship, remain central in matters of identity and subsistence. Daniel (1984) echoes the same sentiment in his study on Tamil personhood in South India.[21]

While Dumont, Hocart and to a lesser extent Marriott were concerned with explaining hierarchy in the caste system, Barnett and more recently Raheja (1988) show how a concentration on the structural principles of caste organisation, such as hierarchy, may obscure more than it reveals. Furthermore, as Raheja indicates, caste attitudes related to hierarchy are just one among a host of other attitudes influenced by kinship organisation, affinal relations, economic circumstances, religious and other observances. Raheja makes a powerful case against a focus on hierarchy which she found hampered her study of social identities and relations of prestations between 'donor and recipient' (ibid.: 241) in Pahansu, northwestern Uttar Pradesh. For Raheja, prestations of the Gujar caste were best regarded in terms of the categories of centrality, mutuality and exchange. Only relations of centrality (epitomised in the *dan,* or non-reciprocal gift) were linked to Gujar dominance and hierarchy. More importantly, relations of mutuality (services from attached groups paid in kind over time) and exchange (payments of short term contracts) expressed the more common category of 'own persons' and a symbolic kinship rather than hierarchy. Raheja's material on complex prestational interaction in a multi-caste village presents similarities between multi-caste and single-caste (associated with tribe) villages which support my assertion that caste and tribe are not different in their notions of transaction. Relations within the Girasia village were also dominated by the notion of transactions with 'own persons', giving substance to the differences made between insiders/outsiders referred to in the previous subsection.

20. In the following text, I use the word *jath* as it was pronounced by the Girasia, in reference to their localised patrilineage. I use the spelling *jath* to distinguish it from 'Jat', a dominant community of farmers in Rajasthan, as well as from *jati*, used by other authors who have used it to refer to a caste, sub-caste or sub-sub-caste (see also chapter 4).

21. Daniel finds the concept of *jati* (which he depicts as 'beyond or beneath caste'; 1984: 2) especially useful in understanding the construction of the Tamil person. According to Daniel, 'By focusing on the caste system, scholars who consider it a uniquely Indian institution (Bougle 1971; Dumont 1970) and those who see it as an extreme manifestation of its rudimentary or vestigial counterparts found in other cultures have both in their own ways subscribed to the creed that to understand caste is to understand India '(1984: 1).

Some of the most useful studies on caste have been those which have studied the system from the bottom up, either starting with the individual or focusing on the poorer communities in India. In the 1980s, studies of lower class and caste communities were undertaken by the subaltern school of Indian historians which developed in response to the elitist renderings of Indian historiography.[22] The subaltern studies group has been concerned mainly with the reasons that subaltern politics, despite its pre-colonial origins and survival through colonialism, was neither able to steer the national movement nor emerge victor in the politics of liberation. The agenda of these historians has been to highlight the distinctive role of subaltern politics in Indian nationalism.[23] More traditionally organised around kin and territory structures as compared to the vertical bureaucratic organisation of the elite polity, subaltern politics, as the historians indicate, is also characterised as more violent and spontaneous than the latter. The subalterns, who may be from diverse ethnic backgrounds, are considered by the historians to be united in their experience of exploitation as well as their resistance to elite domination.

In a critical analysis of the work of the subaltern historians, Das (1987) refers to the implications of their endeavours for South Asian anthropology and history. In particular for anthropology Das feels that the subalternists, in their giving 'centrality to the historical moment of rebellion' (ibid., 312), are relevant in stressing the importance of both history and the analysis of violence in the constitution of tribal and caste societies.[24] The Girasia constitute a section of the

22. 'Subaltern' is a term coined by Gramsci to denote 'peasant', and has been used more recently by the school of Indian historians who have attempted to reconceptualise Indian history through a study of peasant protest . Guha (1982), in the introductory volume of the subaltern project, suggests the two dominant kinds of historical accounts on the rise of Indian nationalism had so far been based on either of the following notions: 1) the (colonialist) notion that Indian nationalism arose in response to the opportunities provided by the colonial structure, or 2) the (nationalist) notion that an indigenous elite (with industrial, mercantile or feudal interests) opposed the colonial structures to lead the country to national liberation. Amin, Arnold, Chatterjee, Guha, Hardiman, Pandey are some of the prominent subaltern studies historians.
23. For Guha, earlier historical writing on India was particularly problematic, 'demonstrated beyond doubt by its failure to understand and assess the mass articulation of this nationalism except negatively, as a law and order problem, and positively, if at all, either as a response to the charisma of certain elite leaders, or in the currently more fashionable terms of vertical mobilisation by the manipulations of factions' (1982: 3).
24. By concentrating on the issues of protest, raised as a result of the nature of colonial domination, the subaltern historians analyse the characteristics of the indigenous

subaltern (non-elite) population in India. In understanding some aspects of Girasia identity, especially in the outsider's shifting use of the label of tribe to describe the Girasia, I find the regional historical relations a useful guide. However, there is little historical documentation on the Girasia and I find this linked to the fact that the occasions of Girasia protest have been very few. In both the later colonial and postcolonial periods the Girasia used flight, rather than violent protest, as a means of struggle and survival. This leads me to what I see as a major weakness of the subaltern approach. In their constitution of the subaltern subject, the subaltern historians are not able to construct the history of the non-violent subaltern. Furthermore, in their reconstruction of violent episodes the historians are restricted by the availability and language of the administrative records, which in turn tend to emphasise the powerlessness of the subjects. In addition, a reliance on historical accounts such as those presented in administrative records, means that it is very difficult to study the relation between everyday life and the historic moment (acknowledged by Guha, Das).[25] In this study I have attempted to go beyond the notion that violent protest is the sole means of restoring history to the subaltern. The grounds for this argument lie in the reconstruction of the reasons for Girasia voluntary isolation, and commence from the oral accounts collected during fieldwork. By doing so I hope to distill the benefits of a diachronic analysis to those of the synchronic analysis as determined by my fieldwork experiences.[26]

Caste and the Concept of Tribe

Academic discourse in post-independence India largely regards castes and tribes as examples of opposed social systems: caste is

---

consciousness of caste communities. Further, through the analysis of the charismatic leaders of the spontaneous subaltern protests, the historians study the nature of individual action within the community frame. The analysis of the effects of historical experiences on the nature of the consciousness of communities remains a critically weak area of anthropological investigation in India. In the book, I address this issue with regard to the Girasia notions of their rights to land and a related identity as well as in terms of their participation in peasant protests in the region (chapters 2, 9).

25. As Das points out, most rebellion in the colonial period, took place in relation to the extension of colonial domination largely through the mechanism of such state institutions as law, bureaucracy, police and medicine.

26. As Das (1987) has aptly stated, 'The relevance of synchrony for the anthropologist is not that it denies time but it allows the present to be constituted as a spectral present rather than a point present. It is not that sequences are not important but rather these are absorbed within the concept of repetition' (1987, ibid.).

viewed as an hierarchic, organic system, based on a complex division of labour, while tribal society is seen as egalitarian and mechanical, based on a simple division of labour. Tribes are associated with a specific territory, with clan exogamy and with few restrictions for women as a means to preserve the purity of the group as compared to caste endogamy and strict rules relating to women. In contrast to caste groups, tribal groups are also considered to be unconcerned with ritual purity, ritual experts or Hindu deities. I suggest there has been little work done to challenge the view on tribe, with some notable exceptions, largely because of the emphasis placed on caste in studies of Indian society. Both the political and academic climates in India after independence in 1947 were such that caste became emphasised as a major focus of study in the social sciences, especially in the emerging discipline of sociology. Anthropology, by contrast, which was regarded as the study of tribes was derided because of its colonial associations.[27] With its colonial connotations, the study of tribes came to be associated with what was perceived as static and unchanging in Indian culture (Beteille 1974). Indian sociology on the other hand was influenced by the American preoccupations with social change and social class (for example the studies of Redfield and Lewis 1955, Srinivas 1955, Mandelbaum 1955, Dube in Srinivas 1955, Singer 1972), which reflected the rising urban and industrial concerns in America (Beteille 1974: 8).[28] A focus on caste also made

27. For example, Madan (1982) observes that by Indian independence there 'existed a tripartite division in the study of culture and society in India. While Indology was regarded as the study of Pali and Sanskrit texts, sociology was seen as the study of Hindu society and anthropology as the study of Indian tribes' (ibid.: 12). Textbooks dealing with the state of anthropology in India often stress the colonial origins of the subject. Most Indians who were trained as anthropologists were seen by the academic, administrative and political community as serving the interests of the British colonialists in the latter's interest of gathering information to strengthen control over their colonial subjects. Dube (1962: 239) claims the 'British hold' existed well into the 1950s in the form of British-trained Indian students. For example amongst the most influential early Indian anthropologists and sociologists, G.S Ghurye and K.P Chattopadhyay were students of W.H.R Rivers, D.N Majumdar a student of T.C Hodson, and M.N Srinivas was a student of Radcliffe-Brown at Cambridge.
28. The shift in theoretical stances between disciplines reflected the wider politico-economic changes and ideals of the newly formed independent Indian government. Dhanagre (1985), writes of the post-1950 academic period as one that was influenced by the impetus given by economic planners (the first 5-year plan for economic growth started in 1950), involving the procurement of large-scale information and evaluation data which in turn guided the funding of new jobs within sociology (ibid.: 325-26). Sociology became the discipline to provide large-scale survey data required by the machinary of development economics. The resul-

possible the study of stratification and inequality in contrast to the earlier emphasis on kinship and ritual (Beteille 1974:15). The shift to caste as a unit of analysis allowed a more regional study and therein moved away from a focus on 'closed' social organisations which the tribal studies had come to represent (also see Fuller and Spencer 1991). Each social system became the subject matter of a special discipline and the study of caste was regarded as having no bearing on the analysis of tribal systems.[29]

Dumont, more so than Hocart, contributed to the view that caste and tribe were separate entities. For both Dumont and Hocart the caste system was manifested through an occupational hierarchy (pure versus impure occupations for Dumont become powerful versus less powerful ritual occupations for Hocart). Dumont's more influential view of occupations once again placed tribal groups outside the system of caste because of their perceived relative unimportance with regard to intercaste transactions. For Dumont, the Hindu ascetic also belonged outside the caste system as he/she was one who had renounced social ties, and thus was excluded from the intercaste exchange system. Dumont's view of social relations and interactions, as either in caste and therefore collectively orientated or out of the caste system if individually orientated, has I suggest, contributed to the outsider perception of 'tribals' as both more individualistic than ordinary caste householders (also see Gardener 1982) as well as possessing an ascetic quality through the renunciation of comforts.

It is interesting to note, however, that for Levi-Strauss, whose work influenced Dumont, castes and tribes were variants of each

---

tant stress on research methodology gave undue emphasis to the quantitative aspect of the discipline as well as a focus on community development programmes, which in turn led to the stereotyping of research themes and priorities (Dhanagre ibid.: 327-28). Furthermore, as Srinivas and Panini (1973) noted: 'The degree of proximity to the states' and governments' policy formulating bodies became an index of academic status and recognition. The newer status criteria transformed the earlier interaction ... into an almost pathological competition for resources as well as recognition' (ibid.: 99).

29. There have been some studies which have corrected this general view. In this context, Bailey's work is a notable example. In relation to the political system of the tribal Konds in Orissa, Bailey observes: 'just at what point on the continuum (of segmentary egalitarian type versus dependent political relations) tribe ceases and caste begins is difficult to say ... the political distinction between caste and tribe is ceasing to be useful, both caste and tribe are being merged ... [however] it is wrong to assume that caste is an automatic solvent of a tribal system' (ibid.: 265-66). More recently, Beteille's work (1986) considers some of the difficulties and problems in the definition and identification of tribes in India.

other, different manifestations of a deeper ideological similarity between social groups which rendered the occupational differences between them as superficial.[30] Along the same lines, an early study by Fox (1967) showed that, despite their peripheral and fluctuating occupations, tribal groups may also be encompassed within the occupational caste hierarchy on the basis of exchange relations. Fox's view is certainly borne out by my own stay with the Girasia. In 1986, the Girasia were sellers in the market only in winter, a period of low agricultural activity when they would supply important items of fuel such as firewood and grass to the nearby town. Although the Girasia were not specialised in any occupation, they met a specialised demand of the townspeople (and sometimes of the villagers; see chapter 6). Based on the observations of the Girasia interactions with other castes I argue that actual occupations are not necessarily significant markers of caste or tribe. This particularly holds true in the Rajput areas, where different communities are from different lineages, all of whom are related through the shared values of kinship related honour, prestige and loyalty.

The definition of anthropology as the study of tribes as opposed to the definition of sociology as the study of castes in India, has had a major effect for the communities concerned. With the focus on caste studies, there has been little attempt to put together the material that existed on tribal India. As a result, I believe, administrative documents and census classifications have become the most impor-

30. In his book, *The Savage Mind* (1966), Levi-Strauss puts forward the view that castes can be seen as transformed variants of totemic systems. For him, while totemic groups (his idea of tribe) use animals or plants to distinguish between social groups, castes use occupations and manufactured objects to achieve the same objective. He demonstrates how the Munda tribe in eastern India and the Bhil tribe of western India use animals and plants as well as manufactured objects as clan names. This in-between position wherein a tribe uses both caste (manufactured objects) and totemic insignia (natural objects) reinforces for Levi-Strauss the notion that castes and totems are variants of each other. He also illustrates how both caste and totemic systems are 'exo-practising' in that they mark difference by the outward exchange of objects (women in the case of totemic societies, and food, services in the case of caste societies), despite the 'superficial differences of endogamy and exogamy (respectively) between the two' (ibid.: 122). Levi-Strauss's observation that, 'Totemism ... could at the cost of a very simple transformation equally well be expressed in the language of the regime of castes, which is quite the reverse of primitive' (ibid.: 129) has implications for the differences based on occupation between caste and tribe in India. His observations reinforce the idea that there is a common ideological basis for social organisation (which I suggest is reflected in the patrilineal basis of caste and tribe in India.)

tant source of information on tribal groups and identifications.[31] It is interesting to note that, while there has been an emphasis on caste in the Indian social sciences, since the Indian constitution came into force in 1951, the task of the census has been to record a person's group identity in caste or tribe terms, 'only if the person is believed to be a member of a scheduled tribe or scheduled caste'.[32] The scheduled (from the word 'schedule' or 'list') groups are underprivileged communities identified as such to get state support under the government's programme of positive discrimination, mainly in the areas of employment and education.[33] Most tribes are scheduled although not all castes are scheduled. The administrative classification of communities as scheduled tribe or scheduled caste, the history of which precedes independence, has played, perhaps, the most significant role in the construction of tribal identities in independent India. The processes of classification have led to often violent claims and counterclaims about identities, both with regard to increasing social status and in terms of accessing economic benefits. This has made the classificatory process itself an exercise in inaccuracy (Beteille 1986) and has been debilitating for poorer communities such as the Girasia, who because of their social marginality and poverty are unable to address the issue of their classification.[34]

I conclude this section by considering academic writing on tribes in India with specific reference to the Girasia. Indian anthropologists' accounts of the Girasia indicate two separate approaches: studies in which the Girasia are portrayed as 'tribal'; and in studies in which they are portrayed as 'tribalised'. The essential difference between the two is that while the latter approach considers the Girasia as Rajputs who have lost their Rajput customs, the former denies

31. More recently, Tribal Research Institutes have been set up in states with large tribal populations, but these institutions themselves remain on the margins of academic work in India.
32. Paper 2, Final Population Totals, Series 1: p. 37-48. Documents of the 1981 census indicate that while only Hindus and Sikhs can have scheduled caste communities, members of Scheduled Tribes can belong to any religion (series 18, pt xiii, A & B).
33. According to the 1991 census, there are 573 tribes and 1,091 castes which are scheduled. The comparative figures for Rajasthan are 12 and 59 respectively. As no enumeration of the non-scheduled castes is made, it is not possible to compare the number of scheduled with non scheduled castes.
34. The reliance on government documents with an implicitly essentialist viewpoint in their definition of communities goes some way towards explaining why Indian anthropology remains evolutionist in its approach to the study of tribal groups (also see Padel 1988).

the Girasia any Rajput connections. Archival research for this book outwardly supports the tribalised approach as it is sensitive to the shifts and changing political and economic contexts in which the Girasia live. However, fieldwork among the Girasia indicates that their increasing distance from state power has tribalised them more in outsider perceptions than in any actual loss of their customs and sense of Rajput identity. The limited academic accounts on the Girasia that do exist, like most work on Indian tribes, locates their apparent social difference as rooted in biology. For example, Meherda who has written a recent account of the Girasia believes that, 'The social organisation and the customs of the Girasia, besides difference in physique and colour, reveal that they are fundamentally different from the Rajputs' (1985: 12). Some writers are more cautious in their categorisations and maintain that, 'The cultural traits observed in the Grasias ... indicate that they are indigenous forest and hill people, although it is possible that there might have been some mixture of blood between the Grasias and the migrated Rajputs' (Dave 1960: 2). James Tod's work on the Rajput States in the early nineteenth century had a great influence on later social scientists' perspectives on the communities in Rajasthan. Tod describes the Girasia as the 'progeny of the cohabitation of Rajput men with Bhil women'. More recently Meherda (1985) has criticised Tod's observations as, 'illogical ... because children born of a Rajput marrying a Bhil woman should have been either Rajputs or Bhil, not Girasia.'

The writers who believe in the tribal nature of the Girasia community also believe that any Rajput customs the Girasia may follow are a result of an emulation of the Rajput lifestyle, in order to gain a higher status in the eyes of the communities of the region. In other words, the Girasia are seen as preoccupied with what Srinivas has termed 'sanskritisation', the process by which a community aims to achieve a higher social status through the emulation of higher caste customs, dress etc. It is in this light that, for example, Sinha (1969) considers the process of state formation among the Bhumij tribals of Bihar. Sinha is particularly struck by the Bhumij employment of Brahmins at ritual occasions, and the Bhumij patterns of hierarchical marital alliances. Sinha attributes the Rajput lifestyle of the Bhumij to their strategy to 'Rajputise'. The notion of tribalisation is opposite to that proposed by Sinha, in that it indicates a reverse process in which the communities in question have lost their Rajput customs over time to become tribals. As early as 1881, Sherring explicitly stated: 'There were instances of tribalisation of Rajputs who went into the Aravalli hills, a scene of turmoil and upheavals as fugitives

... [but while] the Bhilalas were the progeny of Rajput fathers and Bhil women ... the Girasia are described as tribalised Rajputs' (1985 reprint, 89). More recent support for this view has been expressed by Chauhan (1978) in his study on the Bhil of Rajasthan. Chauhan illustrates, through numerous historical examples, how the Bhil were the original rulers from whom the Rajputs wrested power. As a consequence of the displacement of the Bhil onto marginal tracts of land, the Bhil became tribalised. For Chauhan, 'Tribalisation is a process through which an already existing virile socio-political homogeneous unit withdraws itself from the mainstream of the larger culture, and begins leading a secluded life in an inaccessible area thereby redefining its own world view' (ibid.: 29). Chauhan's book is supported by the works of Navalkha (1959) on the Bhil of Banswara in south Rajasthan, Nath (1954) on the Bhil of Ratanmal in Gujarat, and Singh (1964) on the historical perspective of Indian tribes.

On the basis of the Girasia material, I agree with the latter tribalisation approach in so far as the concept implies, above all, a change in the political status of the communities involved. However, I disagree with the tribalisation theorists' belief, that a fall in political status by a community's retreat to marginal lands is necessarily accompanied by a rise in 'tribal' attitudes and customs. On the contrary, I would suggest that, the political isolation of the Girasia, symbolised by their geographical retreat, actually allowed them to maintain a certain lifestyle based on a customary relation to land and other resources. Given the state's derecognition of Girasia rights, especially with regard to common forest and grazing lands, the Girasia could maintain their social organisation and distribution of land among kin only by opting out of the post-Rajput state system. If the Girasia have been able to maintain their customs then surely the so-called process of 'tribalisation' remains very much an outsider's conception. Furthermore, most tribalisation theorists assume that other communities who live in the the same environment as the Bhil will have a greater contact, especially through marital relations, with the Bhil. On the contrary I found that, rather than an increase in interaction, living in the forest seems to have led to a greater rigidity in the social interaction of the Girasia in the Bhakar. If any Bhil and Girasia marry, then according to most Girasia elders: 'The *jath* (lineage) will *nikaal* (literally, throw out) the couple. Often the Bhil community accepts them. Then the Bhil get a chance to call themselves Bhil-Garasia, Doongri-Garasia ... that is why there are a number of groups between the Bhil and us.' The process of tribalisation (de-Rajputisation, as is supposed in the Girasia case), may explain the Taivar Girasia movement through history to outsiders; in the following chapters I suggest that it does not provide a representative picture of the change for the Taivar Girasia. The Girasia 'tribalisation', in outsider eyes, is linked to the sphere of Girasia life which most exhibits their different status, i.e., the role of their women. The more invisible element is the Girasia patrifocal kin structure and a related organisation of resources, which is similar to other castes in the region.

Women, Gender and Differences

A common way in which differences between communities in southern Rajasthan were constructed was with reference to women. Women were used as markers of differences and identities especially with regard to the distinctive ways in which they dressed, including the specific kinds of jewellery they wore; their sexuality, behaviour and attitudes, particularly in public places, and their work-tasks and 'value', considered to be reflected in the institution of marriage payments practised by the communities of which they were a part. An analysis of gender relations is especially pertinent to this study for two interrelated reasons. Firstly, a study of gender roles and relations allows me to look at the politics surrounding the manner in which identities are constructed at the most personal levels within a community and, at the same time, to see how they are used as a means of expressing differences between communities. I see the use of Girasia women as metaphors of identity as reinforcing the notion held by gender anthropologists, that women are markers of boundaries and especially in patrilineal societies are the symbols of tradition.[35] In this book I suggest that the use of women as markers of difference is common to both caste and tribal communities in India. Secondly, an analysis of the sexual division of labour and Girasia notions of work and property enables me to study the interrelationship between the Girasia ties of kinship and their concern with organising personal subsistence and livelihood.[36] Here I argue that Girasia men are embedded in a patrilineal structure which to a great extent organises

---

35. See for example, Douglas 1966, Yalman 1963, Ortner 1981, Whitehead 1981, Fruzzetti 1982, Bennett 1983, Oakley 1983, Goddard 1987, Caplan 1987.
36. Although I see gender as a way into Girasia society, I do not suggest that gender relations determine or constitute the kinship, economic, political or other levels of Girasia organisation. The position that gender relations actually comprise the sphere of kinship, for example, is a position taken by some anthropologists, for example see Collier and Yanagisako (1987) and Collier (1988).

Introduction

the economy, whereas women, excluded from these structures, are subject to the economic vagaries of particular contexts. Important, perhaps, in the economic anthropology of the future, such structural differences based on gender have been largely ignored. Furthermore, I found that although differences in the economic organisation of caste and tribe resulted in differential access to resources for women of both communities, I will maintain that even more profound similarities existed that rendered these differences superficial. To my knowledge this argument has not been made before.

In this section, then, I shall briefly outline some of the similarities and differences in the structural and conceptual aspects of Girasia women's lives as compared to women from other castes and classes. The rest of this section will then contextualise my work on gender in relation to studies on women and gender both in South Asia, and more generally.

Some of the main points of similarity between the structural position of Girasia and other caste and class women relate to the marginality of their participation in important matters of kinship and the economy. For example, both Girasia and non-Girasia women tend to share weaker positions compared to men of their communities, both with regard to the decision-making processes surrounding marriage and marriage payments, and in matters of property more generally. At the same time women of all communities, whether these practised brideprice or dowry, shared an ideological devaluation of their labour. Women married with dowries have been regarded as economic liabilities despite their central role in the economy of the household (for example, Sharma 1984) and I suggest that the work of Girasia women is not recognised in the way their brideprice payments are conceptualised. In both cases, women were the vehicles through which male power and authority, both in the family and in the community, were strengthened. To a large extent, the dominance of the principle of male descent within communities, both caste and tribe lay behind the similar experiences of women in these communities.[37]

There were, however, important differences, which I shall discuss briefly here, between Girasia and other caste women with regard to their sexuality, dress, presence in the markets and agency. Girasia women were perceived by non-Girasia men and women as having a greater 'sexual freedom' (and as 'out of male control') compared to

37. The emphasis on male descent within tribal communities as described, for example, by Orans 1965 and Deliege 1985 reinforces Levi Strauss's argument made in the previous section that castes and tribes are fundamentally similar.

middle- and upper-caste women, who apparently live under greater moral and social constraints. For, as Wadley (1988) tells us: 'According to Hindu cosmology, if a female controls her own sexuality, she is changeable; she represents both death and fertility; she is both malevolent and benevolent. If, however, she loses control of her sexuality (Power/Nature) by transferring it to a man, she is portrayed as consistently benevolent' (ibid., 28). In other words, women's sexuality is considered damaging to (male orientated) society if it is not channelled in the right direction. Individual Girasia women did indeed have the opportunity to prevent their husband from having sex with them and could transfer their sexual favours to other men, often accomplished by initiating a divorce. But, as I argue in chapter 4, even in the instances when Girasia women were seen to be acting on their own initiative, they were only able to accomplish their goals if these also suited their male relatives, especially their father or brothers. Whereas most other caste women were incorporated over time into the agnatic groups of their husband, Girasia women who remained affiliated to their father's group, were not considered 'proper' members of either group. In this sense, they were more vulnerable and less secure than women of middle and upper castes and classes. In their insecurity, as well as in their institutions of divorce and remarriage, Girasia women were in positions similar to a number of other lower-class women in the region, which in a sense belied the popular assumption of the sexual 'freedom' of tribal Girasia women as compared to other caste women.

Girasia men and women saw women of their community differently, or similarly but for different reasons, compared to the non-Girasia. In the Girasia village women lived with caste-type restrictions, they followed *purdah* (veiling to conceal the face or body, also various forms of selusion and exclusion) and seclusion from categories of men, and wives were more 'invisible' and outwardly subordinate than the daughters and sisters of men in the village. In insider perceptions married Girasia women were 'more free' outside their husband's village, whether in the market or in their natal village. Non-Girasia largely saw Girasia women only in the market place, and in turn constructed them as 'free' in comparison with non-Girasia women, especially middle- and upper-caste women who did not go to the market to buy and sell. The outsider and insider images thus coincided with regard to the behaviour and attitudes of Girasia women in the market. Here again I see Girasia women to be very similar to other lower-caste women who gossip and joke in groups in the market where they have come to sell their produce or items gath-

Introduction

ered from the forest. The market places, because they were a considerable distance from their affinal villages, provided the space for Girasia women to come together in ways which they could not in their affinal villages *(huhara)*. In the *huhara*, the occasions for bonding were negligible and the arduous nature of work and subsistence separated women from each other.

It is important to regard descriptions of women in terms of the wider concerns which individuals and social groups may have. Often references to women articulate the differences between communities, and are 'expressed in conscious and unconscious reactions to women's sexuality' (Goddard 1987: 190). The image which presented Girasia women as controlling their sexuality and thus flaunting male control was viewed by non-Girasia to be a result of the 'low morals' of Girasia women and essentially epitomised the tribal nature of the Girasia. The projection of an uncontrolled sexuality onto women of a community other than one's own is often connected with the desire to maintain a distinction and hierarchy between the two communities. This feature is common to society not only in India but also elsewhere. In a study of the traveller-gypsies in England, Okely observes that the problem the gypsies faced was how to maintain a separate identity in the face of constant pressure to become assimilated (1983: 77). Okely illustrates how gypsy pollution beliefs reinforced the ethnic boundary between them and the gorgios (gypsy term for non-gypsies) and how both the gypsies and gorgios 'projected an image of uncontrolled female sexuality onto women of the other group' (Okely ibid.: 202).[38] In relation to the articulation of Girasia identity, I find especially that dress-related attitudes concerning women (such as *laaj-kaadna,* a version of *purdah* described in chapter 4) are used as important markers by both insiders as well as outsiders. In tables 3.1 and 3.2 on apparel and jewellery, in chapter 3 I give some examples of how differences in dress are used as markers of identity. Those within the Girasia community used very small differences in women's attire as markers of differences between themselves, such as the design of a piece of jewellery, the pattern of the skirt or wrap, the number of pieces of cloth or the way these are arranged. For example, a shorter *jhulki* (blouse) and a

---

38. In gypsy-gorgio relations, each had inverted pollution beliefs of the other. For example, the gorgio stereotype of gypsies as dirty was based on their observation of the untidy spaces outside gypsy caravans rather than inside them. For the gypsies on the other hand, inside spaces such as their caravans had to be pure and clean. Observing the well-kept gorgio gardens, the gypsies surmised that the gorgios were dirty inside their homes and in their personal habits (ibid.: 87).

skirt with fewer pleats but in the same style and pattern would make my Girasia companion say 'see, they are Bhil'. The non-Girasia population in the nearby villages and towns could distinguish more generally between women of some groups such as the Rebari (pastoral nomads) and the Girasia, although they often mistook a Bhil for a Girasia and vice-versa, that is, where less dramatic differences of dress were involved. It is also worthwhile noting that the articles of clothing and jewellery which gave the Girasia their tribal identity were all purchased in the market. [39]

At the widest level of this study, I emphasise the similarities between caste, class and tribal women in order to question the way tribal women have been constructed as powerful in literature on India, in contrast to caste women who are described as powerless or covertly powerful.[40] However, in my efforts to deconstruct this popular and simplistic image of tribal women as powerful, it may seem that I am promoting the view that women are universally subordinated in India. As a result, I am aware that my intentions might appear to be directly opposed to the recent work on gender in India which is concerned with the multiple and complex aspects of women's lives.[41] While it may seem that I have flattened the differences between caste and tribal women in order to highlight the similarities in their structural and ideological devaluation, I do not deny an agency to individual women in any community, nor ignore the occasions when they act powerfully. In fact, I consider both perspectives, those that show caste women as powerful and those that show tribal women as subordinated, to be working towards a common important agenda of deconstructing monolithic stereotypes in relation to women. Outlined below, are some of the directions in research which have Indian women as their focus and whose arguments form the backdrop to my work.

Most studies in pre- or post-independent India till the 1970s on the lives of Indian caste women portrayed them as passive victims of the dominantly male-orientated caste ideology.[42] The subordination of Indian women to patriarchal ideologies, institutions and interests

---

39. A similar point is made by Gell, 1986, in his study of the tribal Muria Gond of central India.
40. See for example, Doshi 1978, Mann 1978, Vyas 1978, Meherda 1985.
41. Here I refer especially to the recent work of Raheja and Gold (1994) who find alternative perspectives on women's lives in the songs of rural women in Rajasthan and Uttar Pradesh.
42. Among them is the work of important anthropologists and sociologists like Dumont 1966, Goody and Tambiah 1973, Srinivas 1977.

was considered responsible for their low status in society, especially when compared with the individual rights embedded in the western notion of equality said to exist between men and women in the Anglo Saxon world. The representation of the low status of Indian women in the studies was reinforced by their apparent invisibility (or lack of participation) in spheres of political and economic action outside domestic arenas. In a patrilineal caste culture which constructed the ideal type image of the Hindu woman in terms of the paramount feminine values of submissiveness and subordination, these studies did not challenge the prevailing popular views of women. Instead, I would suggest that in their emphasis on the structural aspects of caste and attempts to present a monolithic description of Indian women, the earlier studies on women reinforced the conceptions of women which were similar to the ideal-type woman delineated in the classic texts on Hindu society. In these texts, Hindu women who were religiously deified in their role as mothers, as both reproducers and nurturers, were regarded as closer to nature, more domestically orientated and less 'pure' than their male counterparts. In this sense, early gender studies on Indian women simply reproduced their position as represented in the historical and mythological texts. Early concerns with the status of Indian women mirrored similar preoccupations in the wider nascent field of women's studies. Most of the women's studies in the early 1970s attempted to locate the factors responsible for the so-called universal low status of women. The status of women in these studies was regarded as a collective and homogeneous entity. The belief in the universality of the low status of women also led theorists to regard gender division in terms of the dichotomies in material and symbolic life, such as nature versus culture, public versus domestic, pure versus polluted.[43] The universality of the reproductive function allowed women to be regarded everywhere as closer to 'nature', while the nurturing functions saw them more involved in the domestic sphere.

Increasingly critical of earlier studies, anthropological work focusing on women and gender relations in the 1980s strongly emphasised the multidimensionality of women's lives. In other words, there are no core universal determinants of status, instead status is the result of a complex and context-dependent mixture of variables. Further, a major difficulty with concepts such as the nature/culture, public/domestic and polluted/sacred of the earlier studies has been the pol-

---

43. Such as Ortner (1974), Rosaldo and Lamphere (1974) among the social anthropologists. Mukhopadhyay and Higgins (1987), make the same point.

ysemic nature and cultural ambiguity of these terms. It is now widely believed that such terms often obscure the finer complexities underlying individual strategy and manipulation within the community.[44] Gender research which takes women's own ideas and voices into account has increasingly led to a deconstruction of the term 'woman' itself, as individual women may oppose or support the dominant ideologies depending on their own life experiences. While some gender theorists believed that women's voices were distinct but suppressed by the dominant male ideology (Ardener 1978, 1981), others believed they were distinct only in as much as they stemmed from a different position within the same social order as men (Moore 1988). In other words, the latter position states that women's voices are distinct but interwoven rather than subordinated to those of men (Keesing, 1982). But it is not enough to record what women or men say and self accounts must also be read between the lines.[45] Humphrey's study on female deference reflected in the Mongolian use of language, and Wolf's study of the position of the Chinese daughter-in-law, for example, indicate how silences or a disobedient use of the language can be a meaningful way of indicating sexual tension and social differences within the community. Both verbal as well as physical gestures are thus equally important languages of communication. In India, this is particularly the case with the institution of *purdah* which is common in some form among the lower-, middle- and upper-caste and class families.[46] The *purdah* attempts to render the physical being and expressions of women invisible, especially to certain categories of men. While some writers argue that the notion of *purdah* cloaks the anthropologist's view of the power women have, other writers elab-

44. MacCormack and Strathern, 1980; Strathern, 1980; Harriet and Whitehead, 1981, for example.
45. As Keesing (1987) cautions: 'Letting women or men speak for themselves is by no means a magical solution to the epistemological and theoretical difficulties of interpreting gender in non-Western settings … .Such self-accounts never answer or even address our questions directly, since the narrator constructs an account within a context of cultural meanings and takes for granted much of what we find problematic: the division of labour, spatial and social segregation of the sexes, ideas of duty and virtue, the rules imposed by gods and ancestors. Moreover it is precisely the hegemonic character of cultures that incorporate and shape the consciousness both of ostensibly dominant men and ostensibly subordinate women which makes gender inequality so analytically problematic. So we must situate ourselves critically within an experienced world as revealed in self accounts and outside it. We must read self-accounts between the lines; they may tell us as much in what is not said as in what our subjects say about themselves and their lives (1987: 33).
46. Mehta 1976, Sharma 1979, Jeffrey 1979, Papanek 1982 are some examples.

Introduction

orate on the use of women (in terms of the manipulation of their dress) as markers of the prestige and status of their men.[47]

Thus while the earlier studies portrayed caste women as passive victims and powerless actors, more recent studies in the last decade have placed greater power, in terms of the capacity to influence decisions, in the hands of caste women (Dube 1986). The confinement of women to certain restricted domains, notably the domestic, these studies argue, does not detract from women's frequently covert contribution in other spheres of social action. Thus while earlier studies on women in the caste system regarded their inequality as synchronous with their collective, structural subordination, more recent studies look at women in individual, powerful roles behind the more public sphere of male interaction.[48] The latter studies are important as they examine individual responses to the structure of gender inequality rather than reproduce the dominant ideology itself. The analysis of both the status of women as well as the material and symbolic meanings of gender division have been part of a wider theoretical exercise to study gender hierarchy, inequality and related gender symbolism.[49] The concept I find particularly useful in studying Girasia society is the connection the organisation of gender has with the concerns of prestige in a society especially so in a hierarchical society.[50] Very frequently differences perceived between individuals and communities in the patrilineal caste context are directly related to concerns of status among the members of the agnatic group. This is especially true in the Girasia case, as chapters 4 to 8 will explain. But more significantly, my experience of Girasia gender concerns leads me to suggest that similar patriarchal contexts of caste in southern Rajasthan and elsewhere may entail different

---

47. Mehta 1976, Jeffrey 1979, Papanek 1982, and Dube 1986, for example, argue that women are powerful behind the veil and, given the patriarchal context in which they live, also because of it. With regard to prestige, Barth (1978) demonstrates how the institution of seclusion or *purdah* was among the three main institutions, the others being hospitality and political councils, which were crucial to boundary maintenance among the Pathans in Pakistan. The *purdah* represented an 'honourable organisation of domestic life ... and among the mechanisms whereby Pathans realise Pathan values and facilitate maintenance of a shared identity' (1978: 106).
48. For example, Mehta 1976, Jeffrey 1979, Sharma 1980, Dube, Leacock and Ardener 1986, Das 1988, Dube 1988.
49. For example, Sacks, Sanday 1981, Rosaldo and Lamphere, Hirshcon 1984, Ortner and Whitehead 1981, Rosaldo and Collier 1981, Strathern 1984, Caplan 1987, Collier 1988.
50. Rosaldo and Collier 1981, Ortner 1981, Collier 1988 have been the main instigators of this approach in anthropology.

gender roles and relations and yet have similar structural implications, especially for women in these communities.

Poverty and Identity

This work is about poor people's perceptions of their poverty, vulnerability and powerlessness and considers their strategies for subsistence with regard to their preoccupations with social identity, status and self respect. In this sense, I am concerned with the general or wider sense of poverty and deprivation, in terms of the hardships as experienced and presented rather than with the more technical measurement and assessment of poverty. This is not to deny the importance of the identification and aggregation approaches in conceptualising poverty (especially Sen 1981). Chambers, Saxena and Shah (1987) identify two areas in poverty related research which have received scant attention. According to them, focusing on the perceptions and priorities of poor people is one of two 'less familiar and less comfortable' (1987: 7) approaches to study poverty (the other being an examination of the priorities and perceptions of the professionals). The focus on perceptions and priorities allows me to discuss what I saw as two primary and interrelated concerns among the Girasia, which was to maintain their self-respect on the one hand and, in the face of increasing economic hardships, to meet their subsistence needs and prevent the degrading economic and social effects of the processes of impoverishment, on the other. Their deprivation was not just a matter of poverty or the lack of income, consumables and wealth but also one of vulnerability and exposure to the vagaries of the weather, ill health, a lack of sustained nutrition and being subject to increasing market costs. The Girasia are classified as a Scheduled Tribe, which identifies them in state administration documents as a socially disadvantaged community. They live in the marginally productive region of Sirohi and have little access to service and resources. All these indicators point to their being caught in what Chambers et al. call the 'deprivation trap' (1987: 10) and its five interrelated clusters of disadvantage, i.e., physical weakness, isolation, poverty, vulnerability and powerlessness.[51]

51. For Chambers, Saxena and Shah, the clusters of disadvantage relate to social and spiritual deprivation as well as its material dimensions. The aspect of physical weakness underlines the role poor health and physical disability play in people's experiences of poverty. While isolation refers to both physical inaccessibility as well as a lack of access to information and services, vulnerability and power-

Introduction

The Girasia in Sirohi live mostly in the hilly and forested areas of the district which are included in what is termed the 'poverty square' of India. This is measured according to four indicators relating to infant mortality, female literacy, numbers below the poverty line and per capita net domestic product; and is centred mainly in the states of Uttar Pradesh, Bihar, Orissa and Madhya Pradesh (Chambers et al. 1987: 26). Furthermore, they experience what Chambers, Saxena and Shah describe as 'peripheral deprivation', i.e., one that is associated with the economic hinterlands as compared with the 'core deprivation' associated with the economic heartlands of India. This means that, with regard to Girasia livelihoods, there are more Girasia who are self-employed in agriculture, fewer landless and tenants and fewer still (next to none) who take up permanent employment outside the village, compared with poor people in the economically prosperous areas. It also means that in terms of the resources of water, land and forests, the Girasia mainly carry out rain-fed agriculture in an area which has lower soil fertility and groundwater potential and access compared to the irrigated agriculture in the core areas. They also have a much higher forest land to family ratio and a lower concentration of landownership than the poor in the core areas.

Apart from their dependence on unproductive land with low water availability, the Girasia also regularly experience drought and famine related scarcity. The need to prevent impoverishment from occurring as a result of scarcity was of primary concern in the organisation, management and planning of the Girasia economy. Their coping strategies were diverse and shifting, depending on the nature and extent of the scarcity, the membership and sharing networks of the individual household units and the extent to which community members had been affected by previous conditions of scarcity. But more often than not each cycle of drought and related hardship made the Girasia less able to cope with the following drought. Furthermore, as Jodha's (1975) study of famine in Rajasthan so pertinently observes, the drought-hit farmer in Rajasthan is most prone to functioning under adverse terms of trade with high purchase prices, low sale prices and high replacement prices. And, unless the farmer is able to protect the productive capacity of his resource base, usually seen as only possible with a drought free period of at least two years,

---

lessness highlight the poor's exposure to physical and political threats, the loss of their assets and the detrimental effects of rising costs on their situation (see also Chambers 1989).

he becomes party to the downward process of pauperisation. Such a process is signalled, according to Jodha, in the irretrievable loss of assets, especially of livestock and, under greater duress, land. In 1986-87, the Girasia showed all signs of responding (adjusting) to the increasing economic difficulties in their lives. As the monsoon in 1986 partially failed, first the part of the crop which was to be stored for fodder was sold and then the smaller animals, especially goats. This was accompanied by an increase in gathering and the collection of food, fuelwood and fodder from the uncultivated tracts and forest areas by some members of the household, while others left to perform wage labour in near and far locations, inside and outside the state. Those members who remained in the village made items for sale in the market town such as baskets, rope, and wooden cots which were sold along with fuelwood, fodder, wildflowers, *lac* resin and honeycombs collected from the forest. In 1986 there was very little milk available to drink in the village and the staple of maize was, as the year drew on, replaced by wheat procured in exchange for labour on famine relief works or bought and exchanged in the market for other items. The Girasia were further subject to adversity as a result of the forest- and land-related restrictive policies of the government, which did not take into account the shifting Girasia dependence on the forest or common grazing land. Moreover, with rising contingency costs related to health care, essential items of clothing, rising brideprice amounts and expenses for ritual occasions, the Girasia faced very difficult economic conditions.

To a certain extent, trips into the forest and to the market were a regular feature of Girasia lives which only became more frequent during periods of shortage. Thus gathering and collecting as well as wage-labour were everyday features of the Girasia economy which supplemented agricultural production. Periods of drought-related scarcity were, however, especially markd by the increased duration and greater number of family members who migrated out of the village to seek waged labour. They had to travel greater distances in search of work which was scarcer in times of famine and drought. Both men and women, young and middle-aged, brothers, sisters, husbands and wives left the village in 1986 to work on building sites, in factories and in fields, mostly to the south of Rajasthan, in Gujarat. The nature of their hardships was never overridingly evident in conversations among the Girasia. Reflections on their economic situation usually manifested themselves in the frequent comparisons which were made between brother households of the lineage, some of whom were 'better off' compared to others. The households considered to be the poorest in the village were the ones which had neither agricultural land, such as was the case with affinal relatives, nor oxen, nor a share in a well, or were those where the household head was disabled and/or had only one wife and no children. The households which were poorest were also those regarded as less 'pure' in their kinship than others. An example of less 'pure' kin was the *ghar jamai* (resident son-in-law) who could only access the productive land of his father-in-law while the latter was alive. Similarly, brothers who married women from unacceptably lower Girasia social groups were considered 'fallen' in terms of purity, and consequently lived on the most unproductive land, as well as on the margins of the village where their descendants formed a separate subgroup and sublineage (see chapter 6).

All members of the village were related through patrilineal kinship and there was an outward emphasis on egalitarianism in the lineage and village. Yet there were economic differences between households which usually followed along lines of descent and marriage. Although there were strict, unstated rules which prevented the borrowing of food grains, money, livestock, clothes, utensils and tools among kin, there were frequent social, including ritual, occasions where individual contributions of goods and money had to be made. Such contributions went a long way to balancing the inequalities in production and consumption between households and did give substance to the Girasia ethic of equality among brothers. Furthermore, it is interesting to note that women marked not only kin differences but also economic differences between household units. Women's labour in the fields, forests, market and home, in their roles as wives, daughters and sisters was more easily contracted and controlled than that of men who were brothers. Yet, despite their significant economic roles, women's contributions to the economies of the household, family and lineage were downplayed, such that Girasia women were regarded as marginal members of their lineage and village. Instead, the fact of their marriage and consequent change of residence was seen as sufficient reason to deny them any ownership rights over the economic assets of the household as well as in the labour of other household members, including their children. The negative ideological construction of Girasia women excluded them from participation in the economic matters of the lineage despite their central role in the subsistence activities of their families under conditions of poverty.

The dialectical relationship between cultural ideologies and control over material resources among caste and class groups has been the focus of recent feminist scholarship in India.[52] There is no comparable work on the so-called tribal groups in India in general and Rajasthan in particular.[53] I see the present work as supplementing the above perspectives in important ways. For example, to a large extent the ideological constructions of Girasia women and the Girasia preoccupation with a *jath* (lineage) identity explain why Girasia women continue to be economically dependent members of their community despite the importance of their labour and the institution of their brideprice, which supposedly acknowledges their work-value in contrast to other caste women married with dowries. Furthermore, the rising Girasia hardships caused by their increasing economic vulnerability and powerlessness has not, as is commonly supposed, led to a decline in brideprice in favour of dowry payments. This is largely because brideprice as a Girasia institution satisfies both lineage and gender hierarchies, the economic needs of the community and the symbolic necessity of the Girasia to distinguish themselves from other social groups in the region.

Tribes in Southern Rajasthan

My research began with a visit to the Tribal Research Institute at Udaipur in Rajasthan in 1986. Statistics compiled at the Institute revealed that the majority of tribal people in Rajasthan were concentrated in the southern region and distributed between three main groups, the Bhil, the Mina and the Girasia (see Appendix 1, List of Scheduled Tribes: Rajasthan). In both popular and academic terms, the Bhil and the Mina are well known among the communities in Rajasthan, whereas the Girasia are little known outside the region of southern Rajasthan. While the Girasia are concentrated in the area around the borders of the two states of Rajasthan and Gujarat, the Bhil are widespread along the tribal belt of India. In Western India the Bhil populate the states of Madhya-Pradesh, Maharashtra, Gujarat and Rajasthan. [54] The Mina are no longer regarded as 'under-

---

52. Sharma 1980, Dube and Leacock 1986, Afshar and Agarwal 1989, Standing 1991, Agarwal 1994 are the most notable examples.
53. Agarwal's (1994) recent work on gender and land rights in South Asia includes material on tribal communities in a very general manner, giving most specific information about the tribal groups in the northeastern hill region.
54. See Vidyarthi, 1978, for example. According to the 1991 census, the Bhil are listed as a Scheduled Tribe in the states of Andhra Pradesh, Gujarat, Karnataka, Madhya Pradesh, Maharashtra, Rajasthan and Tripura (Final Population Totals, paper 2, 1992).

developed tribals', for it is generally believed and recorded in official documents that they have benefited from government schemes instituted in favour of the scheduled castes and tribes. Very little has been written about the Girasia and the material that exists deals in very general terms with the Girasia community.[55] The Tribal Research Institute defined the Girasia in the Abu Road area as belonging to the category of Rajput Girasia and not tribal. In contrast, the other locals of Abu Road as well as the officials of the Abu Road *panchayat* (council of several villages), *tehsil* (council of *panchayats* and smallest administrative unit in the district) and Tribal Area Development departments, all viewed the Girasia as tribal. The 'Rajput Girasia' category referred to by the Tribal Research Institute, I found, was also used in self descriptions by the Girasia in the village where I did my fieldwork. Although the Rajput Girasia category is defined in the census documents as a group which is not tribal, I could not find any figures for such a group elsewhere in the census. Table 1.1 below gives comparative figures on the area and population of Sirohi in Rajasthan.

Table 1.1: Area and Population of Rajasthan and Sirohi

	Area (sq.km)	Population	Tribal Population (percent)
Rajasthan State	342,239	34,261,862	12.21
Sirohi District	5,136	542,049	23.11

Source: Extract from Census statistics 1981 pt xiii A and B, 'facts from figures', n.p.[56]

Of the approximately half a million persons residing in Sirohi district as shown by the table, almost 84 percent (or 445,045 individuals) live in 433 villages and the rest, one-sixth, of the population resides in towns. Within the 5,136 km area of Sirohi district as indicated in the table, there are 125,000 tribals distributed amongst different tribal groups (see table 1.2, below).

55. Dave 1960, Lal 1979 and Meherda 1985 are the only authors I am aware of, who have written an entire book on the Girasia. While Dave and Meherda write more generally about the Girasia in southern Rajasthan, Lal's work, which I find most useful, has more specific information on kinship details of certain Girasia villages in Gujarat.
56. The 1991 census figures show an increase in the figures of 1981 with the total population of Rajasthan and Sirohi at 44,005,990 and 654,029 people respectively. Correspondingly, there is an increase in the percentage of Scheduled Tribes to the total populations, with 12.24 percent for the state as a whole and 23.39 percent for Sirohi (District Census Handbook, pt xii, A & B).

Table 1.2: Distribution of Tribal Population in Sirohi

Major group	population	Minor group	population
Girasia	58,484	Koli Dhor, Tokre Koli	440
Bhil, Bhil Garasia*	51,420	Patelia	102
Mina	14,550	Dhanka, Tadvi	41
		Naikda, Naika*	21
		Bhil Mina	16
		Damor, Damaria	4

* see list in Appendix 1
Source: Extract from the 1981 census table ST-5, 882,883.

Figures in the census indicate that the Girasia are heavily concentrated in the four districts of Pali, Udaipur, Sirohi and Dungarpur in southern Rajasthan (Appendix 2), and in the Sabarkantha and Banaskantha districts of northern Gujarat. Sirohi district in south Rajasthan has the highest number of Girasia among the twenty-six districts in the state of Rajasthan.[57] According to table 1.2, the Girasia population in Sirohi is approximately 60,000 individuals. Combined with the Girasia population in the other districts (see Appendix 2, which includes a negligible population of Girasia living in urban areas) the total population of Girasia in the state of Rajasthan is 118,757 people. As is evident from the table, the total population of the Bhil and Girasia groups is substantially larger than that of the other tribal groups, and accounts for one-fifth of the total population of Sirohi. The Bhil are substantially more numerous than the Girasia and record a total population of 1,840,966 in the state. In other words, there are approximately seven Girasia to every hundred Bhil in Rajasthan. Although spread over the whole state, the Bhil, like the Girasia populate the southern districts of Rajasthan, especially Udaipur, Dungarpur and Banswara, most densely.

Abu Road Tehsil

> A wild hilly region belonging to the state is called the Bhaker ... covered with forest trees, brushwood and grass, as shelter to wild animals of every kind, the only inhabitants being clusters of 3,4 hamlets of Bhils and Girassias' (1st biennal report of the administration of the Sirohi state, 1889,1890, Milap Chand Dewan, 1892)

57. The districts of Udaipur and Pali adjacent to Sirohi have the next two highest Girasia populations (38,257 and 20,198 respectively; from figures for the rural areas in these districts; see Appendix 2). There is an enormous gap after Pali, in the Girasia population of the other districts (from 769 Girasias for Banswara to a few individual Girasias in some districts; see Appendix 2). From the same table we see the Bhil population exceeding the Girasia by large margins in all the districts except Sirohi and Pali.

Introduction

Most of the Girasia in Sirohi district live in Abu Road *tehsil* where I worked. A *tehsil* is the smallest administrative unit in a district. Sirohi is comprised of five *tehsil* (see inset in general map of India). Abu Road gets its name from Mount Abu, the highest point in Rajasthan, situated in the northwestern part of Abu Road *tehsil*. Mount Abu, considered by caste and tribe alike as one of the region's important sacred places, draws a number of pilgrims and ascetics. It is the site of the famous Jain Dilwara temples and was also favoured as the summer capital of the state's colonial officials during British rule. Most of the Girasia in Abu Road live in or around the *Bhakar* (literally, mountainous terrain), the local name for a large, eastern section of the *tehsil* (see map 1.1). The *Bhakar* accounts for twenty-one of the eighty-one villages under the jurisdiction of the Abu Road *tehsil*, although it occupies nearly a half of the land area. Abu Road is a railway town and owes its establishment to the railway line built under the British at the end of the last century. Even now the rail link is a major route in western India, especially connecting Ahmedabad, the state capital of Gujarat, with the central capital city of Delhi, a distance of approximately 1,200 kilometres. Abu Road station is the last station in Rajasthan before the train enters the state of Gujarat. Both the Abu Road station and the nearby market, a major one in the region, see a substantial flow of goods pass through them. Most of the non-tribal population live in Abu Road Town and the villages surrounding the town. The tribal population is concentrated in separate villages in the hilly areas, further away from both the town and its surrounding non-tribal villages. Even where the Girasia or Bhil populations are part of the multi-caste villages, they live separated from the other castes. For example, in the multi-caste village of Ore, six kilometres from Abu Road, three communities in particular were separate from the main village habitation. These were the Rebari (pastoral nomads), the Bhil and the Girasia. The Rebari lived in a separate section closest to the cluster of multi-caste huts of the village community, while the Girasia lived the furthest from this village centre. The Bhil lived at a tangent from both these settlements as well as from the village. Abu Road *tehsil*, as the figures in table 1.3 indicate, has both the highest Scheduled Tribe population as well as the lowest scheduled caste population in the district. The table gives the names of the *tehsil* in Sirohi as well as an idea of the distribution of the highest (H) and lowest (L) Scheduled Tribe and Scheduled Caste populations among them.

Identity, Gender and Poverty

Table 1.3 Distribution of Scheduled Tribe and Scheduled Castes in Sirohi

Tehsil in Sirohi district	Scheduled tribes	Scheduled castes (admin.units)
Sheoganj	–	–
Sirohi	7,771 or 6.20 pc (L)	-
Pindwara	–	-
Abu Road	49,104 or 39.21 pc (H)	13,221 or 13.09 pc (L)
Reodar	–	33,691 or 33.17 pc (H)

L/H, refers to Low or High concentrations
Source: Extract from 1981 Census

Map 1.1 Abu Road *Tehsil*

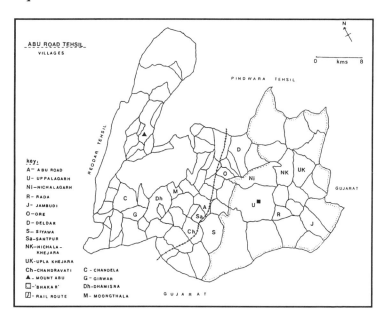

Abu Road *tehsil* is mainly rural in character. When doing my fieldwork and travelling from the railway station of Abu Road in the overused Rajasthan transport bus which operated twice a day, it took only fifteen minutes to leave the urban scene behind. As there are no large towns in the vicinity of Abu Road, soon after the bus began its journey we were in a rural landscape of large and dusty fields surrounding clusters of habitations. The first few stops were at the scattered multi-caste villages. Past these villages, the bus rattled closer to a distant hill range and came to the end of the remains of a road. According to the local inhabitants we had now entered the *Bhakar*. Here the scenery changed to a dry and wooded landscape where visibility was reduced by the surrounding hills. For the first few miles there were no signs of habitation and then occasionally I would see a mud hut in a large field on the slopes of the hill. Once into the *Bhakar*, all the occupants of the bus except the driver and the conductor were Girasia and Bhil. After a ride of an hour and a half up and down the hill slopes within the *Bhakar*, the bus halted on its penultimate stop near the *ashram* (local name given to the government-run tribal boys' residential school). Here all those travellers alighted whose villages lay in the area at right angles to the road. They walked the remaining distance along the sandy paths to their huts which were dispersed among the villages. The villages were at a distance of from five to twelve kilometres away from the *ashram* bus stop and the bus was the only form of motorised public transport. A number of the villagers, especially those living in the villages further away from its route, walked from Abu Road and followed a more direct route through the forest rather than use the bus; this saved them the Rs 1/- fare. The decision of the villagers to walk or ride on the bus depended on the time of the service, as well as on the purpose of the journey. Journeys themselves varied in frequency. The year of my fieldwork was one following a year of drought and low crop yield. Furthermore, the monsoons during the initial phase of fieldwork had been deficient and Girasia journeys to the town for wage-labour, or to sell produce gathered from the forest, were more frequent than when the maize crop yield was good.

This book is concerned with the residents of one Girasia village in the *Bhakar* who belonged to the Taivar lineage of Girasia. The Taivar village was at an average distance of five to nine kilometres away from the bus stop. One of the criteria involved in my choice of a Girasia village was to be able to stay in an interior village with no road, post office or power supply, yet not exceedingly difficult of access by foot. I was unaware that I was also to witness conditions of agricultural failure and drought. In 1986/87, the Girasia faced acute poverty, due especially to the lack of essential food and material goods. Palvi, my 'elder sister', when asked how she would cope, described the previous severe famine when her husband went without food for several days. I was able to experience some of these difficult conditions firsthand; in the next section I consider the ways in which my perceptions and this book are products of the social relationships formed in 1986/87 in the context of the hardships faced by Taivar men and women.

The Context of 'Fieldwork'

The observations made in the following pages must be placed in the specific context of my own relationship with Girasia women and men and the ways, intended and unintended, in which this relationship served my purposes, and to a lesser extent that of the Girasia. Recent social science writing recognises the relation between the 'observed and the observer' as particularly problematic because of the implicit inequalities of power between the researcher and the respondents which, in turn, shapes the translation of cultural experiences made by the researcher.[58] The issue of power differentials, which Barnes has so aptly called the 'colonial paradigm of fieldwork' (1982: 32) in anthropology is especially pertinent for a subject whose methodology in the understandings of 'other' cultures is so crucially informed through the relationships struck up during fieldwork. While one has to accept that some form of such inequalities are bound to exist between the researcher and the researched (Wolf, 1992), to whatever degree of 'native'-ness the researcher can lay claim, the exercise of reflexivity regarding the processes of ethnographic writing and representation remains an important one, not least because in Karim's words, 'the reflexive mode is important to overcome generalisations bordering on racism' (1993: 249). The tendency to racism through misrepresentation applies as much to Indians studying parts of their own culture as to non Indians studying India. The problems in the writing, representation, translation and transmission of human experience and identifications in social anthropology also lie at the heart of questions regarding the study of gender and the representation of women.[59] Locating myself in relation to the Girasia makes this a story of my representations of Girasia representations, and may go some way towards the fulfilment of ethnographic responsibility.

The Girasia saw me as a young, upper-caste, upper-class townswoman associated with the government authorities. It was the asso-

58. Bourdieu 1977, Said 1978, Fahim 1982, Guha 1985, Clifford and Marcus 1988, Wolf 1992, Bell, Caplan and Karim 1993, among others.
59. As Strathern, 1987, Mohanty 1988, Caplan 1988, Moore 1988, 1993 and Bell, Caplan and Karim 1993 have so pertinently shown.

ciation made with regard to the authority of my class, rather than caste or gender which was responsible for the first picture the Girasia drew of me. The villagers first identified me as a family planning agent of the government, despite my assurances that I was interested in their history and culture. My case had not been strengthened by the pursuit of a line of enquiry up to that point, which expressed an interest in genealogies and population statistics. The initial image of me as a government 'spy' (my words), I was to find, led to the first distortion in my view of Girasia society. For example, I was always told of the ideal rather than the actual number of children in a family. There was a significant difference in the two figures as many Girasia men had previous marriages and had thus had children who could be of different generations and, especially with daughters, could be living in other villages. The issues of caste and gender increasingly became important in my relationships with the Girasia as my stay lengthened.

In terms of a caste identity, and in terms of the politics of my own representation, I wanted to present myself as a Rajput (I was asked if I was Brahmin or Rajput) to show kinship with the Girasia. I explained this identity to myself as somewhat grounded in truth as my father comes from a Nayar family in Kerala and the Nayars are considered martial, and very like the Rajputs (!). While, I think, the problem of my caste was, perhaps, never really resolved for the Girasia (and this would have some basis in reality as my mother is not Indian), my being a woman was an enabling factor for both them and me. I got married two weeks before fieldwork knowing this would be an important matter to put women and men at ease in interacting with me as well as allowing me to be visited by my husband without question. I wore *salwar kameez* (long top over cotton pants and a wrap; recognised as an urban dress for young women) rather than the *sari*, initially for convenience and then for the rest of my stay; this seemed to be more acceptable to the Girasia who viewed *sari* clad women as very different to them. On the other hand, they did not expect me to wear their type of skirt and blouse *(ghagra jhulki)* because I was not 'equal' to them (see discussion of seating arrangements below). I was able to get a good idea of what women experienced in terms of their sexuality, details about menstruation, sex and the body and able to share my own experiences with them. I was less able to understand what Girasia men felt about their own and their women's sexuality and related identities, although there were occasions when I could observe this, for instance in the possessive nature of some men and in their fear of women's threats to run away with other men. The access to women's feelings was particularly revealing as regards the differences between the stated and the actual rules and procedures of marriage (see section on marriage by 'capture', discussed in chapter 5). It was the friendships I formed with the women, especially with Palvi, which proved crucial in extracting me from my identity as a government spy. Palvi Bai suggested to the villagers that I was in a similar position to her, on 'training' (English term used by the Girasias to denote the period spent by a few women of the village who attended the government-organised health care programmes held in other towns or villages). 'Training' involved learning about the different ways in which people lived and organised, particularly their nutrition, hygiene and childcare. Thereafter, it was enough for me to say that I was on 'training' and women and men would receive me more openly in their homes.

Being a woman also allowed the Girasia men to dismiss me more easily than if I were a man, and here I found that I had 'entered' into the hierarchies of Girasia interactions. The essence of my fieldwork relationships is powerfully conveyed through the example of the places I was made to, and decided to, sit in. Almost all the Girasia households had one or two *khat* (rope beds on wooden frames) which were used for sitting and sleeping purposes. Whenever a government official came, he (all the government officials were men and the Girasia talk about the government in male terms) sat on a *khat* and the Girasia sat on the ground, the men nearby and the women at some distance. However, when only the men of the village sat together, they all sat on the *khat* and the women sat on the ground. If a male Girasia visitor from another household or village arrived, space for him was made at the head of the *khat* (every *khat* has a head and tail end), while the host, usually the owner of the *khat*, sat at the tail end. Married Girasia women, who came from outside the husband's village, never sat on a *khat* in the presence of men of the village. Among women, sisters and daughters of the men of the village had priority in sitting on the *khat*. Although they could sit together with the married women on a *khat*, usually the daughter-in-law and mother-in-law did not sit on the same one. When I first came to the village, although the Taivars gave me a 'higher' place on the *khat* while men and women sat on the ground, I thought I should sit on the ground to establish equal relations. But when I sat on the ground the Taivars began to have doubts about the status of my agnatic group, for no outsider was conceived of as equal, only higher or lower. I began to sense a lack of response to questions, and later men began to resume their positions on the *khat*. Eventually I sat on a separate *khat* with the women of the local agnatic group. When men were around they would sit on one *khat* and I would sit on another with younger girls who were daughters and sisters of men of the agnatic unit. The seating arrangements reflected the nature of my fieldwork interaction. The Girasia were more relaxed and less subordinate than with a government official, more equal than with the lower castes, and yet maintained a distinction. The seating arrangements also reflected the Girasia concerns with difference and unequal gender relations.

The only government amenities in the Taivar village were a primary school run by one of the four Girasia who had completed a class ten education, a small *ayurvedic* (herbal and mineral tradition of Indian medicine) dispensary, and a veterinary unit. All these facilities were situated in the only two small, concrete buildings in the village, along its central path. The school area was a place where there was always some activity and this was where I spent a large proportion of my time in the village, meeting and talking more freely to women than in their homes. At close quarters to the school unit there were three shrines as well as a government-installed hand pump for water. While most of the houses were situated within their fields and enclosed by fences of dried shrubs and thorns, the area near the school and shrines was a popular spot for the villagers to meet, especially as it lay alongside a public path and was shaded by a large banyan tree. It was more common for men to gather in such a public place than in the closed space of their houses. It was also a way out of the obligations of hospitality for the household. If unable to offer *chai* (boiled tea leaves with milk and sugar) or *roti* (unleavened maize bread) for lack of milk and maize flour, especially in difficult agricultural seasons, it was especially convenient to meet in a public place.

It had been difficult to anticipate the problems or even prepare myself with regard to the Girasia language. I had hoped, and found, that my knowledge of Hindi, the urban language of northern India, would be useful. The Girasia speak an unwritten local dialect. According to Grierson (1907) Girasia or Nyar is a dialect of the Bhil or the Bhilodi group of languages of the central Indo-Aryan family.[60] There are twenty-six Bhil dialects which are linked with the more major dialects of Rajasthani, Gujarati, Khandeshi and Marathi which

60. Grierson's records of Bhili indicate that it is an Aryan dialect closely related to Gujarati and Rajasthani (1907: 5). Relating this fact to the tribal image of the Bhil, Grierson suggests the 'Bhil are non-Aryans possibly of the Munda stock who have adopted a foreign tongue' (1907: 9).

are spoken in Rajasthan, Gujarat and Maharashtra. Girasia or Nyar, Grierson notes, is spoken in the northern part of this linguistic area, in eastern Marwar (now Jodhpur) and southeast Sirohi. Although similar to the Bhili spoken in Mahikantha in northern Gujarat, Girasia is greatly influenced by Marwari, the most important dialect of Rajasthani. 'Rajasthani' is the term for the group of dialects spoken in Rajasthan, and specifically invented for the purposes of the lingustic survey (Grierson, ibid.: 1). Although the native speakers refer to their dialects, the term Rajasthani was employed to distinguish it from western Hindi. More recently, Dave (1960) has observed the correlation of Girasia with Gujarati, which largely supports Grierson's assertions. The samples of Girasia text transcribed in the Devanagari/Hindi script and obtained by Grierson, also coincide, I find, with the language as it is used in the Taivar Girasia village. Familiarity with Hindi helped me to understand the Girasia language. The Marwari dialect uses a number of Hindi words although the accent and pronunciation may be different. It took me approximately four months to piece together the pattern of Girasia language use which I did through taped conversations and the assistance of those Girasia who knew Hindi. Most adult Girasia men, especially those who travel far in search of wage-labour, were able to understand Hindi, and knew Gujarati equally well.

Most of the data used in the tables of this volume was collected four to five months after I became familiar with the unwritten language. The first questionnaire sought to collect general information on household production and other economic activities. This was addressed to male heads of households. Initially I had hoped to collect material from half the Taivar and non-Taivar households. The Taivars lived in a total of 178 households while the non-Taivars lived in 47 households. I was only able to collect information from fifty-six Taivar and fourteen non-Taivar households. This final count of households maintained the ratio of the Taivar to non-Taivar households in the village, which was approximately four Taivar to one non-Taivar. Further, and as far as possible, among the Taivar households I tried to get respondents from the older households, as they were able to supply information for at least three to four other households. A separate questionnaire regarding brideprice amounts, location and members of the natal household, visits to the natal household, and the daily routine was addressed to forty women of all generations. Mostly wives to Taivar men, they came from eleven different non-Taivar groups.

In terms of reciprocity for all the friendship, shared confidences and information given I will probably be found wanting. In the difficult conditions the Girasia lived in, Palvi told me it was not wise to be seen as dispensing gifts or cash freely. The more so as the Girasia had their own codes about what they considered rightfully due to them, including 'gifts'. My inital encounter with the very different view of a 'gift' came when I offered some fruit (difficult to acquire in times of drought) to a young boy. His refusal was later explained to me in terms of the fear of servitude which such non-obligatory, unexplained gifts carried. This same thinking lay behind the Girasia refusal of government offers of free materials for building wells. Most of my presents were to the women who, towards the end of my stay asked me for various items of the sort which they found most useful: a suitcase, sandals, steel locks, utensils, a bed, chairs, a stove. Women like Palvi and other 'sisters' and friends gained, I think, from an association with me, which provided them with an added status in the village. Their visits to me, couched in terms of 'work' allowed them more freedom to meet in a group, away from their husbands. Also, trips to the market together meant their clients took an added (respectful) interest. These and other situations are elaborated in the ethnographic contexts described in chapters 4 to 8 below. In chapters 2 and 3 I look first at some of the early and more recent historical background to the area in which the Girasia live, as summarised below.

The Plan of the Book

Chapters 2 and 3 are mainly historical accounts dealing with groups, institutions, processes and attitudes in southern Rajasthan, to show how the Girasia have become tribalised over time. Chapter 2 considers the historical organisation of the Rajput polity, particularly the central role of a lineage-based kinship in determining a community's and individual's access to resources and related status. The chapter also shows how Rajput kinship is male-orientated and how the importance of men's honour is responsible for restrictions on women's roles and relations. The Girasias share with the Rajputs both the centrality of the lineage as well as the honour-linked roles for women. Chapter 3 is concerned with relatively recent historical processes, especially the administrative measures of the late colonial and early nationalist governments which are shown to have favoured the elite sections of the Rajputs, not the poorer Rajputs like the Girasias. It points to the role of administrators in stereotyping communities as caste or tribe.

The next six chapters are ethnographic accounts. They describe Girasia beliefs, institutions, social processes and experiences and then compare them with other social groups in the region. Chapters 4 and 5 deal with Girasia 'insider' or community orientated notions of kinship, and focus on the ideologies and practices surrounding familial, marital, affinal, conjugal, sibling and adoption relations. These chapters particularly examine the use of kinship as an idiom of identity and differences of descent, marriage and the genders among the Girasia. Girasia kinship is then briefly compared for its similarities and differences with other caste and tribal material in the region. The comparisons show overwhelmingly the similarity in social structures and ideologies despite the claims made by most social groups that those lower than them are less rigid in their kinship and gender relations. Chapter 6 describes how the distribution of resources within the Girasia village further serves to reinforce kinship differences in the group. The chapter also deals with concepts relating to food and the manner in which food is treated as property, further articulating kin and gender hierarchies. Economic relations involving the market are discussed with a particular focus on the cultural aspect of such relations which are seen to strengthen the sense of being a Girasia and thereby different from other caste groups.

Chapter 7 addresses the issue of marriage payments as a means of understanding the connections between kinship institutions, the economy and the structural and ideological position of women. Firstly, it considers the politics surrounding the form of marriage payments in the wider Indian context. In the second instance, the connections between the marriage payments and kinship politics within the Girasia community are explored. At both levels, the relation between women's work and economic 'value' is found to be similar, yet articulated in the form of the contrasting marriage payments of dowry and brideprice. Chapters 8 and 9 concentrate on the religious dimension of Girasia kinship. While chapter 8 describes customary Girasia beliefs, attitudes and actions as expressions of kinship, chapter 9 considers the response of Girasia kinship ideologies and institutions to changing religious affiliations, such as those represented by the Anop Mandal, a little-researched, semi-political and religious organisation which is based on class rather than kin ties. Chapter 10, the Conclusion, suggests means by which we can make sense of the complex social, political, economic and historical contexts in which the Girasia live, and thereby provides an altogether new way of thinking about caste in India.

Chapter 2

HISTORICAL BACKGROUND
The Rajput State and Related Identities

> Going Westwards from Upper India into Rajputana, one enters the most romantic area in the peninsula, a land of ruined forts and ancient strongholds, famous for deeds of valour and self-sacrifice, crowning rugged heights above old and picturesque towns. Many are the monuments to ... warriors, stones carved with a horseman and his weapons and the heavenly bodies, and still frequent are the stones carved with a single upraised arm indicating the place where a widow burned herself upon her husband's funeral pyre.
>
> (Hutton, 1946: 31)

*R*ajasthan has been dominated historically by the Rajput clans. The Rajputs consider themselves members of the warrior or Kshatriya *varna* (occupationally based ideological category) in Hindu social organisation. These strong, patrilineal martial clans, whose presence is noted in the region around the ninth century AD had evolved a specific style of kin-based power which distinctively knitted together the polity and the economy of the region they ruled.[1] The kin-orientated state structure was differentially effected but remained distinct through the Mughal and later the British domina-

---

1. Thapar 1987, 227.

tion of India.² Although increasingly restricted by its encapsulation in the British paramountcy, the formal state structure was not dismantled until the years following Indian independence in 1947. The Rajput rulers relinquished the autonomy of their states to become part of the Indian nation between 1947 and 1956. But it was not until 1969, when the Privy Purses Abolition Act took away the special privileges of the Rajput families that the political and economic influence of the previous rulers on the local population abated. In cultural and social terms, however, today many of the castes in Rajasthan still define themselves in relation to this historical Rajput dominance. The Rajput ethic continues to dominate the psyche of most of the communities in Rajasthan, especially among the rural and land-holding sections. It is an ethic especially linked to the values of honour and shame, and related to a particular style of life popularised by members of the royal lineages.

The Taivar Girasia present themselves as belonging to the Parmar clan of Rajput Girasia; in other words, as Girasia who are descended from one of the ancient Rajput clans. The point of this historical chapter is not so much to prove the Rajput origins of the Girasia and thereby indulge in speculative history, as to recognise the complex dynamics at work in the region where the Rajput state had until recently organised social relations and related identities. The most distinctive feature of the Rajput state, with regard to the Girasia, was the flux between the ruling lineage, which was the centre of power, and the various lineages and sections of Rajput kin. Among Rajput kin, there were communities who were regarded as marginal because of their reduced landholding rights. *Girasia* was a title which denoted a small share in landholding rights. Given the possibility of increasing landholding rights through inheritance and military strategy in the Rajput state, land titles could and did change. In this chapter I suggest that the relation to land and landholdings lies at the core of the perceived and constructed differences in identity and status of the various Rajput groups (clans, lineages and sections within these). In chapter 3

---

2. Following Stern (1977), I use the phrase 'Rajput state' in the singular although there were a number of states under the power of different clans, because each state had a similar political and economic organisation and administration. According to Ziegler (1978), it is only by the early seventeenth century, and as a response to Mughal indirect rule, that one sees the, 'first true Rajput states in the sense that there was a defined and institutionalised basis of power from whom regulations emanated with appropriate sanction and enforcement' (ibid.: 226). At the time that Sherring wrote about the 'Tribes and Castes of Rajputana' in 1881, fifteen of the eighteen princely states were Rajput.

I suggest that a greater social distance, based on differences in landholding rights, arose as a result of the British and later Indian government census classifications; this chapter especially describes how outsider perceptions and attitudes to the Girasia are linked to the nature of the administrative policies of the changing state.

So far historical work on the Rajput State in Rajasthan has been restricted to a study of elite politics and administration.[3] While it is important to study the institutional framework responsible for the economic and social policies, such an analysis does not examine how the majority of the population in the region, which is formed by the lower castes and lineages, are affected by (or affect) the conservative policies of the traditional state [4] and its landed elite. While few historical references exist on the position of the Girasia in the Rajput state, to my knowledge there are no detailed historical or anthropological commentaries on the nature of this association. Without my own archival research for the historical section of the book (this and the following chapter), I might have concurred with the view favoured among Indian anthropologists and administrators, which regards most claims to higher status by communities, especially lower castes and lineages, as attempts at social mobility through the emulation of higher-caste customs (a process which has been called 'sanskritisation', Srinivas, 1957, 1972; and 'hinduisation', 'rajputisation' for tribal groups, Sinha 1962, Chauhan 1978).

Both in the self-presentations of the Rajputs as well as in the writing of commentators on the the Rajput state, references to women are used to describe the characteristics which distinguish the Rajputs from other groups and people in Rajasthan and elsewhere in India. This chapter outlines how the identity and actions of Rajput women have, historically, been dictated by institutions and processes, of which *sati* (self-immolation) and *jauhar* (collective suicide) are dramatic examples concerned with prestige and status amongst Rajput men. The next chapter discusses the strategic use of these customary representations of women to create new Rajput identities in the nation state.

This chapter also provides the grounds to assert that some of the claims of communities at the economic and political margins must be considered seriously if one is to understand the complexities of

---

3. For example, Sharma 1977, Ray 1978, Haynes 1987 Copland 1982, Rudolph and Rudolph 1984.
4. Fuller questions the use of the term 'traditional India' by anthropologists. He shows that the rise of the importance of the institution of caste as a determinant of power was a creation of the colonial policies of British India rather than a feature of pre-British India (1977: 110).

historical and contemporary social categories and processes of identifications. Here, I discuss the nature of the Rajput state in terms of shifting, land-centred, social relations within the state. I focus also on the ways that the Rajputs and their gender relations have been represented by colonial observers and social scientists writing on the Rajput state. The chapter is also concerned more specifically with the Girasia title and related landholding rights as they are recorded in the little archival material that exists.

Organisation of the Rajput State

According to Lyall (1907), the Rajput clans were a warring rather than cultivating caste by occupation, living off the peasants whom they conquered.[5] It was more profitable to wage war than carry on settled agriculture. On the poorer soils there were greater gains in the forcible acquisition of wealth, and on richer soils the Rajputs took up landholding rights in preference to self-cultivation. The most substantive historical records of the area covered by the Rajput states are concerned with land administration. Possession of land seems to have been the prime motive for aggression; land holding signified power. More than the land itself, it was the rights in the produce of the land upon which Rajput dominance was based.[6] Most of the documented material on the Rajput state is available from the Mughal period (sixteenth century until the arrival of the British in the eighteenth century) onwards. The territory of Rajputana was divided among clans of exogamous Rajput warring lords at the time of the first Islamic invasions. The head of each clan was the ruler of the territory under him.[7] Between the time of the early Islamic invasions into India and the Mughal period (eleventh to sixteenth centuries), we find that the territories conquered by, for example, the Rajput clans in Mewar were divided amongst the brothers and sons of the rulers (Sharma 1977: 5-9).

For Ziegler (1978) the key features of the Rajput identity, which also survived the Mughal period, were the Rajput relations of the brotherhood *(bhaibamdh),* and relations by marriage *(saga).* The *bhaibamdh* was a unit of patrilineal descent represented by the clan *(vams/kul),* and branch *(sakha).* While the clan and branches were spread over various territories in and around Rajasthan, the func-

---

5. Sherring notes 119 tribes for the Rajputs (1881: 24); other writers group the Rajputs into thirty-six major clans (Karve 1968, Sharma 1977).
6. Baden-Powell 1892, Stokes 1978.
7. See Lyall, 1907: 225; also *Imperial Gazetteer,* Rajputana, 1908: 14.

tionally corporate units were smaller brotherhoods (*khamp*, or twig) of three to six generations (ibid.: 223). Apart from the families of the royal lineage, the conquered Rajput lineages as well as some (loyal) families from other clans were given rights by the *raja* (ruler) to collect revenue from a small number of landholdings (known as *jagir* after the Mughal unit of landholding).[8] Shah (1982) notes the various levels among the Rajputs in Gujarat below the royal families as, 'the ruling lineages of the smaller and less powerful kingdoms; lineages and owners of large and small fiefs, variously called *jagirs, giras, thakarat, thikana, taluka, wanta;* lineages of substantial landowners under various land tenures having special rights and privileges; and lineages of small landowners' (1982: 10,11). Ziegler (1978) differentiates between the more and less hierarchical brotherhoods. According to him, kinship was the determining factor with regard to the rights to access land among those brotherhoods in the outer-lying states, while clientship or loyalty to rulers of other brotherhoods superseded kinship in gaining access to land in the more hierarchical Rajput states. Thus, landholding rights and related power were determined by a combination of kinship and loyalty. Ray gives two important reasons for the maintainence of extra-kin ties between sections of the lineages and clans. These were firstly, that the Rajput custom of clan exogamy required members of one clan to enter into relations with clans other than their own. Secondly, affinal and other kinship ties provided an essential reserve for the royal lineage in terms of resources and services which were important during infighting within the royal clan (1978: 205-40). Through these kin ties, the Rajputs were able to control widespread areas in Rajputana.

It was the network of kin ties that formed the basis of Rajput political power. The pattern of landholdings largely reflected the kin networks but also represented the individual authority of a powerful landlord. It was the combination of autonomy at one level with subservience at another which characterised the Rajput state.[9] Apart

8. In terms of landholding, Sherring (1881) notes that the Rajputs, whom he called tribes, were divided into three ranked classes: (1) landholders (which included the old hereditary aristocracy); (2) cultivators (only lesser Rajputs were cultivator-owners as in the case of the Girasias and the Bhumias) and, (3) servants, agents and the like (ibid.: 24).

9. For example, in Mewar, according to Ray (1977), 'Each head of lineage possessed the outerlying land and ruled almost as an independent chief. The relations between each chief and his ruler varied from *jagir* to *jagir* as did the relations between him and his kin and the peasants within his *jagir* .... it was the power exercised over the countryside by the Rajput clans and on the highly ritualised relationships that bound these clans to the ruling dynasty at Udaipur that

from kin networks and loyalty, Copland (1982) regards tribute as the main factor on which the power of the state was based. The amount of tribute, Copland emphasises, was an index of power derived from successful conquests and served to differentiate greater rulers from lesser ones. The quest for autonomy and individual power, however, threatened the kinship unity on which the Rajput dominance was based. The strength and commanding force of the ruler was a crucial determinant in the balance of power between closely related kin[10] amongst whom the ruler was regarded as an equal.[11] The system of land distribution caused great rivalry between competing kin on the one hand, and between them and the ruler on the other. The outcome of such rivalry was significant, for the position of the ruler was determined not by heredity, in this case primogeniture, but by the consent and cooperation of his kin and descendants. Individual efforts at increasing power by calling upon the resources of a few kinsmen as opposed to other kinsmen, seriously hampered a solidarity based on kinship among the Rajputs. This was also responsible for frequent fissures within the body of kin.

While the Rajput clans had direct and localised power bases within Rajputana, the Muslim invasions and conquests to follow built up the Mughal empire through delegation and indirect rule, which strengthened hierarchical relationships among the Rajputs.[12] Under the domination of the Mughals, the Rajput *rajas* became holders of the *mansab* (an office showing military title and rank which, while it restricted the expansion of Rajput landholding rights, also legitimised Rajput rule in the recognition it gave to the Rajput titles).[13] The Mughals introduced an organised system of rank and office akin to the Rajput system of *pattidari*, which obviated the previous grants of land revenue by kinship or loyalty. The rising bureaucratisation was reflected in the increasing possession of land deeds *(patta/pata)* which superseded claims based on descent or verbal grants.[14] A

---

the seemingly indestructible Guhilot-Sisodia rule over Mewar for twelve centuries rested' (ibid.: 208). (Mewar was the only Rajput state which significantly resisted subordination to the Mughals and remained hostile to the British). Ziegler (1978) sees these diverse tendencies in terms of conflicting loyalties, of the individual to his brotherhood on the one hand, and to his master or ruler who could be from a different clan or brotherhood, on the other.

10. Ray 1976, Sharma 1977.
11. Lyall 1907, Tod 1920 [1832], Copland 1982.
12. Ziegler 1978.
13. The *rajas* were 'granted *jagirs* in lieu of their salary which was fixed according to the *Mansab* they held' (Sharma ibid.: 292).
14. Ziegler, 1978.

Historical Background

result of the Mughal restrictions on Rajput landholding and the enclosure of Rajput territory was a reduction in the interstate and clan disputes. In other words, even if the kin were strong compared to the ruler they could no longer encroach on his territory, a situation which had previously resulted in the political demise of weaker *rajas* (Ray 1977). Thus the Mughal system in large part supported the Rajput style of government, in the manner in which power in the countryside was delegated through landholding rights. The Mughals did not redistribute landholdings from below, they only controlled them from above. Fuller (1977) draws our attention to some important aspects of similarity between the Mughal system in pre-British India and the Rajput state.[15] In both systems of government there was a permeable local, landed elite (the *zamindar* and the *raiyatwar*). Most *zamindars* originated as peasants, and the critical factor in their ascent was the possession of armed supremacy. The Mughal system was akin to the Rajput in that there was a fluidity between strata; furthermore, in both systems stability was fragile with a permanent potential for disruption.[16] Thus the Mughal intervention did not fundamentally change the Rajput state.[17] Neither did the decline of the Mughal empire critically effect the suzerain-vassal relations between the larger and smaller chiefs within the local state (Copland 1982: 20). Ziegler (1978), however, emphasises that the Mughal domination increased the conflicts of loyalty, to brother versus to another ruler, in the Rajput states.

Under the British, the princely states of Rajputana were administered under the special code of the paramountcy, a form of indirect rule which advocated little interference in the internal affairs of the state.[18] Although non-interference was the overt British policy, there were various forms of covert intervention, particularly in the period following the demise of a ruler who had no direct adult, male descedant.[19] The

15. Fuller's commments are based on Habib's 1963 analysis of the agrarian structure of the Mughals.
16. Rao (1977: 88) notes with regard to the Ahir Rewari Kingdom, south of Delhi (and to the north of Rajputana), that both the loyalty of the Rewari rulers to the Mughals, as well as the Mughal interest only in military service and money, allowed the kingdom a considerable amount of internal autonomy.
17. According to C. Bayly (personal communication), the general picture is one of considerable economic activity up to around 1760, with the decline of the Mughal power facilitating the consolidation of some of the larger Rajput states.
18. Lee-Warner 1894, Copland 1982, Rudolph and Rudolph 1984.
19. For example, Haynes (1978: 32-65) gives a lucid account of the manner in which the British undermined the Rajput ruler's authority in Alwar by substituting a bureaucracy which was loyal to the British.

paramountcy, like the Mughal empire before it, curtailed the possibility of territorial expansion of the Rajput states. This in turn gave rise to interclan disputes within the state.[20] The effect of the British presence on Rajput political administration was to escalate claims to status as a means to ensure landholding rights since land became a fixed commodity and unattainable outside the claims of heredity.[21] The British introduced restraints in the division and transfer of landholding rights in the Rajput state. This was a policy which worked to the advantage of the Rajput elite (Stokes, 1978). I will argue that for marginal Rajput communities such as the Girasia, the restrictions on access to land contributed to their permanently low status in the political economy and social hierarchies.

In south Rajasthan, the Sirohi state, where the Taivar Girasia live, registered only minor direct political interference from the British.[22] Historically, the princely state of Sirohi had been eclipsed by the large and powerful ruling Rajput families of the former principalities of Marwar (now Jodhpur) to the west, and of Mewar (now Udaipur) to the east. Sirohi was continually a source of conflict between Marwar and Mewar, both of whom claimed suzerainty over it.[23] The

20. Copland (1982) notes that when Tod first wrote, a change was already taking place to this effect. Tod himself remarks on the abundant claims of land usurpation between kin (1920, [1892]: 33). This was especially so for the eastern states of Rajputana, which had been more disturbed than the western states by the Maratha invasions (similarly observed by Sherring, ibid.: 6).
21. In 1858 India was formally attached to the British Crown, where previously it had been subordinate to the East India Company. As a result of the proclamation to this effect, the political map was fixed and the states who received patrimony at that time retained the privilege until the end of the British rule (Copland, ibid.: 3).
22. The states of western Rajasthan seem to have been less affected than either eastern Rajasthan or southern Gujarat, either by the dissolution of the Mughal empire in the early seventeenth century, or the incursions of the Marathas from Central India following this dissolution (Copland 1982: 33).
23. Relations between the royal families of Marwar and Mewar had been strained throughout the Rajput supremacy. The two royal families represented two different strands in Rajput rule, reflected in their policies towards outside rulers. The Mewar Rajput rule had been characterised by an adaptive political system, seen in their adjustments to the alien rule of the Mughals (to the extent of providing wives to them, considered the main shameful and dishonourable act by the Mewar Rajputs, who discontinued intermarriage with the Marwar Rajputs on this issue), greater interactions with the British and, through their shrewdness and strategy, have also been able to maintain large landholdings under the Indian Government (Rudolph and Rudolph, 1984). The Mewar Rajputs, known throughout India through the popular folklore of their heroic ruler Rana Pratap, were more interested in the honour and valour of fighting, rather than in polit-

issue was complicated as the Sirohi rulers were descendents of the Marwar royal house but had affinal relations with the Mewar families. On the request of a settlement by the ruler of Sirohi, the British Government (on the advice of Colonel James Tod) legally attached Sirohi to Mewar in 1817 (Banerjee: 212).[24] The rulers most visible in historical accounts of southern Rajasthan were the Rathor Rajputs in Jodhpur and the Chauhan and Sisodia Rajputs in Udaipur. At the time of the first treaty with the British in 1823, Sirohi was ruled by the Deora branch of the Chauhan Rajputs. The Deora Chauhans were descended from the rulers at Nadol in the Jodhpur (then Marwar) state around the end of the tenth century (Erskine 1908: 218). They were known to have migrated westwards, thus crushing the Parmar Rajput hold over the area, first in Jalore to the west of present-day Sirohi. In the early fourteenth century the Deora Chauhan Rajputs captured Chandravati, the Parmar Rajput capital near Abu Road in present day southern Sirohi.[25]

The Girasia Title and Landholding Rights

The Parmar Rajput clan from whom the Taivar Girasia are descended, were the regional Rajput power till the thirteenth century AD. By the end of the fourteenth century, the Parmar Rajputs were no longer in positions of power in southern Rajasthan and had moved further south into Gujarat and Malwa in Central India.[26] The Deora Chauhans maintained their hold over Sirohi through the British period and until Indian independence. Adult Girasia in the Taivar village remembered the last Deora rulers and their *durbar* (court). The ancestors of the Taivar Girasia had sought permission from the Deora Chauhan *thakur* (chief), to live in the *Bhakar*.[27]

---

ical acumen or strategy. The Mewar Rajputs were known to have a more rigid traditional system which remained uncooperative to any foreign rule. After Indian independence, due to a lack of proper organisation they were unable to maintain their privileges in comparison to the larger *jagirdars* of Jaipur and Jodhpur (Rudolph and Rudolph 1984).

24. This decision must be viewed in the light of the bias which Tod had for Mewar. Brookes (1859) notes '[Tod] had arrived enthusiastically in 1818 with the idea of raising her court [Mewar] to the splendour it enjoyed under Sangram Singh' (the ruler of that time; ibid.: 23, words in brackets mine).
25. Erskine 1908: 218; Lala Sita Ram 1920: 130.
26. Russel and Hiralal 1916, Lala Sita Ram 1920, Forbes 1924, Thapar 1966, Lal 1979.
27. The District Gazetteer for Sirohi (1967) notes, 'It is probable that when the Deora Chauhans subjugated the Paramaras about six hundred years ago, they were unwilling to dispossess the Girasias of their land, or were possibly unable

The early British administrators recognised the Girasia as petty landholders who were marginal to positions of state power. The British conception of the Girasias was based mainly on the works of Baden-Powell (1892) and Tod (1832, 1920) for the upper Bombay presidency and Rajasthan respectively. Baden-Powell's book, *The Land Systems of British India* (1892), was among the most authoritative on the subject. According to Baden-Powell:

> A number of old Rajput chiefs were called 'Girasiya' (Grassia of many writers); and, where such still retain in whole or part, territorial estates they come under the head of taluqdari tenures ... But at the present day, the term is applied specifically to a cash allowance or revenue assignation, and not to indicate a landed or proprietary estate. The custom arose out of the dispossession of old Rajput chiefs in Malwa, Gujarat and Central India. The persons (so) harrassed the government and the inhabitants of the former estates that people were happy to give them a share (*Giras* = mouthful) of the revenue to secure protection from plunder. The amount to be paid became an item in the revenue roll of the villages. *Giras* is now paid as a claim established by prescriptive right either by the government or by the *inamdar* (on alienated land) to the descendants of the old chiefs, but only to male lineal descendants ... it is at present day only a matter of cash payment made to certain chiefs who may of course possess other lands or property of other kinds (1892: 280-81).

Two major points arise from the above account. Firstly, the Girasias were dispossessed Rajput chiefs; secondly, the Girasia title, especially in the British period, denoted a cash allowance. Furthermore, although the title was linked to landholding rights in landed estates, the Girasia had claims to alienated land, i.e., land given as a reward for loyalty and service to the chief. Baden-Powell's account supported Malcolm's (1823) writings on central India. According to Malcolm,

> Girasias [were] chiefs who were driven from their possessions by invaders, and established and maintained a claim to a share of the revenue, upon the ground of their power to disturb or prevent its collection. And the *Giras* has been metaphorically applied to designate the small share of the produce of the country which these plunderers claim. (1832: 136)

The important point to note about these accounts is that the Girasias were already marginal to the Rajput state at the time of the British presence in India. However, as the following accounts illustrate, the extent of their marginality varied from one Rajput state to the other. Tod (1920, [1832]) was the author of one of the more

---

to do so on account of the secure position in the mountain fastnesses of the Aravallis which the Girasias held' (ibid.: 103).

detailed accounts of the Rajput states, especially Mewar, in Rajputana. He classified the Girasia landlord or *Thakur,* as one of a class of two (the other being the Bhumia) Rajput landholders in Mewar. The Girasia chieftain, according to Tod was,

> He who holds *Giras* by grant *(patta)* of the prince for which he performs service with specific quotas at home and abroad, renewable at every lapse when all, the ceremonies of resumption, the fine of relief and the investiture takes place ... as opposed to the Bhumia who holds a 'prescriptive possession' and does not renew his grant and so the Girasias come to be known as vassal chieftains (1920: 191).

Tod's observations are echoed in the *Imperial Gazetteer* (1908) which states, 'The Girasias, the original inhabitants of the *Bhakar*, still retain their *bhum* rights ... free of rent or at reduced rates on condition of some particular service such as watch and ward of their villages etc.' (1908: 224-25). For Tod, however, the Bhumias were distinct from the Girasias because, 'The Girasia *pattas* or fiefs were not grants in perpetuity but were movable, perpetual and then hereditary'(1920: 192). Hence the actual entitlement of the Girasia position was not clear. The records indicate that the Girasia in the Rajput states performed services for which they were granted landholding rights. In the Rajput states of Gujarat however the Girasia landholding right was independent of their services to the ruler. For example, Forbes (1924), who recorded Rajput tenures under the British in Gujarat, maintained that the land was mainly divided into *khalsa* (crown lands) and the *Grassia*. While the former had previously been managed by the Mughal and the Marathas and had passed into British hands, the latter was under a Grassia chief and subject to his jurisdiction. The Grassia chiefs paid revenue to the British and were responsible for the maintenance of order within their own state. The greater autonomy and prestige of the Girasia title in the Rajput states of Gujarat may explain their present higher status in Gujarat as compared to Rajasthan. The Girasias are not considered as Scheduled Tribes in the Gujarat census classifications, but as members of the other backward classes (see chapter 3).

Although Baden-Powell, Tod and Forbes all recognised the connection of the Girasia title to land-rights, I would argue that they equated the Girasias with 'fallen' Rajput lineages. In doing so, they disregarded the possibility of the temporary or shifting nature of landholding titles. I found conclusive evidence for the variability in holding and status which the Girasia title could signify in the 1908 agency report of Kathiawar, a Rajput state in southern Gujarat. The report mentioned the establishment of a *Rajasthanik* court in 1873 to settle all disputes regarding the '*Giras* or hereditary estates between the chiefs and the *Bhayads* and *mulgirasia* ' (ibid.: 183). In order to explain the necessity of establishing a separate court to settle Girasia landholding disputes, the report describes the Girasias as those persons,

> who are for the most part the kinsmen of the chiefs or the descendants of earlier holders who have been deprived of their estate ... as each tribe of Rajputs invaded the peninsula, its chiefs bestowed on their relations portions of land they had won. This share was named *Kapalgiras* and passed to the descendants of the original grantees. The more enterprising Girasias continued to acquire fresh lands from their neighbours until they found themselves sufficiently strong to set up as independent rulers ... when a Girasia succeeded in gaining his independence, he became a *talukdar* and assumed the title of *Thakur, Rana, Raval* or *Raja* ... others less enterprising surrendered the greater portion of their land to a neighbouring chief in return for protection and fell into the position of *mulgirasias* or original sharers (1908: 183).

The above report indicates that, even within the single Rajput state of Kathiawar, there were different categories of Girasias. Furthermore, the nature of the difference between the Girasias depended on their differential ability to expand their revenue from landholding rights. More recently, Copland (1982) has examined the layers of power in the princely states, especially in Kathiawar in Gujarat. In a short summary of the various landholding titles, Copland suggests the Girasias were like little kings, or village and supra village leaders.[28] So while a chief had sovereign power over an extended territory, the Girasia had subordinate rights over a village or villages (Copland, 1982: 23). However, Copland argues that the distinction was meaningless over time as the Girassia could become a *raja*.[29] Copland observes that before the Mughal presence, the *Giras* or special rights in land were considered to be a pedigree of ancient repute. Initially grants to temples and religious mendicants, the *Giras* came to be known as donations of tax free land to the relatives of the ruling chief. The Mughals both accepted the *Giras* and extended its coverage. Moreover, Copland argues that the Mughal acceptance of the *Giras* debased it in the eyes of the Rajput rulers who associated its extension with Mughal oppression. After the departure of the Mughals, *Giras* became synonymous with plunder

28. He bases this on the more contemporary anthropological analysis of Cohn (1987) for the Rajput system in the northern province of Uttar Pradesh in India.
29. Based on a report by Wedderburn, Acting Chief Secretary Bombay, dated December 1870; in Copland, 1982: 23.

by the local warlords. Copland notes that this fall in status of the Girasia title had already taken place by 1700. He regards the disputes between the Girasias, mentioned in the Kathiawar report above, as attempts at retrieving a previous status. The use of the prefix *mul* (meaning either ancient, or special or root) could be seen as a step towards creating differences in the types of Girasia privileges.

Copland's analysis indicates that when the British commentators wrote on the Rajput state, the Girasias were already a marginal but not 'tribal' category. This would explain the British classification of the Girasia, mentioned earlier, as 'fallen' Rajput lineages. The British officials were assigned to record the land tenures of a particular area. While each official recorded the nature of tenures and communities in his area, very little collaboration occured on the classification of marginal lands, especially in the Rajput states. This possibly led to different accounts on the Rajput origins of the Girasia. For example, for Brookes (1859) the Girasias in the Mewar State were Rajputs descended from the Chauhan clan. A similar observation for Mewar was made by Sherring (1881). A more recent study by Lal (1979) of the Girasias in northern Gujarat states that the Girasias are a community descended from amongst all the regional Rajput lineages. I find Lal's observation to be true for the Girasia of the Sirohi region as well. From my own fieldwork experiences, I found that there were a large number of Girasia groups divided according to their descent from various Rajput clans and the attached historical privileges.

The Taivar Girasia identify closely with the *Bhakar* or hilly enclosure in which their village is located. In the British administration records, the *Bhakar* was defined as that portion of Sirohi district, 'which consists of ranges of intricate hills, stretching away to Mewar [present-day Udaipur to the East], and has villages of very scattered patches of cultivation' (District Report 1943-44: 55). The *Bhakar* area was one of the last in Sirohi where landholdings were surveyed for the classification of revenue payments. It was not until after 1944 that an official record of the inhabitants was obtained. Until then the *Bhakar* was 'a hilly tract inhabited by the wild and primitive tribes of the Bhils and Girasseas' (District Report 1901, chapter 1). The number of Girasia of the *Bhakar* was roughly estimated at 2,860 in the 1891 census, which was the first to be held in the state (1901: 73). Since the land-settlement operations of 1944, the Taivars have been owners of fixed individual plots of land and the village as a whole is under the jurisdiction of the Abu Road *tehsil*. In their pattern of landholding the Taivars follow the *pattidari* system of landholding common to the region. That is, the land is divided among kinsmen on the basis of ancestral shares, and accordingly revenue is paid to the government (see chapter 6 for a detailed discussion of the Taivar pattern of landholding and production).

According to the Taivar Girasia, their ancestors were given land in the *Bhakar* approximately 150 years previously by the chief *(Thakur)* of the Chauhan Rajput clan, who owned the area surrounding the hilly terrain. This Deora Chauhan *Thakur* lived in Deldar, a village approximately twelve kilometres from the Taivar village. It was common knowledge among the Taivars that their ancestors had come from Jambudi (approximately 22 kilometres from Abu Road in the southern portion of the *Bhakar*); this was another village which was inhabited solely by the Girasia. According to the Tribal Research Institute at Udaipur, Jambudi was amongst the oldest Girasia-inhabited villages in the region. When I visited it, I found the village populated by Girasia who called themselves Parmar Rajput Girasia. In separate accounts, Taivar elders recounted the nature of their separation from the Jambudi Girasia. According to Chela, one of the oldest Taivars: 'there was a dispute over the ownership of a *patta* [unit] of land in Jambudi. Two brothers, our ancestors, left Jambudi on this account. One of their wives was pregnant. As they had no land of their own, they stayed in the households of other castes *[jaths]* away from the village. They also drank water there. When a son was born, they felt the need to own land to provide for their descendants. They approached the *Thakur* of Deldar and requested shelter. The *Thakur* granted them land in the *Bhakar*. The first Taivars stayed in Nichalagarh. They had to patrol the area and also deposit one-seventh cropshare at the *thana* [checkpost].'[30]

Both the Taivar Girasia and the Parmar Girasia of Jambudi told me they were related. The Parmar Girasia, however, stressed that the Taivars were lower than them because their ancestors had drunk water and stayed in lower-caste households. The Taivar version,

30. Remains of the *thana* situated in Nichalagarh still existed at the time of my fieldwork. The *thana* had been for the collection of taxes from the communities settled in the *Bhakar*. I found a community of Muslim farmers living near the *thana*. According to Ajeez Khan, a Muslim elder, referred to as *chacha-ji*, 'To enforce the tax rules on the Girasia, the Sirohi *durbar* imported my Musalman [sic] ancestors from Peshawar [now in northern Pakistan].' Ajeez Khan was a member of the seventh generation descended from the Muslim tax collectors. The fort-like walls of the *thana* had been repaired subsequently. When I saw it, the *thana* housed a police constable and other primary government facilities of the *Bhakar*. Thus the *thana* continued to symbolise the presence of state authority in the *Bhakar*. Few Girasia lived close to the *thana* and many younger Girasia would avoid passing by it.

according to Kalu, was that the Parmar Rajputs were to blame for the split and the subsequent hardship which resulted in the lower standing of the Taivars. For Kalu to even think of the Jambudi Parmars, he said, would cause his blood to boil. Not all the Taivars shared Kalu's sentiments. Taivar membership of the low-caste Anop Mandal association had brought them in close contact with members from Jambudi (see chapter 9). Apart from the Parmar Rajput Girasia, there were Girasia of the Chauhan, Parihar, Rathor and Solanki Rajput clans. Like the Taivar sub-clan of the Parmar Rajputs, there were a number of sub-clans within each clan. At the time of my fieldwork, the Parmar Taivar Girasia had affinal relations with the Girasia of the Parmar sub-clans and other Rajput clans (see chapter 5). Apart from the differences of clan affiliation between all the Girasia clans and sub-clans, there were the differences of 'high' and 'low' (see chapter 5). Landholding rights, however, as among the Rajputs, remained within the local patrilineage and were defined by descent and territory.

'Writing' and Representing the Rajputs

Most of the early Western commentators mentioned above, such as Baden-Powell, Sherring, Lee-Warner, Forbes, Tod, Brookes, wrote on the nature of the Rajput state within the period of the British paramountcy. For Tod (1920, [1832]), the Rajput structure was akin to that of the historical European feudal system. But such a feudal system consisted of rulers who were not usually linked to the ruled by any ties of kinship or cultural similarities. For Lyall (1907), the predominance of kinship as a structuring principle of the Rajput state made it 'tribal', as opposed to the non-kinship based structure of feudal Europe. More recently, I find Fox (1979) combines the views of Tod and Lyall to characterise the Rajput state as constituted by a feudalisation of kin ties, especially in those stages of a development cycle where the lineage elite were successful in consolidating their power at the cost of kin (1979: 95). For Fox, five stages were involved in the foundation of a powerful Rajput lineage. These were, firstly, the growth of the lineage through the stratification and elevation of the *raja* and elite over their kinsmen (mainly by the seizure of the revenue rights), secondly, the fragmentation of these rights between agnatic and a few affinally related kinsmen, thirdly, the difficult control over these intermediary revenue kinsmen who, fourthly, finally break off their loyalty to become a major opposition and, fifthly, if possible found a politically separate lineage with immediate revenue control over the cultivators. Fox bases his model on local-level politics between the kin bodies within the lineage hierarchy and the central authority. He suggests there was a natural tendency for the growth and decline of the lineage elite via territorial and kin expansion which, through the delegation of revenue collection, structured the relation of lineage members to proprietary rights (Fox 1975).[31]

I regard Fox's analysis as an improvement on Lyall's observations because, even if, as Lyall suggests, kin ties supported the political structure of the Rajput state, one cannot assume a homogeneous pursuit by all kin of the policies set by the ruler. In this sense the development cycle of Rajput elite suggested by Fox is much more useful. Often the very character of kin relations among the Rajputs was adversarial in their quest for power, and relationships were governed by the intense desire to increase landholdings to improve upon, or maintain, status and prestige. The motivations for expansion were always at the cost of other kin and were directly opposed to the ideal of a unified brotherhood or a community of kinship. In Mewar, for example, Ray finds that other subordinate clans, by virtue of their loyalty often based on marital affinity, were used to counterbalance the intense rivalry between close factions of kin. Moreover, the potential for such rivalry, and the subsequent need to maintain extensive ties outside the immediate kin group, prevented a local consolidation of power (1978: 209, 215). According to Ray, especially if the ruler was weak, the chiefs under him tended to expand into the crown holdings. In smaller areas the tie between the local chiefs and the people was greater if there was a greater proportion of Rajputs in the population, who then provided a stronger threat to the crown lands.

In the Rajput state, apart from the rivalry between kin in the quest for power, the rewards of landholdings for loyal non-Rajput groups further 'blurred the lines of kinship' (Brookes 1859: 14).[32] While alliances between kin shifted periodically, so did the loyalty of dis-

---

31. Stern (1977: 69) criticises Fox's model of the lineage cycle for its neglect of the effect of the politics resulting from the affinal relationships. For Stern, it was only by the interplay between consanguinity (descent) and affinity (marriage) that Rajput politics was articulated. The hierarchy operative within the Rajput system as a function of this interplay was based on 'the opposition that allows either actualisation or neutralisation of the difference of status between bride-givers and bride-takers from the point of view of each localised lineage segment or clan' (1977: 73). Thus for Stern, as lineage segmentation and marriage cut across state boundaries, the region should be the important unit of study.
32. The landholdings received as a reward for loyalty to the ruler were classified as 'alienated lands' under British administration (Baden-Powell, 1892).

Historical Background

tant kin or non-kin peasant groups. Thus the boundary of the state is shown to be highly fluid between the claims of closer and distant kin as well as with that of the non-Rajputs. It was this fluidity which was affected by the British who fixed land titles to those who were the current rulers. In terms of the shifting basis of power, it seems to me, the Rajput state has close associations with Sahlins' model of the heroic state. Sahlins shows how subordination to the ruler may undercut the solidarity of 'tribalism' based on 'the bonds of kinship and the relation to ancestral lands' (1987: 45).[33] While for Sahlins change in the heroic state occurs through a combination of chance and charisma, Fox sees a cyclic pattern in the nature of solidarity in Rajput political behaviour. Fox (1975) and Stern (1977) both indicate that the 'downward' movement of cadets of successive generations, from a position wherein they possess minor *jagirs* to holdings of land free of the royal share to, finally, the stage of occupant cultivators, was inherent in the Rajput system even before the decline of the traditional state system. Rajput lineages who lost positions of power also had fewer capabilities for maintaining widely dispersed political ties, partly because their reduced status affected the prestigious marital alliances with royal families in distant states. A reduction in political alliances further weakened the threat which the specific lineage or sub-lineage could present within the kin structure in order to expand. The isolation of weaker Rajput lineages was however, not to be taken as a permanent factor, as several such factions could join hands. There was thus the potential for these Rajputs who had been marginalised from powerful positions within their community to regain such positions over time.[34]

Apart from the actual alignments for power which undercut large-scale Rajput kin solidarity, Fox shows how the notion of kinship in

---

33. Using material from Hawaii, Fiji and New Zealand, Sahlins indicates the nature of solidarity when the state is thought to be a creation of the divine king (1987: 35). For Sahlins, this heroic or hierarchic state rested on a solidarity grounded in subordination to the ruler (a solidarity which is contrasted with the Durkheimian organic and mechanical models). Both the organic and mechanical models of solidarity assume a collective consciousness, whereas Sahlins' heroic model bases solidarity on the individual initiative of the ruler.
34. Stokes (1978) argues against the development cycle approach in understanding the transfer of landholdings and related social configurations. Stokes criticises Fox for believing that 'landholdings could be so ductile ... and dependent simply on two variables, the size of the landholding lineage, and the extent of lineage stratification due to political forces' (ibid.: 76). For Stokes, both the amount of land availability, and the scarcity of labour were important factors in determining the nature of landholdings and related power.

the Rajput states provided a symbolic solidarity to link the local lineage and the dispersed caste. The symbolic solidarity (which Fox refers to as ideological), was not based on actual genealogical ties, but on the status attached to membership of the Rajput kin system. Such status concerns were particularly relevant at the wider, regional level where Rajputs defined their status vis-à-vis non-Rajputs. While genealogical ties and the lineage were important in claims to the membership of the minimal Rajput unit at the local level, at the regional level it was more important to articulate a symbolic kinship. The difference between symbolic and physical kinship has important implications for the nature of the relationship between caste and lineage in the Rajput state. Fox suggests that Rajputs think of caste in terms of local lineages, rather than in terms of a dispersed agnatic and affinal group view of other castes. Like the Rajput, the Girasia have a lineage-centred view of caste (this is described in chapters 4 to 8).

Early colonial accounts also played a significant role in assigning specific racial characteristics to the Rajputs. In general the colonial officials and observers were favourably disposed towards the Rajput rulers and sympathised with the wealth and authority of their feudal lifestyle. The descriptions of, for example, Tod, Sherring, Baden-Powell, Forbes and Malcolm, emphasised the noble and brave qualities of the Rajputs, which in turn reinforced the martial image both among the Rajputs themselves, and in the eyes of the other groups. For example in 1881, Sherring quotes Aberigh-Mackay on the chiefs of Central India, to reinforce his own observation of the decline in the stature of the Rajput nobility:

> The saddest thing in all Rajwarra in the present day is the condition of the royal caste. The children of the sun and moon, the children of the fire fountain, seem to have forgotten the inspiring traditions of their race, and have sunk into a state of slothful ignorance and debauchery that mournfully contrast with the chivalrous heroism, the judicious and active patriotism, the refined culture and the generous virtue. The memory of a hundred noble deeds that adorn their annals, is still fresh in the minds of all men, and the names of many Rajpoot princes, of comparatively recent times will never die while a history of India remains. Rana Sanga of Mewar, enemy of the Mogul; Jai Singh Sewai of Jeypore, a scholar statesman, and soldier; Sur Singh, Gaj Singh, Jeswant Singh, the glorious paladins of Marwar, – these are surely names to conjure with – yet they would now seem to excite but little emulation in the breasts of many of those in whose veins their blood flows, and who still bear their undying names (1987 reprint: 8).

The cultivation of the noble and martial stereotype of the Rajput specifically aided the recruitment policy of the British army, which had separate Rajput battalions. The British attitude toward the Rajput princes was reflected in the policy of indirect rule, or paramountcy, in the Rajput states, in contrast to the more interventionist direct rule for the rest of British India. By a separate policy of administration for the Rajput states, the British contributed to the image of the Rajputs as a distinct and special community, in contrast to other communities in India.[35] Rajput values of honour and shame were thus enhanced by the British government, although the latter condemned the way women were used as symbols of Rajput honour.

Rajput Honour and Women

In the Rajput state, as we saw in the previous sections, the power over land and peoples was intimately connected with the interests of the brotherhood, or 'in the shared male substance which allowed it to rule over the land' (Ziegler 1978: 232). Rules of the Rajput code of ethics *(dharma)* stressed above all the solidarity and preservation of the brotherhood.[36] In this context one can understand why Rajput women very rarely occupied positions of power. Some situations, such as the absence of an adult male heir to the throne, did bring women of the royal lineage to important caretaker positions. However, this was more a strategy of the lineage members to enable power to remain within the brotherhood than an acknowledgement of the rights of women. Women and others who were dependent on the brotherhood and ruler, were seen in the Rajput's code of honour as objects of a ruler's protection. Any violation to women or other dependants, symbolised subordination. It is common knowledge in Rajput folklore and oral history that, in cases of military defeat at the hands of a conquering lineage, women committed *jauhar* (mass immolation) as a means of preserving the status of their defeated and 'shamed' brotherhood. Here the body of women becomes a marker of the honour of the brotherhood ('male body'). Thus, to a significant extent, the priorities of women were essentially determined by the status concerns of the patrilineal brotherhood.

35. The British policy of non-interference in the Rajput states was, however, also related to the scant and meagre resources in these states, which were largely irrelevant to the economic needs of the empire.
36. In a translation from the the seventeenth century Marvari chronicle, *Nainsi-ri-khyat*, Ziegler (1978) notes the three basic elements of the Rajput *dharma* to be avenging the death of one's father, maintaining the brotherhood, and fighting for one's master. Ziegler considers the last element a contribution of the Mughal polity, which especially reinforced hierarchy within the Rajput system.

At the level of the individual noble families, women were also constantly concerned with the prestige of their men. The most dramatic symbol of the structural position of Rajput women in the household was that of *sati,* or the custom that demanded that widows burn on the funeral pyre of their husbands. The royal families were especially known to observe the practice of *sati*. It was understood that whenever a *raja* died, his wives died with him. Most cremation areas of royalty in Rajasthan recorded handprints of the royal wives as they proceeded to the *sati sthal,* or place of *sati*. *Sati* was indigenously conceptualised in terms of the honour and status gained by the wife, and her kin, for her sacrifice to the husband's lineage, rather than as an oppressive institution for women. An early British officer notes that at the *sati* he witnessed, the widowed woman was not afraid but impatient to become *satimata* (or the holy *sati* mother; British accounts in Stutchbury, 1982). The British officers condemned and banned the practices of *sati* and infanticide in the early nineteenth century, although these customs were reified in exercises relating to the social classification of communities for the purposes of colonial administration (see, for example, Mani 1986). Reports of female infanticide occur in other dramatic colonial accounts of social practice in the Rajput State. Female infanticide was believed to be practised by the highest royal families who were restricted, in their preoccupations with hierarchy, from forming marital alliances with any other Rajput clans except those of the same or higher status. Clans at the top of the ladder would prefer to kill their daughters rather than bear the shame of having to marry into lower status clans.[37] Parry, for example, observes that, 'The Rajput ethic sets little by store of human life and finds it understandable that a man should rate the honour *(ijat)* of his lineage higher than the life of his daughter' (1979: 215). It was predominantly concerns of status and prestige which orientated Rajput values.

Sati was not a custom specific only to the Rajputs but also to the orthodox sections of the Hindu community.[38] Among the conservative sections of Hindu society, *sati* was seen as a natural extension of the duties of a wife. Ideal Hindu wives were those who sacrificed their own interests for their husband and his children. In this sense *sati,* as the sacrifice of the body, was the ultimate gesture in the portrayal of wifely devotion. As girls, women were brought up in Brahmin and Kshatriya households, and most middle- and upper-class

37. See Goody 1979, Parry 1979.
38. For example, Gupta 1974, Mani 1986.

households in India, to be submissive and obedient.[39] The values of self-sacrifice and *sewa* (service) were expectations of them which increased with age (Dube 1988), and were seen as the specific qualities of wives. Wadley (1988), for example notes that, 'Classical Hindu norms focus almost exclusively on the norms for the Hindu woman in her role as wife' (ibid.: 29). Kapadia (1966) stresses, *'pativrataya*, or being devoted to the husband alone ... not merely implied fidelity but made service to the husband the only duty of the wife, and her main purpose in life' (ibid.: 169). Girls grow up waiting for marriage. They are made aware of the attempts of various relatives to find grooms for them and must feel fortunate if a groom is 'available'. Marriage and related transactions are theoretically irrevocable institutions and divorce is socially stigmatised. The bride must work hard at her in-laws' home to allay any fear of non-acceptance. Her parents may have to meet continuing demands for dowry. They cannot refuse these demands in the apprehension that their daughter is sent back to her natal residence, which would be detrimental to the social standing of the father's family. Further, parents might face difficulties in finding a second husband for their daughter. Sometimes the inability to meet dowry demands has resulted in the death of the bride at the hands of her husband and his immediate family. The moral pressure the girl's parents exert on her to succeed in her marriage, in turn, obliges her to accept any situation at the house of her husband. The sacrifice the wife makes, by immolating herself on the funeral pyre of her husband, can then be seen as an extension of the indissoluble tie which marriage to him symbolised, and the values of *sewa* she had been brought up with.

Sati and female infanticide were relatively infrequent practices among the lower Rajput lineages. Although *sati* was not a frequent practice amongst most sections of the populace, it was common for all people to worship at the *sati* shrines.[40] More restrictive than the occurrences of *sati* and infanticide in the daily lives of most Rajput women, were the rules for their seclusion, reflected in their dress, physical presence, participation and attitudes. The adoption of the Muslim institution of the *zenana*, or separated women's quarters, ensured that women lived apart from men. Similarly, the institution of *purdah*, connected with veiling the body and other forms of exclusion, separated women both from men and from certain categories of women. Papanek (1982) observes that some form

39. For example, Kakar 1986, Das 1988, Dube 1988, Wadley 1988.
40. For example, see Gupta 1974 on *sati* worship in eastern Rajasthan.

of *purdah* exists in all Hindu and Muslim communities in India. Furthermore:

> The restrictions of free movement outside the house by married Hindu women derives from an extension of the avoidance rules underlying Hindu purdah. The Hindu woman is expected to cover her face before elder males of her husband's kindred, but not the younger, and also since the members of her husband's village and his friends are his fictive kin, she must in practice cover her face outside the home in the village where she lives and in others where her husband's relatives may live (ibid.: 19).

The institutions of *purdah* and *zenana* should not be taken as an indication of the powerlessness of Rajput women. Rather, they reflect the fact that power, for men or women, was connected with control over women. This explains why Rajput women who occupied positions of power 'became the instruments in cementing and perpetuating a tradition that was most oppressive to women themselves' (Mehta 1976: 18). In the traditional state *zenana* and *purdah* were practices also followed by women of other communities. Mehta (1976) shows how men of the Oswal (Jain) business community in Udaipur (formerly Mewar) worked for the royal court and were influenced by its ethic. The Oswals followed the Rajput practices of *zenana* and *purdah* and restricted their women from work outside the domestic environment, primarily to show their social proximity to the Rajput nobility. The higher one went in the Rajput hierarchy of power and nobility, the less men engaged in cultivation and the more women secluded themselves. The royal families, and those who could afford to hire labour on their fields were able to 'save' their women from work outside the domestic environment. In this context, women's work was a marker of the status of the family. A woman of higher, or nobler, family was an important exhibitor of her husband's wealth and status. Women of the lower, or less noble, Rajput families who were unable to hire and command services, continued to work within and outside their households and were less restricted by *zenana* and *purdah* which they observed to only a limited extent. For example, in the village of Ore, located just outside the *Bhakar* in the Abu Road *tehsil*, the wealthier Rajputs (thirteen households) owned the largest plots of land, produced for home and the market, owned wells, agricultural machines and engaged labourers to work on their farms. The women of this community did not work outside the house, and always maintained *purdah* to certain categories of relatives within the household, and to all people when they went out of the house. Ore also had a Rasput community of four households. The Rasputs were defined, and defined themselves, in terms of their former occupation of *begar* (forced labour) and as servants in the Rajput households. Their women would fill water pots, clean utensils in the upper caste Rajput homes, and also accompany Rajput women when they went out of the house. At the time of my fieldwork, the Rasputs farmed land previously given to them by the Rajputs, and produced more for the home than the market. Although they observed a similar lifestyle to the Rajputs, their wives worked outside the house on the fields, wells and on the slopes of the *Bhakar* from where they collected wood. These women did not observe *purdah*. The Ore example suggests that Rajput status and honour, reflected in the degrees of the seclusion of women, is linked to the role of women in production. Degrees of the seclusion of women were more indicative of economic and prestige-related differences rather than cultural or ethnic differences between communities. In the Girasia case however, the 'freedom', or non-seclusion of women has been increasingly used by the non-Girasia as a means to denote cultural difference and inferiority as my following chapter suggests.

The present chapter has made use of limited historical material to understand the nature of the Girasia position in the Rajput state. The period of my fieldwork was approximately forty years after the direct rule by the Rajput rulers. The Rajput control over the region was still very dominant in the collective memory of the Girasia, particularly in terms of how the Girasia perceived their past and related identity. The possible reason for the scant historial references to the Girasia could be that their history was linked to that of the higher lords of the Rajput lineages and clans. This would be the case if the Girasia were enfolded within, yet marginal to, the wider state structure. For most Indian historians it has been important to record the nature of the royalty rather than the other, particularly lower, levels of the Rajput state structure. For example, Guha notes that Indian history has tended to be, more often than not, an account of the elite sections of society (1982: 1-9). The lack of documented material on the Girasia, I feel, reflects the orientation of the historians rather than the weakness of the Girasia claims to Rajput origins. In the information provided by the historical records I find a disjunction in the documentation on the Girasia. While the historical records of the period when the Rajputs ruled make mention of the Girasia as lower and marginal adjuncts to the state, most official records of the independent Indian government from 1947 onwards refer to the Girasia as a cultural category distinct from the Rajputs. In these latter records the Girasia emerge as 'tribal'.

Academic observers on Rajasthan also consider the Girasia as 'tribal' in conjunction with the local Rajput elite and the local government.[41] The following chapter indicates how the recent views on the Girasia reflect their relatively recent status as a cultural category distinct from the Rajput in the closing decades of the British rule.

---

41. Carstairs 1955, Dave 1960, Vyas 1978, Meherda 1985.

Chapter 3

RAJPUTS AND GIRASIAS IN INDEPENDENT INDIA

Identity Politics and Administration

In Rajasthan today, most communities continue to identify with the historical Rajput state.[1] The previously dominant Rajput families have in large part maintained positions of wealth and prestige within their communities. Other communities continue to stratify themselves according to their historical association with the Rajput nobility.[2] Now no longer in the sole context of the Rajput state, I see Rajput identity as having to continuously define itself in relation to history. The pressure to justify status in terms of a previous glory is one of the factors which informs Rajput identifications today. In this chapter, I suggest that the attempts to form a homogeneous and undifferentiated Rajput identity are largely in response to the emerging political concerns of communities in the nation state. The more homogeneous the Rajput identity, the more vehement are the denials regarding connections with the lower and peripheral Rajput lineages. I further

---

1. According to Mathur (1986), there are two hundred groups in Rajasthan. In terms of size, the ten largest groups are the Jats, Brahmans, Chamars, Bhils, Rajputs, Mahajans, Minas, Gujars, Malis and Kumhars.
2. For example, the Brahmins who live in the village Ore, sixteen kilometres from the Taivar village, call themselves the *raj-purohits,* which means literally the priests of the *raja* or rulers.

suggest that such processes contribute to the increasingly tribal image of communities such as the Girasia. Two other important factors responsible in viewing the Girasia as tribal are: 1) the British and Indian administrative measures which weakened the Girasia control over land, and, 2) the notion of 'tribe' held by the national leaders of independent India and reinforced in academic studies.

The first section of the chapter considers contemporary Rajput identity. The most determined effort to reinstate Rajput custom in the 1980s has been in relation to the traditional structural position of women. I suggest that the Rajput and other outsider constructions of Girasia women are related to the slower change in the attitudes towards their own women as well as an accelerating deterioration in the economic position of the Girasia as discussed in the following section. (More recent class-type identities of the Girasia are discussed in chapter 9, framed by the kinship, economic and religious concerns of the Girasia described in chapters 4 to 8.) The second part of this chapter traces the administrative attitudes and resulting government classifications of landholdings and communities. The section also shows that the policies of the Indian national leaders towards 'tribal' communities affected the Girasia position within the modern Indian State.

Rajput 'Custom' and Women
Communal Politics

Rajasthan in the late 1980s witnessed a public outcry, mainly among sections of the urban, educated elite, at the incidents of *sati* in some of its villages. Recent practices of *sati* in Rajasthan are performed against legal rules banning the practice of widow-burning. The *sati* at Deorala village in Sikar district in September 1987 involved the self immolation of a woman named Roop Kanwar and was followed by great speculation as to whether she was forced to kill herself or had done so voluntarily.[3] While some of the population, especially the feminist organisations, condemned the act and urged a speedy police investigation into the matter, thousands of other people visited the *sati sthal* (place of *sati*) to pay homage to the *sati-ma* (goddess), who had become *sada suhaagan* (achieved a holy permanence in her marital state).[4] Sections of the Rajput community, villagers of Deorala and

3. The village had had three other *sati* temples built over the past seventy years. In the same region other *sati* cases (1981, 1983, 1987) had been prevented by the police (Report in the *Illustrated Weekly of India*, no.4, October 1987).
4. Idem.

some national politicians who were Rajput, meanwhile, made public their outrage at the restrictions and investigation of what was to them a central Rajput custom. Measures to restrict the occurences of *sati* were posed by them as a threat to Rajput identity and to counter this a temple was erected to commemorate the *sati* of Roop Kanwar. The Deorala *sati* issue resulted in a massive rallying of support around a collective reinforcement of Rajput identity and tradition.

Two issues emerge most strikingly from the whole incident. The first has to do with the ways in which certain customs of the Rajputs were being used, especially by Rajput politicians, to create a communal basis for their power. Further, the Deorala case pointed to the manner in which such incidents have been used by community leaders and politicians to resurrect a Rajput identity based in the past, in order to exhibit their strength and solidarity to an electorate in the present. The second point to note is how central *sati* is to the construction of Rajput identity and, consequently, how images of Rajput tradition are projected most forcefully in terms of the actions of Rajput women. Although *sati* in Rajasthan today is a means of political action at the national level, at the time of the Rajput states it occured as a result of the gendered political action within the household and the lineage. But what is significant for the purposes of this book is that, whether *sati* was used to signify the honour of the patriarchal household in the traditional state, or its more recent use as the means for Rajput men and women to gather political support under the wider regional Rajput label, Rajput women remain at the centre of the symbolic constructions of Rajput identity.

Both the political use of community identitites and the central role of women in their conceptualisation and presentation are issues that have been noted for other communities in India. According to Kothari (1970), a seasoned analyst of Indian politics, the Rajput is just one more example of caste communities adjusting to democracy. Kothari believes that for any political system to be stabilised in the Indian context, it is necessary that its earlier procedure and symbols are both traditionalised and internalised. More recent studies on national political processes especially emphasise the increasing relevance of religion ('communalism')[5] in the creation and political use of collective identities in India.[6] The communal aspect of Indian politics

---

5. Communalism in the Indian context refers to the creation and political use of community identities based on religion. It is essentially conceptualised in negative terms as the process is based on the aggressive and divisive propagation of religion (Chandra 1979, Vanaik 1990).
6. For example, Chatterjee 1982, Engineer 1989, Chhachhi 1989, Pandey 1990, Vanaik 1990, Sarkar 1991, Das 1992

is linked directly to the processes of nationalism and the emergence of the nation state in India in these pertinent recent studies. The meaning of communalism, first used to describe the nature of Hindu-Muslim conflicts which accompanied the partition of India, is now applied more generally to describe the creation and violent assertion of community identity in India. Communal identities are powerful mechanisms for mobilising actions and, like national identities, cut across smaller scale identities such as those of caste, class, kinship, gender and region. Unlike national identities, communal identities are perceived to have their basis in religion and are seen as divinely sanctioned. Contrary to work on nationalism and identity elsewhere[7] we find that in India, with the rise of the nation state, the formation of macro religious, 'communal' identities has been encouraged through the processes of nationalism and colonialism preceding it.

Most of the recent studies on communalism focus on the role of the state and politics at the national level as encouraging the formation of communal identities.[8] What has been less visible has been the impact of such processes at the micro-level, in the relationships between and within communities. I believe it is here that studies on gender and religious conflict have much to offer. Compared to the work on political leaders and state processes in communalism, there are fewer studies which have women as their central focus.[9] Chhachhi (1990), for example, notes how women are used as symbolic representations in the creation of contemporary communal identities in India. Given the central part women play as markers of community identity, their role in the representation of communal identities comes as no surprise. However, what is of interest is the process by which women become key symbols of a newly created 'tradition'. Chhachhi emphasises that 'tradition' is reconstituted in a selective manner by the fundamentalist elements, both men and women, of the respective communities. Citing the Deorala *sati* case as one of two examples to illustrate her argument, Chhachhi suggests that the two specific areas to which the fundamentalists have turned in their selection of symbols of community identity have been, firstly, the stress on a martial tradition, and by extension on masculinity, and, secondly, the choice of the female symbol as passive and subordinate in contrast to the more aggressive images of women contained

7. For example, Anderson, 1983; Gellner, 1983.
8. Engineer's work (1989) is among the few studies which also discuss the dimension of attitudes, prejudices and stereotypes in the creation and maintenance of communal identities.
9. Chhachhi 1989, 1990, Sarkar 1991, Das 1992 come to mind.

in historical and mythological texts. Chhachhi sees the call for a return to tradition in *sati* and other communal action, as a means by which certain sections of the communities in question combat the threat they perceive in the state's erosion of their patriarchally based authority.[10] One of the reasons why women play a crucial role in signifying contemporary communal identities is because, as Chhachhi suggests, women seem to be more easily identified with what is considered 'natural', the home and the domain of kinship, which are at the same time the 'natural' symbols of community identity. It is in their role as a repository of community honour that women themselves become most controlled by their own communities.

While the Girasia have not been directly involved in the processes of communal politics, at least till the early 1990s, the emerging different constructions of Rajputness have, I suggest, indirectly made the Girasia claims to being Rajput even more remote than before. So, while especially the upper and middle classes of Rajputs select specific symbols of the past to assert a strong, collective identity in the present as a means of acquiring powerful positions in the nation state, the lower class of Rajputs such as the Girasia continue to emphasise the physical aspects of Rajput kinship. The physical ties of kinship, rather than symbolic associations, are given a much more central place in the political strategies of the lower classes than they are among the upper Rajputs as the following chapter describes. Women, however, continue to be used as an important means of presenting the differences between communities in the region as the following lines and tables reveal.

Everyday Differences

The incidents of *sati* are not widespread in the Rajput community as a whole. The Girasia, as the lower-caste Rasputs of Ore, did not have either the customs of *sati* or female infanticide, nor did they observe *purdah* outside their affinal village. During my fieldwork, the institutions of *purdah* and the related manner of dressing of Rajput and other caste women were more constant reminders of the differences between communities than the instances of *sati* or infanticide. While men of the different communities of the region dressed in terms of the status of their occupations (most poor farmers wore a cotton

10. What unites the fundamentalists, according to Chhachhi, is their opposition to the state's 'capitalist interventions' seen in the decline of the traditional patriarchal family. What the state had eroded was essentially the power to maintain property within the family previously effected by restricting the inheritance powers of women, and controlling the sexuality of widows.

cloth *dhoti*, and shirt or *kurta*), women dressed in a distinctive manner (see tables 3.1, 3.2 on apparel and jewellery of women in the region). Groups of Girasia men and women could tell other groups apart from the manner in which their women dressed.[11]

Although only differences in attire and jewellery were pointed out to me, I found similar designs in the apparel and jewellery of Girasia, Rajput and other caste women of the surrounding villages. The tables show that although the Girasia did have differences in apparel and jewellery, these were only a matter of degree and occurred to the same extent between women of different castes. In terms of what Girasia women thought about their dress, as far as I could gather, there was no conception of their clothes and jewellery as oppressive and, since dressing was so central to being a Girasia and a woman, women seemed to enjoy the fact that people noticed what they wore. The length, colour and design of the dress of individual Girasia women was often a topic of conversation among women, especially on ritual occasions when the heavily pleated skirts, made up from up to nine metres of cloth, were worn. Although the cloth and tailoring expenses were borne by men, the wrap and jewellery were more directly dependent on men's purses and strategies. While the wrap was 'gifted' by brothers (see chapter 4), jewellery was connected to brideprice payments (see chapter 7).

Despite certain similarities in dress, the Rajputs and related (Rasput, Parmar) communities in the villages (including one prominent Chauhan Rajput village leader) stressed the tribal nature of the Girasia. This image of the Girasia also influenced the nature of the non-Girasia and Girasia interactions. For example, on one visit to Abu Road town with my Girasia women companions, I was able to see how the townsfolk *(hindu-lok)* treated the Girasia. It was a hot day, and we were sitting in the shade, in the verandah of a house along the market road. A woman of the house came out, and shouted at the Girasia women to get out. It was only when I said in Hindi that we were there for a short while only and would clear the potential mess she was complaining about, that the woman retreated from her aggressive stance. Meanwhile, the Girasia women were already packing up without attempting to confront the woman.[12]

11. Although the Girasia could tell through minute differences in dress and jewellery the different categories to which persons of the lower castes belonged, the upper Rajputs and other castes in the region could differentiate lower-caste groups to a lesser degree.
12. On another occasion, while waiting for a bus at the station, I saw a middle-class boy spit at a Girasia girl who was in a party of Girasia returning from a *mela* (fair).

Table 3.1 Apparel of Girasia Women and Some Non-Girasia Women

No.	Items of clothing	Approximate cost (1987 prices)	Material and design	Occasion worn	Other caste women
1.	*Ghagra* (skirt)	Rs. 150/- onwards (includes stitching)	Thick pleated cotton usually plain blue with red piping	All the time at work outside and inside the home	Cotton skirt especially worn by lower-caste rural women. *Rebari* women wear skirt of mid-calf length, heavily pleated, of dark coarse cloth with dull piping. *Bhil* women wear ankle-length skirts of no particular design. The cloth is usually cheap and thin. The skirt has few pleats. *Rajput* and other middle- and upper-caste women in the neighbouring villages wear a full-length skirt, with no large pleats. The material is of fine cotton, sometimes with a mill print. The skirt is popularly called *Lehnga*.
2.	*Jhulki* (blouse)	Rs. 35/- (for cloth only)	Medium cotton, usually plain green with red piping, tied in two places and covering the stomach	Especially to work outside the house. Sometimes substituted by a bodice inside the house.	Blouses are worn by all rural women, however they differ in material and design. *Rebari* women wear short, backless blouses with silver ribbon in the design. *Bhil* women wear short, plain cotton blouses. *Rajput* women wear long blouses in the same pattern as blouses of Girahya women, however, the material is of fine cotton or polyester mix. The blouse is popularly called *Kanchali*. Other middle- and upper-caste women wear short blouses of fine cotton.
3.	*Odhani* (wrap)	Rs. 30/-	Medium to thick cotton, usually red with mill print of yellow design	Worn all the time	Worn by all rural women who wear the skirt. While *Rebari* women have wraps of coarse cloth sometimes in a similar print to *Girahya* wraps, *Bhil* women wear differently patterned wraps of thin to thick cotton. *Rajput* and most other middle- and upper-caste women wear fine muslin wraps of single, often pale colours.

Table 3.2 Jewellery of Girasia Women and Some Non-Girasia Women*

No.	Items of Jewelry	Approximate cost (1987 prices)	Material and design	Occasion worn	Other caste women
1.	*Borejyu* (forehead ornment)	Rs. 25/-	Small silver plated ball of two separate designs	Worn all the time by mother or daughter	Gold plated for upper- and upper-middle caste village women. Silver in different designs for *Rebari* and *Bhil* women
2.	*Domene* (side of face ornament)	Rs. 314/-	Broad (approximately one and a half inch) silver chain attached to two sides of the *Borejyu* above	Worn at fairs, ritual occasions	Gold and silver in different designs for upper, middle, *Rebari* and *Bhil* women
3.	*Oganya* (ornament for upper ear)	Rs. 106/-	Silver plated hook-like attachments ending in small silver betel-shaped leaves	2 or 3 worn all the time in both the ears	Differently designed upper ear ornament
4.	*Toti* (ear stopper)	Rs. 320/- (including 5 below)	Large, round silver designed ear stopper, Previous to this a wooden ear stopper is used to enlarge the ear hole	One or the other always worn	
5.	*Jhumra* (hanging ear ornament)	See 4 above	Inverted umbrella-shaped silver attachment to 4 above	For rituals; sometimes to the market or fairs	Differently designed ear ornaments in gold and silver
6.	*Ado Roto* (nose ring)		Large gold ring with design near nose-hole, attached with gold chain to the ear	Rarely worn; for festivals or rituals	More popular amongst middle- and upper-castes
7.	*Horki* (small loose choker)	Rs. 360/-	Rigid collarbone type; thin silver plated or (cheaper) aluminum imitation	Worn all the time, the cheaper ones by daughters	Gold- and silver-plated chokers worn
8.	*Varle* (large loose choker)	See 9 below	Large and hollow rigid collarbone type silver choker worn below 7 above	For special occasions such as fairs and rituals	
9.	*Jhabiya Varle* (8 above, + attachment)	Rs. 1,032/-	3 groups of chains with bells, all in silver, attached to 8 above	Only certain special occasions	

- 76 -

Table 3.2 continued

No.	Items of Jewelry	Approximate cost (1987 prices)	Material and design	Occasion worn	Other caste women
10.	*Hathpon* (ornament for the back of hand)		Silver central design with chain attachments to rings for fingers and band for the wrist	Usually worn by bride at marriage ceremony	Worn in silver with similar design by other caste women, especially at marriages
11.	*Baliya* (bangles for arm)	Rs. 30/- (for plastic set) Rs. 10/- (for aluminium set)	Usually five bangles made from thick white plastic (previously ivory) on each arm. Each set is preceded and followed by 1 aluminium armlet	Worn all the time, fixed by iron solder, only removed voluntarily at death of husband	Most middle- and upper-caste women of the *Mali, Khandelwal, Purohit, Nai, Luhar, Kumhar, Ghanchi* and *Meena* castes wore both upper arm and lower arm bangles. *Rebari* women also wore both kinds. *Sargada* women wore only the lower arm bangles
12.	*Choori* (bangles for upper arms)		Ivory or plastic	Only worn by one elderly woman in the village	
13.	*Lac Choori* (bangles for lower arm	Rs. 25/- for set	Bangles made from backed and glazed clay in colours of black, red, yellow and green	Worn all the time by unmarried girls. Soldered but broken with use as well as before marriage. Can be re-used by applying heat to cracks.	Worn by *Khandelwal* caste girls. Otherwise all young girls may wear thin, coloured plastic or glass bangles. (Glass and gold bangles are worn by middle- and upper-caste women in urban areas).
14.	*Karla* (anklet)	Rs. 14/- for cheap alloy set	Silver or made from cheap alloy, worn on both legs	Worn most of the time. Many women had replaced these with several rounds of black thread.	Worn in silver by most middle- and upper-caste women.
15.	*Kandora* (waistband)	Rs. 10/- (cheap alloy)	Silver but more commonly of cheap alloy	Worn occasionally for festivals as a long necklace by both boys and girls	Worn in silver by most middle- and upper-caste women.

Table 3.2 continued

No.	Items of Jewelry	Approximate cost (1987 prices)	Material and design	Occasion worn	Other caste women
16.	*Nath* (nose stud)	Rs. 2/-	Silver plated small round nose-stud	An optional, seldom worn	Usually gold, popular among middle- and upper-caste women
17.	*Dama* (ring for two fingers)	Rs. 75/- (silver)	Silver or cheap alloy	Worn sometimes, not common	
18.	*Veeti* (ring)	Rs. 3/- onwards	Of various metals and designs	May be worn by men and women	Usually gold
19.	*Angothiyo* (big toe-ring)	Rs. 1-2/-	Silver or cheap alloy	Especially worn by bride	Worn in silver
20.	*Polri* (small toe-ring)	Rs. 1-2/-	Silver or cheap alloy; ideally there should be three on each foot	At least one or two worn regularly	Worn in silver or gold
21.	*Moto Pulyu* (broad choker)	Hand-made Rs. 14/- for material	Coloured beads set in white bead choker worn around the neck	Girls wear this for fairs and occasions of dancing	
22.	*Nonko Pulyo* (narrow choker)	Hand-made Rs. 6/- for material	Coloured beads set in black plastic thread	Worn by all women and girls permanently	Worn by *Rebari* men and women, although pink and red beads are used rather than other colours. Middle- and upper-caste women may wear the same with gold coloured beads.
23.	*Aariyu* (long necklace)	Hand-made Rs. 14/- for beads	Mainly white beads with coloured beads in symmetric design	Worn more often by young girls	
24.	*Konejyu* (brooch like decoration attached to blouse pocket)	Hand-made Rs. 3/- for beads	White beads and coloured beads on string hanging from a safety pin	Especially worn by young girls	

*Note: Most silver jewellery owned by a man may be worn by his wife or their daughters only while the latter lives in her natal home.

Most members of the groups in the villages and the towns I met treated the Girasia as inferiors; however, there were others who were more ambiguous about their relationship with the Girasia and this tied in with the views Girasia men and women had on whom they considered 'upper', 'lower' or 'equal' to them. According to Chakra, the castes lower *(neenchu)* than the Taivars were the Mina and Bhil, Musalman (Muslim), Sargada, Heeragar, Regar, Meghwal (all leatherworkers who had switched jobs to work with dyes, or as farmers and servicemen in the town), Ghanchi (oil-presser, who had turned to growing and selling vegetables), Kasai (butcher, usually Muslim), Harijan (untouchable, cleaned refuse), Nai (haircutter), Dhobi (washermen), Moyla (Muslim potter), Luhar (ironsmith), Dholi (sang songs for festivals in return for grain), Cheepa (tailor who exchanged his labour for grain), Jogi (lived on alms) and Bajaana (collected used plastic items to sell). The Taivars did not have a term equivalent to 'tribal' to describe the communities whom they considered lower, or whom the non-Girasia considered as 'tribals' apart from the Girasia (for example, the Bhils). The castes the Taivars considered equal were the Kumhar (potter), the Rebari (pastoral nomad) and Mali (who grew flowers traditionally but were currently major producers of vegetables for the market). The higher castes were those who 'kept difference' *(pher-raakhe),* such as the Bhat (caste of chroniclers), Guru Brahman (low-caste astrologers), Rajput, Purohit, Brahman, Vaishnav (priests now in government service), Jain (salesmen and traders) and the Soni (silversmith). Chakra's list indicates that there were more castes in the lower category than the upper or equal category. In equating[13] themselves with the Kumhar, Rebari and Mali castes, the Girasia also acknowledged their lower Rajput status, reinforcing the Taivar self-descriptions as Rajput Girasia as opposed to Rajputs. Chakra's ordering also fitted in with the rank of 'tribals' in the caste-rankings elsewhere (Babb 1975, Mayer 1966, Gupta 1974, Chauhan 1978).[14]

Differences between groups in the region apart from those of class and caste which were signified by the dress, behaviour and economic role of women were also based on the different experiences of

13. The 'equality' with the Kumhar, Rebari and Malli was practised only in commensal (chapter 6) rather than marital terms (chapters 4, 5).
14. For example, in Babb's study (1975: 16), in central India the *adivasis* (tribals) were ranked the highest in the lower-middle caste category, above potters, tile-makers, black-smiths, gardeners and barbers. This category was higher than the low caste comprising washermen, basketmen and watchmen as well as the lowest caste of shoe-makers and ex-leatherworking farmers.

administration in the region. The following section outlines the manner in which administrative classifications have helped to marginalise the Girasia.

'Tribe' in Official Classifications

Following the decline of the Rajput state, the major changes which affected the Girasia relation to natural resources as well as their Rajput identity were the administrative policies of the nascent Indian government. The 'tribal', forest dwelling image of the Girasia, I suggest, is largely a consequence of their association with the *Bhakar*, a relationship which has been reinforced by the state's restrictions on Girasia mobility and expansion. In economic terms, their impoverishment through the experiences of famine and drought has further contributed to the marginalisation of the Girasia in outsider eyes. The following lines trace some of the issues and ambiguities in the offical classifications of tribal groups.

Early Debates

Indian independence in 1947 brought to an end the nationalist struggle by the Indian National Congress (INC). It was a period of high nationalist fervour, and recorded attempts by the middle-class elite to forge an Indian identity (Chandra 1979). The structural changes in the classifications of peoples and land in the modern state were based on extended debates which characterised the decades of the 1940s and the 1950s. From the Girasia point of view, from this time onward one is essentially dealing with three kinds of identity: the collective regional Rajput identity which becomes more and more based in the past, the collective Girasia one, continuously formed and maintained through actions in the present, and a vague or national identity, very much on the margins of the Girasia perceptions. With the dissolution of the Rajput states ended their separate administrative relation with the central government, and the marginal communities within the former territory of Rajputana were treated as other marginal communities of the Indian union despite their different historical experiences.[15]

15. The British themselves had observed a difference in the tribal population of the paramountcy whom they saw as, 'better off than the rest of India, as the more primitive conditions of the states were congenial to them' (Singh 1985: 114).

The policies of the nascent Indian government towards the 'tribes' become clearer when they are seen in the context of the early debates about tribal identity which were, in large part, driven by the desire to shake off the colonial mantle. The tribal policy was one more issue with which to resist the British, and, at the same time, to widen the basis of popular support for the Congress. For the British administrators, tribal people were non-Hindu (British formulations were largely informed by the Brahmanical model of Hindu caste organisation). It was considered in the interests of these non-Hindu communities that the British officials, advised by anthropologists (notably Mills, Hutton, the early Elwin, Roy) and missionaries, made the tribal tracts 'totally and partially excluded areas' to be directly administered by the colonial authorities. The British official stance was enshrined in the Government of India Act of 1935 (Singh 1985). The Indian leaders of the national movement saw this policy of exclusion as part of the well-known British strategy of 'divide and rule'. There was some truth in the nationalists' argument, as the British policy restricted their contact with the tribals, regarded by some historians as an explanation of the weak tribal participation in the national movement (for example, Bates 1988). Moreover, most nationalists, Gandhi included, had also been opposed to the form of exclusive missionary contact in the 'excluded' areas which had converted the tribals to Christianity.

In contrast to the British policy of exclusion, the Congress advocated an assimilation of the tribal communities into 'the mainstream of Hindu civilisation' (Ghurye 1959, Singh 1985). By promoting the assimilationist view under their banner, it seems to me, the Congress reinforced the notion that the tribals were non-Hindus. This was reflected in their view that contact with the Hindu mainstream was considered a solution to 'tribal backwardness'. Shortly after independence, however, the Congress government reintroduced the restriction on the access to tribal areas. This later Congress legislation was in direct response to the rapid rate at which the non-tribal communities were buying up tribal land and impoverishing 'tribal' existence (see for example, Furer-Haimendorf 1982). Whatever the extent of sympathy for the tribal population, at the level of the administrative discourse, the Congress, dominated by elite, upper-caste Hindus, was the only spokesperson for free India. Even if it did oppose the British administration of tribal areas, it did not contest the British classification of such peoples. The Indian government, contrary to the nationalist formulations, extended the British category of 'tribal' people formulated within British India to include the marginal communities who had been part of the British Paramountcy. While the British administrators differentiated between categories of landholders in the Rajput state, no Indian government records clarify this point and the whole state of Rajasthan has been considered a 'backward' state in the government plans for the allocation of state funds. In the euphoria of a free India and in the first stages of planning for development which followed, the Congress believed that the processes of modernisation and industrialisation would percolate to 'uplift' the tribals and bring them into the Hindu fold (Bates 1988). Most of the government surveys relied on the studies of anthropologists and sociologists who were themselves steeped in ahistorical approaches (as we saw in their formulation of 'tribe', chapter 1).

The Census

In terms of the census, which started in 1881 and has since been held every ten years, the year 1941 is a watershed; in the following decade political control changed hands at national level and the administration of the country came under the Indian National Congress party. In the years following 1941 we find the region of south Rajasthan fragmented for administrative purposes. While the areas to the south of Sirohi, such as Palanpur and Danta in Gujarat, were included in the Rajputana census in 1941, after Indian independence they were separated along with Sirohi to form a part of the separate state of Gujarat. (Under the British, Gujarat had previously been within the larger Bombay Presidency.) In 1956 Sirohi again became a part of Rajasthan. Accompanying the shifting boundaries of Sirohi was the administrative indecision regarding the classification of social groups in the region. The constitution, which came into force in 1950, specified that 'backward' groups were to be 'listed' as Scheduled Tribe, Scheduled Caste or Other Backward Classes, in order to dispense government aid. The reservation policy of the government was based on the notion of positive discrimination, or a discrimination in favour of the lower castes and underprivileged sections of the community, for an equitable distribution of state funds. The policy confused the issue of identity of the marginal communities, as each vied with the others to be included as 'lower', 'tribal' or 'under-privileged'. Some communities asserted 'lower' caste positions in the census to claim the benefits of the government-reserved employment for the underprivileged. Other communities found the 'lower' or marginal positions assigned to them in the census unjust. Remarking on the possible inaccuracy of the classification, Beteille (1986) states that the problem in India, with regard to the concept of tribe, was, 'to identify rather than define tribes, and scientific or theoretical considerations were never allowed to displace administrative or political ones ... the conceptions of those engaged in the listing were neither clearly formulated nor systematically applied' (ibid.: 299).

It was only after the enactment of the Scheduled Castes and Scheduled Tribes List Modification Order of 1956 that the Girasia were included in the Scheduled Tribes List in Rajasthan (but not in Gujarat, the neighbouring state; census reports 1961, 1981).[16] Furthermore, from the 1951 census onwards, the populations of the Girasia and the Bhil Girasia were subsumed under the single category of Girasia and were distinguished from the Bhil category. In some cases, sections of the Girasia population were included in the Bhil category.[17] Thus in some areas the Girasias were classified as a separate tribe, in others they were bracketed with the Bhil Girasias or even subsumed under the Bhil rubric, while in areas to the south of Rajasthan they have been included in the category of Other Backward Classes. The reason given for the inclusion of the Bhil-Girasias in the Girasia category was that, 'they appeared to be an intermediate, being a mixture of Bhils and Girasias, and they can be elevated and absorbed in the Girasia tribe according to certain customs prevailing among the Girasias' (Dave 1960: 5). However, as both later censuses and fieldwork have shown, there was neither an absorption nor an exchange of cultural practices between the two groups. The Taivar Girasia considered both the Bhils and the Bhil-Girasia as members of the Bhil community. The distinction from the Bhils, according to the Taivars, was in terms of royal Rajput descent, the privileges of landholding and a purity reflected in their food habits (see next below). Only recent government reports (Appendix 1) differentiate between groups of Girasia, such as the Bhil-Girasia, the Doongri Girasia, and the Rajput Girasia.

16. This explains the leap in population for the Sirohi district at 26,530 Girasia and Bhil-Girasias, of whom 19,225 were in Abu Road. The number of Girasia of the *Bhakar* was roughly estimated at 2,860 in 1891, at 7,754 in 1901 and 17,830 in 1941.
17. Dave (Assistant Commissioner for Scheduled Castes and Tribes in the Bombay region in 1960) noted at the time that all the tribals in the Revakantha and the Palanpur area immediately south of Sirohi were recognised as Bhils after 1921, while no Girasias were listed. However, in the 1901 census report for the same region, the presence of 825 Girasias had been recorded. Similarly, in Mewar to the east of Sirohi, Dave noted a dramatic increase in the Girasia population in 1941, which he explained as resulting from certain groups of Bhil and Gamit referring to themselves as Girasias. This was before official records included the Girasia in the list of Scheduled Tribes.

The shifting census categorisations with regard to the Girasia, a relatively small community in the Indian context, reflects the administrative uncertainty regarding their classification as a tribe, caste or 'Other Backward Class'. The 'tribal' and 'other backward classes' categories, because they are linked to state aid, have been particularly erratic in the census lists. Their categorisation has also led to the most protests. These protests are viewed by outsiders as more than a means to rectify administrative errors. Srinivas (1972) for example, saw the Backward Classes movement in South India as essentially one to gain mobility in the caste system (1972: 114).[18] The Taivar Girasia have not agitated for increased political or economic rights although, as I suggest in the following pages, the nature of the administrative classifications had an impact on the Girasia relation to natural resources and their identity in the region.

Forests and Tribes

All the forests in the Rajput State were considered part of the domain of the *raja* or *jagirdar*. Koppers (1948) notes that all the land, forest, water and animals were the property of the king (ibid.: 136). The Rajput king's domain was a product of his marriage to the land, which was often referred to as his wife (Ziegler 1978: 233). Those inhabiting the forest could only do so with the acknowledgement, if not the consent, of the ruler. The forest was an integral part of the ruler's domain. In the Rajput state there was no absolute boundary between the forested and non-forested areas. It was common practice for defeated chiefs to move into less fertile areas with difficult access, both as a protection from the enemy and when land was scarce.[19] Similarly, Lyall (1907) gives defeat and the scarcity of land

---

18. There have been widespread political debates and 'anti-reservation' protests in India regarding the implementation of the Mandal Commission report. The Commission had been constituted in 1975 to amend the number of backward classes and the related reservation of 55,000 government jobs. The Scheduled Castes and Tribes have 22.5 percent of government jobs reserved for them. With the Other Backward Class job reservations at a recommended 27 percent, the total percentage of reserved government jobs was to rise to 59.5 percent (*India Today*, 15 Sept. 1990). While the Mandal Commission identified 3,743 castes and subcastes as part of the backward classes, an independent study made by the Anthropological Survey of India has identified 1,051 caste and sub-castes as members of the backward class category (*Times of India*, 1 Oct. 1990).
19. For example, Brookes (1859) observes that the hilly forest regions surrounding Rajputana were instrumental in the art of Rajput warfare. Brookes recalls the case of Jugmal, son of Oodey Singh (of the Chauhans of Mewar) who, when dis-

as the two prime factors for the frequent Rajput recourse to the hills (ibid.: 207). Deliege (1985) believes that one of the consequences of extreme Rajput political fragmentation, after the period of Mauryan and Gupta empires until the Muslim invasions in 1192, and their subsequent defeat, was a reason for their, 'expansion into hilly tracts and their penetration into tribal areas' (1985: 41). The forest was considered politically threatening as it harboured political escapees; it was thus an important and to some extent influencing factor in Rajput relations, reflected in the frequent recourse and shelter provided to the defeated lineages. It was usually the policy of the *raja* to settle people in the forest, either as loyal informers or watchmen for a marginal tax. By allowing only loyal communities to reside in the forest, the ruler theoretically extended his control over it. Through his proprietorial relation over the *jungle*, the *raja* enhanced his powerful image over his people (Haynes 1987). The subjugation of the forest was more to control the rights in revenue, and exert authority over its inhabitants than to exploit its resources (ibid.: 4, 5).

The colonial classification of forests as a separate administrative category was governed by a commercial intent, and served for the first time to delineate the forest as a distinct, commercial entity. The British officers classified 'productive' forests and 'wastelands' on the basis of their saleable potential. The British classification largely ignored local usage. For the local population even the 'wastelands' were important as grazing lands, for fodder, wood, fuel and medicinal purposes (Haynes 1987, Singh 1986). Within the Rajput State the forests were often under the jurisdiction of the local rulers rather than the king. In order to increase state control over the productive forests the British urged that forest areas be centralised under the authority of the king. The separation of forest tracts as distinct entities and their centralisation under the ruler was the first step in the dispossession of the rights of the forest inhabitants. It also worked against the autonomy of the local chiefs.[20] In curtailing Rajput war-

---

possessed of Udaipur in 1572, 'sheltered in the hills causing the plains of Mewar to be desolated, with a view to impeding the imperial forces, whilst he effectively intercepted the traffic between Delhi and the coast' (1859: 14).

20. The increasing centralisation recorded by Haynes (1978) in Alwar, in Rajasthan, was achieved by an increase in bureaucratisation in the late nineteenth and early twentieth centuries. Haynes argues that the whole idea of the rising centralisation of wasteland management contradicted the *jagirdars'* conception of an autonomous equality. It was favoured only by the *raja*, as it helped him to gain greater control over the *jagirdars* (ibid.: 32-61).

fare and fixing land titles, the British effectively prevented the lower lineages and spatially peripheral Rajput communities from rising in the Rajput hierarchy.

The government classifications of land and forest were of immediate significance to the Girasia. The 'settlement' (term indicating the classification of land for revenue) of land was a major colonial exercise, the aim of which was to, 'create a vested interest of the cultivators in the soil by fixing a reasonable cash rental, and, granting them hereditary rights over their holdings' (1943-44 Sirohi district administrative report: 56).The *Bhakar* was among the last areas of Sirohi to be settled and was known for its resistance to the cash-rent or *bighoti* system.[21] According to the *Rajasthan District Gazetteer* (1967), 'Up to about 1867, little if anything was known of the *Bhakar* or its inhabitants: the latter were said to be jealous of intrusion and wonderful tales were told of their strength, lawlessness etc.' (ibid.: 103). Between 1911 and 1914 most of the land in Sirohi district was settled (surveyed and classified for land revenue) except the *Bhakar* and the land of a few *jagirdars*. The administrative lassitude in imposing the cash rent system in the *Bhakar* stemmed from the fact that the *Bhakar* was remuneratively the least important in the region. The forest of the *Bhakar* was considered poor in quality timber, the resource in which the British were mainly interested. Erskine (1908) observes that, 'the Bhakar or hilly tract to the south-east bears evidence of having been at one time well wooded, but the forests have been for the most part destroyed by Bhils and Girasias' (1908: 222). According to Erskine, the shifting cultivation carried out by the Bhil and Girasia was the main reason for the depletion of the forests. During fieldwork, older Taivar Girasia villagers talked of a previous system of shifting cultivation, *valra,* whereby the forest was burnt and seeds were cast over. A system, they said, which required only watching, as compared to the more labour intensive techniques of the present agriculture. Erskine approved of the measures taken by the colonial government to prohibit what he described as *walar* or *walra* system of cultivation by the Bhil and

21. Since the turn of the century the British had attempted to introduce the *bighoti*, or cash-rent system (based per *bigha* unit of land), as opposed to the *batai,* or crop-rent system (based per plough), prevalent in the region. During the period 1918 to 1924 the former was accepted by the Mahajans, who were a well-to-do community, and some *jagirdars.* By the end of the settlement period most of the cultivators paid under the *bighoti* system. All the cultivators who accepted the rates of *bighoti* were granted permanent hereditary land tenures, based on the continued adherence to the payment of the rental (1943 to 44 Report: 62).

Girasia in Sirohi in order to prevent the destruction of the trees which it entailed.[22]

Whether the British classifications directly effected the *Bhakar* inhabitants is difficult to say. But their classification indirectly contributed to the ideological separation of the forest-inhabiting communities from the rest of the region's communities. In their confinement to the forest, the Girasia gained a Bhil, or an archetypal 'tribal' aspect. The contemporary outsider construction of Girasia identity is largely coloured by the Bhil image, a powerful symbol in the region. (As mentioned in note 1 of this chapter, the Bhils are among the ten most numerous communities in Rajasthan.) The Bhils command awe and have been regarded as hardy and chivalrous, both in local perceptions as well as in India more generally. The fearlessness of the Bhils was depicted in such titles as the 'Lord of the Pass', 'Forest Lord', 'Lord of the Frontier' – descriptions which are also recorded in British accounts (Tod I-8, 116, 469, in Deliege 1985). On the other hand, the Bhils are also objects of disdain, particularly for their meat-eating habits. The opposite or negative image of the Bhil is linked to their relation with the forest or *jungle*. In Abu Road, the Bhils were frequently described as *jungali*. Although literally meaning inhabitants of the *jungle, jungali* also denotes a 'primitive' and 'savage' lifestyle. (The savagery is considered to be epitomised in the consumption of the flesh of wild animals and buffalos domesticated for the purpose, a major factor in the outsider construction of Bhil impurity.) By extension, all the communities living in the *jungle* gain a *jungali* or Bhil aspect. Carstairs (1956) writing about the Bhils of Udaipur notes that the Rajputs regarded them as 'remnant Dasyus' (i.e., aboriginal populations who were used as slaves). Carstairs' work also documents instances of cruelty which the established Rajputs inflicted upon the Bhils of their region. The Girasia highlight the negative image of the Bhils when they refer to them as buffalo-eaters *(paada khava vale)*. Some Bhils deny the Girasia their superior position. For example, Dola, a Bhil from Deldar village

22. The southern Aravalli section of Rajasthan, where the *Bhakar* is located, is a geographical area which includes Bhilwara, Chittorgarh, Udaipur, Sirohi and Dungarpur. It is an area of uniform vegetation described as 'grass/wood/scrub complexes' (Singh, in Haynes 1987: 16 to 20). For the southern Aravalli area, Haynes (1987) notes an intense deforestation for the period 1860-90, a slow minor regrowth from 1890 to 1910, and a general decline from 1910-80. There is a slow increase in arable land from 9 percent in 1860, through 14 percent in 1930 to 29 percent in 1980. This has been mainly at the cost of the grass and scrub lands, which have registered a continuous decrease in grass, wood and fodder. In 1980, almost all of the 66,000 hectares of temperate broad leaved forest in Rajasthan was in Sirohi (Haynes 1987).

(twelve kilometres from the Taivar village) said: 'The Girasia and Bhils were all one community. We were all Rana Bhil, that is the highest *[unchi]* Bhil and above the Thori Bhil and the Maryan Bhil. We all sat around one day and there was a dead camel. Those who ate the meat of the dead camel were called Girasia and those who abstained were the Bhils'. Other sections of Bhils living in Ore, however, acknowledged the superiority of the Girasia.

The upper-caste Rajputs identify with the chivalrous aspect of the Bhils. The Bhils are popularly believed to be the previous rulers from whom the Rajputs wrested landholding rights. Symbolically, this relation between the Bhil and the Rajput is reflected in the *tilak* ceremony of the Rajput coronation, in which a Bhil is said to anoint the forehead of the ruler with the blood from his finger (Tod 1920, Carstairs 1956, Mayer 1960, Deliege 1985). According to Koppers (1948), the old State emblem of the *rana* (ruler) of Udaipur figures a Bhil standing next to the *rana*, an honour given to the Bhils, 'whose forefathers had assisted in the battle of Haldighat against the Mohammadens' (1948: 115). Koppers goes on to note that the Bhils of Udaipur-Kherwara for this reason consider themselves 'pure' and above other Bhils, although, 'there are still limitations to purity as the Bhils are meat-eaters' (1948: 115). Most of the lower-class communities of Rajput, Bhil and Girasia in the region of Sirohi shared the common experiences of a drought-related poverty which made claims of superior status particularly difficult to sustain.

Scarcity and the Common Economy

While the colonial state mainly settled landholdings in the *Bhakar*, a greater penetration of the Girasia economy took place under the Indian government which had many more indigenous uses for the forest products. At the time of my fieldwork, the Indian government had a wide-ranging interest in the forests of the *Bhakar,* especially in the plants for medicinal purposes. There are many indigenous uses for other products such as *lac* (tree resin), the leaves of the *khakra* tree, fibres of the date palm, berries, and *tendu* leaves for the Indian cigarette. It has been noted for other forest regions (Singh 1986), but can equally well apply to the *Bhakar,* that the state appropriation of the forest resources has been at the cost of the common property rights of the forest dwellers.[23] The notion of common property is one

---

23. Singh (1986) points out, that common property rights of the forest inhabitants had not been recognised either in the British formulation of the forest policy of 1865, or the Indian Forest Act of 1927.

that is applicable to the economy of the region and includes the collection of wood, grass, weeds, leaves, cowdung, berries, fruit, bark, also common grazing lands and water for drinking purposes and for cattle. It is in the utilisation of these raw materials by the lower strata in the region that a common economy is recognised. Singh (1986) suggests that it has been impossible to ensure the welfare of the forest dwellers and others sharing common property resources because of the government's failure in legitimising common property claims. In the pursuit of so-called 'wider national interests' the government, by contracting the forests to industrial firms, has aided the privatisation of these resources with the benefits accruing to the urban rich who use the finished products, items (such as tables and chairs), which are neither used nor available to the forest people. Other items which the forest people use (especially the direct forest products) which were previously freely available to them have, as a consequence of the privatisation of the forest, to be bought back from the state. In this sense, the state ensured the pauperisation of the very large section of the population dependent on common property.

Apart from the detrimental economic effects, state extraction from the forests may also have political implications for its inhabitants. Haimendorf (1982) gives increased economic dependence following the alienation of tribal land as one of the major factors in the political disruption of the Reddi, Chenchu and Gond tribal communities in Andhra Pradesh (ibid.: 149). In the *Bhakar* region however, the government has protected the autonomy of the landholdings of the Taivars. There has been no sale of land to other communities. Moreover, the tax rates for landholdings remain relatively low, at approximately one and a half rupees per *bigha,* depending on the productivity of the land. Despite its extraction from the forests in the *Bhakar* and restrictions on forest-products used by the Girasia, the forest department provided relief work for the Girasia during the year of my fieldwork.

The uncertainty of the monsoons, and the relatively unproductive landholdings of the Girasia and the other inhabitants of the *Bhakar* (see chapter 6) and the nearby villages has increased their dependence on the sale of the forest products. Food substitutes from the forest were crucial for subsistence especially during drought and famine conditions.[24] The absence of alternate strategies for subsis-

---

24. During my fieldwork I was told that when there was a dearth of maize flour, and little money to purchase wheat, the bark of the date palm tree was often ground along with a handful of wheat grains to meet the food requirements of the household.

tence is reflected in the pursuit of forest related activities despite the risk of imprisonment or fines stipulated by the Forest Act [25] and enforced by the forest officers who regularly patrol the area. Especially in times of drought, as in the year of my fieldwork, most Taivar households were able to survive only through the sale of wood and grass cut from the forest. For such purposes groups of villagers would leave the village a few hours before dawn so as to conduct their sales as soon as possible after sunrise in order to avoid the forest guards. Fines and imprisonment were difficult for the Girasia to sustain and there were cases where the Taivars had become bonded in debt to a junior forest or police official, who was subsequently able to appropriate the forest products for his own benefit. With the introduction of unsympathetic middlemen, the government has both alienated and further distanced itself from those 'tribals' and 'forest-dwellers' it so categorised for the disbursement of state aid.

In the illustration of the Girasia dependence on the forests, I do not suggest that the Girasia pursue their extraction from the forest with a view to its conservation. In fact there was a conspicuous absence of an ethic related to conservation of the environment, a romantic notion often attached to people inhabiting the forest. But what may once have seemed a balanced environment (where extraction does not exceed the natural regenerative capacity), has long since been affected by the growing poverty of its inhabitants. Even Girasia men and women in their forties can remember greater affluence in the immediate past. 'Affluence' for the Girasia was in terms of the least possible dependence on the market for their staple cereal requirements. According to Jevali Bai, a Girasia mother of ten daughters: 'We never used to visit the market as much as we do now. When there are good rains, we need only go to the market once in two to three months, and there was a time when I went only once in twelve months and that too to look for some clothes. Nowadays at least one member of each family goes every week to the market.' This rising dependence on the market is due partly to the failure of the monsoons, but is also a result of the reduced forest cover due to the intensive settlement pattern relative to earlier times. The congestion of settlements has followed the restrictions in forest area usage stipulated by the forest authorities.

The *Bhakar* area has had some very damaging famine conditions as a result of scarce rainfall. The Taivars also had memories of famine passed down from their immediate ancestors, especially in

---

25. Section 26 and 33 in Act XVI of 1927.

1899 and 1901-2. For this period the district records report a very low amount of rainfall, of five inches and seventy-five centimetres and five inches fifty-one centimetres for the monsoon months which was in contrast to the annual average of seventeen inches for the period from 1895 to 1905. A number of elderly Taivars record their births at the time of one famine or another. Dala, one of the oldest inhabitants of the Taivar village at the time of my fieldwork, said he was born in *athaavna re kaal*, the famine of 1908. He remembered his parents talk about the *Undariya*, the plague of rats which took place in the 1890s, and the *Sapno* and *Hathaavno* famines which took place before his birth.[26] The 1908 report for Sirohi records loans to agriculturalists of the magnitude of Rs. 48,000 and suspensions of land revenue to the order of Rs. 25,000 as relief for the 1899-1900 famine. It is difficult to envisage the impact of these famines on the Girasia and Bhil communities. There are government reports of widespread relief measures in the form of famine work, depots in Sirohi to buy wood, grass and to sell subsidised grain. However aid to marginal communities often came with strings attached.[27]

The situation of undependable monsoons and the resultant scarcity has continued till the present. The year of my fieldwork (1986-87) was the third consecutive year of poor rains and the *Bhakar* Girasia predicted widespread suffering if the crop failed the next year (1987-88). After the monsoon failed in 1986-87, the Taivars sold their corn-stalks and grass which normally serve as fodder for livestock, fully aware that this would entail starvation for their livestock but having no choice in what was a question of their own survival. The monsoon failed again in 1987-88 and most livestock perished. In the following year (1988-89), although there was enough rain, many villagers died

26. Dalaji died a year after this interview was held, a victim of the scarcity of 1988. The 1908 *Gazetteer* on Rajputana notes that famines occurred in 1746, 1785, 1812, 1833 and 1848, although further details were unavailable (ibid.: 223). Later, from 1868 to 1869 there was a great scarcity on account of the famine, as a result of which 50 to 75 percent of the cattle perished for want of fodder in the state of Sirohi. The failure of the 1868 monsoon also affected the Bombay Presidency and the Deccan. Tensions, arising from conditions of indebtedness among famine-stricken villagers, led to peasant riots in 1873. Three years later, the great famine of 1876 to 1878 took place. In 1878 the irregular monsoon was followed by epidemic fever and plague (Vol. II, 1909: 34). The plague reappeared in Bombay in 1896 after the monsoon failed in 1895, and was followed by another major famine of 1899 to 1902, which in turn resulted in an epidemic of cholera. Up to 1904, one million deaths due to plague were recorded in the Bombay Presidency.
27. For example, in the Bombay Presidency, the political agent records how the relief work paid each Bhil Rs. 1/- per rat that he killed during the plague.

as a result of reduced resistance to disease in constitutions weakened by the previous four years of low-level subsistence. When I revisited the village in December 1988, I was given an approximate figure of a hundred deaths (from a population of 1,400 persons) which had occurred. Most of those who died were village elders and children. The number was so large that mass funerals for twenty people were held. The Taivar Girasia felt that famine and scarcity had occured more regularly under the Indian government than when they were a part of the Rajput State. Girasia members of the low-caste Anop Mandal organisation (chapter 9) associate the difficult conditions for the Girasia with the exploitation of the *sarkar* (government). For them, the decline was symbolised by the first land survey (1944-56) when 'the government absorbed all the productive powers of our land'. It was to oppose the government control over them that the Girasia abandoned their village during the period of the initial surveys held in the 1940s.[28] Often distantiation was a method used to retreat from conflict within the village and community itself (as I discuss in chapter 8). Haimendorf (1982) indicates the effects of state-enforced restrictions of mobility on the social relations within a tribal Chenchu village. According to Haimendorf, 'The procedure of placing spatial distance between those who could not live in peace was no longer practical when larger numbers of families were compelled in one permanent village and this resulted in frequent occurences of violence, murder, rape and theft'(ibid.: 146). I suggest that, as a result of state restrictions on Girasia mobility within the *Bhakar*, the Girasia experience the famine and drought to a greater degree than when they were able to cultivate any part of the forest they chose. It is in this sense that the Girasia also experience the increased presence of the state administration after Indian independence.The experience of a forest-related subsistence, and the notions of common property were shared by the

---

28. Padel (1987) conceptualises the survey as a tool in the larger framework of orientalist power. The Girasia response of flight, to state intervention has also been reported as a tactic of other marginal communities. Hardiman (1987), notes a similar means of protest in Gujarat, 'In 5 years before the British annexation of Valsad taluka in 1802, the *adivasi* cultivators twice deserted the area in protest against heavy tax demands. After the establishment of British rule, they returned but between 1828 and 1833 again migrated en masse due to exploitation by moneylenders' (ibid.: 70). Gardener (1982) observes that the Tamil Paliyan hunter-gatherers use, 'non-retaliation and actual geographic retreat as the main responses to conflict or hostility' (ibid.: 467). Fuller (1977) claims that flight was a characteristic of pre-British India, where there was a surplus of land and a shortage of cultivators. 'The cultivators' ultimate sanction against oppressive rulers was flight to unoccupied land, of which there was plenty' (1977: 69).

Taivar Girasia, the lower castes, and other poor sections of the villages bordering the *Bhakar*.

In this chapter I have indicated that the present, 'outside' identity of the Taivar Girasia is informed by their increasing marginalisation from the regional groups and other communities who identify with the Rajput ethic. These latter communities have in turn needed to delve deeper into history to assert their positions of difference and dominance. This is reflected in the increasing politicisation of potent symbols of Rajputhood, of which *sati* is one example. Deprived of their traditional kin-based power, many of the significant elites have joined the national-level political parties. Although they still rely on their previous glory to get votes from the people, the lineage-type hold is giving way to a different but diffuse sense of Rajput identity which, at the same time, excludes the Girasia who are considered to have no Rajput heritage. The Girasia may have been equally disregarded and distanced by upper-caste Rajputs in the days before Indian Independence.[29] However, subsequent administrative classifications and political changes have added substance to the middle- and upper-caste outsider claims of difference from the Girasia in the nation state.

---

29. As indeeed the Bhils were (Carstairs 1956).

Chapter 4

BEING A GIRASIA
The Lineage and the Village

*I*n the previous two chapters I outlined the historical nature of Girasia marginality and the outsiders' constructions of Girasia identity. In this chapter I turn towards understanding Taivar Girasia views on what it means to be a Girasia. In conversations, members of the Girasia community continuously evaluated other Girasia men and women in terms of the two contrasting, yet interrelated social institutions of descent (relationships of one's own patrilineage), and marriage (relationships with other patrilineages). The Girasia evaluations were always made with reference to the 'village' or space occupied, owned and associated with a specific lineage and descent. The village was called the *kaka-baba-re*, meaning place of the father's brothers. It was also known as the *piyar* or natal village and *huhara* or affinal village. The village in spatial and genealogical terms was thus associated with men and provided a map of male social relations. Women were less visible in the language and images of lineal kinship but through their change of residence at marriage created realationships beyond the village and linked specific villages across the region. Despite an inability to read or write, an isolation from the media and a general ignorance of national affairs, the Taivar Girasia were extremely well informed about the members of their community in other Girasia villages of the region. The main channels for the flow of personal information were the connections established through marriage among the members of the different villages. In this chapter I show how descent and marriage, in the context of the Taivar village, are central to the sense of being a Girasia.[1] Furthermore, I suggest that the institutions of descent and marriage have different implications for Girasia women compared to Girasia men which are at the same time similar to gender differences elsewhere in the region.

The first section discusses the centrality of the Girasia lineage and related social units such as the sublineage, the 'family' and 'household'. It considers the nature and implications of agnatic solidarity as well as differences. The second section describes how the meaning of descent and kinship based differences are articulated in everyday life in the village for daughters, sons, brothers and sisters. This is further elaborated in the final subsection describing the relations between Taivar husbands and wives.

The Taivar Lineage and Related Social Units

In the region of south Rajasthan as well as in most of northern India, the caste (sub-caste or lineage) or *jati* of a person is invariably one of the first questions addressed in personal introductions. *Jati* is a genus of social classification which may account for the least inclusive level of 'family' and also, depending on the social relation of the speakers may vary in meaning to include a group of families, the sub-lineage, the lineage, the clan or group of clans (the level of 'caste'). According to Das (1977), *jati* is the social unit of a caste which identifies it with descent, locality and cult (ibid.: 57). Inden and Nicholas (1977) illustrate a similar usage in the Bengali conception of the *kula*. At the lineage level the *kula* includes all the male descendants of a common ancestral male together with married wives and daughters. The Girasia *jath* (lineage) is similarly the social unit which includes all the male and female descendants of a common ancestral male. The Girasia *jath* is an exogamous and virilocal unit. Unlike the *kula*, incoming wives are not included in the Girasia *jath* category.

The very first Girasia of the Taivar village whom I met, told me, '*hemo Parmar Rajput Girasia*' (we are Parmar Rajput Girasia). By this I was supposed to understand that they were the superior category of

---

1. I am aware that by concentrating on the institution of marriage, I will be emphasising the role of women as wives, wherein they appear most dominated by men. However the idea of being related to a man is central to the lives of Girasia women, and, apart from birth, marriage is the only way of achieving these relationships.

Girasia called the Rajput Girasia, who traced descent from the Parmar clan of Rajputs. In the surrounding region, the Parmar label is used as a prefix by some of both the lower and higher Hindu castes.[2] Later I heard the villagers give a different introduction to Girasia of other villages, to whom they would specify that they were 'Taivar *jath*'. Members of other villages would refer to specific Girasias of the Taivar village as, for example, 'Ramla Taivar' or the person Ramla of the Taivar *jath*. In these conversations, the *jath* essentially denoted the autonomous localised lineage and was the common suffix used by Girasia in intergroup introductions. The qualification 'Taivar' referred specifically to the common ancestor Tava (Taivar literally means 'from Tava'). The Taivar village, I was told, had five generations of Taivar Girasia all linked to Tava. Members of the Taivar lineage formed the dominant group, both numerically and with regard to landholding in the village. The few male members of the Taivar lineage who had moved to other villages retained their lineage title of Taivar Girasia, but lived as minority groups with reduced rights in villages of other lineages (see below). The few Taivar Girasia in other villages returned to their natal village to participate in the rituals of the lineage including marriages and funerals of their lineage relatives.

In conversations amongst the Taivar Girasia, the natal village was always referred to as the *kaka-baba-re*, or the home of the father's younger brother, *kaka,* and father's elder brother *baba.*[3] The *kaka-baba* was the classificatory category denoting 'father's brother' and linked all members of the lineage through the relations of male siblingship. In other words, all men were either F *(bapa),* FB *(baba or kaka),* FBS *(bhai)* or extensions of these categories (for example, FF was *mota bapa,* or simply *mota,* FFB was also *mota* and FFBS simply *bhai*). All women who were not sisters *(bai)* were either FBW *(babi/kaki),* FBD *(bai)* or FZ *(bua).* There was thus a difference in age and seniority, reflected in the terminology for the father's brothers *(kaka-baba)*[4] but their wives, and all the father's sisters were called *bua* (although some-

---

2. For example, Deva Ram Parmar is among the few outsiders employed by the government to work in the Taivar village. He is a member of the *meghwal* (untouchable) community whose traditional occupation was in leather-curing, but who currently manufacture plant dyes.
3. *Kaka* and *baba* are also used as terms of address and reference. While *baba* for the Girasia means father's elder brother, it is also a term of respect. In the north Indian kinship pattern, *baba* is used to refer to father's father while *kaka* is the father's younger brother (Karve, 1968).
4. The presence of lineal seniority is common to the lineage levels in the Rajput structure. This is reflected in the Taivar positions of legislative authority in the village (see chapter 8).

times in cases of reference the prefix *nonki*, meaning smaller, may be attached to refer to *nonki bua*, or the younger aunt). Thus the lineage was an extended form of the FB category and bounded by the agnatic relation. A reference to the patrilineal relationship is inbuilt in the names of the lineage members in the Taivar village. When referring to each other they would use two names, for example, Ramla Deeta, or Ramla (son) of Deeta, and Dhanki Deeta, or Dhanki (daughter) of Deeta. In practice most of the women were referred to as *bai*. Although the Girasia terminology did not distinguish between daughters and sons, women were absent in lineage genealogies.

In the Taivar village there were eight sublineages each named after the sublineal ancestor. For example, members of the Vaijjath sublineage were descendants of Vajja, a 'son' of Tava the founder ancestor (see figure 4.1, the kinship diagram). Each of the sublineages lived in their own section of the village called *phalli*. As the sublineages grew and divided, the sections *(phalli)* became more numerous.[5] The Taivars also divided their village into three broad *phalli* sections. These were called the *Neechali* (lower), *Beechali* (middle) and *Uppali* (upper) according to the scale of ascent into the hills (which was from the northwest to the southeast). It was generally understood that the households in the lower section (Neechali *phalli*) were older than those in Beechali or Uppali *phallis*. This corresponded with the oral versions of Taivar history discussed in chapter 2, which indicated the Taivar ancestors had settled in the Neechali *phalli*.

Whenever we talked of the 'family' referring to the most important and smallest self-sufficient unit, the Taivars always mentioned the sublineage, or *hojvan*, whose male members were called *haga-vale* (or 'true'-ones, and denoted sons born of the same parents). The 'family' or sublineage could be spread over one or more *phallis*. For example the largest sublineage, which was the Vaijjath, had its households distributed mainly over two *phallis*. Each *phalli* had its own leader *(patel)* as well as its own ritual mediators (described in chapters 8 and 9). The *phalli*-wise sectioning of the sublineage presented checks to the domination of any single sublineage in the village and lineage. It was not so much that there was a practised egalitarianism within the lineage, as that sections of the sublineage had equal aspirations to inequality, as I will demonstrate in the fol-

5. The sublineage households determined the extent of the *phalli*. For example, when some households of the Lailath sublineage grew to a strength of nine households, the area of their households and fields came to be known as *Baliya Kua* rather than *Beechalli phalli* of which it was a part. Thus the number of *phallis* at any time could only be an approximation.

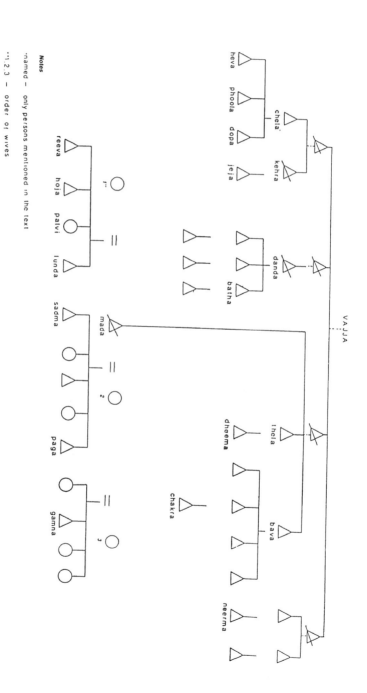

Figure 4.1 The Vaijjath Hojvan (sublineage)

lowing chapters. Table 4.1 shows us, for example, that the Vaijjath sublineage has the largest number (51) of households in the village. The Vaijjath households mainly occupy two *phallis* Beechalli and Malwa. There were households in the Taivar village which belonged to Girasia who were not members of the Taivar lineage but who were affinally related to the Taivars. Table 4.2 shows the distribution of the 47 non-Taivar households in the Taivar village.

Table 4.1: Distribution of Taivar Households According to Sublineages and Geographical Location

No.	Sublineage	(Hhs)	N	G	P	B	V	M	BK	Na
1.	Vaijjath	(51)		4	3	23	2	19		
2.	Devath	(20)	20							
3.	Raijjath	(27)	15	10				2		
4.	Khetrath	(14)	13/1							
5.	Lailath	(33)		23		1		9		
6.	Gokhlath	(9)								9
7.	Billath	(6)						1		5
8.	Rehmath	(18)								18
	Total	(178)	49	37	3	23	3	22	9	32

Key: Hhs = Households

The *phalli* names are abbreviated in the table as follows: N = Nichalli, G = Ghata, P = Palri, B = Beechalli, V = Vera, M = Malwa, BK = Baliya Kua, Na = Naal

Source: Primary Fieldwork Data

Table 4.2: Distribution of Non-Taivar Households According to Geographical Location

No.	Non-Taivar	(Hhs)	N	M	B	G	V	Na
1.	Bubariya	(7)	6	1				
2.	Peesra	(9)	2	1	1	3	2	
3.	Khair	(5)			3	1		1
4.	Khokhariya	(3)			1	2		
5.	Gamaar	(5)	1			3	1	
6.	Dungaicha	(1)						1
7.	Khejariya	(2)						2
8.	Vanhiya	(1)						1
9.	Ninoma	(5)	4					1
10.	Kunwar	(4)	4					
11.	Parmar	(5)	5					
	Total	(47)	22	2	5	9	3	6

Key: Hhs = Households

The *phalli* names are abbreviated in the above table as follows: N = Nichalli, M = Malwa, B = Beechalli, G = Ghata, V = Vera, Na = Naal

Source: Primary Fieldwork Data

The table indicates that non-Taivar households were affinal members of eleven non-Taivar Girasia lineages. The non-Taivar households were also dispersed among all the geographical sections in the village. The Taivar Girasia occupied 178 out of a total of 225 households in the village. The remaining households were comprised of Girasia (non-Taivars) who were affinally related to the Taivars. They lived in the village but were rarely allowed to own productive land. No other castes lived in the Taivar village, with the exception of one household of a *Jogi* (low-caste man who lived on alms). The Taivar household was most frequently a nuclear unit in that it housed a couple and their children. But a Taivar household was often a joint household, in the sense that, besides the couple and their children, a household could have an adopted (permanent) brother's son, a visiting (temporary) brother's daughter, or the elder parents (if the household was of the youngest son), two or more wives of the husband, a resident son-in-law (the death of the father), or the son and daughter-in-law and their child (they established their own household). Although a joint household could have the two conjugal pairs of a father and his son, no two adult married brothers lived together. Married brothers would often, but not always, live in adjoining households. The adjoining households could also be those of a man's son, his father's brother, or father's brother's son. The physically adjoining households were functionally separated in two major ways. Firstly, the households were separated in the daily production and consumption of food and in the distribution of cash income earned by the individual members of the household. Secondly, the households were separated with regard to the labour of the wives. Each household could, however, cooperate with the adjoining household and other households with regard to sharing the implements for production, including oxen to harness ploughs, rights to crop shares, shares in well-water (an important but scarce resource), and all services which involved the collective labour of the 'brothers'. The 'brothers' participating in joint production activities outside the household, nearly always belonged to the same sublineage of the lineage.

Although the Taivar households, in terms of separate hearths, were predominantly comprised of a couple and their children, a number of households had elders or other categories of relatives also resident. Sixteen out of fifty-six households had elders of the generation above the male head, staying. Fourteen out of fifty-six households had other categories of adult kin staying (see table 4.3). Amongst the households I was most familiar with, were those of Lunda Mada in Beechali *phalli* and Dopa Chela in Malwa *phalli* (see Fig. 4.1, the kinship diagramme on the Vaijjath sublineage). Both Lunda Mada and Dopa Chela had their own individual portions of land, allocated to them when their eldest brothers had bought wives. Lunda Mada was the youngest son of Mada from his first wife. Mada, now deceased, was a Taivar of the Vaijjath sublineage. He had had three wives and fourteen children from them. Lunda lived next to his brother Gamna, the youngest of Mada's sons who had inherited his father's house *(gair)*. Lunda had two wives, Haluri and Tibri, and eleven children from them. As his wives were not on good terms with each other, Lunda built two adjoining rooms so that each wife could have a separate living space and hearth *(chula)*. Next to the outer wall of his house was the temporary construction of his only married son, his daughter-in-law and their child. Dopa Chela was the youngest son of Chela from his only wife. Dopa had one wife and nine children from her. He had two elder brothers Heva and Phoola, the school master. Heva lived in Beechali *phalli*, while Phoola lived with Dopa. An adjoining household had been built for Phoola when his wife was there. But once she left him, Phoola rarely stayed there. Dopa's elderly father Chela, and his mother, popularly called Maji, also stayed with him. A temporary shelter was built on the other side of the house from Phoola's section for Chela when he became sick.[6] The two *chula* for Dopa's wife and his mother were in the same hut.

Table 4.3: Number of Elders and Other Adults Resident in Taivar Households

Kin category	Elders resident No. of Households	Kin category	Other adults resident No. of Households
F, M	5	D-in-Law	4
only F	1	yB	4
only M	6	eB	2 (unmarried)
M, GM	2	Z	1 (unmarried)
GM	1	ZS	1 ('guest')
FyB	1	yBS	1 ('adopted')
		eBS	1 ('adopted')

Key: F= father, M= mother, GM= grandmother, yB= younger brother, eB= elder brother, Z= sister, ZS= sister's son, BS= brother's son, D= daughter

Source: Primary Fieldwork Data

---

6. Subsequently Chela's sickness was diagnosed as tubercolosis and he died one year after my fieldwork.

The complicated household arrangements among the Taivars at once contests the neat categories of joint and nuclear households used to describe social organisation in northern India. Early studies, such as those of Kapadia (1966) and Karve (1968) maintain that a joint family in the north operated in the context of a pooling of resources among closest male kin and their wives who lived under one roof and shared the same hearth, living and ritual space. In contrast, the nuclear family was regarded as a household of one brother, his wife and children, who formed an independent production and consumption unit.There have been long standing debates regarding the definition of the joint family, particularly in relation to the impact of westernisation and urbanisation in India (Parry 1979 discusses these in some detail). Some studies have claimed that the institution of joint families is dying out as nuclear families are more suited to the needs of modern, urban living. Other studies have countered these claims by the observation, for example, that despite increased mobility and migration towards towns, the nuclear families continued to maintain ties of a pecuniary as well as ritual nature with their parent joint households. Shah (1974) questions several generally accepted notions of the Indian household such as, for example, (1) that joint households have been more common than nuclear ones in the past, (2) that there has been an inevitable evolutionary shift from one to another, and (3) that joint households were more characteristic of rural as compared to urban India. Earlier, Mayer (1960) had stressed the need to distinguish a joint family from a joint household. According to him while the joint family was a 'corporate property group of patri kin, not necessarily a discrete living unit' (1960: 182), a joint household was one 'where there is more than one man and where incomes and expenses are pooled' (1960: 181).

The Girasia household had both joint and nuclear characteristics. Furthermore, the 'joint family' was comprised of several households who shared some movable property in common (for example agricultural implements and bulls), but not land, contra Mayer. However, like Mayer, I find the distinction between income and consumables as opposed to non-consumable, movable goods an important one in the Girasia case. To take an example, a few goats were kept by each household for milk, but were also a source of meat. Goat-meat was normally only consumed together with brothers, frequently at a feast following a ritual occasion of the sublineage. Goats could be lent and borrowed but were never gifted between households. Dhanki's husband had borrowed a goat from Andu's husband, his father's brother of another sublineage. A few days after the feast, when

Dhanki passed Andu's house, Andu reminded her about the payment. Thus goats may be lent, but are not shared. Food and money were also not shared among households. In general the Taivars preferred not to borrow food or money from their brothers *(bhai)*. Duda said money was preferably borrowed from a money-lender than from brothers in the village. Even though he acknowledged relatives could lend at a better interest rate (Rs. 10 per 100 compared to the moneylenders' rate of Rs. 25 per 100), he felt it was best not to spoil relations with brothers by borrowing, except as a last resort.

In terms of the patrifocal caste ideology, the sharing of resources in the Indian joint family reflects the solidarity of the agnatic group. It is in this sense that the joint family has been regarded as an ideal, and upheld in mythological and folk texts as well as in popular opinion. In contrast, the nuclear family is regarded as a threat to agnatic solidarity in that it divides the lineage property between brothers. As a consequence, nuclear families are popularly seen to originate as a result of negative interaction, in the form of a rift between brothers, often attributed to the instigation by their respective wives. One is therefore given to believe that nuclear households reflect stronger conjugal ties at the cost of agnatic relations. Although the nuclear aspects of Girasia households were related to the separation of women's labour in production activities, I will argue in the last section that these nuclear aspects do not necessarily reflect a greater autonomy of the household from other sublineage households. In terms of the autonomy of the wife's position, the nuclear aspects of the Girasia household are not significantly different from the joint family life for affinal women in other caste households. For example, as in other joint-caste families, among the Taivars women were often blamed for conflicts between men. But as Parry (1979) has pointed out, quarrels between women are often a facade behind which men carry out their own kinship strategies. The fact that the differences between men are not directly articulated, according to Parry, emphasises the value placed on the ideal of brotherhood (1979: 179). While the partition of Girasia land is more a stage in the development cycle of the household,[7] the only forced partition of the Girasia household of one man and his two wives is usually a result of conflict between a man's wives (see below).

So far I have outlined the major Girasia categories which give meaning to the term 'village'. These various categories are however

---

7. In anthropology, the fact that households may be differentially constituted at different points of time is captured in the concept of the development cycle (for example, Goody 1976).

translated in different ways into action by daily life in the lineage. The following section looks at the meaning of the categories of lineage and sublineage for individuals in the lineage.

Experiencing Age and Gender Differences

Childhood and Adolescence

All children belonged to their father's lineage and the Taivars strongly believed, as Kalu told me, that, 'Women contribute the *peth* (stomach container) for the child who is actually made by the *aadmi ka paani* (water of the man)'. Girasia children contributed significantly as workers in the Girasia economy. Conceptually, however, the birth of a boy was considered important as he would maintain and reproduce the agnatic structure of the lineage. The birth of a girl was also welcomed, preferably after a boy, as she would bring her father a brideprice by which he could maintain and try to expand his economic standing in the lineage. Daughters as brides also provided a network of affinal relations potentially useful for their father and brothers. The ideal number of children, I was told, was five, three sons and two daughters. According to one Taivar man, 'Too many sons divide the household assets into very small, inefficient portions. Too many daughters carry away [deplete] household resources when they get married'. Whenever I asked Taivar men to list the number of their children, they would only mention their sons unless I specifically asked about their daughters. When I remarked about the absence of women in lineage genealogies I was told, 'Our daughters will marry and leave the village'. The important work contributions of the daughters were thus not recognised.

In the Girasia household both parents 'work', although the mother works closer to the home in the year after childbirth. If the child born is the second or third, its care is delegated to the eldest child. The child is initially encouraged to play on its own and later joins its own age-group amongst kin. But already at an early age children begin to help their parents. As soon as a girl can carry an earthen pot of water, she begins to help her mother outside the household. When she is able to handle an axe she goes to cut wood in the forest and later to the market place with her relative-companions (i.e., daughters of her father's brothers). Boys help in drawing water from the well, herding goats and cows, and practice with their bows and arrows. (Bows and arrows are useful to hunt rabbits and birds consumed in the lean winter season. They are more frequently kept as a warning to thieves, and are also carried by men as a means of protection on journeys outside the village.) Boys perform more chores outside the household and travel greater distances at a much younger age than do girls. In terms of responsibilities, Girasia children become adult much faster than children in upper- or middle-caste and class Hindu households. In fact the Girasia do not have a word for 'child' which is different from 'unattached young adult'.[8] Bosa was approximately ten years old and one of the few Girasia boys who attended the small primary school in the Taivar village. When his parents and baby sister had to go to Gujarat for a few days, Bosa was left to look after their home. He had to care for his younger sister and brother, to cook unleavened bread, feed the few goats and the dog, and also go to school. At other times, I would meet him on the forest path returning from Abu Road town where he had gone to sell leaves with *lac* gum resin which he had collected, or to buy kerosene oil, or other small household requirements.

Children reduce their mothers' domestic work-load and later her work in the fields and forest. The daughter is a major co-worker in domestic duties especially related to food processing. An important function which children perform is as messengers or bearers of information. Wives and mothers are not free to move in the village in the absence of a purpose governed by work. They also do not go for social visits to the houses of husband's kin unless sought out by the women there. Women seldom form working groups with women of other households. With households scattered in the *phalli* on the hillsides children, who usually have unrestricted access to all households, become major carriers of gossip, information, and entertainment. Children are especially vital to the survival of handicapped men. Laga had lost his leg a few years previous to my fieldwork, when he worked as a labourer in a mining company in Gujarat. With the loss of his leg, he became unable to journey long distances in search of wage labour in the low agricultural season. His capacity to work his own field declined as well. A year later his wife left him. Laga's greatest grudge against her was that she had left *pethas* (full of stomach) and carrying his child (chapter 5 discusses the options women have to leave their husbands). While male household heads can seek help from their brothers for major activities such as house-building, well-repairing and the seasonal ploughing and threshing activities, most of the day-to-day work is done by the women and children. The

---

8. S*ora* means boy as well as young man; *sori* means girl as well as young woman; in the region, the terms are *chora* and *chori*.

Taivars often imply that a lack of children is the cause of a brother's poverty. Heva, the eldest brother of Dopa, had only one daughter from his first wife who had died a few years ago. He could not maintain his house or fields and was forced to give his daughter in marriage to a man who was poor enough to be willing to leave his own fields, and become a resident son-in-law *(ghar jamai)*. Lunda's eldest brother Hoja, was similarly inconvenienced by a lack of children. His last wife had died leaving him childless. Hoja adopted one of Lunda's sons to stay with him and work on his fields. When Lunda's son brought a wife, Hoja helped them build an extension to his house, although he said he was expecting the couple to leave him after a while. Later during my stay, Hoja bought himself a wife, a woman who was deaf and dumb, but all that he could 'afford' in brideprice terms.

For Taivar children, an older female in the household is the main source of physical care and comfort. The oldest female is usually the mother *(aai)*, sometimes the father's other wives (called *mahi* or mother's sister) and in some cases the father's mother *(moti aai*, or big mother). With an increase in age of the child and the number of siblings, the contact of the child with the mother lessens. Children's relations with the father's other wives often depend on the relations between the wives. At a young age, the children of two wives may play together but more enduring ties are formed between siblings of the same parents. Haluri, Lunda's first wife (although slightly younger than Tibri the second wife) had six children from Lunda, while Tibri had five children from him. I would always see the daughters of Tibri form a separate work and play group. Sometimes Lunda's sister's daughter would join them. Palvi, Lunda's sister was a 'friend' of Haluri whom she called *vahu* (or brother's wife; while Haluri called Palvi *bai*, or husband's sister). Palvi was not friendly with Tibri although she was kind and chatty with Tibri's daughters (who called Palvi *bua,* or father's sister). Relations within their own generation greatly colour Taivar childhood, and for a Taivar girl especially provide a contrast to her later years in her husband's village *(huhara)*. For daughters, the important relations in their father's village are of two kinds: 1) those with 'friends,' (daughters of their father's brothers, and daughters of their father's other wives; both called *bai*, or by their names) and 2) those with her 'brothers' (sons from the same mother, sons of the father's other wives and sons of the father's brothers; all called *bhai* or by their names). This distinction between friends and brothers reveals that all male relations of the girl are defined by the kinship categories of father, brother and husband ('lovers' could be 'brothers', but 'lovers' who could become husbands were never 'brothers'). The same is true for boys. Boys of the same generation are 'friends'[9] and all the women are mothers *(aai),* sisters *(bai),* or wives (whom they call *aurat* in reference. Husbands never directly address wives and often take the name of the eldest child instead. Women 'lovers' are seen as potential wives).

Girasia children choose their 'friends' from the restricted universe of patrilineal relatives. For girls, 'friends' are those with whom they shared confidences. Matters relating to menstruation, sex and boys are learned from friends rather than from mothers. Palvi complained that her married daughter Zenu had never told her whom she was seeing at night, an activity Palvi was certain of, as Zenu always insisted on sleeping next to the door of the hut. Palvi said she had felt *sharm* (shame) in talking to her own mother about *gaaba aave* (literally, the cloth coming; the soiling of the clothes was an indirect reference to menstruation).[10] Apart from sharing information on bodily functions, it is with this group of 'friends' that the Girasia girls go to the forest to collect produce for the home and the market, or to the town to sell the produce and make small purchases from a part of their earnings, such as small trinkets, *tili* (dots for the forehead), *sipiyo* (hair clips), *aariyu* (cheap necklaces), *kajal* (soot for the eyes), *kanch* (small mirrors) and *kangi* or combs. A number of young girls and some boys would buy packets of coloured beads and make necklaces for themselves or their friends.

Often friendships divide the relationships among sisters and women of different age groups. Girasia boys in contrast have fewer 'friends' (sons of their father's relatives) than girls and move more on their own in the forest and the market. Work in the forests allows young Girasia girls and boys to meet away from their parents and lineage relatives. It is common knowledge that taking goats to the forest, or collecting firewood and grass is often an excuse for young adults to meet. Such a meeting can involve varying degrees of physical interaction. Often the elders do not object and every one knows,

9. Boys, unlike girls who called their friends *hakhi,* do not have a special term for friends.
10. Palvi said she had learnt all about *gaaba* from her friends (*hakhi,* women friends). She told me how *'gaaba aave tho ugman mein aave ya poonam mein'* or, 'The cloth comes either on the night of the new moon or on the night of the full moon.' Further she explained that *'gaaba ugman mein aave aur jheele tho sori hove'* or, 'When the cloth comes at the new moon and you bathe [indirect reference to sexual intercourse], then you will have a girl.' Similarly intercourse during menstruation on the night of the full moon would result in the birth of a boy.

in any case, that their girls will marry men of other villages. There was however one occasion, during my stay, when an objection was raised. Lunda's second youngest daughter Temli came home after a day in the forest and mentioned to her sisters and mother how Soka, the son of Deva of the Lailath sublineage in Baliya Kua, had pulled her hand, implying a physical interest in her. Temli said she had run away from him as he was slightly drunk. Temli's mother told Lunda, who told Heva and Hoja, his *bhai*. Soon the matter was known to most of the households in the Beechalli, Malwa and Baliya Kua *phalli* where members of the Vaijjath and Lailath sublineages lived. Palvi told me that there had already been several incidents which had caused friction between the Vaijjath and Lailath sublineages. For example, most of the Vaijjath households (except those who fought over well shares, chapter 6), refused to attend the *kandiya* (funeral of a child) at a Lailath household after the Temli incident. I found that every ritual or festive occasion ended in a fight between the members of the two sublineages. Each dispute led to an impromptu *panchayati* (sitting of the elders, ritual and 'traditional' leaders). The Vaijjaths demanded a fine for bad behaviour, and the Lailaths always refused to pay.

For Girasia girls, relations between females ('friends' or 'sisters') are especially strong during adolescence. On the other hand, the intimacy with their brothers is greatest between the ages of 3 to 4 years and 10 to 12 years. In adulthood and especially after marriage, the relationship of a sister with her brother is more important than with her 'friends'. Women marry into different lineages and become divided also by the different lineage interests of their husbands.[11] Girls usually go to fairs accompanied by their brothers; accompanying a sister on a long journey is a practice carried over into a man's adulthood. It usually involves coming and going to the husband's village, especially when he is unable to accompany his wife. In some cases, as in the first pregnancy, it is customary for the woman's mother or brother to bring her back to her natal home for the delivery. Chakra's brother's wife was having her first child and waited impatiently for her brother to come and take her home. When he did not arrive for a few days, Chakra's brother left her at Abu Road market from where news reached her home and then her own brother came to collect her. But these are sensitive issues between

11. In their natal home, in the first stages of childhood, girls play with their brothers. Later they go together to the forest to cut wood and may even go to the market together. Apart from working together, the girl often cooks for her brother and father, especially if her mother is occupied elsewhere.

wife-giving and wife-taking lineages and therefore require diplomacy (I elaborate on this in chapter 6, when I describe the politics of food transactions between lineages). Brothers and fathers also arranged a girl's *hagai*, or marriage by brideprice settlement (see chapter 5). Girasia women maintain the title and affiliation of their father's lineage after their marriage, but have no share in the property which their brothers inherit. Although not stated explicitly, there is a definite expectation of assistance from a brother who, along with the family title and property is regarded as inheriting a responsibility towards his sisters. After marriage, the natal lineage is accessible to a Girasia woman through her brother and his children, since sisters may stay only in their brother's households when they visit the village. Thus ties between sisters are emotionally important, while those between brother and sister are structurally important.

For a brother, the cross-sibling relationship is also important because through his sister he can form contacts with 'reliable' men, with whom he may later want marital, political or economic alliances. It is usually the sister who suggests potential wives for her brother, or his sons, from the village of her husband. In all these respects, the brother-sister relation is an important one, both when the sister is within the natal village and when she marries into another village. The brother-sister relationship is reflected in institutionalised gifts given by the brother at festivals, either when the woman returns to her village or when her brothers make the special trip to their sister's affinal home. The major, and often only, 'gift' from a brother to his sister is the *odhani*, or cotton wrap. The *odhani* is an institutionalised 'gift' usually presented at the agriculturally based festivals of *holi* and *dussehra*. Those sisters who have given birth to children in the past year are given a different colour (yellow) wrap than the others (who get red wraps). The gift of the *odhani* symbolises the brother-sister relationship, particularly the protective, sheltering role of the brother. The *odhani* is the single most important item of clothing for Girasia women. Among its many uses, the most obvious is its use as a covering for the head for protection against sunlight, and from the cold in winter.[12] The *odhani* is also used to wipe perspiration off the face as well as to wipe children's faces and noses. Parts of the *odhani* function as flexible 'carrier-bags' and are used to carry, for example, forest produce, grain, wheat or flour, unleavened bread to work, or

---

12. Very few villagers and almost no women had woollen clothes. Temperatures could drop to 5 degrees centigrade or even lower in the winter months of December and January.

as the bride's means to transport her bridal food. Sometimes a second, older *odhani* serves to connect two earthen water pots bought from potters in a nearby village, which are then carried on the head. Most importantly, the *odhani* is used to veil the body. While women bathe they remove their skirt and blouse, but wrap up in the *odhani* (younger women tend to cover their breasts while older women do not). Similarly the *odhani* allows wives to veil their faces from certain categories of their affinal relatives. In this sense the *odhani* is indeed a symbol of protection, which allows women to keep their *laaj* (respect). Finally, the *odhani* is a symbol of separation, for the action of veiling classes wives as distinct from women of the husband's lineage.

Apart from *haga* (true) brothers who give their sisters the *odhani*, there is another category of men known as *dharm bhai* (social brothers) who give *odhanis* to their *dharm ben* (social sisters). These are men, usually affinal relatives of the girl's parents, who live in the village of the girl's husband (as opposed to her own brothers who live in the girl's natal village). The *dharm bhai* are the first relatives in the affinal village whom the girl can turn to. Dhanki said she was really pleased to have two *dharm bhai* in the Taivar village, especially as she had no *haga* (true) brothers of her own. Apart from the occasional ceremonial gift of the *odhani* the *dharm* brothers have no vital role to play in the girl's life in the *huhara* (affinal residence). But the position of the *dharm* brother reflects three important features of Girasia social relations: 1) the primacy given to the sibling relationship, 2) that for a woman, her affinal village could be a hostile place; 3) relationships which are not based directly on patrilineal ties are couched in a patrilineal idiom.

The brother-sister relationship, and the other intra- and inter-gender relationships, especially of Taivar women, are affected by the institution of marriage. In chapter 5 I describe the processes and implications of marriage, while in the rest of this chapter I outline the nature of the lineage's control on adult gender relations, particularly of married women who come from other villages and lineages.

Living in the Husband's Village

Girasia women talk about the differences between their natal and affinal villages in terms of veiling, greeting, seating, work, cooking and the consumption of food. Despite the different nature of work and relationships in a woman's affinal lineage, in this section I suggest that, unlike other upper- or middle-caste women, Girasia women are structurally weak in both their natal and affinal lineages. (Individual women may, of course, assert different degrees of control over their husbands.) I further suggest that there are few differences between Girasia and non-Girasia when it comes to the relationships between husbands and wives.

The first time a Girasia woman enters her husband's village and household she is confronted with expectations of her which are different from those in her natal home. She must now interact with a new set of relatives to whom her husband is bound in blood and loyalty. Both the husband and his sublineage control his wife's relationship to work and entertainment, which in turn contrasts with her life in her natal village *(piyar)*. The control of the *huhara* (affines/affinal village) is manifested in the requirement that a wife must cover her face *(laaj kaadna)* before certain categories of male affinal relatives. She must veil her face from her husband's father *(hahur)*, husband's elder brother *(jeth)*, both elder and younger husband's sister's husbands *(jamai)* and her husband's sisters son *(jamai)*. She need not observe *laaj* (shame) in front of her husband's mother *(hahu)*, husband's younger brother *(devar)* or husband's sister *(nanad)*. According to most women I met, *laaj kaadna* represented a mixture of shame, deference and respect. As a bride one is supposed to appear ashamed to face older men because of the fact of sexual relations with the younger relatives of these men. (It is taboo to have sexual relations or even to look at men older than one's husband). Deference and respect are accorded by lowering the eyes and covering the face.

The different kinds of social relations in the *huhara* are also implicit in the manner in which women greet other members of the village. For example, I found that on encountering a male relative of the husband at close quarters, wives bow and touch the ground with their finger tips holding each side of their wraps. Apart from their husband's male kin, women do not veil their face from other relatives, although they use their wrap to acknowledge friends, natal relatives and *dharm* relatives (who are, as it were, between natal and affinal kin). When greeting other women friends, both women touch hands and then fold them in front with the expression '*ram-ram*'. (*Ram-ram* is a common greeting in the region especially among the rural and lower castes and classes). When women meet their natal kin such as their *mahi, moma* or *bai* (MZ, MBD and MBD), they flick the left side of their wrap. Whenever women met their *dharm* relations *(bai, bhai)*, they touch their hands to the sides of their forehead. There is no specific form of greeting between husbands and wives, who usually ignore each other in company.

As already discussed in chapter 1, in her husband's village a wife never sits on a *khat* (bed) in the vicinity of men of the lineage. If she does, I was told, it implies that she is, 'indicating the importance of her own [father's] lineage rather than her husband's lineage in his village'. A wife should never be seen idling and her presence in any other part of the village is justified only if it is related to work. A similar situation exists among wives in other caste households and villages. Usually the domestic work within the household totally occupies the new bride whose work load is great, as both her mother-in-law and sister-in-law give her a large portion of their own work tasks to complete. In the neighbouring Girasia village of Rada, Gumla Vanhiya's two sons had brought very young girls as wives (approximately thirteen to fourteen years old). These girls get up before dawn and are constantly busy grinding flour, fetching water, cooking and cleaning. While men can eat food cooked by their sisters, mothers and their children, their wives cannot expect these women to cook for them. This distinction is further reflected in the convention that the bride never uses the utensils of her husband's lineage for her own food. She uses her own brass plate and water vessels *(vadku, lota)* to eat and drink from. These are often the only items that a bride brings with her from her parent's house. Her husband and their children from her, eat from her vessel but according to Haluri, 'No-one else of my husband's lineage will be given food in this'. Apart from cooking food for themselves, wives also cook for the husband and any visiting relatives. If the wife is from a lower lineage,[13] no-one from the husband's village will eat food cooked by her. If her parents come to visit her, her husband will cook for them. (Men cook for all auspicious gatherings, such as funerals, marriages and all religious celebrations). Duda told me that if his daughter went away with a man of a lower lineage, he would not eat her *haath re roti* (literally, unleavened bread made by her hands) as she was considered even lower, than her lower-lineage husband.

In the initial stages of marriage, the conjugal relationship was most important for the wife as the husband's attitude defined the relations of his own lineage members towards her. Even though the wife is still considered as a member of her father's lineage after marriage, the payment of brideprice transfers the hold of her father's lineage both on her production and reproduction as well as for her

---

13. Ideally Taivar men obtained wives from affinal lineages equal to them in the hierarchy. Sometimes however, they would marry women of lower Girasia lineages (see chapter 5).

subsistence (see chapter 7) to her husband's lineage where she has to work in order to justify her consumption. Girasia wives are evaluated as 'good' or 'bad' in terms of their work in the home as well as outside. Husbands often beat their wives if they are 'disobedient' *(kena ne mana)*. The most frequent occasions are when *roti* (bread) is not made on time or the water-pot is empty. Whether wives get beaten, however, varies with the temperament of their husbands. According to Haluri: 'Lunda used to beat me often and for no fault of mine . He never beats his second wife. I left once because of his behaviour to live with another man. But I had my children in Lunda's house and they used to help me in my work. When I went to this other man's house I had to work all over again as a new bride. This was too much for me so I came back'. (Palvi, Lunda's sister, explained to me that her brother had always been aggressive but, in contrast, Reeva their eldest brother was very *shant* (peaceloving) and never beat his wife.

Over a period of time, it is the wife's capacity to work and to bear children that determines the level of acceptance and interaction in her husband's village (a common situation in other caste households). This is reflected in the belief that it is worthwhile to spend money on a *shadi* (the ceremonial marriage; see chapter 5) if the wife has given birth to a child in her husband's household. In cases of infertility, or of difficulties in bearing children, the Girasia wife may expect social tension. Usually the husband takes another wife, and if the age difference between the two women is not great, there may be a lot of resentment. Often, however, over the passage of time, an alliance may also spring up between the two women. For example, Vanju told me that the most upsetting feeling she had was when Bunba slept with Sali on the *khat* while she slept on the floor. But she said, 'Sali and I get along well. She has had only one son during all these years, and we have a lot of work to share'. During my stay in the Taivar village, Sali approached me for medicines which would enable her to get more children. She was fearful that Bunba might take another wife because she had given him only one child. But there have been several cases where husbands have brought second or third wives, even when the previous wife or wives have produced a number of children. For example, Haluri had borne Lunda three children and was upset that in spite of this he had brought Tibri, his second wife. While Vanju and Sali lived under the same roof, Haluri and Tibri had separate quarters.[14] Often

14. According to Haluri, Lunda spent some nights with her but more often with Tibri. There were also times when he slept alone on the *meri* outside the house.

the physical distance between households allows greater possibilities for intimate relations to develop between husband and wife. As the husband is separated from his own natal household and from other adult members of his lineage (only the youngest son would have his parents staying with him), the influence of older men and women is less. For example, Valli *bai* said she confided in all matters with her husband, even about the pains of *gaaba aave* (menstruation). A number of women like Haluri and Palvi, who were 'captured' in marriage (see chapter 5), had their first menstruation in their husband's household. They said that their husbands would be the only ones to know of their *gaaba*. They could cook both for him and the children during *gaaba*, but could not give them water. However, separate households are usually built after the couple have had several children; before this the couple stays in a separate enclosure adjoining the husband's father's house. Although in some senses the husband becomes a confidant to his wife, their relationship remains hierarchic in the sense that the wife's wishes are considered secondary to the wishes of the husband and his lineage. An arrangement of scattered nuclear units is also disadvantageous to women as it prevents them from meeting other women of the village with any frequency.

Although taking a wife *(aurat lana)* is seen as the first step in establishing a semi-autonomous unit (household) and signalling the division of the father's property, in reality the separation of households is a more gradual affair, largely because it has to contend with two opposing desires. These are, firstly, the desire of the son for sexual rights in a woman and his desire for a separate household and, secondly, the subsistence pattern of his father's household and the labour the son (and subsequently the daughter-in-law) contributes to it. Usually these opposed tendencies were resolved by building a temporary extension to the father's household when the new bride arrived. At the same time, property is earmarked for all the sons, thus symbolically acknowledging the partition of the household. After marriage, there can be a continued sharing of resources (of money income and consumption) with the parent household, although the cooking area is separated. The son may still eat at the hearth of his mother but his wife cooks at her own hearth. Sometimes the wife and mother-in-law do cook at the same hearth, especially if the age difference between them is great. When Homa married he and his wife stayed with his parents. When he was a bachelor, he would sleep on the *meri*, or raised and roofed wooden platform. While the platform stored corn-stalks, usually the goats were kept under it, enclosed by a bamboo fence. When his wife arrived, they slept in the temporary enclosure which had been built at the side of his father's hut to house three cows and two bulls (who were then shifted to the goat enclosure). Homa told me of plans to prepare a more permanent structure. He has two options: either to build a more permanent extension to his father's hut, or to build a separate hut at some distance, depending on which part of the field will be his. When the first child is born, it will be necessary to have a more permanent structure. Some wives, however, like those of Deeta and Bhula, gave birth to their children while they were in temporary accomodation. It will all depend on how much time and collective labour (*halmo*) Homa is able to organise to help build the hut without disturbing the normal work routine.[15]

Girasia women participate equally with their husbands in the work sphere and are direct contributors to the income of the household (see chapter 6). Although husband and wife work and eat together, they rarely socialise together (unlike brother and sister). The husband often goes to *panchayatis* (lineage councils) or rituals, matters which concern only his lineage. At other times the husband will talk and smoke *bidis* (cigarette of tobacco leaves) with his lineage brothers at a public place or clearing in the village, at a distance from his hut. Over time the wife becomes more acquainted with the village and lineage members of the husband. With the birth of their children, often followed by a *shadi* (marriage), there is a decrease in the workload of the woman; further reinforced when she becomes mother-in-law (similar in other caste households). The decrease in the workload for older women is a strong incentive for a woman to remain in her current husband's household, as is evident from Haluri's account above. The birth of a son, who will look after her when she is a widow, is of primary importance. The decline of a woman's work with age is much less than that observed for men. Amongst most elderly couples in the Taivar village, women are continuously engaged in the small chores of the household while the men remain inactive and seated on the *khat*. On the death of her husband, his wife is (ideally) meant to return to her brother's household

---

15. A hut required large logs of wood to be cut for the frame, two special kinds of mud to be brought and mixed, a large quantity of cowdung to be collected and clay tiles to be crafted for the roof. At the same time the *kothi*, or large clay bins to store grain, would also be made. All in all, I was told, it could take six months to a year to build, particularly as most of the work was done in the really hot summer months of May and June to ensure the structure was well baked. The summer months are also in between agricultural seasons, when kin were more free to help.

and village. This depends on the age of the wife. If married for a short while only, and still in her reproductive span, she would certainly have another husband. In the case of an older widow, her fate is more ambiguous. Usually older widows have no father's household to go back to. Their brothers are themselves dependent on their sons and do not want the burden of a marginally productive member. Often the old woman stays on in the household of her husband's son by her, although it is not regarded as his duty to feed her. I was told that on the twelfth day after her husband's funeral *(nyath)* the widow's legal ties with her husband's lineage are dissolved and no lineage member has any obligation to look after her. However, as far as I observed, there are few instances when such measures are taken. Yet most elderly women work hard to prevent the eventuality of an exclusion from their husband's lineage. Rathi *bai* lost both her husband and her son in quick succession. Her two young grandsons lived together in a hut adjoining their father's brother. Rathi *bai* (who died the year following my fieldwork) would complain to me how difficult she found her task of watching over the fields because her knees were constantly troubling her. But she said she did not complain to her grandsons as she might have to leave, and she had nowhere to go.

Wives in the Taivar village are constantly referred to and distinguished between in terms of the lineages of their fathers and brothers. Although after marriage women are referred to as the 'wife of so-and-so' rather than 'the daughter of so-and-so', there is always a statement which follows, qualifying her father's lineage. For example, Lunda's two wives are known as Gamarin (a woman from the Gamar lineage) and Damarni (a woman from the Damar lineage). The lineage title of the father reinforces the woman's status as an outsider to her husband's agnatic group and, furthermore, legitimises her restricted participation in it, as the following example reveals. When I asked a Taivar man why wives could not participate in all affairs of the lineage he responded, 'The *panchayati* [legal lineage council] is between us lineage brothers, women of other lineages have no place here; how can they decide about matters concerning our lineage'. In her natal village too, a woman's lineage identity is subordinated to that of her father, brothers and father's brothers where, unlike them, she has no decision-making capacity regarding lineage matters. The fact that, on marriage she will live in another lineage also weakens her position within her own lineage. For example, when I asked a villager about the absence of the rights to property of his daughters and sisters, he commented, 'A woman gets married and goes to another village anyway, so how can she do anything for our lineage'.

Despite what I see as a similarity rather than a difference in the structural positions of women in their natal and affinal households, most Girasia women stress the differences between the two. The natal village is often referred to as a place where there are few expectations of work. Few women live as wives in their natal village. Palvi is among the few; she continues to reside in her natal village after her marriage to Jama. The reason she gave me for her return to the Taivar village was that she took the advice offered her by a ritual mediator (*bhopa*) who had suggested that she may be able to prevent the death of her children by returning to her natal village. She explained,

> My husband Jama accepted the situation and would come at regular intervals to stay with me as he had to tend the house and fields in his own village. But now our eldest son is looking after them and so we both stay here. My father and brothers did not give us any share of the land but allowed us to reclaim a bit of land on this hill where we live at present.

The general Girasia perception of a son-in-law such as Jama is one of poverty and of an inability to organise production or manage the land, on the one hand, and a related femininity, on the other ('only women move to other villages'). While Jama is thus portrayed as weak, Palvi, his wife, is relatively strong, outgoing and uninhibited, especially when compared to other wives in the village. She would sit on the *khat* rather than on the ground where other married women sit. Unlike other women she did not cover her face in the Taivar village. She said this is because, 'I have no *huhara* [in-laws] here, only my brothers'. Despite Palvi's unrestricted movements, she does not participate in *panchayatis* where the policies and strategies of the lineage and households were made. Moreover, she is careful to maintain a respectful attitude to her brothers. For example, she would offer to help their wives with work and sometimes feed their children with extra food or provide them with medicines stored at the childcare centre. Palvi was also an experienced *huwani* (midwife) and because she belonged to the same lineage as her brothers she could be trusted to deliver their children. Some men are also *huwani*, but because of the practice of *laaj kadna* (where men may not see their younger brother's wives) they can only deliver the babies of their older brothers' wives and are instead called to other villages. There were other incidents which stressed the differences between natal and affinal villages. One of the more dramatic ones occurred the day I was returning from a visit to Beechali *phalli*. Bheema's wife was crying bitterly outside the fence of her household. The first thought that struck me was that Bheema had beaten her. But Dhanki, who was walking with me, told me that someone had died in the woman's natal lineage and therefore she had to cry outside her husband's household rather than inside, emphasising the outsider status of the affinal lineage.

Despite the structurally weak position of the Girasia wife, she may at an individual level influence the affairs in her household. Non-cooperation[16] is the most frequent method of resistance used by the Girasia wives I came across. Other means of asserting independence from their husbands is in the relationships wives form with other women in the village and with other Girasia men in the market. The confidence to refuse to work also comes from the wife's links with her father's lineage. A woman may expect her brothers and father to help her at the times when her husband has treated her harshly. Often the brothers see the bad treatment of their sisters as an insult to their whole lineage. But there are limits to the help or interest that brothers have in their sister's affairs (see chapter 7). Although the Girasia women are restricted from socialising in their *huhara* (in-laws village) this is not the case in the market where they meet people from their natal or other villages as well as people of other castes. The contrast between the market and the *huhara* is reflected in two ways: firstly, wives were not required to veil themselves in the market; secondly, the market, fairgrounds and other public areas outside the husband's village are areas where women can form relationships with men of other Girasia lineages. Girasia men often perceive the market as a threat to their marital stability. In the Taivar village, new brides are not permitted to visit the market frequently or on their own. Husbands usually accompany younger wives to the market, which they did not do once the women get older. For example, while the four women of the *anganwadi* childcare centre made trips together to the town every month to see their employer, Babli, the youngest of them, would always be accompanied by her husband. He was constantly suspicious that she would form an extramarital relationship with another Girasia man and leave the work in his household. I was told that for quite a few years and especially until the end of a wife's reproductive period, the husband accompanies her on trips to the market and elsewhere. Within

---

16. I regard women's non cooperation in domestic affairs as an example of what Scott (1985) describes as 'everyday' forms of resistance.

the village too there is constant gossip among the women about certain women and men who were believed to be meeting the opposite sex. I was told in confidence about four women, and of many more men. Naturally, it was difficult to verify the number of these extra-marital relationships.

From the actions of Babli's husband it is clear that Taivar men do not expect other wives to work for the Taivar interests by spying on their wives in the market. Both the market and the forest, unlike the affinal village, are areas which are outside the husband's control. It is in these spaces that women become powerful and threatening to men. On one of her trips back to her natal home, ostensibly for a ritual occasion, Dopa's eldest married daughter engineered the abortion of the illegitimate child she was carrying (she feared her husband would suspect the child was not his). I was told that she *pani toda* (literally, broke the water, meaning killed the foetus) with a stick in the forest of the *Bhakar*. Palvi told me that women also go to Abu Road town for the *hui* (literally, needle, referring to the injection used for abortions) if they had the money. These examples show, above all, that Girasia women can and do exert some degree of control over their bodies and circumstances. Furthermore, despite belonging to different natal lineages, Girasia women can still have some bases for solidarity in the affinal village. Often, for example, women can be related even if they are from different patrilineages. Sali and Dhanki are close friends and whenever they could, they visit each other. Later I learnt that although their fathers come from different lineages, their mothers were sisters of the Damar lineage. Sali (a Khairadini), and Dhanki (a Bubarni) were married to Bunba and Nota respectively, two *haga* (true) Taivar brothers of the Raijjath sublineage.

The relationships between Girasia husbands and wives indicate that marriage implies a different kind of relationship for Girasia men compared to Girasia women. The overriding experience for women is one of restriction based on the fact that while Girasia men remain in the familiar environment of their *kaka-baba-re* (village), and amongst relatives and friends, Girasia women spend their lives in different agnatic groups and villages. In their structural role as wives, Girasia women are set apart and become symbols of difference in the agnatic groups of both their husbands and their fathers. In this role they help men to construct differences between and within lineages. This chapter has shown that, despite the limited agency of individual Girasia women, in their structural roles as wives Girasia women are not 'free' as depicted in the outsider constructions of 'tribal' women. In fact, there were more similarities than differences between Girasia and other lower-class women of the region, as the discussions of poverty and marriage payments (see chapters 6 and 7) will reveal.

Chapter 5

ACROSS VILLAGES
Marriage Ideals, Practices and Strategies

*I*t is not unusual for Taivar men and women to have several marriage partners in their lifetime. Two features of their marriage practices are, on the face of it, unique in the Indian context: firstly, their practice of polygyny, which is not a 'stated' rule; and, secondly, their claim to making 'equal' marriages. The present chapter examines how these practices fitted in with the boundary, status and identity concerns of the Taivar patrilineage and its members. I look at marriage from the perspective of the lineage as well as individual women and men and will analyse it in two contexts: that of the ideal structure and some deviations I had the opportunity to observe. This chapter also places the Girasia material in the context of similar practices in the region.

In the first section, I present voices and views of marriage experiences to describe, firstly, how the Taivar Girasias talked about their marriage processes. Secondly, I show by these accounts how Girasia girls and women had different perceptions of marriage and related processes compared to Girasia boys and men.[1] Thirdly, the descrip-

1. My use of the words girl or woman and boy or man is mainly to differentiate between the categories of just married (younger generation) and long married (older generation) men and women. In the latter case if a woman is 'captured' in marriage she may be already 'married', while in the former case, it may be the girl's first marital relationship.

tions indicate that not all women have the same experiences or views on marriage related practices. Above all, the diverse accounts show how lineage and sublineage concerns diverge or converge with individual interests and perceptions. In the second section I move on to describe the ideal-type notions surrounding Girasia marriage and affinity. The third section then considers the variations from the ideal marriage 'rules' and explores what is negotiable in Taivar affinal strategies. Finally, I discuss Girasia marriages with reference to the wider concerns with hierarchy and difference and relate this to similar preoccupations in other communities in the region, particularly the Rajput and the Bhil.

Processes of Marriage

The Taivars distinguish between two processes in establishing a conjugal relationship or marriage[2] namely, that of *khichna* (literally, 'pulling'; or 'capture') and *hagai* (or 'engagement'). This section explores the nature and implications of these processes through the accounts of individual Girasia women and men. The narratives of Girasia marriage experiences must be seen in the wider context of the narrator's own location in her or his community. The first account is that of Palvi, a Taivar woman who is a 'daughter' of the Taivar patrilineage. This is followed by accounts of a woman from a different patrilineage married into the Taivar lineage, and of younger men of the Taivar lineage.

Marriage by 'Capture' (Khichna) and 'Engagement' (Hagai)

Palvi Bai, the daughter of Mada Taivar was approximately forty-five years old at the time of my fieldwork. Unlike other wives in the Taivar village, who come from other villages, Palvi lives a married life in the same village where she had been born and brought up. She is one of two other such women (in fifty-one Vaijjath households) who did not stay in the village of their husbands *(huhara)*. Palvi had returned home to her *piyar* on the advice of a *bhopa* (ritual mediator) following

2. So far I have used the term 'marriage' as if it contained a similar meaning for the Girasia as that used in the anthropology of Anglo-Saxon and northern European societies (i.e., a social ceremony which binds two individuals in a legally and religiously sanctioned relationship); however, as the material in this chapter indicates, this is not the case for the Girasia where the religious or ceremonial and the legal aspects of marriage are separated.

the death of her first two children at her husband's village.[3] She explained to me how she first got 'married':

> When I was slightly younger than Savli the daughter of Dopa [approximately twelve years old], which was a time after my mother had died and my father brought another wife, I was sent to work in Puni *bua*'s [FZ] house. Puni *bua* lived in the village Sawaliagarh near Pindwara [approximately seventy kilometres from the Taivar village]. Hoja-ji, my *haga* ['true', denoting from the same mother] elder brother left me there. There was no-one to work in *bua*'s house which is why I was sent. Their maize fields were at a slight distance from the house. I would go with *bua*'s son to tend them. One day we were on our way there when I was pulled away [*khichna*] by a boy like Jonya, the son of Chopa [approximately fifteen to sixteen years old]. My pot of water broke. He dragged me and then lifted me over his shoulder and took me to his home [*gair*]. Two months later my father came and took me back to our home with the promise to the boy's people [*huharo*] that I would be sent later as I was still too young [to be a bride]. After a year had passed and Rs. 500 *dapa* [brideprice] had been settled, my *hahur* [father-in-law] and his brother came to get me. They belonged to the Damar lineage. After a while my husband [*admi*] bought two more wives [*aurat*], the second after only four or five months of my arrival. He gave *dapa* for them as well. For three years I worked hard there but they made me work too much. My in-laws [*huharo*] called me *kali* ['blackie'] because of my dark complexion. At this time I went home for the *Diwali* [festival in November]. There I met Jama-ji, my present husband of the Peesra lineage. He had come to leave his sister, who is married in the Taivar village to Deeta Taivar [in the FB category to the narrator]. He heard of my unhappiness from my stepbrother Kheema. Kheema arranged for Jama to *khichna* [pull me] away from there. This time I was willing. The financial settlement was made by Jama to my first husband. He paid *dava* [a sum over and above the brideprice]. This arrangement took place without the knowledge of my father. [The words in brackets are the author's.]

Palvi's story shows at once the powerlessness of being 'captured' as a bride, as well as its use as a strategy for getting out of oppressive circumstances. In her first capture, neither she nor any of her family knew of the event before it occurred. In the second case both Palvi and her brother actively sought to encourage her 'capture'. The second 'pulling' could, however, only be accomplished without the knowledge of her father. There were very real economic reasons which would have caused her father to prevent her from leaving her first husband, as I outline in the following sections. Marriage by cap-

---

3. As a result of spending her married life in her natal village, she called other wives in the village (i.e., women from non-Taivar lineages) either *bhabhi* (eBW) or *vahu* (yBW), which were terms of address used by her brothers as well.

ture is not unique to the Girasia. Gupta (1974) for example, in his study of the multi-caste village of Awan in Kota district in eastern Rajasthan, describes five types of second marriages *(nata)* practised by all but the highest castes. One of the types of *nata* was the *bhagalana* (literally, run and bring a wife) and the second type was the *rajimarji*, or eloping by mutual consent (1974: 151).

Palvi's experience was not uncommon for her generation of wives in the Taivar village. While most women seemed to accept the fact that *khichna* was something that might happen to them, both women and men distinguished between the 'proper' and 'improper' procedures of *khichna*. Khichna without the consent or connivance of the girl was an improper (*khoti*, or bad) way to arrange for a wife. Not only could the boy's family expect an aggressive return encounter with the girl's father and father's brothers, but they would also have to pay a *dava*, or 'attack' price, over and above the *dapa* (brideprice). A suitor who takes a wife away from another husband (rather than from her father) has to pay *dava* (see also chapters 7 and 8). If the girl leaves her husband once the brideprice is settled, her father and brothers will have to return the brideprice amount to her husband. To prevent this from occurring, Palvi and her brother Kheema arranged for her *khichna* without her returning to her father's house. But there was an even more appropriate way of getting married which was through the process of *hagai* or 'engagement'. Even a wife who has been captured must undergo the *hagai* ceremony for the purposes of the brideprice settlement if she is to remain a wife. When the parents of a boy approach the parents of a girl of the 'right' lineage for marriage, the procedure that follows is called *hagai*. In the non-Girasia region of south Rajasthan, as well as in most of Hindi speaking north India, *sagai* is the term used for a couple's engagement. The Taivar Girasia *hagai* focuses on the settlement of a brideprice amount which formally establishes the conjugal relation for the wife-giving and wife-taking lineages. *Hagai* is considered the proper *(hau)* way to arrange marital relations both by Taivar elders and even by those wives who had experienced *khichna*.

The institutions of *khichna* and *hagai* are separate from the Girasia institution of *shadi* (a term used to denote marriage for the non-Girasia Hindu groups in the region. In the non-Girasia case, both the ceremonial and the legal co-occur in formally establishing one's conjugal partner in life). The Girasia *shadi* involves long, social and ritual ceremonies and is accompanied by a number of feasts held over several days (like the non-Girasia north Indian Hindu weddings). Unlike non-Girasia middle and upper-caste Hindu weddings, the Girasia *shadi* usually take place after the woman has been resident for some years and often after the birth of her children. Thus a Girasia *shadi* does not indicate the commencement of a couple's conjugal relationship, as it does among the non-Girasias. Among the Girasia there are thus three processes through which the relationship between a husband and wife is formed, those of *khichna, hagai* and *shadi*. While the first two deal with the legal and financial relations between sublineages of various lineages, the *shadi* is more ceremonial and symbolic, and mainly involves the sublineages within a lineage. The categories of *shadi, khichna* and *hagai* are not exclusive of each other. For example, a *shadi* may be performed for a wife who is 'brought' by *khichna* or *hagai*. The following passages look more closely at some of these distinctions through the eyes of those connected with the Taivar Girasia lineage.

Dhanki belonged to the Bubariya lineage of Girasia and was married to Nota Taivar. Her account of capture was both similar to and different from that of Palvi. According to Dhanki:

> I was working on my parents' fields, a slight distance from home when three youths came and got hold of me. I was as high as Savli [approximately twelve years old][4] and my breasts were as small. Of the three youths who caught me, I could identify who was to be my husband as he caught my hands. They alternately dragged and carried me. My *ghaghra* [skirt], *odhani* [wrap] and *jhulki* [blouse] all got torn. My body was bleeding. I cried and cried. After a while they stopped and said if I would not come quietly they would put thorns in my head. When we reached his home, I refused to go in. The boy's *bhabhi* [sister-in-law] was kind to me. I slept next to her at night. Next day my parents came and they refused to give me. While they were talking, I ran back to my house. My father willingly took me back. Then Nota [the present husband] came in *hagai*. In the case of *khichna* if the girl does not want to go then it is her decision.

Dhanki's account shows that she was less willing than Palvi to accept her marriage by *khichna*. The degree to which a girl is forced or not to accept her situation also depends upon the circumstances of her family. Dhanki comes from a smaller and relatively well-off family as compared to Palvi. Dhanki's father has one wife and five daughters while Palvi's father has three wives and sixteen children. Palvi was sent to work at her father's sister's home, an indication that Palvi was not required at home. Her father's delay in visiting Palvi when she was 'captive' was probably due to the unsettled matter of her brideprice. The negotiations indicated that her father was willing

---

4. Whenever women explained their ages at their first marriage to me, they did so with reference to younger Girasia children with whom I was acquainted.

to give her away provided he got the right price. Dhanki's father, in contrast, came the day after her 'pulling', indicating his unwillingness to consider the boy, let alone negotiate a brideprice.

Girasia women showed mixed responses to their experiences of *khichna*. While for some it was traumatic, for others it was amusing and yet others were shy to talk about it. But none were shocked and I got the impression that all Girasia women were socialised to expect such an occurrence. According to both Taivar men and women, *khichna* was very much on the decline as 'government police' were beginning to have access to their area. The Taivars, and the Girasia in general, were scared of court cases as they knew legal matters involved the expenditure of money. The Taivars also feared a contact with townspeople, who were perceived as possessing alien ways as reflected in their language. According to Dopa and Hoja, two respected men of the village, '*Khichna*' at present requires a fifteen rupee fine imposed on the ambush party if the wife-giving group is not willing to part with the girl. Nowadays the word *khichna* is substituted by the word *chori*. *Chori* (literally 'stealing' in Hindi), is not as traumatic for women as *khichna*, I was told, because it was usually the woman's decision to run away from home with the boy. It was referred to as 'stealing' because it was without the knowledge or consent of the girl's parents and therefore without an agreed settlement of brideprice. The boy's parents might or might not be aware of their son's plans although they were known generally to support him unless the woman was of an inferior and unacceptable lineage (the categories of 'good' and 'bad' women are explained below as well as in chapter 7). During my fieldwork Kakra, a Raijath Taivar boy 'stole' *(chori)* a girl with the connivance of his mother's brother who lived in the same village as the girl. Kakra told me how his maternal uncle *(moma)* had told the girl about Kakra's wish to meet her. Their meetings were after dark and outside the boundary of the fields around the girl's house; they had met twice. On learning from the girl that she was willing to come to his house, Kakra took Honya (his FBS) with him on the appointed night when the girl would come away with him. Although the girl was of the 'proper' lineage and an engagement could have been arranged, according to Kakra and his father, *chori* was the only possible way to get the girl as her parents would object to give her to a household where there was already another wife. I asked Kakra where his other wife was. He said he had gone through an 'engagement' with another woman several months before but due to a disagreement over the payment of the brideprice amount and the subsequent quarrel that developed, the girl had not come to stay as his wife.[5] As a result of the *chori* Bunba said he would have to pay Rs. 5, 000/- *dapa* approximately Rs. 2, 000/- more than the current brideprice rates in their community (see chapter 7).

Contact with a girl of one's choice is usually made at fairs, or in the market. Gopa, a young Taivar boy, had his marriage arranged by his father and uncles. He was living with his first wife when he saw a girl of his liking at the market place and enquired about her village and lineage. He found he had affinal relatives in her village and pursued the matter with them. He then visited her house with his lineage relatives and friends. He said he was pleased to find that her family was *shant* (or peaceloving and amiable) and the girl was a worker *(kaam karne vali)* rather than lazy. The next time Gopa saw the girl at the market place he proposed to her. She agreed and returned with him. Three to four months later, her fathers and brothers were expected to collect the brideprice payment and fine for her stealing *(chori)*. Gopa's second marriage by *chori* was in contrast to his first marriage in which 'the girl was brought in *hagai*'. He described his first marriage as follows:

> I was in class seven. My *baba* [FeB] Duda had enquired and arranged for a match through relatives [FBWB] in Iqbalgarh, Gujarat. My father, uncle, me and a few of my friends (boys of the same generation in the lineage) went by bus and foot to the house of this girl. We had dinner there which we had paid for in advance. Then the elders sat in a group to finalise the *dapa* [brideprice] which was decided at rupees eleven hundred. We left the next morning with my wife. However in the following days the girl did not work properly or respect my uncle [who had adopted Gopa as a son]. She never gave him *roti* [bread] on time. After staying for a short while she went to visit her parents. She stayed there for a long time. [Words in brackets are the author's.]

In the above account Gopa justifies the reason for a second wife by giving the long absence of his first wife and her previous bad behaviour as the main cause. He also suggests that one of the reasons why his first wife took so long in returning was that she had probably found herself another suitor. These were only rumours, he said, which he and his uncle Duda would investigate soon. At the end of my fieldwork period, six months later, nothing had been done about this matter. Although Gopa's second wife came to stay, neither her father nor her uncles had come to take the brideprice nor had Gopa

---

5. I visited Bunba's house a few days after Kakra brought his wife by *chori*. The girl was quite happy with the arrangement (Bunba's household was one of the few well-off houses in the village).

and his uncles gone to demand a return of the brideprice for his first wife (*agal aurat*, literally, previous wife). Gopa did say that his present wife's father and uncles were expected but that an accident, resulting in the hospitalisation of one of her uncles, had prevented them from coming.

In general, the decision to get a wife through an engagement commences at the level of gathering of information. A boy's father explores the availability and reputation of a girl in her natal village through discussions with the wives of his brothers (most likely with those BWs who are genealogically closest) in his own village. Usually wives of men in the boy's village are keen to bring their sisters as wives from their natal village as this provides them with a closer association with their natal village. The main criteria for the selection of a wife are mainly her physical capacity and her mental makeup. In the words of one Girasia respondent, an ideal wife is 'someone who is neither lazy nor quarrelsome'. There is not much emphasis on beauty although being tall *(moti)* and fair *(gori)* are added qualifications. To assess these qualities, the groom, his father and father's brothers attempt to see the girl in a public place, such as at a fair or at the market. The girl's family soon know of this interest through their female relatives who reside in the boy's village. On the pretext of a visit to these relatives, the father of the girl and his closest brothers survey the fields and house of the boy's father to ensure the future wellbeing of their daughter and also the economic status of the potential alliance. The settlement of brideprice is related to the assets, especially in land, held by the boy's family. The lower in economic status the boy's family are in comparison to the wife-giving household, the stronger the position of the wife-givers to ask for a higher brideprice. With equal assets the decision between wife-giving and wife-taking households takes longer (see chapter 7).

The two processes of marriage by 'capture' and by 'engagement' impose both similar and differing demands on members of a lineage. After the *khichna* it is the wife-giving *(aurat-re)* lineage which makes the effort to negotiate and settle a brideprice. *Hagai,* on the other hand, is mainly initiated by the wife-taking or husband's *(aadmi-re)* lineage. The question of group boundaries is of major concern for the lineage especially when, as in marriage by capture, the marriage is not arranged by the girl's sublineage. On the other hand, marriage by capture is a quick way to procure a wife's labour and sexual favours; arrangements and negotiations for an engagement may take several months. Marriage by capture also involves more of the individual groom in the decisions about whom to marry, although this has to be eventually approved by the lineage. As Dhanki's account above indicates, women have had the only rights to veto the decisions made by men of another lineage.

Khichna and *hagai* are not mutually exclusive institutions, in that a marriage by capture is followed by the procedures of an engagement, especially regarding the settlement of the brideprice. These processes are further formalised by a ceremonial marriage *(shadi)* wherein a woman's associations with her husband's lineage is symbolically acknowledged.

Marriage by Ceremony (Shadi)

In the following lines I discuss briefly some of the economic, ritual and symbolic implications of the ceremonial marriage for the Girasia patrilineage and its members. For convenience the rituals and procedures of a *shadi* have been outlined in the table 5.1. In the popular practice of the Hindu region, *shadi* is the term used to describe the social and ritualised celebration of a man bringing his wife away from her natal home to live with him. It involves an intricate and elaborate religious ceremony at the house of the girl after the payment of a dowry. The marriage is usually consecrated by a Brahmin priest and sanctions the entry of a girl into sexual and reproductive relations with a man of the appropriate affinal group.

It is usually the first time that she enters the domestic space of her husband's household, meets his family members, and it may even be the first time that she speaks to her husband. The Girasia *shadi*, like the non-Girasia *shadi*, also involves long rituals over a span of three to seven days. The rituals are interspersed with the distribution of food among sublineage and lineage members (see further in chapter 8 on kinship and ritual, and chapter 6 on economic distribution).[6]

The Girasia ceremony is especially similar to the non-Girasia in terms of the symbolic meanings of the various rituals performed. The *peethi* (turmeric) ceremony (see table 5.1) is considered the central ceremony of a *shadi*. Whenever I asked women why they should have to undergo a marriage ceremony, they would reply it was for *peethi chadhana* (the application of the turmeric paste). Both the bride and groom remained tinged by the yellow of the turmeric for several

6. The Girasia *shadi* is a complicated affair, and difficult for an outsider like me to understand. As on other ritual occasions, only some older Girasia, more often men, were able to tell me the significance of the detailed ritual procedures. Similarly, in the non-Girasia Hindu weddings of friends that I have attended, I cannot claim to have understood all the details, and meanings, of each ritual performed.

Table 5.1 Details of a Girasia Wedding (The groom's house)*

No.	Main Ceremonies	Duration	Activities involved	Place	Main actors
1.	*Mata Manana* (celebrating the clan mother)	mid-morning to evening of first day	(a) 2 handfuls of earth are obtained from the field and placed in a brass plate containing a light *(diya)*, vermillion powder *(sindoor)*, water and wheat grains	Field of the household	Eldest women, probably mother of groom
			(b) Brass plate is placed on the floor at the selected site for ancestor worship *(path)*	Verandah of the household	
			(c) Groom is bathed and then lifted to sit facing the selected site	Verandah	
			(d) Earth is removed from the plate onto the floor, powdered and with a sprinkling of water is used to paste *(leepna)* the site	Verandah	
			(e) The site is decorated in a geometric design with wheat grains	Verandah	
			(f) The main agricultural and food processing implements are tied together and the hagavale dance, pound and sing, rotating the implements 7 times in an anti-clockwise direction.	Veranda	
2.	*Peethi me behna* (sitting in turmeric paste)	Early morning of the second day to afternoon of the third day	(a) Jewellery of groom is removed, all his clothes except the loincloth are removed (for the bride the skirt is left on). The groom sits on an upturned dough-kneading dish *(kaasroth)* in front of the site with his feet on the ploughing blade *(halvani)*.	Verandah (in front of site)	Wives of father's brothers
			(b) Paste of turmeric powder, wheat-flour and water is applied *(peethi chadhana)*. The remainder is placed on the wraps of married women present. The paste is removed after it covers the whole body and sesame seed oil is applied. The same procedure is repeated 7 times.	Verandah (in front of site)	Wives of father's brothers
			(c) After the final *peethi chadhana*, the bride and groom are bounced up and down on a rope after which they are again bathed.	Field near verandah	Young adults

Table 5.1 continued

No.	Main Ceremonies	Duration	Activities involved	Place	Main actors
3.	*Mata Manana* (celebrating the clan mother)	Third day afternoon	Complicated drawing of figure of clan goddess, goat is killed in offering. Other offerings are cooked rice and wheat flour *(matar)* in 5 leaf containers. Later this is distributed as blessed food *(prasad)*.	Verandah, on wall next to the site	Specialist within the Jath
4.	*Peravna* (clothing)	Fourth day morning	Cloth and cash (rs. 2/- or Rs. 5/-) gifts are distributed	At groom's ancestor site only	Mother's brother of groom, his father's sisters.
5.	*Hangarna* (adorning)	Fourth day mid-morning	(a) Wedding garments are put on groom, new skirt sent to bride in groom's discarded loincloth (b) After the groom is ceremonially dressed, he and his relatives gather at the edge of the verandah and then proceed to the gate at the boundary of the house. Here the groom waits as his mother performs a short ritual in which she anoints the groom's forehead with red paste from the brass plate and throws balls of turmeric paste (from his body) and ash in four directions. (c) the groom jumps over the threshold. The father of the groom leads the procession to the place of marriage accompanied by singing and the beating of drums.	Verandah in front of site Entrance to household compound	Father's elder brother, father
6.	*Peniwa* (the 'marriage' ceremony)	Fourth day afternoon and evening	(a) The groom's party approach the firesite *(chowk)*. The bride sits completely veiled in the groom's discarded loincloth (b) The *chowk* is prepared for each couple c) The bride is lifted and placed near the groom. They are given sacred items and then move around the fire (7 times in an anti-clockwise direction with the bride ahead for 3 circles and then the groom for 4).	In the shade of the peepul tree, between the two households	Father's elder brother of the groom, father's sister's husband

* Note: The bride and groom have separate ancestor sites *(path)* but similar rituals performed at these sites. Except for the last, all rituals are initiated at the groom's household.

days, even after the paste has been washed off. (In north Indian Hindu marriages, turmeric is regarded as a substance of purity and auspiciousness and is used especially at marriages; see Khare, 1976.) I was told that the turmeric paste may be applied any number of times to a Girasia man, but only once to a woman. In other words, men could undergo *shadi* as many times as they liked, but a woman could do so only once. Furthermore, as Palvi explained, turmeric was only applied on a *kunwari* (girl-virgin). It is particularly inauspicious to apply the paste to four categories of women: the *dokri* (old woman); *randole* (widow), *pethas bairi* (pregnant woman); and another *kunwari* (unmarried girl), all of whom are either unreproductive or considered potentially so. When I pointed out that Girasia brides usually had children, Palvi replied that they were childless before they came to their present husband's household. In the middle- and upper-class Hindu weddings, the bride was ideally 'given away' by her father to the groom in a 'pure' state in the ceremony of *kanyadan* (literally the giving of a girl-virgin). In the Girasia case as also among other lower castes, in contrast, virginity is not a criterion for marriage. In fact, marriage is considered worthwhile only if the woman has been able to prove her child bearing capacity. To a large extent, I suggest, the differences between Girasia and ideal Hindu marriage practices and concepts are ones of degree, and are driven mainly by the different and unequal economic constraints under which they live.

The *mata-manana* ceremonies before and after the *peethi* are celebrations of the clan mother who is invited to bless the occasion. By celebrating the clan mother, the Girasia essentially celebrate the patrilineal principle (also see chapter 8). Such ceremonies are practised all over India. Khare (1976), describing the *matra-pujan* (literally, mother-worship) among the Kanya Kubja Brahmins of north India points out how the ceremony of the *kul-devi* or the *mata* (mother), 'helps dramatise the solidarity of the agnatic group with their dead and living ancestors ... and socially and ceremonially emphasises the dominant descent (patrilineal) principle of northern Hindu society'(ibid.: 199-200). Apart from the similarities in clan mother worship, the importance of the Girasia groom's old loin cloth being used to send the bridal skirt and later used to veil the bride, ritual sanction by the circling of the fire in *peniwa,* which includes an awareness of the right and left, are all details reminiscent of the popular style of non-Girasia Hindu marriages. The dress of the groom and the raised sword he carries with him to the *peniwa* (see table) are peculiarly a Rajput custom.

Despite similarities, the Girasia rituals of marriage actually reinforce the boundaries of the patrilineage, as do the marriage rituals of other castes. The differences between the two are, I suggest, mainly a result of the different economic situations in which these communities live. I was told that the major reason why Girasia marriages take place so infrequently is the prohibitive cost involved. During my stay in the Taivar village, no *shadi* was held. May and June are normally the months of the Girasia marriage season, but this applies only in a year of good rainfall. The summer of 1987 was considered a year when the people were too poor to get married. To see a Girasia wedding I had to go approximately eight kilometres further into the inaccessible terrain of the *Bhakar*, to the Girasia village of Rada. The examples I use in this next section are drawn from my observations of the *shadi* at Rada.[7]

The marriage at Rada was to take place in a Taivar household where two brothers were the grooms (*lada, veed*) simultaneously. It is not uncommon to have several marriages of members of the same sublineage at the same time. A very frequent statement made to me about the Girasia *shadi* was that, 'A father and son may be married at the same time'. In other words, due to the major expenditures involved, a *shadi* can simultaneously celebrate the marital relations of both father and son.[8] In the context of scarce resources, caused,

7. Rada, a smaller village than the Taivar village has only two sections and forty Girasia households. Rada is regarded, more or less, as an extension of the southeast Naal section of the Taivar village. Twenty-five households in Rada are of the Billath sublineage of the Taivar lineage. The rest of the households are of the Vanhiya lineage of the Girasia, who claim to be related to the Taivars, on the wife's side. This fits in with the fact that some residents of the Taivar village had received a *nootar* (an invitation to the *shadi*, in the form of a handful of uncooked rice grains and yellow turmeric powder). Some of the wives of Taivar men had sisters in Rada who were married to Taivar men, other Taivar men had their own sisters married to Vanhiya men. I was able to attend the wedding as I accompanied the Taivar relatives invited to Rada. Being accompanied was crucial from two points of view – firstly, for negotiating the unknown rocky and forested terrain, and secondly, for the assurance of hospitality. At a *shadi* it is etiquette that everyone attending is fed by the host. Some of my Girasia *hakhi* (friends) took advantage of my going by joining me. For example, Haluri *bai* who came with me, said she had not been invited even though her step-sister was the mother of one of the grooms. The young and unmarried daughters of Mada and Lunda, as well as the young son of Dopa, also came with me. Often young Girasia are enthusiastic about social gatherings outside their village, as there is always the possibility that they will meet a potential spouse.

8. In Rada, Palvi and I stayed at Gumla Vanhiya's place. His wife was also called Palvi. Gumla lived next to his father's elder brother who had two wives. The elder wife was a Taivarni, and the sister of Phoola Taivar's father. Gumla said that

for example, by conditions of drought, the ability to perform a *shadi* is more an index of wealth than an essential in sanctioning Girasia marital life. (Amongst the non-Girasia Hindus a *shadi* is considered essential before the commencement of the marital relationship. In this case, the pomp and splendour of the *shadi* is used as an indicator of wealth and status, to differentiate between the wife-giving and the wife-taking households.) The implications of delaying the marriage until sufficient funds are available means that the marriage is no longer simultaneous with the entry of the bride *(ladi, veedni)* into her husband's household. This is reflected in the fact that when Girasia women get married, they may already be mothers.[9]

The economic constraints of a Girasia marriage mean that some wives do not undergo the ceremony at all. Even when there are funds, I was told that men usually wait for a woman to have a child before they spend money on a *shadi*. This can be for either or both of two reasons. Firstly, to see if the woman is fertile or not *(sora howe heke*, literally the possibility of having children). If she is infertile, this necessitates taking another wife (although both could participate in the *shadi* at the same time after the second wife has borne a child.) Secondly, a child is considered to bind a woman more effectively to her husband's household (see, here, the reason given by Haluri for returning to her first husband, chapter 4). Economic reasons also underlie the fact that, unlike the non-Girasia weddings, in a Girasia *shadi* all the ceremonies are performed by various relatives of the bride (especially the FZH) or groom (mainly the FeB), rather than by different Hindu castes.

In the following section we may see how the experiences of marriage fit in with the ideal notions of marriage and affinity held by the Girasia.

The Stated and Unstated Rules of Marriage

The Lineage

The most frequent interactions between Girasia lineages revolve around the arrangement of marriage partners. The affinal *(huhara)* relation is considered essential for Taivar men and women. There

---

because she could not have children, the younger wife had been brought, and the previous year he, his father's elder brother and their respective wives had all had their *shadi* together.

9. In Rada, the two brides were breast-feeding their children in between the rituals.

are virtually no single Taivars. Only two men in the village were 'single' at the time of my fieldwork. However they too had had wives in the past. While a man may ideally have as many wives as he chose, women may not have more than one husband at a time. Marriages are predominantly virilocal, and women from other lineages come to live in the Taivar village. At any point of time, therefore, the village contains two categories of women: (1) The daughters and sisters of men of the Taivar lineage. These are women who have inherited the lineage name from their Taivar fathers. They do not inherit any property. They live in the village until they marry into another lineage and village. They return to visit their *piyar* (natal home) on certain occasions. (2) The wives and mothers of the Taivar men, who belonged to different lineages in different villages and married into the Taivar lineage. Apart from these two categories there are a small number of Girasia women who are not married to the Taivar men in the village; these are the sisters or wives of the non-Taivar Girasia men.

The Taivar marriages are prescribed, and at the time of my fieldwork the Taivars could only take wives from, and give wives to, the members of fourteen Girasia lineages (see table 5.2). The fourteen Girasia lineages are the Dungaicha, Gamar (Solanki), Bubariya (Parihar), Dhangi (Solanki), Damar, Peesra (Parmar), Vanhiya (Bansia), Khairadi (Rathor), Chauhan, Khokhariya (Rathor), Angarin (Chauhan), Parmar, Gorina (Solanki), Raidara.[10] These Girasia lineages and villages were spread over the Abu Road tehsil, both in and out of the *Bhakar*, in the Reodar and Pindwara *tehsils*, and also up to Palanpur in Gujarat.

The fourteen affinal Girasia lineages all trace descent from five major Rajput clans. While the Peesra and Parmar are like the Taivar in that they are Parmar Rajputs, the other lineages belong to the Solanki, Parihar, Chauhan, and Rathor Rajput clans. In Rajput historical literature and mythology, the four clans of the Parmar, Chalukya, Parihar and Chauhan were the *agnivanshi* Rajputs (from *agni*, fire, and *vansh*, lineage, denoting those Rajputs who were descended from the fire-lineages). Amongst the *agnikulas* (fire clans), the Parmars and Chauhans are considered the superior lineages (Karve, 1968 b: 166).[11] Apart from the fire-lineages, there are other

10. The names in parentheses refer to the Rajput clans of which these were lineages.
11. It was on Mount Abu (the highest mountain in the region) that, 'the four *agnikulas* were brought into existence by a special act of creation ... Vashishtha invited the gods to assemble at Mount Abu where a great *yajna* [sacrifice] was performed in the *agnikunda* [fire-pit] and the four tribes of the Kshatriyas were created by

Rajputs, who are divided into the *suryavanshi* (sun-lineages) and the *chandravanshi* (moon-lineages).[12] Both the *suryavanshi* and the *chandravanshi* Rajputs have been historically predominant in the regions to the north of Sirohi.

Although the Girasia lineages are all descended from the *agnivansh* Rajputs, the Taivars distinguish between the *unchi* (upper) and *neenchi* (lower) categories of each of these lineages and claim to marry women only from the upper category. Those Girasia lineages with whom the Taivars have no affinal relations are frequently considered 'lower'. For the Taivars, 'lower' Girasia lineages are comprised of those Girasia who have married outside the Girasia community, particularly into the Bhil community. The Girasia image of the Bhils, shared by other communities in the region (chapter 3), acts as a powerful social sanction against Girasia marriage outside the prescribed lineages. Occasionally some Taivars have married Bhils but no such marriages had taken place for a number of years before the time of my fieldwork. I was told that in the Taivar village the Khokhariya, Dungaicha and Bubariya wives all belonged to the upper categories of the prescribed Girasia lineages. According to Phoola: 'We [*hemo*] Taivars have connections with only the *unchi* Bubariya. We can eat *roti* from their women, which means we can marry them. We have no relations [*beti-vyavhar* or exchange of daughters] with the *neenchi* Bubariya because they eat buffalo meat [*paada khave vala*].' In other words, the lower Bubariya are those Bubariya Girasia who have intermarried with the groups who eat buffalo meat, i.e., the Bhils or others lower than the Taivar Girasia. (For the Taivars, we see that the Bhils are an archetype of a 'lower' rather than 'tribal' category.) The distinctions between high and low are also made within the Taivar lineage and serve to distinguish loyalties among sets of brothers. For example, in the Taivar village there is a continuous conflict between the two largest sublineages, the Vaijjath and the Lailath which revolves around the individual marriages made by their members.[13] As a result of such controversies over time

---

the gods, the Parmars by Indra, the Chalukyas by Brahma, the Parihars by Shiva and the Chauhans by Vishnu' (Lala Sita Ram 1920; 8, 9).

12. The *suryavanshi* are divided into three major clans: the Guhilot, Kachwaha and the Rathod (Karve 1965: 166).

13. While the Khetrath and Devath sublineage members largely supported the latter at *panchayatis* (village councils), the Raijath, Rehmath and Gokhlath sublineage members supported the former. Although there were internal divisions within the sublineages on matters such as water and land divisions (chapters 6 and 9), the Taivar lineage, if it were to split, would do so between the Vaijjaths

the number of lineages has increased and consequently so have the maritally prescribed categories.

Within the prescribed universe of marital lineages, there are some lineages whom specific Taivar Girasia may not marry. For example:

(1) A Taivar son cannot take a wife from his father's lineage. A daughter cannot take a husband from her father's lineage. This then excludes the father's brother's daughter or the father's brother's son (FBD/FBS) and the father's brother's son's daughter or the father's brother's son's son (FBSD/FBSS) from the group of potential affines.
(2) A Taivar son cannot take a wife from his mother's lineage although a daughter can marry a man from her mother's lineage. For the son this excludes the categories of mother's brother's daughter (MBD) and the mother's brother's son's daughter (MBSD). But a son may marry his mother's sister's daughter (MZD), as she has the lineage affiliation of her father (and not of the ego's mother's brother). However, this is only possible if the ego's mother's sister is not married into the lineage of his father. In other words the lineage of his mother's sister's husband (MZH) should not be that of the ego's father or his mother. The daughter may marry her mother's brother's son.
(3) A Taivar son may marry a woman from his father's mother's (FM) lineage or from his mother's mother's (MM) lineage provided they do not fall into either of the above two categories.

Considering the rules from both the male and female ego's point of view, it is clear that the rules are not universally applicable to men and women. As is illustrated in point (2) above, while a son may not unconditionally marry a woman from his mother's lineage, a daughter may take a husband from her mother's lineage. A son may however marry his MZD (if the MZ is not married into his lineage) as her children are not considered part of their mother's lineage (which is also the male ego's mother's lineage). Thus the marital link between the ego's parental lineages cannot be replicated by the male ego in the form of S-MBD relation, or into the same wife-taking, wife-giving equation, but it may be inverted by a female ego so that the wife-

---

and the Lailaths and their respective supporters. The Taivars themselves had split from the Madariyas, their ancestors in Nichalagarh. . Similarly the households in the village Rada (described in the previous section) are an offshoot of the Taivar households in the Naal *phalli*.

givers become wife-takers, as is the case when the daughter marries the MBS. The reasons for these restrictions are because of the consequences that marriage has for hierarchy between both sets of affines (see below), as well as for individuals. The possibility of this one-sided replication (i.e., through the daughter) of the relation between the wife-transacting groups is a reflection of the gender hierarchy, as the status of the lineage is not affected when women of the lineage (daughters and sisters) marry into other lineages; this is dealt with in greater detail below.

The Girasia 'stated' rules of marriage show characteristics of both the north and the south Indian models of marriage as described by Dumont (1959). For example,

1) The north Indian marriage pattern disallows marriage with close cognates, into the lineages or clans of the ego, ego's M, FM, and MM (the four clan rule; Mayer 1960, Karve 1965, Parry 1979). According to Parry, although the Kangra Rajputs followed the four clan rule, the marriage of the ego into the MM clan was 'readily tolerated' (1979: 225). The Girasia only disallowed marriages of the ego with his and his mother's clans. In other words, the north Indian restriction on marrying cognates does not apply to the Girasia descendants of the MM or FF category. Thus the male and female ego may marry their FM(B)D, MMB/D or the FMB/S, MMB/S respectively. The south Indian pattern, on the other hand, shows a preference for cross-cousin marriage (i.e., of the male ego with the MBD/FBD). As has been seen, the Taivar Girasia, practise restricted parallel cousin marriage within their rule of marriage to close cognates. In other words, a Taivar male may marry his MZD only if the MZH was not of the same lineage as the ego's father. A Taivar female can, however, unconditionally marry her MBS.

2) The north Indian pattern is said to manifest hypergamy while the south Indian pattern shows a concerted attempt at equality (isogamy) between wife exchanging groups. Dumont (1980) indicates that isogamy, or minimal status concerns, are to be expected when one is marrying a close relative as in the south Indian case (ibid.: 116). The Girasia follow the south Indian pattern within the prescribed set of affines, but manifest a concern with hierarchy with Girasia groups who fall outside this set.

3) In terms of the position of women, the Girasia pattern closely follows the north Indian pattern of virilocality and village (lineage) exogamy which have been linked to the distinct social

roles of women which are, for example, portrayed in the images of the 'free daughter' and the 'controlled wife'. The south Indian pattern blurs this distinction, for a woman has continued access to and even responsibility to her natal family, a role which marriage does not disrupt (Ram 1988). Despite the strong tendency towards the dichotomisation of social roles between a woman's natal and affinal lineages, the continued right of the natal lineage over the person of the Girasia wife (excluding the access to her labour and reproduction), as well as the close brother-sister bonding, modify the complete separation as witnessed in the lives of north Indian women.[14]

The Girasia position with regard to the north-south ideal types of kinship and marriage becomes clearer when we go beyond the Girasia rules given above. Observations of Girasia households show up certain patterns which are not apparent in their stated rules. For example, observations indicate that Girhaya men on an average have had at least one or two wives before their present wife. In a weighted sample of fifty-six Taivar households (out of a total of 178 Taivar households in the Taivar village), twenty-three male household heads, who had wives during my fieldwork, also had previous wives.[15] Another practice not articulated as a rule, I found, was that whenever men have had previous wives, the wives are usually consecutive rather than simultaneously present. Reasons for the presence of consecutive wives are observed to be 1) the high death rate of wives (it is hard to ascertain whether this is due to the diseases related to reproduction, maltreatment or from general conditions of malnourishment at the husband's home), 2) an informal type of divorce where the woman leaves her husband, either due to his desire or by the volition of the woman herself, often at the encouragement of a prospective husband (see in the section on divorce in chapter 7). While most men have had consecutive wives, a small number of men (nine men of the fifty-six households) had two wives at the time of my fieldwork. The low reproductive capacity of the first wife is the most common reason given for bringing in a second wife. (To what extent the husband himself was infertile it was not possible for me to ascertain). In some

---

14. Goody and Goody (1990), question the view that stresses there is a complete separation of the wife from her natal kin in north India (see chapter 7).
15. Of the twenty-three men, sixteen had one wife previous to the present one, five had two wives previous to their present one and two had three previous wives. (Similarly, seven out of a sample of twelve non-Taivar households had one to three wives in the past).

instances the amount of brideprice is a limiting factor in taking a second wife. There are other cases, however, which do not follow this line of reasoning. For example, both Cheema Hela and Lunda Mada had children from their current wives and yet they both brought in second wives. I was told, furthermore, that Cheema could not afford the brideprice. Sometimes men have been persuaded to accept wives. For example, Palvi said her brother Lunda was forced to accept Tibri, his second wife, on the persuasion of Tibri's father and uncles. This was a result of the relationship between the Vaijjath and the Damar lineages, described below.

A further unstated rule is that in general past wives, but more so the concurrent wives of a man, are from different affinal lineages. According to the opinion of several Girasia wives, 'It is not considered "proper" [*hau-ne or theek-ne* or *khoti*] for two "sisters" [i.e., two women of the same lineage] to share a husband'. In one instance when a second wife ran away from her husband, the move was welcomed generally because the man's other wife was of the same lineage as his second wife. The unstated rule of separating the lineages of a man's wives, as well as the presence of a number of such prescribed potential affinal groups indicates that through marriage the Taivar men are diversifying rather than consolidating their affinal links within the marital community. However, what may appear as the multifarious ties of individual men in a lineage has a pattern of consolidation when viewed at the level of the sublineage, as is shown in the following example of the marriages of men in one Taivar sublineage.

The Sublineage

Although the lineage is the exogamous unit where the ultimate sanction for a Girasia marriage rests, it is the sublineage which is the main unit involved in marriage transactions. Most of the fifty-one households of the Vaijjath Taivars have marital links to the west of the Taivar village, and to the south into Gujarat.[16] Half the Vaijjath Taivar men from amongst the sample of fifty-six men who had had one previous wife (eight out of sixteen), have wives from the Damar lineage of Girasia (see table 5.2). Vaijjath men can have only one

16. There is a small population of Girasia in the north of the Taivar village and some pockets in the Northeast, but Dopa, a Vaijjath Taivar said, 'We do not maintain contact through marriage with them because the Bhils come between us'. 'Between us' here refers to the spatial proximity of the mixed Bhil-Girasia groups of the Udaipur region. Among the houses contacted during my fieldwork, there was only one case where a Taivar girl married in the northeast.

Damar wife (unstated rule) and their sons from Damar women can not marry Damar women (stated rule). However, a man's sons from his other wives can marry women from their Damar stepmother's lineage. In fact I noticed that most sons of Vaijjath fathers and non-Damar mothers, showed a preference for Damar alliances. In doing so they maintained the link between the Damar and the Vaijjath lineages in each succeeding Taivar generation. For example, Lunda's second wife Tibri was a Damarni. She was also Lunda's FBWBD (see kinship diagram, figure 5.1 below). Lunda's first wife Haluri was a Gamarin (of the Gamar lineage). His eldest son from her also married a Damarni (see kinship diagramme, figure 5.1 below) as did Lunda's sister and his brother's son.

Table 5.2 Affinal Lineages of Wives in the Taivar Village

Affinal Girasia lineages	Taivar Girasia sublineages								
	V	L	R	D	Kh	G	Re	B	Total
Dungaicha	4	7	1	–	1	1	1	1	16
Gamaar	4	2	–	2	–	1	–	1	10
Bubariya	2	2	2	–	–	–	–	–	6
Dhangi	4	–	–	1	–	–	2	–	7
Damar	8	3	1	–	–	–	1	–	13
Peesra	1	3	2	1	1	–	–	–	8
Vanhiya	2	–	2	1	1	2	2	–	10
Khairadi	1	1	1	2	–	–	–	–	5
Chauhan	1	2	2	2	–	–	–	–	7
Khokhariya	–	1	–	–	–	–	1	–	2
Angari	–	–	–	1	–	–	–	–	1
Parmar	–	–	–	1	–	1	–	1	3
Gorina	1	–	–	–	–	1	–	–	2
Raidara	–	–	–	–	–	1	–	–	1

For a total of 90 women and 54 men

Key: V-Vaijjath, L-Lailath, R-Raijjath, D-Devath, Kh-Khetrath, G-Gokhlath, Re-Rehmath, B-Billath

Source: Primary Fieldwork Data

Apart from the Vaijjath Taivar men, men of the other Taivar sublineages also have marital ties with the Damar lineage, only these are fewer in number (as table 5.2 shows). The affinal ties of the father's brothers in other sublineages provided greater marital contacts for sons of the Vaijjath Taivars born of Damar mothers. For example, Dopa, whose mother was a Damarni, married a Sawanni (or woman from the Sawan lineage). Dopa's wife's maternal grandmother was married to Dopa's FFB (see kinship diagram B in figure 5.1 below).

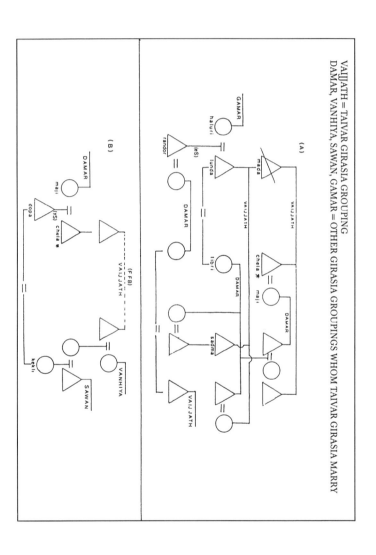

Figure 5.1 Vaijjath – Damar Marriages

Therefore, apart from the preference which Vaijjath Taivar sons have for Damar wives, they also tend to marry women from the lineages of their father's brother's affines. The marriage connections of all the sublineages are seen to further alliances over the consecutive generations of the lineage. The marital connection of the male ego with the affinal lineages of his father's brothers is another dimension in the bond between close agnates. For example, even when marrying women of lineages other than the Damar, Vaijjath Taivar sons would prefer to marry women of those lineages which are affinally related to their closer uncles, often of the same sublineage. The preference for Damar wives may also be linked to the important role played by existing affines in arranging marriage partners.

Marital relations served to reinforce the male sibling relation as they connect more people, for example, the FBWZ and the FBWBS/FBWBD are related through their own marital ties apart from the agnatic ties traced through their uncle (FB). Marriage strategies thus add another dimension to the agnatic relations in the lineage. In other words, relations through women bring some men of a lineage closer to one another. Sublineages which are genealogically closer are more likely to have more overlapping affinal connections. In this sense marriage reinforces the genealogically based relationships between close kin.

Two tendencies serve to obscure the sublineage's marital preferences at the level of the lineage. Firstly, different sublineages within the lineage tend to have relations with a number of other lineages. Secondly, there was an overlapping of affinal lineages among sublineages. So while at the level of the sublineage which is the real unit in setting up marriage contracts, one is aware of the existence of preferred affines within the larger set of prescribed affines, at the lineage and exogamous level sublineage preferences balance out to show an apparent minimal hierarchy within the Taivar Girasia system. Although affinal relations are important, it is through membership of the lineage brotherhood that women are made available as wives. In this sense, the lineage's ties through descent are reinforced and more valued by Girasia men, than those established through marriage connections. Moreover, a consequence of the diverse ties among the Girasia lineages is to ideologically reinforce a strongly related community of lineages which provide potential and existing affines. (When a member of a lineage is related affinally to another lineage, all members are considered affinally related to the other lineage. For example all the fourteen lineages mentioned above are called *huhara* lineages by all the Taivars). Within the affinal lineages there were higher and lower categories. For Taivar Girasia men to marry these lower categories of the prescribed lineages involves a negotiation with other members of the Taivar lineage and sublineage, particularly regarding the degree of 'lowness' that is acceptable. In the following section, I outline the nature of these negotiations surrounding marital alliances.

Marriage Negotiation and Lineage Boundaries

Marrying out of the Girasia community, i.e., either up into higher caste groups, or down into lower castes or 'tribal' groups is theoretically impossible. While the upper castes maintain a distance from the Girasia both in marital and commensal terms, the Girasia maintain a distance from the lower castes, specifically in marital terms (and from the Bhils in both marital and commensal terms). There are a few scattered stories of marital alliances with other castes which are known to have occured in the mythological past but there were no specific cases known for men in the Taivar village.[17]

According to the stated rules of the Taivar Girasia, marriages with Girasia lineages other than those prescribed are unacceptable. Yet, in practice, members of the Girasia lineage do marry 'lower' Girasia women. These marriages are hedged by negotiations and the lineage is able to reassess its status when certain breaches in the rules of marriage occur. The mechanism for adjustment is very similar to the procedure among the upper and lower Kangra Rajput *biradaris* where, as Parry observes, the 'status of the male line is continuously readjusted to take into account the prestige of its recent alliances' (1979: 204). It is concerns of status which affect the way a breach of rules is regarded in the community. Dumont (1980) has also observed that status is the essential principle which regulates a group's desire for endogamy (ibid.: 113). It is to prevent a considerable adjustment in the status of the lineage that the Taivars do not want to contract 'lower' marriages.

17. For example Nana, a Madariya Taivar from Nichallagarh recounted the story of how his sublineage originated in the alliance between his ancestor Madari and a Rebarin (woman of the Rebari community of pastoral nomads). Madari was sent out of the village after he married the Rebarin. On the way, seeking a place to live, he saw a Rajput chief being ambushed by Bhils. He rushed to the rescue of the Rajput and was rewarded with land near Mewar (Udaipur). Because Madari had been so brave and earned a name for himself, he was called back to stay in the village and all his descendants are now called Madariya Taivars. The story indicates that acts of bravery may excuse an improper marriage. I suggest also that the rules are more flexible because Rebaris are among the category of 'equal' non-Girasia (see also chapter 3).

Wives from lower castes are tolerated less than those from equal or higher non-Girasia groups. Frequently, however, 'lower' marriages are made among the Girasia. I found in the few instances where the men of the Taivar lineage have brought in 'lower' Girasia women, there follow conciliatory measures undertaken by other members of that sublineage in order to amend their fall in status relative to other sublineages in the lineage. The favoured conciliatory measure is in the form of the hosting of feasts where discussions and negotiations take place concerning the nature of compensation expected from a man and his sublineage for his incorrect marriage.

There is, in reality, a hierarchy of Taivar sublineages in the village based on the 'purity' of their affinal relationships. The three Taivar sublineages, Billath, Gokhlath and Rehmath, living in Naal section in the Taivar village are considered of a lower social standing in the village because, 'Their grandfathers [*mota*] had married lower women'. During my stay in the Taivar village, Taivar men of other sublineages would not eat at the houses of men of the three sublineages in order to avoid eating food cooked by their wives. The Naal men organised a feast as a means of negotiation and they got their sisters to cook to ensure their other sublineage brothers would attend the occasion. The attendance of the other sublineage brothers at the feast was the major exercise of the negotiation. At the time of the feast it was believed by some Taivars of the Vaijjath sublineage that the Naal men would be slowly accepted, although Palvi thought that they would always be considered lower whatever they did. The Taivar (Rajput) Girasia case then seems to agree with Dumont's as well as Parry's assertion that, 'castes are ideally endogamous units, though it must be stressed that the real objection is to miscegany with inferiors and not to unions with superiors' (1979: 123).

To some extent marriage with 'lower' women could have lasting effects for the sublineages in that they could link generations of Taivars to the lower non-Taivar lineages, as we saw in the Damar-Vaijjath alliances discussed above. However, if the second or third wives of a man are not from 'lower' lineages, lineage sanctions will purge these lower connections. Lineage sanctions are a very real fear, for a man may be disinherited and dispossessed of his property (synonymous to stripping him of his identity and social roots) and told to move out of the village. Although no Taivar was able to give me an incident of the expulsion of a Taivar man, a non-Taivar Girasia man was driven from the village during my stay. The man had fought with Gona Taivar, whom he accused of sleeping with his wife when he was away on *mazdoori* (wage-labour). (An accusation which was considered very likely to be true by my Taivar friends.) Gona died two days after the fight, and whatever the other Taivars had felt earlier as a justification for his beating disappeared as all the members of the Taivar sublineages combined to destroy the non-Taivar's house and, 'kill him if they got him'. Meanwhile the man, his wife and child, had fled into the forest. Gona was a member of the Gokhlath Taivar sublineage of Naal *phalli*. A result of his murder and the resultant action (described in chapter 8) by the other sublineages, was the reduction in the 'inferiority', or social distance of the Naal sublineage from the other Taivar sublineages.

So far I have been dealing with the marriages of Taivar men and I have shown that despite lineage sanctions, in some cases adjustments were made. But the restrictions on the marriages of Taivar men are different from those on the marriages of their sisters or daughters. This is related to the fact that the marriages of men affect the collective status of the natal lineage to a greater extent than the marriages of women of the same natal lineage. If a Taivar woman marries into a lower lineage, it is mainly her own relationships with her natal household and sublineage members that are affected, but the status of her natal lineage remained unchanged. As a consequence of this practice there are fewer sanctions on the marriages of women than on those of men. The relatively relaxed attitude surrounding the marriages of Taivar women reinforces the point I made earlier, that the Girasia wife-givers do not use their women as a means of increasing their status in comparison to castes who practice hypergamy. A crucial element in the flexible attitude to women's marriages is that Girasia women do not inherit any property or 'gifts', as do women of other castes (see chapter 7).

Although there are not many restrictions on women who marry outside the community, the loss of the brideprice is a strong incentive for father or brother to control the marriage. Further, from the viewpoint of most adult women, the prospect of wearing the distinctive jewellery of the husband's household is a symbolic representation of Girasia womanhood and identity which prevents them from choosing to marry a non-Girasia. But the important difference between the genders which favours women is that men are disinherited following an improper marriage and cut off from access to the resources of any lineage, while women who marry improperly are more easily allowed to return to their parental home.[18]

18. During my fieldwork, I came across only one instance of an improper marriage. Puni Taivarni was the daughter of old Rathi *bai* whose Taivar husband had died

Apart from marital ties with other castes, there are a few cases of restricted exchange and bride-service arrangements. Restricted exchange is called *homo-hata* (literally, face-to-face). The Taivars, Phoola told me, do not favour *homo-hata* for two reasons. Firstly, he said, there was no exchange of money and thus it was the poorer families who resorted to *homo-hata* when they had no money to pay the brideprice. *Homo-hata* was therefore associated with families with scant resources. Secondly, in the event of a disagreement in one household, the other household would be simultaneously affected because, 'A man's sister in another household is treated in the same manner as he treats his wife'. When I asked why this was not suitable, the Taivar Girasia said that *homo-hata* was contrary to the preferred ideal of maintaining a distance, or difference, from affines in contrast to the closeness between agnates. Parry (1979) observes that the two types of reciprocal arrangements, of *batta satta* (one brother-sister unit marrying another brother-sister unit) and *tarvadla* (a more generalised exchange where, say, three brother-sister units could be related through marriage) are prohibited among the the dowry giving upper clans *(biradari)* of the Kangra Rajputs. According to Parry the main reason for the restriction was that the marriage arrangements, 'contradict the unilateral ideal of *dan*' (ibid.: 209).[19] Parry noted, however, that there were no restrictions on exchange marriages among the lowest (Rathi) clans of the Kangra Rajputs, who exchanged women for brideprice (ibid., 210). A greater difference between the upper and lower Kangra Rajput clans was, according to Parry, in the practice of *rakhewa*, or the inheritance by a younger brother of his deceased elder brother's wife. Another difference lay in the ease of divorce amongst the lower Kangra Rajput lineages.

---

a few years previously. Puni had gone away with a Punjabi truck driver who had spent a night at the Abu Road *dharamsala* (free or cheap board and lodgings). Rathi bai said her daughter would visit them once a year from Punjab and tell them about her good food and clothes. They had, however, never seen her husband. Nyama *patel*, a village councillor, said that when a Taivarni went away with a non-Girhaya, her father and his *haga bhai* would track her husband down, extract money and take the girl back. Nyama said that usually no-one would dare to take their women.

19. *Dan*, is the Hindu form of 'gift', or donation, given without thought of return, and considered to bring spiritual merit to the giver. Similarly, the notion of *kanyadan*, or the gift of the virgin daughter from the wife-giving lineage to the wife-taking lineage, earns the bride's father spiritual merit which is contradicted if his agnatic group also accepts women from their daughter's affinal group. Both *dan* and dowry are institutions which support hypergamous marriage exchanges among the higher clans of the Kangra Rajputs.

The Girasia material illustrates that even when there is no concept of *dan* attached to the exchange of women, restricted exchange is not a preferred means of marriage. Furthermore, the Girasia practices indicate differences between *homo-hata* (*satta* in Parry's terms) which is not a preferred means of marriage, and a more common form of the *tarvadla* type of marriage for which the Girasia have no name. Apart from the few restricted exchange marriages, bride-service arrangements were the focus of other negotiations between wife-givers and wife-takers. The Taivar institution of the *ghar-jamai* (resident son-in-law), like the *homo hata* mentioned above, is not preferred, and is equally perceived to be practised by poor families with few shares in land and water. In the case of the *ghar jamai*, the wife-taker is poor and instead of paying a brideprice, the groom performs bride-service. The groom does not inherit the in-law's property as in other bride-service societies.[20] Among the Taivars, bride-service takes place under two conditions: firstly, the groom-giver is poor compared to the groom-taker; secondly, the groom-taker should require a resident son-in-law in the absence of sons or adopted sons to look after his land. The position of the *ghar-jamai* is of an extremely low status in the village, and mockingly equated with that of a wife. According to a male Taivar, 'It is wives, and not husbands, who move between villages'. A *ghar-jamai* is, 'poor in his village, and so he is treated like that in ours'. Not resident in his natal village, as other male members of his lineage, but changing residence on marriage as do the female members of his lineage, the *ghar jamai* becomes a socially ambivalent individual. He neither participates in the decision-making process nor occupies a position of authority or importance in either his natal or his affinal village. The lack of authority of the *ghar-jamai* is essentially related to his absence from his natal village and his 'wife-like' position in his affinal village. Both the wife-like position, and the lack of authority contributes to the image of the *ghar-jamai* as a 'weak' (or *ese-hi,* just like that) man.

To take an example: Jama, Palvi's husband belonged to the Peesra lineage and had land in Moongthala (approximately 10 kilometres from Abu Road). Jama had not married as a *ghar-jamai* but came later when it was decided that Palvi could not have children in his village. Jama's other married son and daughter-in-law stayed to look after the land in his village. For all purposes Jama was treated as a *ghar-jamai.* He was always on the physical and social margins of any

---

20. See for example, Gell 1988, Rosaldo and Collier 1981, Strathern 1984.

feast or ritual celebration. Palvi and he had been able to clear a bit of the hilly and unproductive land near her *haga* brother Reeva's house.[21] Palvi and Jama did not own a well, nor did they have a share for irrigation purposes in her brother's wells. They were able to use the well only for drinking and bathing purposes and for their livestock. They could thus grow crops on their land only if there was a heavy monsoon. Their son would send them a few bags of corn from Jama's village where they had better quality land. Palvi's youngest son, Bika, had a fight with Dopa's (her FBS of the same sublineage) youngest son. The boy's grandmother, Maji, came to hit Bika with a large stone. According to Bika, Maji said to him: 'What have you come here for, in any case you don't belong. This is not your village. Your father [Jama] has been given land by us. How dare you fight with us.' Maji's retort highlights two interrelated characteristics of the institution of *ghar-jamai*. Firstly, even though Palvi was a Taivarni and Maji was not, Maji saw Palvi's family as outsiders, because of the low status of Palvi's husband. Secondly, not only were *ghar-jamai* considered outsiders and of low status but their children were also treated in an inferior manner. Moreover, Maji considered her claims to status within the Taivar lineage as relatively greater than Jama's, although both had no absolute authority, or status, in comparison to Taivar men.

Living outside his own lineage, the *ghar-jamai* is denied the opportunity to exercise authority. However on some occasions, especially in times of conflict within the lineage, *ghar-jamai* were used as intermediaries between conflicting parties (usually sublineages). In such situations the fact of being an outsider (i.e., of another lineage) was seen to provide a greater impartiality. However, such positions of authority were temporary and were not fixed in the persons of specific *ghar-jamais*. (Some *ghar-jamais* may acquire other politico-ritual skills which single them out for attention, greater acceptance and authority within their affinal lineage; see chapter 8).

Most often, what determined the appropriateness of a marital alliance at the sublineage and individual levels were the Taivar Girasia concerns with status and difference. In the next section I discuss similar concerns among the non-Girasia castes.

21. Palvi said that nobody had helped them clear the land. But the fact that Palvi could stay on in her natal village and build her *gair* was itself a sign of support from her brothers and the sublineage. Palvi belonged to the Vaijjath sublineage, the largest in the Taivar village, and her father Mada had been the *sarpanch*, as well as the primary *bhairu bhopa* (ritual mediator) at the sublineage shrine.

Marriage and Hierarchy in the Region

Both from the marriage rules and from observation it is clear that in ideal terms the Girasia follow a pattern of generalised exchange, in so far as they take a wife against brideprice from one lineage and give a wife against brideprice to another lineage. The exchange of wives, however, only occurs among a restricted community of Girasia. For the Taivar Girasia it is the 'upper' Rajput Girasia set of lineages which provide suitable marriage partners. The Girasia lineages within the 'upper' category are considered equal in status (the fact that they intermarry reflects the fact that they are equal, and vice-versa). Thus marriage exchange is neither hyper- nor hypogamous but rather isogamous. In other words, there is a lack of concern among individual Taivar household heads to use marriage as a means of aligning with other Girasia households for greater status within the lineage. At the outset, the Girasia tendency for isogamy represents an anomaly with respect to the north Indian Hindu marriage rules. Hindu marriages, especially the Rajput, illustrate a singular preoccupation with status.[22] Below I show how the Rajputs may have isogamous marriages, like the Girasia.

Hindu texts and customs indicate a gradation between two inverse types of marriage practices. The hypergamous, or 'correct' marriage (*anuloma*, with the flow), is a signifier of the high status of the caste group. It is symbolically and materially manifested in the transfer of dowry and the 'gift' of the virgin bride. Hypogamy (*pratiloma*, against the flow) defines the other, and lower end of the marriage hierarchy, considered to be characterised by the transfer of brideprice. Poverty, impurity and low status are compounded to characterise brideprice practising hypogamous groups in Hindu society.[23] Attempts to achieve a higher status are found especially between groups adjacent in the caste hierarchy (Tambiah 1973: 200). According to Tambiah, the larger the fall through the status structure in terms of matrimonial alliances, the more the likelihood that the marriage be considered *pratiloma*. Tambiah's observations are important as they point towards a continuum rather than a dichotomy between the tendencies of hyper- and hypogamy in caste marriages. This is further illustrated in Parry's work on the Kangra Rajputs.

Parry notes that the practice of hypergamy among the members of the top *biradaris* (who have prestige related titles or wealth) forces

22. Dumont 1966, Mayer 1960, Karve 1965, Kapadia 1966, Parry 1979.
23. Relational purity as reflected in marriage practices is a general means of ordering power relations in the Hindu caste hierarchy, with superiority attached to the traditionally purer groups (Dumont 1980).

the lower *biradaris* into hypogamy.[24] Hypergamy results in an abundance of brides for the top *biradaris* and a shortage of brides in the lower *biradaris*. On the one hand, a consequence of fewer brides in the lower *biradaris* creates inflated dowry rates for the wife-givers from wife-takers of the equal *biradaris*. On the other hand, status is gained by wife-givers if they give their daughters to the upper *biradaris*. The conflict is usually resolved in favour of hypogamous marriage exchanges among the lowest *biradaris* in exchange for brideprice rather than dowry payments. The lower *biradaris* also resort more frequently to sibling exchange marriages and show a greater acceptance of divorce (ibid.: 228). Parry's work points to the simultaneous presence of both hyper- and hypogamy within the same caste. He also observes the existence of a transitory isogamous phase where repeated marriages, which result in an accumulation of women at the top, over time tend to break up into endogamous units on the basis of a mutual agreement, 'to boycott their superior and inferior affines' (ibid.: 228). But, Parry continues, the resultant isogamous phase is itself a temporary phenomenon and later becomes transformed into a hypergamous relation of wife-exchanging units. The pattern of wife-exchange among the Kangra Rajputs leads Parry to propose, 1) that hypergamy and isogamy can be mutual processes within the same community, and further, 2) that isogamy is not a stable configuration and therefore is not clearly distinguishable from hypergamy. The Girasia pattern, in contrast to Parry's proposition, tends towards a more stable configuration of isogamy. In isogamous marriages, as in the south Indian case, Dumont stresses that as the individual often marries a close relative, there is little concern with increasing status (ibid.: 116). There may be a high degree of fusion between isogamous groups instead.[25]

24. Parry (1979) describes the Kangra Rajput ideal of hypergamy among the four clans (*biradari*) as, 'Wives are taken from the *biradari* immediately inferior to your own, but preferably from your own *biradari;* and daughters ... given to your own *biradari,* but preferably to the *biradari* above' (ibid.: 200).
25. For Dumont, castes are 'endo-recruiting' (ibid.: 112) in the sense that both marriage (endogamy) and the transmission of group membership (descent through both parents) are within the group. This distinguishes caste from tribe, in that tribe tolerates marriage outside the group. Further, for Dumont, the endo-recruiting tendency of castes distinguishes them from the exogamous marriages of clans, apart from the clan feature of unilineal descent. However, at the level of more than one clan I believe that Dumont's distinction between caste, clan and tribe collapses. For example, both the Girasia and other Rajputs have clans, and emphasise patrilineal descent as well as endogamous marriages within a group of clans (which I see as caste). Therefore it is not possible to say that a

The main difference between the upper and lower *biradaris* in Kangra lies in their tendencies for opposite marriage practices, which according to Parry, introduces a 'caste-like barrier' (ibid.: 233) between them. I would suggest that the differences between the Rajput Girasia lineages and the middle and upper Rajput lineages in the region is a similar type of division, only more impenetrable. The major difference between the lower Kangra Rajput *biradaris* and the Girasia lineages is that while the former are attached through marital linkages to the wider hierarchical community, the Taivar Girasia have no marital links outside their isogamous community. In chapter 7 I suggest that, because the Girasia are removed from a hierarchical marital system, they are able to view their institution of brideprice with pride. Because the upper *biradaris* in Kangra exchange women for dowry, brideprice payments of the lower lineages are regarded, by members both of the upper and lower lineages, as shameful. Another practice shared by the lower Kangra lineages and the Girasia is the practice of polygyny. Although polygyny is considered despicable by the Brahmanically-orientated Hindus, the ideal of Brahmin monogamy is frequently compromised by a secondary (inferior) marriage due to the barrenness of the first wife (Dumont 1980: 110). The royal lineages, on the other hand, made polygyny a more frequent practice in order to enter into politically and economically beneficial relationships (Stern 1977). The Brahmans and the Kshyatriyas, the two upper castes of the Hindu hierarchy, were also among the groups who were allowed an access to the largest number of wives from amongst the other castes (Tambiah 1973).

Often the standards of emulation of a group are set by those with the highest socially condoned authority, which in the Rajput case have been the royal families. The royal Rajput practice of polygyny was different from the ideal Brahmanic practice of monogamy.[26] According to Plunkett (1973), polygyny allowed the royalty to marry into high-status, non-royal houses, as well as equal status, royal

---

    caste is a closed group at only one level (i.e, versus tribe), as its closure varies from level to level within each caste community. Dumont is however justified in stressing that marriage as well as descent are important vantage points from which to study the closure of social groups.

26 This may be regarded as a symbol of the conflict between the authority of religious power of the Brahmins based on the knowledge of the texts, and the political power of the Rajput Kshatriyas based on conquest and military might. History has shown that strong Rajput rulers could continue their distinctive practices despite the potential opposition from the Brahmins, as the former possessed the necessary authority to enforce these customs.

houses. Such an arrangement, 'also permitted alliance and exchange between houses without violating the North Indian norm that prescribes the avoidance of cousin marriage' (ibid.: 79). Furthermore, Plunkett observes that Rajput brides were more solicitous of their natal clan in comparison with their loyalty to the husband's clan (ibid.: 70; Plunkett's observation had also been made earlier by Tod in the 1830s). The loyalty of the Rajput wife to her father's clan is a distinct break from the Hindu custom where a transferral of the loyalty of the wife to her husband's group indicates her accomodation to its patriarchal ideals.

Most of these distinct Rajput customs are also practiced by the Girasia and thus show that although regarded as degraded customs among non-Rajput Hindus, they are considered a model for emulation amongst the Rajputs. Where the Girasia and Rajput cases differ is that the preoccupation of the Girasia lineage and sublineage is with the maintainence of their status, in contrast with the Rajputs who were historically preoccupied with increasing their status.

The Girasia identify with the Rajputs on the one hand, but distance themselves from the Bhils on the other. Despite the Girasia-stated differences from the Bhils, I saw similarities between the Girasia, Rajput and Bhil institutions. Below, I show how the similarities between Bhil and Girasia practices, as between those of the Rajput and Girasia outlined above, are comparable, despite indigeneous constructions of difference. I use the Bhil community for comparison, as they are the other group in the region, besides the Rajput, who are numerically dominant and equally, if not more, present in Girasia conversations. From Deliege's work (1985) on the Bhils, I observe certain similarities between the Bhil and Girasia kin structure and process of affinal linkages. According to Deliege, status is largely absent as an ordering principle between Bhil exogamous clans. Bhil clans are a loose cluster of dispersed lineages and, as with the Girasia lineage, they form a territorial kin group. Further, Deliege notices a 'reluctance for the repetition of Bhil marriages and a tendency towards the extension of affinal ties ... with no groups occupying the permanent status of wife giver or taker' (ibid.: 125,127). Deliege finds the Bhil wife-giving group superior to the wife-taking group for a limited period of time only, i.e., not a permanent hierarchichal relation between affines, as is the case among other castes.

In a system where the wife-giving group is in a position of potential superiority at marriage, as among Girasia and Bhils, its potentially high status could undermine the authority of the male kinship unit into which the woman marries. If the position of the wife-givers is allowed a permanent superiority, the incoming wives and their (father's) lineage would work against the wife-taking (husband's) lineage's interests. In the situation of temporary superiority only being granted to the wife-givers, I see an importance of the patrifocal ties of the lineage, both among the Girasia and the Bhils. Furthermore, the relative equality between the wife-giving and wife-taking lineages has implications for the structural position of women. In the Rajput case, where the wife is treated in accordance with the relatively low status of her natal lineage, women build stronger links with their affinal lineage, but in the Girasia case, and I would suggest in the Bhil case also, the wife is treated as an inferior by both her natal and affinal lineages because of the absence of a permanent hierarchy between groups who exchange wives.

The role of individual choice in the selection of a marriage partner is another striking distinction popularly perceived as a means of distinguishing the Bhil from other castes. Elopment is a common means of initiating marriage among the Bhils. Although Deliege seems to suggest that eloping (which the Girasia call *khichna* or *chori*) is an unplanned act of individualism, I would suggest that it may not be as random a phenomenon as it seems. From the observations discussed in chapter 4, it is clear that prior information as to the status of the girl's lineage is always procured by the men, and in cases of *chori* the willingness of the woman is ascertained. I would, however, agree with Deliege that eloping is not only socially condoned but is even encouraged as a means of lessening the expenses otherwise incurred in an engagement ceremony. Furer-Haimendorf (1982) makes a similar observation of the Gond tribals of Andhra Pradesh. According to Furer-Haimendorf: 'There is a fairly general view that whereas in the old days marriage by capture [*pisi watana*] usually occured without previous agreement between all the parties concerned, nowadays the capture of the bride is frequently staged as a mere formality in order to avoid the expense of the full wedding ceremonies necessary in a marriage by negotiation' (ibid.: 165). But there is no doubt that the individuals concerned make their own decisions, or at least men initiate decisions and women willingly or reluctantly go along with them. The individualism, noted by Carstairs in his study of the Bhils of Udaipur (for example, as 'sturdy ego formation of the Bhils'; 1956: 180) is also reflected in their marriage choices. Such individualism is correlated with the ideal of an egalitarian ethos, the reluctance to centralise authority, or to subscribe to too many rules. Yet as we have seen, egalitarian tendencies among the Girasia are circumscribed by considerations of status and the related sanctions applied by the lineage.

Carstairs contrasts Bhil marriages to Hindu marriages in terms of the personal or qualitative nature of the relationship. He feels that among the Bhils spouses share a closer relationship. From my observation of Girasia relationships, it seems that such a conclusion needs to be qualified by the markers of production and consumption. In the sphere of production, where the major input was in terms of women's labour the couple shared a closer relationship (in terms of consultations for decision making). However, in the sphere of consumption (the feasting and sharing of food) and in the sharing of resources and the products of labour, the Girasia man has a closer relationship with his male kin in the sublineage and lineage.

In this chapter I have concentrated on the ideals and variations in Girasia affinal arrangements as a means of indicating the boundaries of the lineage and the related role of women. I have also shown that patrifocal concerns with status blur the distinctions between caste and 'tribal' communities.

Chapter 6

RESOURCE MANAGEMENT AND THE DIVISIONS OF KINSHIP AND GENDER

*I*n this chapter I examine the Taivar Girasia economy through the social categories which have been discussed in the previous two chapters. The first section describes to what extent notions of male siblingship in the lineage (*kaka-baba* relations) translate into economic sharing in practice. The distribution and control of economic resources in the Taivar village was determined, above all, by the nature of the sublineage divisions within the lineage and, further, by the genealogical divisions within the sublineage. What was clear from the distribution of land and water resources among the Taivar Girasia was that it was not so much 'tribal' or egalitarian (as denoted by the *bhaiachari* system) but rather lineal *(pattidari)* in character like other farming communities in the region. From an emphasis on the lineage in economic organisation, I will move to focus on the economic aspects presented by the affinal relationships of the lineage. The economic relations between Girasia affinal lineages, unlike relations of descent, are governed by stipulations of payment rather than sharing, thus further emphasising the difference between the natal and affinal villages for women. In the second section I use food transactions to illustrate the difference between the natal and the affinal lineage (us [*hemo*] whom we eat with and others [*beeja*] with whom we do not eat certain foods, a common distinction in most parts of India). The rules regarding food consumption among the Girasia particularly affect women as wives and are symbolic of the differences between the Girasia lineages. In the final section I discuss the economic and social aspects of the market which are central to Girasia lifestyles. I suggest that the market plays an important role because it is spatially, socially and economically 'between' the natal and affinal Girasia lineages. This has important implications for Girasia women and men. Further, I argue against the commonly perceived isolation of 'tribals' from the market, to stress the manner in which the Girasia influence what is produced and sold in the market.

The Lineage and Subsistence: Land, Water, Labour

In this section I outline how the major resources, especially water, are shared by members in a sublineage in order to produce their staple cereal. The climate in the Abu region is temperate-monsoonal and the agriculture practised is seasonal. The land in the village is taken up by the following uses, as gleaned from the information provided in the census documents:

Table 6.1: Land Use in the Taivar Girasia Village[1]

Total area (hectares)	3,631 (36 sq.km)
Land use (hectares)	
forested area:	3,294
irrigation:	40
no irrigation:	175
no use:	122
Water source:	wells, rivulets
Staple crop:	maize

Source: *District Census Handbook*, 1981: 56-7

Maize is the major crop for the Taivars and most other farmers in the Sirohi district. It is sown once a year before the monsoon rains in July, and harvested in the period between the end of October and the beginning of November (and called the *barsati phasal* or summer rain crop). Rainfall in the initial stages of growth is crucial for the

---

1. I do not give the name of the village for obvious reasons, although I know full well that the village will be recognisable to locals and others familiar with the area. Neither do I use a pseudonym for the village, referring to it instead as 'the Taivar village' (village of the members of the Taivar lineage of Girasia).

production of *makka* (corn). According to Lunda, 'In a good production year we get approximately 13 *makki bori* [jute sacks containing approximately 80 kilograms of maize grains]. Then we have food for the year and enough to sow seeds for the next season'. In the year of my fieldwork the production of *makka* per household, as table 6.2 reveals, was only approximately 2 *bori*, or 160 kilograms.

Table 6.2: Quantity of Corn Produced in 1985 and 1986 for 56 Taivar Households

| Quantity | Number of households | |
(kgs)	1985	1986
0- 50	3	30
50-100	14	11
100-150	2	2
150-200	16	7
200-250	4	0
250-300	5	3
300-350	3	1
350-400	4	0
400-450	0	0
450-500	1	0
500-550	1	0
550-600	2	0
600-650	1	0

Source: Primary fieldwork data

The above table is an appropriate index of the hardships I witnessed in 1986. The previous year was considered a bad production year with approximately seventy percent of the households producing less than 250 kilograms of corn for the whole year. In 1986, seventy per cent of the households produced less than 100 kilograms of corn and thus registered a fall in crop output of more than half that of 1985. Whenever I asked a Taivar what was the most fortunate economic position, I was told that it was to be able to have two full meals a day, of which one should be with *makka-roti* (unleavened bread made from maize flour) for every day of the year. Although foods gathered and hunted are more important from the nutritional point of view, it is the production of maize that is related to prosperity. In the latter part of my stay in the Taivar village, the households which were consuming *makka-rotis* could be counted on one hand. Most households had run out of their supply of corn and were instead consuming *gainhu-roti* (bread made from wheat flour) which had been bought in the ration shops in Abu Road town (or earned in wage labour on government famine relief projects). Duda voiced a general opinion when he said that nothing compared with the taste of *makki-roti*. He felt the bread made from wheat had neither the same flavour nor the same 'heat' (energy) as that from maize. To preserve the taste of the maize, he said that he avoided the use of chemical fertilisers distributed by the government as the fertilisers not only reduced the flavour, but also 'burnt' the soil (particularly damaging when there was no rainfall).

Besides maize, some Girasia irrigate wheat in the winter season *(hiyala)*. Sharing the field with wheat could be *jowar* (millet), *jou* (barley), *channa* (gram), or *rayda* (rape-seed). Only a small proportion of Girasia cultivate a winter crop and the fields for this occupy a smaller area than for maize.The sowing and harvesting of wheat takes place between November and March. From April to June the fields lie bare the next sowing season. As crops other than maize required irrigation, access to well water, the main water source other than rain water, determines the quantity of winter crop sown and harvested. Most of what is consumed by the Taivars in the way of food is either grown or gathered from the *Bhakar*. The surrounding villages and nearby town rarely provide any contributions to the daily Girasia subsistence needs during a good monsoon period. However, in lean agricultural periods following a slack rainy season, most households augment the low quantities of corn produced by purchasing low-quality wheat from the markets. Cheap low-quality wheat is provided by the government 'ration' shops. Wheat is also given as payment for wage-labour on famine relief work sites (at the rate of seven kilos per day or Rs. 14/-). The amount of wheat consumed by a household is a good indicator of the shortfall in the annual production of corn. While the quantity of corn produced fell during fieldwork (1986 to 1987) in comparison to the year before (see table 6.2 above) the quantity of wheat bought rose in accordance. For example, in 1985, thirty-five out of fifty-six households obtained[2] less than 500 kilograms of wheat, whereas in 1986, thirty-five out of fifty-six households procured between 400 to 1,400 kilograms of wheat.

The different capacities of households to produce food create an economic differentiation in the ideally egalitarian social context of the lineage. Differences in food production are related to differences in landholdings and the ownership of water resources. Resources and produce are both shared and individually owned and consumed

---

2. I use the word 'obtained' rather than 'bought' because, while some wheat was bought, other amounts were received as payments for wage labour.

according to certain rules. Differences in the quantity produced depend upon the number of brothers sharing resources, particularly water and land. One characteristic attributed to tribal (or single clan communities) has been a customary sharing of resources, especially land. This aspect has led observers to classifiy 'tribal' landholdings under the category of *bhaiachari* (Baden-Powell 1892: 265).[3] In contrast, land in multi-caste villages is regarded as ancestrally divided into separate shares *(patti)* amongst male family members, known as the north-Indian *pattidari* system of land tenure. The Taivar Girasia, however, had both *bhaiachara* and *pattidari* aspects in their economy. The Taivars follow the regional *pattidari* (lineal) system in their division of land and water. There are elements of the *bhaiachara* (collateral) or communal-brotherly sharing during some occasions in the production, distribution and consumption of food. For Stokes (1978) the *bhaiachara* is essentially a tribal form of joint tenure by the nature of its origin (through conquest), the nature of the ownership of land (without subordinate tenancy) and the impermeable character of the system. These three aspects of *bhaiachara* could equally well be applied to the Girasia. They are the sole owners and occupiers of the *Bhakar* land, they do not practice subordinate tenancy nor does land pass to any non-Girasia or outside the control of the lineage. However, in contrast to a joint ownership of resources in the Taivar village, the Girasia have a lineal transmission of rights in ancestral shares within the sublineage, as the rest of this section will show.

3. There has been some ambiguity with regard to the classification of the *bhaiachara* tenures by the British in north India (Baden-Powell 1892, Fox 1971, Stokes 1978). According to Stokes, the British administrators mistakenly used *bhaiachara* to, 'indicate any joint tenure (where land revenue was apportioned at land, or plough rate), which did not follow ancestral shares' (ibid.: 6). Stokes supports Baden-Powell in his claim that the *bhaiachara* was a truly tribal form of joint tenure, which originated not as a grant from a ruler but as a result of the, 'colonisation of an empty tract of land' (ibid.: 6). Stokes, however, also points out that beyond this intitial difference, the lines between the *bhaiachara* and *pattidari* tenures were difficult for Baden-Powell to distinguish. For Stokes, the importance of the *bhaiachara* system lay in the exception it provided to the historically fluid nature (development cycle) of landholdings as portrayed by Fox (described in chapter 2). The *bhaiachara* system was based on a local kinship system which was homogeneous and compact. Its members resisted the entry of outsiders by, 'containing the urge to seek higher status and subordinate tenants' (Stokes, 1978: 87). For Stokes, *bhaiachara* holdings were especially possible in areas of abundant land. Furthermore, separate forms of land tenure could exist within the same caste. For example, Stokes finds *bhaiachara* communities and lineages as well as the overlord tenure communities of Jats living next to each other in the Mathura and Aligarh districts of Uttar Pradesh (ibid.: 86).

All the Taivar Girasia in the Taivar village own *patti* or units of land. Fifty-six households surveyed owned one-half to 3 *bigha* of land (see table 6.3 below). Thirty households own 2 *bigha* (half a hectare) of land. There is an absolute restriction on the transfer of land outside the lineage. The few affinal relatives who reside in the Taivar village own virtually no land and especially have no rights over productive land in the village. *Ghar-jamais* (resident sons-in-law) do not inherit land (as we saw in chapter 5). Even when land is mortgaged *(girwi)*, it is mortgaged amongst lineage brothers in the village.[4]

Table 6.3: Distribution of Landholdings in the Taivar Village for 56 Taivar and 12 Non-Taivar Households

Land *(bigha)*	Taivar hhs	non-Taivar hhs
1/2		1
1	3	
1 1/2	1	
2	30	2
2 1/2	2	
3	11	6
4	3	1
5	4	
6	1	1
12	1	

Note: hhs= households, 1 bigha = 1/4 hectare
Source: Primary Fieldwork Data

Each household is surrounded by its own plot of land *(khet)* for the rain-fed crop *(barsatu phasal)*. Several households also have rights to land in the surrounding hills *(donga khetar)* where wild grasses are gathered. Irrigation is possible mainly on the flat land in the Taivar village. The most fertile land in the village is the area near the dry river-bed.[5] Especially after a heavy monsoon the fields nearer the river have the added advantage of siphoning water from the river via canals *(haran)*. Most wells are also situated on the flat land. Land in the flat and fertile area is divided according to well shares (*kua-mathe,* literally on, or at the well) and usually between the sublineage broth-

---

4. For example, Duda's younger brother had 'kept' (*rakhna*) land with Dopa who lived next to him and was a prosperous member of a different sublineage.
5. According to the agricultural extension officer of Abu road *tehsil,* with a good monsoon and no irrigation the average produce of maize would be seven to nine quintals per hectare (one quintal is a 100 kilograms) for the flat land as compared to four to five quintals in the hilly parts.

ers of that *phalli* section of the village.[6] As the flat land had been acquired by the older lineage households in the initial stages of occupation in the village, subsequent households are forced to own shares rather than individual land or water holdings in the fertile area. At the time of my fieldwork, a Taivar Girasia's access to both land and water sources was determined by the resources of his father as well as the number of *haga* ('true', of the same father) brothers in the sublineage. An access to well water is very important due to the unpredictable frequency and quantity of the monsoonal rainfall. Most households are dependent on the monsoons to water their annual maize crop. Households also have shares in the wells in the lower lying area, to meet daily consumption needs, including drinking water for livestock. The few wells situated on the flatter land then become the main source, other than the monsoon, for irrigation.[7] Below, I concentrate on the distribution of shares *(bhag)* in wells among shareholders *(bhagidar)* in order to understand the relationship between the economic and social divisions in the Girasia lineage. Thirty-six out of sixty-eight of the Girasia households in the Taivar village (56 Taivar, 12 non-Taivar) have rights in a well (see table 6.4 below, on well shares).

Table 6.4: Distribution of Well Shares in the Taivar Village for 56 Taivar and 12 Non-Taivar Households

Shares	Taivar hhs	Non-Taivar hhs
1	4	
1/2	2	
1/3	3	
1/4	9	
1/5	5	1
1/6	1	
1/7	4	
1/8	7	

Note: hhs= households (for 56 Taivar and 12 Non-Taivar Households)
Source: Primary Fieldwork Data

6. Lal (1979), who studied Girasia landholdings in the nearby area of northern Gujarat, found that households having larger holdings were located in the *dhar* (arid) sector where the land was extremely poor, while households having smaller holdings were situated where land was more fertile (ibid.: 105, table XIX). Therefore the size of the holding was not indicative of the productivity or the prosperity of the owner. The same was true for the Taivar Girasia.
7. Although the water table was high and approximately eight feet below the river bed, the subsoil was extremely rocky and difficult to dig. It was therefore impos-

Of the 36 households only 4 have individual wells. The remaining 32 households have between one-half to one-eighth shares in a well, with the majority (27 households) having between one-fourth to one-eighth share in a well. Below I describe the division of water shares among the households of the major (Vaijjath) sublineage in the Taivar village. (Twenty-three of the 51 Vaijjath Taivar households live in the Beechalli *phalli,* see table 4.1 above.) The 23 households in Beechalli *phalli* shared the water of 2 wells. The water and related crop shares are distributed amongst the brother-households in the sublineage in terms of their descent from the lowest (or youngest) common sublineage ancestor, whom I shall call K for convenience. The members of the Vaijjath sublineage are descendants of the four sons of K, who were NK, RK, LK and AK. Beechalli *phalli* was dominated by the sons of LK, RK and NK in that order. Other descendants live mainly in the Malwa *phalli.* For example, most of the sons of NK live in Malwa *phalli* with the descendants of AK. The descendants of LK occupy the maximum number of households (12) in the *phalli*. The descendants of RK live in 5 households, those of AK in 4 and those of NK in 2 households. In this example I consider the well shares of the sons of LK (well W1 in figure 6.1). I then briefly examine shares in the second well (well W2 in figure 6.1) which are divided between the sons of NK and RK.

Mada (LK1), Thela (LK2) and Bava (LK3) are the three sons of LK. Mada and Bava had constructed the well W1. Of Mada's seven sons, five have shares in W1 (two are not included as one had fought with his brothers, and the other lives as an affinal relative in a village in Gujarat).[8] Mada's sons have constructed an *arhat* (Persian wheel) at which they and their household members (men, women and children) take turns to draw water for irrigation. Bava's four sons have shares in W1,[9] and operate a diesel pump ('machine') on the same well. Thela's only son Dheema does not have a share in the well-water for irrigation purposes because his father had not contributed to the construction of W1. However, Dheema has a share in the crop produced by the well water used by Bava's sons. This is because he had contributed the maximum amount of money towards buying the water pump, which is registered in his name.

---

    sible for most fields, especially on the slopes, to have access to any ground water at all.

8. Seven of the Vaijjath Taivar men lived in their affinal villages in Gujarat.
9. One son was an absentee shareholder as he was employed as a railway clerk in Ajmer; the only Girasia in the village to have succeeded in obtaining middle-class employment in a town.

The well water drawn by both the Persian wheel and the mechanised pump is used to irrigate two separate 3 *bigha* plots of land. This is land inherited from LK and divided between LK1 and LK3 who had built the well.[10] All shareholders helped to repair the instruments and had contributed money towards the purchase of seeds, fertilisers and fuel (in the case of the machine owners). Each shareholder *(bhagidar)* in the Persian wheel gets up to 100 kgs of wheat a season, which amounts to one-sixth of the total output. Reeva, the eldest of the five brothers, has contributed the most labour in the construction of the *arhat* and therefore owns two shares of the well. Shareholders in the machine get much larger shares of wheat (up to 200 kgs) both because there were only four main sharers and because of the higher productivity as a result of the efficiency in water management. Each shareholder was also able to take home 50 kgs of *rayda* (rape-seed) to process for cooking oil. One-third of the *rayda* was used at home and the rest was sold in the market (at a rate of Rs. 500/- per quintal, 1986-87 prices). According to Chakra, whose father has a share in the machine, all the shareholders would meet at Dheema's house to decide the quantity of seeds to be sown and the quantity of fertiliser to be used. *Rayda* had been first sown in their fields three years previously. The shareholders continue its production because it gives a good yield and also requires less water than wheat.

The second well (W2) is run by a Persian wheel and has eight shareholders, who are the sons of RK, AK and NK. Dopa Chela, a descendant of NK, who lives in the nearest household in the adjacent Malwa *phalli* has an individual well on his land as well as a share in W2. This is because Dopa's father had jointly built the well with his brothers. Dopa's own well is a *paoti* (pulley-system well) which is not an efficient source of water for more than one field. Dopa, who lives on comparatively flat land, had built his own well with some help from his sons, and the help of one of the sons of the descendants of AK who lives near him. AK's descendant takes only drinking water from this well and also shares a portion of the small barley and millet crop grown around it. With the *paoti*, Dopa is able to water his corn crop in a weak monsoon and grow barley and millet apart from the 200 to 300 kilos of wheat he gets from the use of W2. Dopa's is among the few relatively prosperous households in the village. In Beechalli *phalli*, which has a concentration of Vaijjath households,

---

10. Each device was allowed to draw water for a stipulated amount of *beedi* time, or time it took to smoke an Indian cigarette, which was approximately ten minutes. The *beedi* time was measured onto a circular thread spool attached to the top of the wheel.

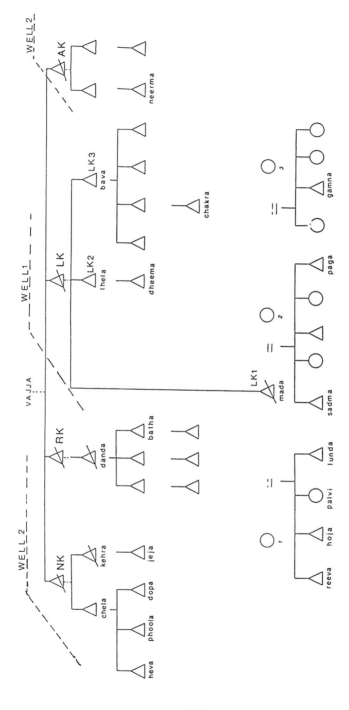

Figure 6.a Well Sharers in Beechalli *Phalli*

none are very prosperous although the machine owners on W1 are able to procure good crop outputs.

Usually, 'true' *(haga)* brothers form a shareholding group in a well and also irrigate a common section of land around it. The *haga* are all required to bring their ploughs *(hal)* and oxen and are later accompanied by their wives who sow the seed. Each house has one or two ploughs and, usually, a pair of oxen. The ploughing is done by all the brothers together in their shared plot in the fertile area. Ploughing involves furrowing *(kheriya)* and levelling *(mairi)* the land. The same ploughs are later run over the harvested crop in order to thresh it. While each household has its own oxen and plough, two or three households share the *mairi* instrument. The plough and the oxen, like pots, pans and earthen vessels, are considered the property of the individual sublineage households.

The possession of a plough and oxen allows men to realise their rights to water and land. Dopa has two oxen and was able to draw water at his pulley well and also contribute towards running the wheel on W2. Neerma (descendant of AK), who also lives in Malwa *phalli* is among the poorer householders in the Taivar village. He gave the reason for his poverty as the inability to buy an ox. Neerma's father has not helped to build a well. (His father's grand uncle had left the Taivar village in the Sapna famine, and Neerma has few *haga*.) Thus Neerma does not have shares in a well, nor can he build his own well without the help of oxen. He has crop shares in the irrigated land of his brothers and may use water from their wells for his household, but he can not use their well water for crop production. Therefore the sharing between sublineage brothers who do not contribute major inputs to production is restricted to crops and water for household consumption. Similarly, the non-Taivar households who do not possess wells or have 'true' brothers in the village are allowed by the Taivars to use water for consumption purposes only. This allows the non-Taivar households in the village to survive, but not prosper.

The water for household and for personal use is usually obtained from the well nearest the household. Palvi's *ghar-jamai* household in Beechalli *phalli* is equidistant from the wells W1 and W2 but she and the members of her household use water from W1, which belongs to her *haga* brothers, rather than from W2, which belongs to her other sublineage brothers. When Palvi's goats return from grazing in the forest they drink water from W1. Whenever households have disagreements, the drinking rights of livestock are the first to be restricted. Only when the quarrel is very serious does it affect the rights of the Taivar to use water for personal consumption. Thus, while water used for personal and livestock purposes is negotiable between kin, water for the irrigation is not negotiable and is based on gendered rights through descent.

Sublineage members share not only water and land resources but also a degree of work together. The occasions for collective labour *(halmo)* usually revolve around the work surrounding the joint management of water and land shares and is thus the labour that is shared between the *haga,* work which women did not do. The collective labour *(halmo)* involved in ploughing, weeding, threshing and harvesting the irrigated crop is contributed by members who share the same well-water. This is in contrast to the production of the maize crop which involves no water sharing and is ploughed, harvested and threshed by members of a single household. Whenever an operation requires a number of workers, outside the context of well sharing, a *halmo* (collective labour group) is called *(halmo bulana)* by the household which requires the help. Most frequently, a *halmo* takes place when assistance is required to transport large quantities of materials. For example, the *halmo* takes place at times when the grass in the *donga khetar* had been cut or the maize requires immediate weeding. All members who participate in the *halmo* are provided with specific types and quantities of food (see the next section). Unlike brothers working on irrigated land, the *halmo* work resembles daily wage labour for kind, and not one in which kin or the *haga* and sublineage brothers have rights in or duties towards.

Thus far, I have described the context of Taivar kinship within which the division of resources takes place. Accompanying this division is a specific ideology related to the consumption of food, which I shall deal with in the next section. But first, I will deal briefly with the forest as a resource that contributes to Taivar subsistence.

The Girasia gather wild cereals *(kodara, kang, mal, kura, homa),* vegetables, *(kankoda, jhumka, turiya, valoda, jhalra, koli, phong, ahor, gudi, vedon, seel, toison, bokhlo, puar, kohra)* and fruit *(ber, tibirna, dongra, chibra, mahua,* wild dates, mango and papaya) from the forest. The forest produces the cereal *kodara* and the wild vegetables immediately after the rains. Berries and dates are found in winter and summer. The Taivars also grow some vegetables around wells, and on the thorn fences directly outside their huts during the rainy season. Gourds, beans and local vegetables are grown in the rainy season, with chillies being grown in the later periods. Green chilli is an essential item and a favourite vegetable in the Girasia household. The Girasia occasionally purchase the cheapest seasonal vegetables from the market, these can include potatoes (Rs. 2-3/- per kilo) and aubergine (Rs. 1-2/- per kilo) in the winter and onions (Rs. 2-3/- per kilo) and chillies (Re 1/- per kilo) in the summer. Otherwise the Taivars purchase damaged vegetables from the vegetable sellers at Abu Road township for very low prices. In spite of the conditions of scarcity, I was struck by the fact that the Taivars constantly eat small snacks such as roasted chick peas, roasted sesame seeds with molasses, cucumbers, berries, mangoes, wild fruits and roasted maize when the crop was good. Although I did not make a survey of their nutritional intake, my observations would suggest that a high percentage of Taivar vitamin, fibre and protein intake comes from this level of consumption. Food that is gathered or grown on a smaller scale forms just as important a part in the Taivar diet as the staple cereal, particularly when the monsoons are weak or fail altogether. Apart from cereals, vegetables and fruit, the Girasia eat meat. The most regular supply is in the herds of goats owned by individual households. These are usually sacrificed on an occasion when there are members of more than one household present. Often birds and rabbits are hunted by the men and boys, but they form an irregular supply and are usually consumed by individual households.

In the next section I describe how the proscriptions relating to food consumption reflect the concerns of the Taivar Girasia with identity and status. The Taivars have very fixed ideas regarding which food may be consumed on one's own and which food is to be shared.

Food Transactions and Status

Both raw and processed food has a particular value among the Girasia. I find that I can best describe the position of food as one which is similar to other Girasia property, such as land, labour and water. The most distinguishing characteristic of food is that, like other forms of property, it is shared (under certain conditions) amongst natal but not affinal kin. In this section I concentrate on food transactions within the lineage as yet another means of understanding the nature of the boundaries constructed by the Taivars which have implications for the lives of Taivar women. The Taivars believe that sharing food brings auspiciousness. In this sense food is seen to contribute, even if indirectly, towards the cure of social and physical ailments.[11] Food is therefore not only a serious category related to the

---

11. All aches, pains, minor and major sickness required an appeasing of the afflicting spirit by the offerings of food (either directly or through the medium of adults or children).

immediate satisfaction of hunger, but also one which reflects the ideals of the community and addresses wider issues of solidarity and equality. I use the example of a *nyath* (death-related feast) to illustrate the nature of food transactions between households and sublineages within the lineage and with other lineages.

Nearly every study on the social organisation of caste groups in India has a section on the nature of food transactions. The importance of food transactions lies in the fact that, apart from marriage, commensality is the major indicator of differences in status between caste groups. For Dumont (1980), for example, differences between types of food, and the social relationship of those who consume, is an expression of purity and/or pollution, which in turn sets up a hierarchy between groups. In a recent study, Raheja (1988) challenges Dumont's assertion that hierarchy is the main principle governing the nature and directions of prestations within and between caste groups.[12] Raheja's illustration of the elaborate nature of Gujar transactions is useful in understanding those exchanges between the Taivar Girasia which are based on differences, not necessarily conceived in hierarchical terms.

Living amongst brothers, as the Taivars do, there is nevertheless a strict code amongst members of the sublineage with regard to the consumption of food. Underlying the Girasia etiquette regarding food is a strong sense of not burdening a brother with the necessity of providing hospitality. The Taivars consider hospitality to contain the seeds of obligation, which implies letting others have a means of controlling oneself (see also the section on the context of fieldwork in chapter 1). To prevent the burden of hospitality from falling on kin, all Taivar social occasions which are followed by the distribution

---

12. In order to account for all the types of prestations between the communities in the multi-caste village of Pahansu (north-western Uttar Pradesh), Raheja argues that the relationships of centrality, mutuality and exchange are more important than hierarchy as a principle foregrounding relationships within the Gujar dominant caste, and between the Gujar and fourteen other castes. The Gujars have the prerogative to offer *dan*, or gifts, to other castes in the village in order to transfer ritual inauspiciousness away from them (relations of centrality). The Gujars also give shares of the produce to the service castes 'attached' to the Gujar household, in the sense that they provide specific and routine services (relations of mutuality or *len-den*). Fixed 'contract-like' transactions take place with members of 'non-attached' castes who provide temporary services (relations of exchange or *badla*). Within these relations of centrality, mutuality and exchange there is a further relative gradation, according to the notions of sharing and payment, between those who are *lage-hue*, or considered a part of, and those who are considered *alag* (different or separate) by the Gujars.

of food, take place outside the household. Apart from the concern with hospitality, meeting in a public place also indicates a desire to increase the accessibility of the occasion to other brothers. Meetings amongst a few kin of a household occur only when certain private matters have to be discussed and often invite comments of conspiracy from other households. The frequent collective gatherings for ritual occasions, which occur several times a month, also take away the need for Girasia hospitality. At all these occasions the members of a sublineage or sublineages participating contribute stipulated amounts of food. As I shall describe in detail, using the example of a funeral feast later on in the section, the collective consumption of food is in contrast to the daily organisation of meals.

Continuous small-scale consumption and the different work patterns of household members reduce the importance of the daily meal as a social occasion in the Taivar village. Often the main meal of *roti* and a watery curry is stored in a large earthern pot *(kothi)* for household members to eat as and when they wish. Members of the family who go to the jungle to herd the goats (either the young or the elderly) or to cut wood (adult men and women), carry their *roti* with them. Similarly, family members who go to the market to sell wood or cots, also carry their *roti*. This food pattern is partly a result of famine conditions. In times of abundant rain and good crops the family works nearer home and consequently eats together more often. In times when maize is sufficient, most households eat *rab* or *doe* (a mixture of cornflour porridge, salt and chillies to which buttermilk is added) in the mornings. Roti is usually eaten either in the late afternoon or as the evening meal, or when working away from the house. In large households, it is particularly tedious and time-consuming for women to make *roti* for all the members and therefore there is a practical side to its restriction to one meal. Women are, however, subject to a number of constraints with regard to the consumption and distribution of food.

Implications for Women

The importance of food in marking Taivar relationships is particularly evident where women were concerned. Like food, women are superficially property-like, because they are 'detachable' and serve to define the boundaries of the Girasia groups within which the movement of food takes place. I do not suggest that women can be equated with food or considered as property. On the contrary, I suggest that their 'detachability' from the natal group gives them the appearance of being like food and other forms of Taivar property. However, unlike food and other property, they carry aspects of the natal group of which they are extensions (a similar point has been made by Strathern, 1984).

As already mentioned in chapters 4 and 5, the participation of wives in cooking and eating at feasts is restricted. In general, the activity of cooking is not regarded as degrading, above all when performed for special occasions. In feasts prepared outside the domestic space, whether for the brothers or for the deities of the lineage, it is the Taivar men who cook and distribute the food. Within the household, the women prepare the daily meal. In the context of the food prepared for household consumption, a wife's cooking is controlled. For example, when 'guests' (relatives) visit households, the husband cooks for them as a sign of respect. Only if the guests are themselves slightly inferior in lineage status does the wife cook for them, as she does for her own kin when they visit her husband's village. Moreover, if the daughter of a lineage marries into a 'lower' affinal lineage, her own natal lineage members also eat food cooked only by her husband, thus compounding her degradation.

From these observations, it is clear that wives are considered as bearers of impurity who can transmit inauspiciousness (impurity, sin, immorality) when dispensing food to those beyond their social and structural positions. The sisters and daughters of Taivar men are not able to assume positions of ritual authority but, unlike wives, they may eat with Taivar men and can cook for their feasts. Wives are distinguished from sisters, I was told, because they come from other Girasia lineages, with whom food is not shared but paid for, as the following example illustrates. Nota, a Raijjat Taivar, had no children from his earlier wife nor from Dhanki his present one. He paid Rs 550/- in brideprice for a third wife. He was able to get her 'cheap' *(kem dapa)* because she was a widow and had five sons to look after. On the death of her husband, the woman had returned to her lineage as she was still in the fertile span of her life and could find another man to live with. She bore Nota a son. (Nota could not 'buy' her other sons as they were members of her former husband's lineage). The woman had the baby at the home of her brothers and decided not to go to Nota's house (possibly because of the expected hostility from Dhanki and the work load placed on her as a 'new bride'). She was, however, expected to give Nota 'his' child. So the woman brought the baby to Abu Road where she gave it to Dhanki and Nota. What surprised me was that her brothers returned her brideprice, which I was told was expected of them. When I questioned Dhanki as to the reason the woman was not given anything in return for the conception, Dhanki replied:

> When the woman was pregnant with the child here, we spent money on 2 kilos of *ghee*, 10 kilos of *atta, ajwain, hoonth* etc. to feed her. This totalled to Rs 140/- plus. We are not asking for this to be returned.

Implicit in Dhanki's explanation was the notion that the expenditure on food undertaken by Nota was a sufficient compensation for the woman. The expenditure on food was taken as an adequate repayment for reproduction, by both the wife-giving and the wife-taking lineages. Food was often considered acceptable in exchange for work. Children who are often 'adopted' into households for the purposes of their labour (see chapter 7) are not paid, but given food. For the child's parents, the feeding of the child is considered a sufficient compensation for their work. While 'adopted' boys can inherit land from their adoptive fathers over and above the food they receive, girls are only given food (just as wives are only fed for their reproductive services, described in the example above).

The affinal lineages from where the wives come are lineages with whom a Taivar may eat food. The context of eating together is more symbolic than representative of the actual situation, since affines usually pay, either directly or indirectly, for their food. For example, at an engagement ceremony at the girl's house, the boy's family either bring their own food or pay the host family in advance for the meals consumed during their visit. Eating together implies, however, that members of the groups are of a similar (marital) standing. The fact that the affinal lineages are of a similar commensal standing is also reflected by the fact that wives then cook for men of both their natal and affinal lineages.

The ability to provide food is central to Girasia notions of well-being and reflects the way in which they perceive most social institutions and processes. For example, the brideprice itself is considered a payment to compensate for the expenditure made by the bride's father in feeding and clothing her, and not for the loss of her labour as is commonly supposed. Furthermore, the prospective bride's male kin visit the boy's village to inspect his land and assets, 'to be assured their daughter is fed well.'[13] The attitude towards food reflects the

---

13. Rosaldo and Collier (1981) show how in brideprice societies men establish their claims over women by distributing produce off the land to the wife-givers. Among the Girasia, there was no distribution of produce to win wives. The bargaining power during *hagai*, or the financial settlement of brideprice, depended on the survey of the groom's assets. The lower the capacity of food production

relationship between the wife-givers and the wife-takers throughout the period they are so related. For example, Chakra Taivar's sister-in-law was pregnant with her first baby and it was expected that she would go to her natal home to have it delivered. But she could not go on her own accord and had to wait for her mother or her brother to come and collect her. On other occasions, Chakra's brother had usually accompanied her to her village. But this time it was different. Chakra explained that, if she left earlier, her father and brothers would feel that her husband's lineage were avoiding the cost of feeding her during her pregnancy. However, because she was pregnant with a baby which would belong to another lineage, no urgency was expressed by her natal kin for her return.

From the above it is clear that the aspect of a woman's life which is most controlled by her natal and affinal families is related to her consumption of food. Among the Girasia an access to food is determined by gender and age and above all, is related to the concerns with status of the lineage, especially its male members. I would argue that, while women have an access to the productive resources mediated through men, they have no power in the distribution of food which, because it is connected to status and prestige, is a highly politicised process among the Girasia. In other words, when the distribution of food is a question of status, women are distanced from its control. Middle- and upper-caste women become in charge of distribution systems only when they are sufficiently attached to their husband's group (i.e., as mothers). Girasia women who are never sufficiently attached to their husband's lineage take a greater part in the distributive processes in their role as daughters and sisters rather than as wives, but as they live in their huband's village may do so only on special occasions and are thus further removed from a control over their lives than other caste women.

Collective Occasions

For work requiring collective labour *(halmo)* which involves the whole day, the person initiating the *halmo* has to provide *raab* or *doe* in the morning, and *roti* or *gugri* (boiled corn) in the evening. For jobs of less than a day, *gugri* is usually distributed, followed by *doe,* while

---

of the boy's family, the higher the amount of brideprice demanded. In the reverse case, the girl's side had a reduced base to bargain from. With equal assets, the decisions took much longer and were closer to the average brideprice rate (see chapter 7).

roti is made only when there are few helpers involved. (*Doe* and *gugri* are more divisible than *roti* and therefore practical when a large number of helpers are present). A primary incentive for the Taivars to participate in a *halmo* or collective work party is the distribution of food that takes place afterwards. Dhanki had spent several days working in the forest collecting grass and leaves. The day before she wanted these transported, she *halmo bulana* (literally, called a *halmo*). Usually it is women, young men and children who participate in those *halmos* which are not for ploughing or ritual activities. Dhanki informed the households of her husband's sublineage, who then sent a member or two. Dhanki told me, 'We call *halmo* first among the houses of the sublineage, because we give food on these occasions.' In other words, whenever there is a distribution of food involved, as much as possible, the hosts must first see that their closest relatives are fed. Although frequently only one member from each household attends the *halmo*, the food obtained was usually taken back to the household and shared.[14]

Collective Taivar consumption, as I observed during fieldwork, only takes place at feasts. At all feasts there are stipulated contributions of food which are made. The collective contribution and consumption is reinforced by the fact that all occasions where more than one household consumes food together have an attached ritual significance. Girasia feasts are occasions where the special foods such as *laphi, churma, matar* or *khichri* (see the following account of a funeral feast) are made. The largest feasts occur at the annual *Bhakar baosi* (mountain deity) worship and the *Shitala satam* (pox goddess) celebration. Annually, there are also the *beej* (literally seed, meaning ancestor worship) and *phulera mata* (mother deity) rituals of worship, which are organised by each sublineage separately. In addition, every three months a *rati jaga* worship ritual is held in each of the four shrines *(devra)* to the protector spirit *Bhairu*. At these occasions groups of sublineage members host other sublineage in the village. (In chapter 8, I describe the ritual occasions of the Taivars and the involvement of the sublineage members). At the feasts accompanying the ritual occasions, contributions to the feasts are almost always mandatory and involve equal contributions from all the sublineage member-households. Death and marriage are the only lifecycle stages which are celebrated. Births are not celebrated by feasts, nei-

---

14. Even amongst those children who were given a midday meal at the school, which was subsidised by aid agencies, I found a number of them taking their portions of *daliya* (wheat porridge) home.

ther is puberty. Moreover, as I noted in the previous chapter, marriage celebrations are not frequent. Below, I use the example of a funeral feast because death and sickness involved the Taivars in the most frequent ritual feasting.

Funeral feast for Pema's daughter-in law

Pema Taivar is an elder of the Khetrath sublineage and also among the leading *patels* (lineage leaders) who lives in Nichalli *phalli*. His son Natha and Natha's wife and baby stayed in the house adjoining Pema's house. During my sojourn in the Taivar village, Natha's wife (of Vanhiya lineage of Girasias) died. She had been ill for the past year with *bukhar* (fever). Pema and Natha organised her funeral in the Taivar village. The real ceremonies *(nyath)* began only after approximately a month, as I was told it took time to inform all the relatives and gather all the material *(saman)* for the rituals and feasts.

The body of the dead person is buried on the day of the death (in a north-south direction with the face turned towards the east; this is the direction the deities come from; see chapter 8).[15] The clothes worn by the dead person are torn in one place so that the *jeev* (soul) is not identified when it returns. The face is cleaned with water and a coin is placed in the mouth. Water is sprinkled in the grave. Between the time of the death, and the burial, no members of the deceased's *haga* household drinks water, or smokes. Food is eaten without *masala* (spices). After returning from the burial, the *haga* members perform *kulla* (washing the mouth with water) and also wash their faces, hands and legs with water. All the male members of the bereaved familiy tie white turbans after which water-drinking and *beedi* smoking commence. Women of the nearby households bring *roti* for the bereaved family when they come to *rona* (cry loudly with women of the household). Within the next week a group of children, not less than five in number, will be fed *laphi* (wheat flour boiled in water, molasses and clarified butter). Only after this ceremony (the first *kandiya*) can family members consume clarified butter, milk, butter-milk or tea.[16]

15. In some cases I was told that the body was cremated. In fact, burying was done only in cases where a *bhopa* (ritual mediator) or a child had died. However, due to the economic hardships of the previous years, and the need to sell wood for money, the numbers buried had increased.
16. When young children die the first *kandiya* excludes the death ceremonies. But for adults the first *kandiya* is used to meet and decide on a date for the *nyath* ceremonies. It is only when the *nyath* is over, that women of the household stop the

Identity, Gender and Poverty

The actual funeral consists of three consecutive ceremonies: (1) the *hankaudar* (or ritual departure of the soul from the body); (2) the (second and major) *kandiya* or 'feast', and (3) the *nyath* ceremonies (ritual of blessing and consecration). Before these ceremonies could begin, Pema spent approximately Rs. 1,245/- on a number of items (see table 6.5), mainly on the food required for the rituals and feasting. The expenditure for both funerals and weddings is a large amount of money in relation to the income of a Taivar household. The largest sums of monetary income come from the lump sum payments for the Girasia bonded, seasonal wage labour and from brideprice amounts (see chapter 7). Whereas marriages may be delayed in the absence of finance, there is no such choice with funerals, considered ritually more important.

Table 6.5: Expenditure on the Funeral of Pema's Daughter-in-Law.

Item	Quantity (kg/sp)	Expenditure (Rs/-)
Wheat	200	300/-
Molasses	30	120/-
Refined clarified butter	5	125/-
Crude clarified butter	0.5	30/-
Mustard oil	1.5	33/-
Chick-peas	10	40/-
Goat	1 pc	200/-
Dried red chillies	2	24/-
Salt	8	4/-
Turmeric (whole)	1	20/-
Garlic pods	0.5	12/-
Spices (cumin, black pepper, coriander)	–	10/-
Red turban cloth	80 hds	140/-
Red cloth	12 hds	32/-
Thin red cloth	1 pc	24/-
Beedi-cigarette	–	80/-
Matches	1 dz	1.50/-
Services of the Kombariya	–	50/- (or 1 goat)
TOTAL Expenditure		1,245.50/-

Key: sp=spelling, pc=percent, hds=hands, dz=dozen
Source: Primary fieldwork data

---

ritual crying for the deceased. The crying before the *nyath* usually takes place each morning, or when any 'guest' comes to visit.

Resource Management and the Divisions of Kinship and Gender

As we go through the three main ceremonies, we see how each of the items in the table are used. Only the male members of the Taivar lineage attend the first *hankaudar* ceremony. Both men and women of the deceased woman's immediate natal family *(hagavale)* join in at the end of the *hankaudar* ceremony. The *hankaudar* is essentially performed to break the earthly connections of the *jeev* (soul). In Pema's household the *hankaudar* lasted from 11.30 pm (the night before) until 5.30 am (the next morning). A major part of the time is spent in the construction of the ritual site *(path budiyo)* by four ritual specialists called *khoont*.[17] The head *khoont* was a non-Taivar Girasia of the Bubariya lineage who lived in the village. The other two *khoonts* were Taivars, while the fourth was Pema's *bhanej* (sister's son, and therefore a non-Taivar). The head *khoont* was assisted by a specially appointed *kotwal* (guardian) who was also a non-Taivar Girasia of the Ninoma lineage, living in the Taivar village.

Once the ritual site had been prepared for the *hankaudar* ceremony, the *churma* (wheat flour fried in oil and molasses) was made. Once the *churma* was brought, all the food offerings (large sugar crystals, dates, coconut, *churma*) were put on the ritual site and the ceremony of departure began.[18] After the ceremony, the *path* was

17. The *path budiyo* commences with the purification and marking of the ritual site with moist cowdung and wheat flour (the latter is placed over a matrix design made with the cowdung). As is the case in marriage ceremonies with the bride and groom (chapter 4), the *khoont* does not leave the *path* unattended at any time. The initial *path (sona)* is covered with two cloths *(ausar)*, first white and then red. On top of this the second *path (rupa)* was constructed with animal and abstract designs drawn in rice grain. While the second *path* is readied by one *khoont*, the head *khoont* prepares a grass doll (of *dab* grass) and the other *khoonts* prepare a sacred stick and grass ring. Finally, four balls of wheat are made sacred by touch and recitation and shaped into four *diya* (lights) which are placed at the four corners of the *path*. The *path* was then ready for the *hankaudar* ritual.
18. In front of the *path* is placed a broken earthen water pot into which cotton thread *(kokri)* is hung from a bamboo pole tied to the rafter. Mango and *beel* leaves are tied to the string and the grass doll and a toy grass ladder are placed in the broken pot. A red cloth covers the string, doll and the contents of the pot. Vermillion powder *(sindoor)* is sprinkled in the base of the pot. Then offerings of milk are made by all kin, who each pour five small thimblefulls of milk into the pot. This is done, I was told, because '*Jeev gaay ki poonch ko pakar kar aage badhta hai*' (the *jeev* progresses by catching the cow's tail; Hindi translation by Phoola). In the order of relatives, the milk is first offered by the husband's immediate male family members, then by the eldest male, down to the youngest 'sister' of the deceased woman. After this, the doll representing the female *jeev* (because the dead person was a woman), 'climbs' (in the audience's imagination) the seven steps of the ladder. At each step *yamdoot*, the god of death asks, through the *khoont*, for a *dan* (prestation of money) in return for the sins committed by the *jeev*

dismantled and the floor was freshly coated with cowdung and water *(leepna)*. Where the body had been buried, a plain stone was set up and worshipped. The *churma* that was distributed after the *hankaudar* was more in the nature of a *prasad* (blessed food) than a meal. So far, the materials used in the *hankaudar* had been provided by Pema.

The actual feasting started later in the morning with the *kandiya*. For this occasion all the Taivar male heads of households brought 2 *paili* atta (1 kg and 200g of wheat flour), 1 *dheenga* (log of wood) and *pattal* (leaves on which the food is served). For the *kandiya* a meal of *daliya* (wheat porridge), *dal* (lentil soup) and *goat* (spiced mutton curry) was prepared. While the meal was cooked, new white turbans *(kanjiya)* were tied to all the *haga vale* (natal male kin of the husband and of the deceased wife). The preparation and the consumption of the meal lasted from 10 am until approximately 3 pm. While all Pema's brothers in the Taivar lineage contributed equal shares to the feast, the deceased woman's natal kin *(piyar-vale)* were given food as guests. The *kandiya* is also a time when some *panchayati* (customary dispute settlements) are held, as it is an occasion when all the brothers gather. Usually both the accused and the accusor parties in a dispute are required to feed the *panch* (who are the sublineage elders and ritual specialisits; chapter 8). To initiate a *panchayati* at a *kandiya* is one way of reducing the expenditure on the frequent sittings of the *panchayati* while at the same time gaining the audience of the collective of brothers. After the *kandiya*, the heads of the *kanjiya-vale* (white-turbaned ones) are shaved.

The *nyath* ceremony follows the *kandiya* and has two interrelated focal points. Firstly, it allows the natal and affinal lineage members of the deceased, and the deceased woman's husband to send the *jeev* (soul) to an untroubled resting place in the 'other' world. Secondly, it allows the natal and affinal members the *jeev* leaves behind to return to their own routine life. To achieve the first objective, all the men and women (sisters and daughters) of the Taivar lineage, as well of the lineage of the deceased woman, gathered together in the field

---

during its lifetime. The dead woman's natal kin paid amounts of Rs. 2/- to 5/- at each step. Progressively, the steps are destroyed and after the last step is broken the *jeev* is considered to have cut all connections with the people on earth. The pot and its contents are then buried by the four closest male relatives of the deceased's husband. These men also perform *dhoop* (burn incense, and break a coconut) for the departed *jeev*. On their return they are asked by the head *khoont* 'how many of you have returned', and must reply, '*Mu aave tho mua, jeeviyo ve loajariya*' (four men and five *jeev* went, but four men and four *jeev* return). The red cloth and grain is given to the head *khoont*.

outside the household to pour water on the *peetal ghoda* (literally, brass horse, although it looked like a cow to me; approximately four and a half inches in height). The *peetal ghoda* was brought specially for the occasion by a *kombariya* (a man from the particular Girasia lineage who 'owned' the brass animal).[19] I was told, 'Without the *kombariya* there can be no *nyath*'. The *kombariya* was introduced to me as a *neench* lineage, or lower Girasia. The *kombariya* had come from the village Ranora, which was approximately thirty-two kilometres from Abu Road and to the east of the Taivar village. He was accompanied by his son, brother, brother's son, sister (all of whom belonged to the Gamar lineage) and the wives of the three men (who were all lower Bubarnis).

The final ceremony of the *nyath* involved the tying of the red turbans (*tateru*), an indication that the relatives could return to a 'normal' life. All the eldest male brothers in Pema's sublineage, the eldest representatives of the other sublineage (*bhopas* and *patels*; see chapter 8), as well as the four *khoont* sat in two rows to receive the gifts of red cloth, money (amounts of Rs. 1/- and Rs. 2/-) and tobacco (*bidi, zarda*) from Pema's *jamai* (DH, BDH). These offerings were then counted (forty-two red cloths had been presented). After the prestations, the red turbans were tied, first on those among Pema's family who wore the white turbans and then on the other Taivar elders. One red turban was tied to 'every *bhai*' (in practice, to every male household head) in the village. The head *khoont*, because he was a Bubariya (non-Taivar), received the cloth but did not tie it on his head. After the turbans had been tied, the congregation had a meal of *khichri* (wheatflour and lentils boiled together with salt and chillies). As with all the meals, Pema's sublineage brothers prepared the

19. The *nyath* commenced with all the *piyar vale* (natal kin) of the deceased placing pieces of white cloth around Natha and his son. Then each man, followed by the women, poured three handfuls of water over the *peetal ghoda*. According to Phoola, water was used because it was like the *ganga* (the Ganges water considered holy by the Hindus). Women of the deceased's natal (non-Taivar) kin poured water on the *ghoda* before the deceased's male, or female affinal kin (i.e., Natha's natal kin). No Taivar woman had been present at the *hankaudar* ceremony. Even during the *nyath*, both affinal and natal women stayed close to the household, only emerging for the *ghoda* ritual, or for the feast that followed. After pouring water on the *ghoda*, each person also placed a few coins, or handfuls of wheat, or corn grains, on the sheet placed near the brass animal. These were for the *kombariya* and were picked up by his son. (Pema himself would give a separate 'payment' of Rs. 50/- or a goat; a matter which had not been settled completely beforehand). At the end of the water pouring (*peetal ghoda*) ceremony small pieces of molasses were distributed (similar to when disputes were settled) and the men proceeded to the next ceremony.

food under Pema's supervision and the guidance of the other Taivar elders. The night of the *nyath* was spent in eating, drinking (although Pema did not mention the expenses on liquor) and in the entertainment of songs and dances provided by the *kombariya* and his family.[20] On the morning after the *nyath*, Pema tied red turbans on all men of the deceased's family. The guests then ate a meal of *daliya* and left to return to their own villages.

The *nyath* ceremony was based on the the understanding that all the lineage brothers would participate and contribute to the feast. In this sense, the Taivar sublineages and the lineage acted as collective hosts to the visiting Girasia from the affinal lineages. While the lineage brothers contributed food for the *nyath*, members of the other affinal, non-Taivar lineages only contributed non-edible items, such as money and cloth. There was thus a hierarchy, between those who were similar and equal members of the Taivar lineage, and the affinal lineage members, who were 'equal but different'. The lowest position in this hierarchy was occupied by the lower lineage *kombariya*, who provided the services of the brass horse and the entertainment. All the ritual specialists in the *nyath* ceremonies were Girasia who were related to Pema. Two of the *khoonts* were Taivars and members of Pema's own lineage, the other *khoonts* and the *kotwal* were members of Pema's affinal lineages and finally, the *kombariya* was a member of a lower Girasia lineage. That only Taivar men made standardised contributions of food, demonstrates that food can be shared and eaten without obligation (*sharm*, shame) by members within a lineage. All the other lineages were guests who ate food which belonged to, and was cooked by the Taivars (in spite of the fact that the guests, or affinal lineages, including the deceased's lineage contributed a substantial amount of money towards the *nyath*).[21]

The social differences between those who contributed and consumed food and those who only consumed it was further reflected in the prestation of the red turban cloths. The *jamai* (DH, BDH) affinal

20. The *kombariya* and his son took turns to play the *harangi* (stringed instrument), while his two brothers played the *dholak* (drum) and the women played the *majira* (bells). They earned money from the Girasia audience as they performed.
21. The various rituals and feasts must be carried out in proper detail, as there is always the fear that a dissatisfied *jeev* may return to harass the living. I was told that it was especially the *huhara vale* (affinal relatives) who have to fear the sickness and death the *jeev* might inflict. It is well known that the *huhara vale* of a woman always gave her more trouble than her *piyar vale* (natal kin). In a recent study, Lambert (1990) has pointed to similar beliefs regarding spirit-induced fevers, aches, and pains, among the Brahman, Gujar, and Rajput caste families living close to Jaipur, the capital city of Rajasthan (ibid.: 13).

lineages presented the turbans which were then used by Pema to honour his own lineage brothers. The *kombariya,* who was neither in the brother category nor a member of the equal affinal lineages, was paid an exact amount for his services. The transactions of food and money at the *nyath* indicate that there is a gradation among the Girasia along kin and caste lines, which is very similar to that in multi-caste communities (for example, Raheja 1988). Those Girasia relations which revolved around rituals and feasting, were relations among kin (agnatic and affinal) and were distinct from the purely economic service-orientated relationship with some castes in the market (discussed in the final section of this chapter).

In their food transactions, I found the Girasia as preoccupied as other caste members with degrees of purity and pollution and the importance of the collective rather than the individual (Selwyn 1980, Khare 1976, Dumont 1980, Marriott 1976, Raheja 1988).[22] In the *nyath* ceremonies, relations between the Girasia are expressed by the transfer of substances which, apart from food, are the materials used in the ritual (for example, milk, cow dung, water, fire, grains, fruit, sugar). The use of these substances as pure or sacred materials in the rituals is similar to their use in rituals by other castes. This reveals that the Girasia, like other caste Hindus, believe in the 'active' power of substances. Furthermore, the Girasia also believe that for food to be beneficial it has to be exchanged with other members of the community. Among the Girasia, as with the non-Girasia castes, the benefits of sharing are qualified by the notions of kinship. The Girasia, like other Hindus, experience their commensal relations as an idiom of kinship. It is in this light that the feasts and the occasions where food is collectively consumed become important as indicators of inclusion or exclusion from levels of their community. In this latter role, the Girasia and other Hindu systems of food transactions become a 'powerful instrument of social control' (Selwyn, 1980: 315). One major difference, however, between the Girasia and the upper castes is that the Girasia exchange food more within, rather than outside, their caste boundaries.

The rules relating to the distribution of food allow the Taivar Girasia to 'buy' the services of other Taivars (in the *halmo*), of other Girasia (such as the *kombariya*) and, above all, allows them to attend the social and ritual occasions in their lineage. It is in this sense that I see

22. While most of these studies concentrate on transactions at the boundaries of caste groups, Khare (1976) and Raheja (1988) are notable exceptions, as they provide an equally detailed analysis of both inter- and intra-caste transactions.

food as occupying a property-like position among the Taivars. Girasia women are restricted in both their consumption and participation in the processing of food, in a manner which is similar to their weak control over the other resources such as land, water, and labour.

The Market and Girasia Identity

The Girasia role in the market economy was most forcefully brought home to me in the comments of a Marwari businessman in Abu Road. Chaganlal is a Marwari dealer in printed mill cloth. According to him, a large proportion of the small shops in Abu Road town owe their survival to the Girasia.[23] Chaganlal himself earns his livelihood solely by the sale of cloth to the Girasia (for their *ghagra, jhulki, odhani, dhoti, saafa*) and by tailoring Girasia garments. Although Chaganlal complained that he had to spend time 'talking to' (convincing) the Girasia, he said that he made good money especially in the marriage or festival season (when he could get up to a hundred customers a day). Chaganlal's observations, I believe, are important in dispelling two related misconceptions regarding the 'tribal' or other marginal groups. The first is that 'tribal' economies, have been historically self-sufficient and isolated in their economic relations; the second is that in their contact with market economies marginal groups participate as subordinate and peripheral economic agents. A third point, I observed, regarding the market dimension of Girasia lives, is the manner in which relationships with other castes and other Girasias in the market serve to define Taivar Girasia identity, not only as a distinct community but also as a separate lineage of Girasia.

As buyers, the Girasia have always purchased a large proportion of their basic needs, apart from the food they produce in good monsoon periods, from the market. The Taivars bought a large quantity of low-priced items and a few relatively expensive items from the Abu Road market.[24] The clothes of women are especially expensive

23. Apart from the town's market, the Girasia have service-orientated, economic relations with some of the neighbouring villagers for the procurement of certain village-specific goods. But for a majority of their economic transactions, the town acts as the larger economic centre.
24. The few household items bought regularly are groundnut or mustard oil, sugar, molasses, tea, matches, snuff, soap and spices (whole turmeric, salt, coriander and cumin seeds and garlic pods). Sometimes wheat grains are bought, as mentioned above. Most houses have one kerosene lamp and buy oil to light it. Other houses may have small luxuries in their inventories, such as a lock, scissors, a

and are bought once or twice a year, although wraps *(odhani)* are bought more frequently.[25] Jewellery, particularly the silver ornaments, forms another major portion of the expenditure of a household. As sellers, the Girasia occupy important, but peripheral positions, reflected in the temporary and shifting spaces from where they sell the seasonal items demanded by other villagers and the townsfolk. The impact of deforestation, famine, drought and policies restricting the sale of forest products (discussed in chapter 3), have been responsible for weakening the position of the Girasia as sellers in the Abu Road market.

The Girasia have economic relations with only some of the service castes in the nearby villages. For example, they have no contact with the washermen *(dhobi)* or the barber *(nai)* castes, as each Girasia household is self-sufficient in these functions. On the other hand, the Girasia did have economic interactions with those castes who included the manufacture of products in their services. For example, among the service castes in Ore and Deldar villages, the Taivars exchange or buy items from the *kumhar* (Hindu potter),[26] the *moyla* (Muslim potter)[27]

---

bag, a few cups and saucers and a bucket. Apart from the separate stores which sell cloth and jewellery (the silversmith and the bangle-seller), most other items are purchased from a general store. All items for the Taivar rituals are purchased from the market. The more regular ritual requirements (such as coconut, molasses, incense) can be bought at the same general provision store. For the special ritual requirements, the Taivars seek special shops in the nearby villages.

25. Typical *ghagra* prices in 1986-87 were from Rs. 150/- onwards and for a *jhulki* were approximately Rs. 60/-.

26. The *kumhar* is the only artisan to make the clay horse *(ghoda,* at Rs. 7/- each) which the Girasia 'sacrifice' *(chadana)* to the mountain god *(Bhakar baosi)*. He also makes the clay *dhoopkarni* (incense holder, Rs. 0.50/-) which holds the sacred ash at the Taivar rituals. Furthermore, among the *kumhars*, there is only one special family living in the village Molela (a day's journey by bus from Abu Road) who make the clay tablets *(murti)* representing the five deities in the Taivar shrine *(devra)*. The potters of Molela are the only source of the painted clay images in the whole of Rajasthan (each two-foot tablet costs Rs. 60/-). The fact that the Molela potters also supply the clay tablets to a number of other communities indicates that, although the clay forms are worshipped in different communities by different names, the images and forms worshipped are common in the region (especially popular are the images of the clan-mother and goddess *kul-devi* and the male protector Bhairu, described in chapter 8). For special ritual items made of steel, such as the *guruj* and the *hankal*, the Girasia travel to specific households of ironsmiths in neighbouring villages.

27. On a more regular basis the *kumhar* in the nearby villages provide earthen drinking water pots *(matka,* at Rs. 3/-) and earthen well attachments *(dhak,* at Rs. 0.75/- per piece). The *kumhar* (Hindu potters) made only water pots, in the range of vessels used in the household. Earthen vessels for cooking such as the *tolri*

and the *meghwal mochi* (shoemaker).[28] The Taivars often buy the items from the artisan castes in cash, in kind or on credit, depending on the season and their own sales in the market.

Duda explained to me that in times of a good rain and abundant crop, the Girasia sold ten to twenty kilos of their *makka* (corn) at a time. Two to three years ago, he remembered, the price for 10 kilos of corn was between Rs. 10/- to 12/-. Now he could sell the same amount of corn at Rs. 25/-, because corn was not easily available. However, he would not sell the little he had because he only sold corn when he had produced it in excess. In other words, the Girasia sell only when they have an abundant corn crop, which is also when the price in the market is at its lowest. The Taivars were more cautious in selling their corn crop in the year of my fieldwork, although nearly all the households sold bundles of dried foliage *(vanda)* at prices ranging from Rs. 8/- to 15/- per bundle. *Vanda*s were usually sold in the months of November and December. For most of the other months of the year the *bhara* (bundle of sticks collected from the forest) are sold at prices ranging from Rs. 3/- to Rs. 6/- per bundle and weighing approximately six kilos. Bundles of the more expensive and strong *khaida* wood, called *gaitha*, are sold in winter and are an important source of heating in the town and nearby villages. Individual wooden poles *(khoonti)* and *vans* or bamboo sticks (Rs. 20/- for a bundle of 20) are other items sold by the Girasia.[29] Often the households from Nichalli *phalli* would take their bundles of wood to the Ore and Deldar villages which were closer to their end of the Taivar village. The groups of women who carry the wood loads would also take a *gola* or earthern pot so that they can bring buttermilk in exchange (a payment in buttermilk is preferred by the Girasia in times of famine when they have little milk and few milk

---

(pot), *tava* (earthen plate to roast bread) and *gola* (for porridge) are made by the Muslim potters called *moyla*. The Muslim potter, unlike the Hindu, frequently carries his wares to the *Bhakar* on a donkey.

28. Unlike the potters, the *mochi* (shoe-maker) in Deldar talked of a declining trade with the Girasia. He used to sell many more pairs of sturdy and long-lasting shoes to the Girasia for prices between Rs. 60/- and Rs. 100/-. In recent years he complained that his trade had suffered with the introduction of cheaper plastic (pvc) shoes in the town's market, which cost only Rs. 12 to 15/- a pair. The Girasia in the Taivar village continue to buy only the less expensive items from the *mochi*, such as the *belon-ki-rai* (leather plough harness, at Rs. 15/- per piece) and *belon-ki-moori, dori* (leather mouth and horn piece for a pair of oxen, at Rs. 30/- a pair) and the *gophen* (sling, costing Rs. 5/- to 6/-).

29. Hence the whole population of the Abu Road *tehsil*, not just the Girasia, are involved in the deforestation of the *Bhakar*.

products). Some households would sell a couple of goats in the winter to the Muslim *kasai* (butcher) who visited the Taivar village for his meat supplies which he knew would be cheap following periods of drought or scarcity.

Duda said that the year of my fieldwork differed from other years because the Girasia were selling *dheenga* (large logs of wood at Rs. 20/- to 30/- each), which they normally used for their own purposes as well as *handoo* (livestock fodder, at Rs. 15/- per bundle). He said they were forced to sell these items because of the *kal* (famine). Most of the items fell in value as the winter progressed because more and more Girasia entered the market as sellers and there was an excess of supply. For example, the *dheenga* which cost Rs. 20/- to 30/- in November fell to Rs. 15/- in December. The same was true for some processed items, such as bed frames. Soma complained that at the end of December he had to go further away from Abu Road to find a suitable price (Rs. 25/- to 30/-) for a bed frame which had taken him two days to cut and design.[30] When the market for bed frames declined, the Taivars would often produce *khat-pag* (bed legs) which were sold for Rs. 10/- each. As sellers in the market the Girasia occupy subordinate positions. With rising inflation in the Indian economy, the depleting resources of the forest and the dependance on the vagaries of the monsoon, the Girasia role as voluntary sellers of goods and services is becoming more and more difficult to sustain. So far the Girasia have been integrated as buyers and sellers within the regional economy because they can fulfil the demand for certain forest requirements, and so far the price of being called 'tribal' is an easy one to pay for what the Girasia value as a restricted dependency on the the market.[31]

Above all, the Taivar contact with the market served to distinguish the rich and the poor in their lineage, as the example of Neerma's household below illustrates. Furthermore, in their role as wage labourers, the Taivar wives, daughters and sons reinforced the differences based on age and gender within the lineage. As the winter progressed, and particularly after a negligible corn harvest, the

---

30. Some Girasia households possess and use all the instruments of a carpenter *(hutar)*.
31. Gell has made a similar observation, more succintly. In an article on tribal market participation in Bastar, Gell noted: 'The effect of the market is to establish a stereotype of tribals, and tribal-Hindu relations, in which tribals retain actual control over their resource base, at the expense of becoming symbolically peripheral to Hindu society... For the Hindus it is the establishment of symbolic hegemony, for tribals, real security' (ibid.: 490).

members of a Girasia household diversify into various occupations. For example in Neerma's household, he made baskets,[32] while his wife collected wood to sell as *bhara*. Neerma's daughter had left home even before the corn harvest, to seek work as hired labour for the season at a tobacco firm. Neerma's unmarried adult son worked as a daily wage labourer on a construction site in Abu Road. Younger children in the household were occupied with less skilled jobs and usually collected forest produce, such as berries, *lac* (tree resin used in bangle production), *khakra* leaves (used as disposable plates by wayside restaurants). They were also employed by the *beedi* (Indian cigarette) factories to pluck the leaves of the *tendu* tree, which earned them Rs. 0.25/- for two bundles of 100 leaves.[33]

The division of tasks in Neerma's household is also present in the relatively prosperous Girasia households, but to a lesser extent. As far as possible, in the latter households the male heads would not work as hired labour. Usually the women and children of the eldest man go first in search of wage labour. Young adults are the first to leave home to work as waged labourers and are the longest to stay away. Palvi's unmarried daughter and married son had gone together with Neerma's daughter to work for the *seth* (employer) in Umjha in Gujarat. They would be away for a total of four months and would come home only for the few days at the *rati jaga* (night celebrating *Bhairu*, chapter 8). Although the Girasia take a greater risk by searching for employment in the seasonal market, they do not prefer longer term or more permanent employment, as it does not fit in with their agricultural and ritual cycles. In this sense they approach the market as sellers to 'collect' earnings in the same manner as they gather forest produce or harvest crop according to the season.[34]

As buyers the Girasia influence the market of small-scale producers to a significant extent, so much so that cloth dealers like Chaganlal produce only Girasia cloth and jewellers design special

32. Anything not made from clay or wood in the Taivar household inventory, is made from grass or reeds. The most important multi-purpose item in a household is the *hoodla* (or large basket made to transport grain, ritual food, cow dung, small children, crops etc). Neerma's household was among the poorer families who made *hoodla* to sell in the market at Rs. 10/- .
33. The *tendu* leaves are dried, and then soaked before they are cut and filled with tobacco to make *beedi*.
34. A similar tendency has been noted by Bird (1983) for other forest people, the Naiken hunter-gatherers of the Nilgiris in South India who took up wage labour at the nearby plantation only when they needed the money. Bird illustrates how plantation labour was considered by the Naiken as an extension of their customary, gathering mode of existence.

Girasia ornaments. The buying and selling of jewellery is centrally linked to Girasia brideprice payments and is discussed in the following chapter. At the level of low-priced items, the Girasia make the potters produce clay horses. The Hindu potter at Ore said he would have liked to stop the production of clay horses as they involved a lot of time and brought very little money. The fear of the Girasia deities prevented him from terminating this small-scale production. The Girasia are able to influence the market because they concentrate on buying certain specific items. They exhibit little desire to acquire a different lifestyle or to invest in modern appliances, except perhaps in a bicycle, water pump, watch and radio. The tendency to reject consumer items is grounded in the association of these items with a non-Girasia identity (a similar observation is made by Gell, 1986, noting the conservative nature of consumption of the rich Maria Gond tribals).

The social significance of the market for the Girasia is as important as the economic. Taivar men and women like to visit Abu Road because they can meet other Girasia lineages and buy *chai* (sweet tea), *pakora* (deep fried savouries) or *pan* (betel nut and leaf to chew) after they had sold their head loads. Young girls like to buy small coloured beads for necklaces. Such desires would bring even Savli, the daughter of the relatively prosperous Dopa, to the market with a head load of berries or wood. Young adult men and women get to 'see' (view) each other in the market. Often couples meet for the first time in the Abu Road market. In the absence of literacy and communication through letters, the market is an important means for wives to procure information about their natal village. Moreover, in the market wives are less observed than in their husband's village. The Hindu townsfolk described the Girasia to me, 'like foreigners', to whom the moral values of the Hindu *dharma* do not apply. So while Hindu women should not be seen idling or chatting to other persons, especially other men, if Girasia women do so it is because, 'they are different'. The market environment thus supports the independent and individualistic behaviour of Girasia women by providing them with an environment with fewer social sanctions than in their husband's village.

Abu Road market is also a place where sensitive Girasia matters may be settled, and where certain factions in a dispute can meet away from the eyes of other lineage members. In this sense Abu Road provides a relative degree of privacy, although it is very likely that a Girasia would meet or be seen by a relative. Abu Road market is also a convenient place to carry out transactions without the need for hospitality. In the example of Dhanki and Nota, mentioned above, they had arranged to meet his 'hired wife' in Abu Road, where they took possession of his child. Meeting in Abu Road ruled out the need for either party to visit the other's village. In this sense the Abu Road market, rather than the nearby villages, is spatially an important part of a Taivar life which is pre-occupied with maintaining both a distance and an accord among kin and with outsiders.

In the present chapter I have looked at the sharing of resources, the related transactions of food and the role played by the market as a means by which the Taivars differentiate between their brother-members within the Taivar Girasia lineage, affinal members of different Girasia lineages and, finally, between other caste members in the surrounding area. The sharing of economic resources and food emphasises the differences between genealogical and affinal relationships among the Girasia. Market relations are in contrast to, but at the same time reinforce differences between those whom the Girasia consider as kin and others who are in the non-kin category. The market is also a place where Taivar women exert an independence away from their affinal village, and which at the same time also constructs the Girasia as 'tribal' in non-Girasia perceptions.

Chapter 7

GIRASIA BRIDEPRICE AND THE POLITICS OF MARRIAGE PAYMENTS

*A*s a feature of Girasia society, brideprice immediately, if superficially, distinguishes it from dowry paying, upper-caste Hindu culture. In the present chapter I suggest that Girasia brideprice transactions are similar in function and meaning, if not in form, to the dowry payments in the region.[1] While a number of studies have been made on the Indian dowry system and its relationship with concerns of prestige and hierarchy,[2] there has been little research on brideprice and bridewealth transactions, although many lower-caste and 'tribal' groups are known to practise them. While popular caste opinion in the region considers a brideprice payment as a reflection of a group's morals, gender theorists have in contrast championed the cause of brideprice as it supposedly acknowledges the work 'value' of women.[3] The positive valuation of women embodied in the concept of brideprice is, on the face of it, a contrast to the popu-

1. In the text I use the word 'brideprice' to describe Girasia marriage transactions, because firstly, only cash is transacted between the wife-exchanging groups, and secondly, the payment is not made to the bride but to her father, or in some cases to her brothers.
2. Khare 1972, Van der Veen 1972, Goody and Tambiah 1973, Vatuk 1975, Sharma 1976, Parry 1979, Fruzzetti 1982, Kishwar 1987, Goody 1990, for example.
3. For example, Kishwar 1987.

lar image of the 'economic liability' of wives in dowry-practising communities. In this chapter I question this view to show that Taivar brideprice payments do not improve upon the structural gender inequalities found in dowry-paying communities. The ideology of Taivar brideprice constructs women as economic liabilities although objectively they are not so.

In this chapter I first consider some of the important issues raised in studies on marriage payments generally but more specifically in relation to caste status and hierarchy in India. I then describe the notion and practice of brideprice payments among the Taivar Girasia with specific reference to the economic transactions involving property, adoption, divorce and the death of a spouse. The third part of the chapter compares the structural inequalities of women in brideprice and dowry-paying communities. The similar processes at work in both societies which devalue women's labour contributions allows me to question the use of brideprice to describe some communities, especially 'tribal' communities, and dowry to describe others. In the final part of the chapter I outline the impact of a rising inflation in the market economy on the levels of Girasia brideprice payments. Contrary to popular academic opinion which states that dowry is replacing brideprice as an institution,[4] I suggest that brideprice is firmly established within the Girasia community and is manifested in continuously rising amounts. Apart from an economic rationale to brideprice payments, there is also the important component of identity maintenance in Girasia marriage transactions, which promotes a lineage identity at one level and a sublineage identity at another. I argue that the continuation of brideprice as a Girasia institution is related to the fact that it satisfies both lineage and gender hierarchies, the economic needs of the community, and the symbolic requirements of the Taivars to distinguish themselves from other caste communities.

Some Issues in the Studies of Marriage Payments

In anthropological studies on marriage payments, Goody's work (1973) is notable for the connection it establishes between the system of property distribution and the nature and direction of the marriage payments. For Goody (1973), the transfer and control of property follows two distinct patterns. In the first case, goods are transferred

---

4. Shah 1982, Kishwar 1987, for example.

from the groom's kin to the bride's kin (bridewealth) where the control remains with the elder generation and the property is distributed beyond the lineage group in a collateral manner. In the second pattern, goods are transferred from the bride's father to the bride (dowry). According to Goody, the distinctions in the form of control over property are influenced by the mode of production, which in turn determines whether the form of marriage will be monogamous or polygamous. Goody based his observations on the high statistical frequency with which dowry societies were plough-using and monogamous (the Asian type) in contrast to the polygynous, brideprice societies which practised hoe-cultivation (the African type). Tambiah's (1973) model of marriage payments in India was similar to Goody's more general model of marriage payments for Asia and Africa. According to Tambiah, dowry was, 'wealth given with the daughter at her marriage for the couple to use as the nucleus of their conjugal estate' (1973: 63). He defined brideprice as, 'the transfer from the bridegroom's family and kin, to the bride's family and kin certain goods in return for which certain rights in the bride are transferred' (ibid.: 61).

Among the Girasia, and in contrast to Goody's model, plough-farming co-occurs with brideprice payments. Furthermore, within the Girasia economy which defines itself in terms of plough-production, there is a centrality of female labour. The importance of female labour in plough based economies is in contrast to the connections Boserup (1971) made between types of economies and the forms of marriage payments and practices. Boserup, like Goody, argues that it is the centrality of female labour in hoe-cultivation which determines the nature of the marriage payment (bridewealth). Moreover, she proposes that bridewealth societies because they acknowledge the 'value' of women's labour must give them greater independence. On the other hand, she emphasises that, the marginality of female labour in plough-based societies results in the greater dependency of women on men and is reflected in the fact that dowry payments are made. More recent work, for example, Ram (1988) has shown that dowry payments may co-exist with a centrality of female labour in the economy.[5]

5. In her study of the Mukkuvar fishing community in South India, Ram (1988) suggests that, although the fishing community does not have land, the sea is treated as its symbolic equivalent and women are ideologically marginalised from the actual event of fishing as they would be from agricultural production, although they contribute most of the on-shore labour. Ram highlights the difficulties with the simple correlations made between the mode of production,

In the more recent studies, the focus has been on the meanings and implications of marriage payments for members of the community in which they are practised (Comaroff 1980). Correspondingly, recent work on Indian marriages has also placed a greater emphasis on the concerns of status and hierarchy in marriage transactions (Goody and Goody, 1990). The stress on social status and prestige is also made by gender theorists such as Ortner 1981, Moore 1985, Collier 1989 who argue that marriage payments must be studied in relation to a community's concern with hierarchy and the unequal access to power between men and women. Ortner and Collier suggest that it is hierarchy, rather than production or kinship, which determines the relations of marriage payments to property.[6] I agree with Collier that the related concerns of prestige, status and the cultural notions of women are crucial determinants of the form and meaning of marriage payments. However, I also believe that production and the access to resources are important (Goody 1973, 1990) and feed back into cultural notions of difference and hierarchy (Humphrey 1985).

In India, classical (Brahmanical) literature suggests that the opposed forms of brideprice and dowry, the range of marriage exchanges between them, as well as a hierarchy among all these types, are all encompassed within caste society.[7] The literature stresses that the prestigious nature of marriage with dowry payments is a characteristic of upper castes, as compared to the less prestigious, brideprice marriages of the lower castes (Tambiah 1973). However, as Parry's study of the Kangra Rajputs (1979) has shown, both brideprice and dowry payments can exist within the same caste. Where dowry is practised by the upper and landed families and brideprice

---

marriage payments and a society's means of valuation. Her work emphasises that there can be 'no easy relation between community status and women's work, as women perform both waged and unwaged, productive and unproductive labour' (1988: 343).

6. Earlier, Meillassoux (1976) suggested that it was control or access to the capacity of human reproduction, children and labour, rather than the ownership of property per se which determines the type of marriage transaction. Collier (1988), however, points out that in Meilassoux's case it was status that determined the access to resources, and the access to the labour of women that determined status.

7. Tambiah (1973), divides the eight classical marriage rites *Brahma, Deva, Arsha, Pragapatya, Asura, Gandharva, Rakshasha and Paisaca* (Tambiah's translation from Manu III: 21 ,34) of the four *varna* , into the four categories of marriage. The categories of marriage are ranked with dowry at the top, followed by marriage with bridewealth, free romantic union and, finally, forcible abduction and seduction.

by the lower and poorer groups, as among the Kangra Rajputs, marriage transactions are related to the hierarchical differences of prestige and affluence between lineages or families within a caste. Sometimes even dowry and brideprice transactions may occur simultaneously in a single marriage arrangement. Among the Lewa Patels of Nandol (Goody and Goody 1990) for example, brides received both a dowry from their own father as well as an indirect endowment[8] from their father-in-law. Goody and Goody's point that both dowry and brideprice can co-occur as aspects of a single marriage payment reinforce my own observations of the Purohit (upper-caste, lower-middle class Brahmin) families in Ore village. The Purohits have both a brideprice practice, which they call *vyavhar* (literally, courtesy or gesture) which involves the transaction of a nominal amount of money (Rs. 47/- to 50/-) and also a direct endowment, where the bride's father or uncle give her livestock. All the above examples point to the range of marriage payments that can exist within a caste, sub-caste or even within a single marriage arrangement. These observations strengthen my assertion that Girasia brideprice reflects not a 'tribal' but a lower-caste and class phenomenon.

Apart from mapping a hierarchy between the groups of different castes or between the different lineages or families within a caste, marriage transactions also reveal a hierarchy based on gender, where wives are ranked lower than husbands. The cultural notions of gender roles in India have crucially affected the transmission of property in practice. Despite the differences in the expectations of work of women from the lower and upper castes, similar notions of the role of wives informs the range of castes. The cultural ideal which stresses that a wife's primary responsibility is her huband's welfare (see chapter 3) alters the bilaterality of property transmission, noted by Goody (1973), in practice.[9] In other words, in the actual practice of property transmission, the divergence of property becomes male-orientated (from father to son and son-in-law) although the divergence may be caused by the movement of the woman from one household to the other. Thus, the ideal of dowry at marriage as a 'gift' to the daughter from the father (a time when she inherits movable goods, designated as her share of her father's property) thus in

8. Goody and Goody term the latter payment an indirect dowry rather than brideprice, in order to highlight the fact that the bride was the direct recipient. Moreover, there was no notion of sale, or purchase, attached to these prestations.
9. According to Goody, 'dowry systems distribute relatively exclusive rights in a manner that does not link property or patrimony to sex' (1973: 26).

practice becomes a 'payment' to the husband and his family.[10] The wife-taking group usually exerts a control over the bride and the wealth that comes with her. Sharma (1976), on the basis of her work among women in northwest India, highlights the difference between the theory and practice of marriage payments. She observes that, although dowry is believed to go *to* the bride, it only goes *with* her. According to Sharma, the control of a girl's dowry lies in the hands of her mother-in-law.[11] The actual control or final ownership of the property transferred as a result of marriage,[12] also depends to a large extent on what constitutes the dowry payments. For example, Tambiah (1989), in a revised definition of dowry, shows it to consist of: 1) gifts for the bride which remain in her personal use, 2) gifts for the groom's joint family which are put into circulating use, i.e., in getting other brides, and 3) gifts to the wife-taking group of women. I see the consumable nature of the dowry payments, in contrast to a Girasia brideprice in cash, as making it more difficult for the wife to retrieve her share, or establish her claim (a point also made by Sharma 1976).

Goody (1990: 216) has noted that dowry only appears like a 'gift' to satisfy the conflicting demands of a devolution of property between siblings, as it prevents the sister from having any future claims in her father's property. In contrast, among the Girasia I find that there is very little room for ambiguity in the nature of the marriage transaction, and in the related rights in property, as the following lines describe.

Girasia Brideprice

The Girasia marriage payment is called *dapa* (literally, *da* meaning to give, and *pa*, to get) and denotes an amount in cash given to the father of the bride by the father of the groom. The *dapa* or brideprice

10. Goody and Goody indirectly acknowledge this in the form of an ideological tension between 'the jointness of the conjugal estate and a woman's separate holding in it' (1990: 198).
11. Goody and Goody are critical of Sharma's analysis, and suggest that not all couples live with their husband's parents. Moreover, if the dowry is retrievable by the bride and her family, then the mother-in-law's control over it is inevitably restricted (1990: 188).
12. Dowry payments may not always be synchronous with marriage, and as Goody (1973, 1990) points out are related to the economic resources of the household in question. In the case of richer households, the daughter is able to take her dowry at marriage while the daughter of a poorer household may wait till the death of her father.

is transacted only in the form of money, as far back as the oldest women could remember. The only variation over time has been in the actual amount. The payments made for the eldest to the newly married Taivar women ranged from Rs. 80 through Rs. 100, 500, 1000, to between Rs. 3,000 and Rs. 4,000 at the time of my fieldwork. The brideprice money could be paid all at once or delayed, depending on the process or type of marriage (i.e., sooner at *hagai* than at *khichna*, see chapter 4). Usually an initial payment is made and the remaining brideprice amounts transferred over the span of a year, frequently in three instalments, approximately every four months. The Girasia brideprice transaction is not a simple transfer of the brideprice received for a daughter to another (wife-giving) group for a daughter-in-law. Brideprice money is put together by pawning an item of jewellery and in a small part was obtained by borrowing money from relatives. The whole or part conversion of the brideprice payment received to silver, and vice versa, in differing amounts, is usually substantially supplemented by the wage-labour income of all the household members. Other contributions, from the geneologically closer sublineage members, are only in denominations of tens rather than in hundreds.[13]

In 1986-87, brideprice rates were between Rs. 3,000 to 4,000/- for young women who were brides for the first time. There were, however, a range of brideprice rates for 'better' or 'worse' wives. More brideprice was paid for younger as opposed to older women and, within the same generation, for those who were more physically fit and reproductive.[14] Women with physical handicaps had low brideprice rates attached to them. For example, Hoja Mada paid Rs. 500/- as brideprice for Velki, which he himself considered to be quite a low amount. This was possible, he explained, because Velki was deaf and dumb. Hoja Mada's wife had died several years previously. At the time of my fieldwork he was in his late forties. Hoja decided to bring a wife to look after his household, more so because his 'adopted' (younger brother's) son had brought a wife and was setting up his own household. It was not because Hoja could not afford to pay higher rates, but more because he was seen as someone who was older and had a weak social status that he could not expect to get a 'better' woman as a wife. Although brideprice reflects the importance of the labour of women, this direct connection is not made by

13. The Girasia strove to keep all debts to a minimum, not just vis-à-vis the Hindu money lender or affines, but also within the lineage.
14. As the amount of money transacted varied according to the 'type' of bride, I use the term brideprice rather than bridewealth to describe Taivar marriage transactions.

the Taivar Girasia. When I asked Teja why he accepted a brideprice for his daughter, he said, 'I have not fed and clothed her so that she may work on another's field'. The Taivar Girasia view brideprice not so much as recognition of a woman's contribution to the household nor as a payment for the loss of a productive member, but as a compensation to the father and his agnatic group for the past expenditure on her maintenance, particularly consumption of food.

In most of the conversations I had with the Taivars on *dapa*, I got the impression that it was regarded as a major Girasia institution. The Girasia take pride in their custom of brideprice, especially the high rates they pay. They are aware of dowry payments, but feel their system is proper because it does not require them to, 'buy a man'. In contrast, the inhabitants of the surrounding villages who pay dowry look down upon brideprice because it amounts to 'buying a woman'. I suggest that Girasia brideprice is an institution which is enhanced as a symbol of their identity because it places them in a distinct opposition to outsiders.[15] Apart from the sense of Girasianess evoked by their practice of brideprice payments, the *dapa* also legitimises the husband's control on his wife's labour and procreation, as the following sections reveal.

Brideprice and Economic Transactions

Labour

As among other lower castes and classes in the region, Girasia women work at home as well as in the fields and forests and make trips to the market. Some of the early to mid-morning chores of the women are filling earthen water pots, sweeping, collecting dung, grinding grain, making food and feeding livestock, in that order of priority. The day usually ends with filling water pots, making food and feeding the livestock. Other domestic assignments include a weekly to fortnightly washing of clothes and the monthly repasting of the floor with a mixture of cowdung and water *(leepna)*. During the

15. Berreman (1972), studying categories and interaction in an urban town in Uttar Pradesh (north India) suggests that the social or economic arrangements of a community often act as indicators of identity, and are the 'focus of self-esteem' (ibid.: 575). The Pahari Hindu community he studied were proud of their brideprice marriages in contrast to the dowry marriages of the plains Hindus. Later in the chapter I show why not all brideprice paying communities necessarily have the same pride in their marriage transactions.

agricultural season, women sow the seeds, weed, water and cut the cobs and stalks of the maize. Women are also carriers of grain to and from the market. In the lean season they carry head loads of wood and grass *(vanda, bhara, gaitha)* and berries for sale. The chores of the household are shared by women of all generations but the burden is heaviest on the new bride. Girasia men are more usually involved in activities which require a certain level of specialisation, such as carpentry, basketry and the construction and repair of the house and well. In agriculture, the specific male task is to plough the field and channel the water in cases of irrigation. Usually the agriculturally specified male activities are those concerned with the cooperation of the lineage brothers, as outlined in chapter 6, above. Otherwise, in the household, men substitute women wherever extra labour is required. Men seem more like stop-gap workers and were mobile between jobs. (Children also functioned in this manner although they undertook lighter tasks than men).

As in other castes, the main difference between Girasia men and women lies in the control over each other's labour. Girasia husbands control the labour of their wives and children. The power to control a woman's work and her procreative capacity lies in the hands of her father and brothers and becomes most clear at times of brideprice negotiation. There are, moreover, monetary incentives involved in the allocation of women's work, as Teja's example below reveals. Teja was annoyed because the village council *(panchayat)* had not resolved the dispute regarding the brideprice payment of his daughter. He said it all began when his wife was sick and admitted to the hospital and he had needed Rs. 500/- for her treatment. A Girasia of Siyawa (an affinal village of the Taivars, approximately twelve kilometres from Abu Road) had agreed to loan him the money, provided Teja gave him his daughter. Teja agreed and the girl went to Siyawa. According to Teja, after a short while had elapsed the man bought himself another wife. Teja first heard that his daughter and her co-wife *(mahi)* quarrelled, through a villager of Dhamaspur (also in Abu Road *tehsil*). The Dhamaspur villager said he would take Teja's daughter provided Teja gave him the money to repay the debt and money for the brideprice *dapa*, which totalled Rs. 1,100/-. Teja told me he had agreed to this man's offer but initially kept it secret as he had organised a *panchayati* (meeting of the village council) to ask for the return of his daughter from her first husband as a result of her ill-treatment at his house. Teja essentially wanted a *kayda* (compensation) payment of Rs. 100/-, which he claimed was justified as his daughter had worked on the fields of the Siyawa villager. In sum,

Teja said he would return Rs. 400/- rather than the initial sum of Rs. 500/- which he had borrowed. As the above example emphasises, women become wives as a consequence of the monetary transactions between men. A brideprice in cash greatly enhanced a gendered access to material benefits.

Property

Marriage marks the division of Taivar property which passes exclusively to male heirs. This division takes place in the lifetime of the father, unlike the property division among north Indian middle and upper castes. In the latter case, the division often only takes place after the death of the father as in the Indian *dayabhaga* system (Tambiah 1973, Parry 1979). The Girasia are, however, co-partners in the joint family property at birth, as in the Indian *mitakshara* system (see Tambiah, 1973, for a discussion of these two major schools of property transmission stated in the classical texts). Girasia women, whether at marriage or otherwise, inherit neither the movable nor immovable property of their natal lineage. Often the only item the bride brings to her husband's house and village are a metal plate *(vadku)*, a small metal drinking pot *(lota)*, the clothes she wears, and the few pieces of cheap jewellery acquired as gifts or purchased over the years. Sometimes the bride may be 'gifted' her favourite goat or calf, if she belongs to a richer family. At her husband's house the Taivar wife is given silver jewellery which she can wear but which remains the property of the husband and his sons by her. While the jewellery she wears displays the status of her husband, the pot and plate are symbols of the wife's 'outsider' status. Girasia women do not have any rights in their children. Where their husband dies or when they become a wife to another man, a Girasia woman is separated from her children. This is essentially because children are regarded as their father's property (born of his 'water', see chapter 4). When a Girasia man dies, his children are brought up by his father's brother's wife and the mother is encouraged to leave (in practice this depends on whether the woman is in her reproductive age span or not, see subsection on death, below).

Like other caste women, Girasia women cannot have a share in the immovable property of their father. In most upper- and middle-caste households, in the absence of a brother, the daughter may inherit the father's land. In the Girasia case, however, and unlike other castes, in the absence of sons the father's land passes to his male collateral relatives (in the FB category). Thus Girasia property transmission is determined by gender apart from descent. For example, in the hypogamous-type of *ghar-jamai* (resident son-in-law) marriage, after the death of the father-in-law the land reverts to the father's brothers, and does not pass to either the daughter or the son-in-law, who must return to the latter's village. Tambiah (1973) has pointed out that in the Hindu-Indic model of inheritance, lineal relatives are preferred over collateral relatives for the purposes of inheritance. In other words, daughters may be preferred as heirs to father's brothers or their children. On the other hand, the West African, non-Islamic, bride-wealth societies stress male survivorship and the reversion of property to male collaterals, women being excluded as heirs (Goody, 1973). As in the Hindu model, Girasia inheritance is lineal and stresses partition and adoption. However, as in the West African case, Girasia women are rigorously excluded as heirs and are displaced by the father's collateral relatives.

The difference between Girasia and other caste women in terms of their actual control over property might not be different in practice, in that the relationships between brothers and sisters in both cases are similar. Ideally, relations between middle- and upper-caste Hindu sisters and brothers are non-conflictual because there is no competition for the irreplaceable economic resources such as land and water shares. The dowry is considered to be the daughter's share of her father's wealth (although a movable and replaceable part). The relations between a sister and her brothers are tense only if the sister claims a share in the immovable property on the death of her father. In order to avoid displeasing their brothers, most middle- and uppercaste women give up even their marginal claims to a share of their father's property. It is such a common practice for a sister to forgo her share in her father's property and thereby ensure her brothers' 'protection', that most families do not expect otherwise. There are very few exceptions to this practice, because women look to their natal households (i.e., their brothers) to provide a means of security, especially in times of disagreement arising in the husband's household. Not surprisingly this expectation is greatest in the initial period in which the wife stays in her affinal household. The protective role of the natal household weakens over time and simultaneously the wife gains a footing in her husband's household. Relations between Girasia brothers and sisters are ideally 'good' as there is no uncertainity about land ownership. There are also expectations of 'protection' from the brother (described previously in chapter 4). The absence of conflict among cross-siblings over parental property and the brideprice money, as well as the affinal contacts generated by the sister, keeps the relations between Girasia brothers and sisters harmonious.[16] Both in the Girasia and other castes, we see not only a minimal control of women over material resources, but that women trade even the partial control they may assert, for a greater security.

Similarly, in both the Girasia brideprice and regional dowry cases, the movement of wives not only facilitates inheritance in the form of a flow of money or goods, but also redistributes rights between the natal and affinal male-headed households. Women in other castes strengthen their husband's household by bringing in dowry. They strengthen their brother's household by forgoing their claim on the immovable property in favour of their brothers. Girasia women strengthen their husband's household with their labour, children and food. They strengthen their brother's household by providing brideprice and transferring their consumption needs.

Adoption

The gendered control of property is also reflected in the pattern of Girasia child adoption. I observed that there are different rules for the adoption of male and female children, because of the lineal and gendered transmission of property. Boys are adopted within the village by a father's brother while girls are adopted in an affinal village by a father's sister. For Girasia boys, it is usually a permanent adoption whereby the boy is most likely to inherit land from his *kaka* or *baba* (in this case also his adoptive father). Gopa, who lived with his *haga kaka* (father's true younger brother) Duda, said he would inherit Duda's land. Gopa would not get a share of his father's property, nor would he share his adoptive father's inheritance with his brothers. The adoption of girls is a more temporary arrangement compared to the adoption of boys. Girls usually stay only until their marriage. Then they either return to their natal village to be wed or, as was usually the case, would form a marital alliance in the village of their adoptive mother (aunt). In both cases, the brideprice goes to the girl's father and not to her adoptive mother's husband. An adopted boy's brideprice, however, was paid by his adoptive father and not his natural father. In other words, the adoptive father has a greater control over a boy's labour and the related brideprice money than an adoptive mother has over a girl's labour and brideprice.

In the ideal pattern of inheritance among the upper and middle Hindu castes, the preferable order for inheritance is the son, his grand-

---

16. If the brothers have tensions amongst themselves, the sisters usually take sides as well.

son, his great-grandson, the daughter's son, the brother's son and, lastly, the adopted, 'outsider' son (usually a distant relative's son). The Girasia preference, on the other hand, is in the order of son, father's brother, father's elder brother's son, father's younger brother's son, father's father's brother's son and so on. The major difference between the Girasia and the upper Hindu is that the Girasia adopted son is treated as the son, and the daughter's son does not inherit property.

Divorce

Like adoption, divorce also reflects the preoccupation of Girasia men with transacting money and labour, and is determined by brideprice concerns and negotiations. Descriptions of divorce are, however, made by men and women in terms of a woman's assertion of independence. The Taivar term for divorce is *pairi-melo* (which translated as 'send back').[17] 'If a woman is unhappy, she simply runs away.' This is how a Taivar man described a woman's attitude to marriage. The spontaneity of a woman's action is meant to convey her disregard for the authority the brideprice transaction has given her husband and is therefore couched in terms of her lack of responsibility for the work at her husband's household. To a casual observer, a Girasia woman's decision to go away might seem freely determined but usually the decision to 'run away' is dependent on men of other affinal, or potentially affinal lineages. Often the difficulties faced by a woman at her affinal home are conveyed to her father or brothers through the unofficial channel of 'relatives' and 'friends'. Frequently the news reaches a wider circle of persons than those of the natal and affinal villages. Interested suitors might approach the woman's brother and might even encourage them to take her away. It is then that she 'runs away' with her second husband. A woman's ability to leave her husband is determined primarily by how suitable a wife she was considered by men of other lineages.

While a woman may run away and thereby initiate a divorce, a man resorts to a separate set of procedures to break the marriage. According to Phoola (who spoke to me in Hindi), a man will want to divorce his wife when she causes him displeasure, particularly in two ways: either she does not prepare *roti* for when he is hungry *(samai pe roti nahi dena);* or she answers back, especially to any reprimands her husband might give her *(moonh pe bolna)*. The frequent general complaint was that wives are lazy and shirk their work to

---

17. Other terms with the same meaning were *naasotka* and *haathsawera*.

wander around (*bina kam kare ghoomna*; also see men's reasons for procuring additional wives, chapter 5). According to Phoola, if the wife continues in her displeasing behaviour, the husband first beats his wife. If she continues in spite of this then the husband and his family members, with the counsel of the other lineage members, explain to her what is expected of her and the deviance her behaviour constitutes. If the woman remains adamant in her behaviour, a complaint is sent to her parents to return the brideprice. The parents often try to convince their daughter to remain and to prepare food when the husband demands it. Despite all these measures if the situation remains unchanged, the wife's brother is summoned and she is handed over to him *(sompna)*, and it is expected that the brideprice will be returned. On the other hand, if the wife is willing to work in her husband's household but it is her husband who wants her to leave, then there will be no return of the brideprice.

The main concern of the husband following a divorce is with the loss and replacement of labour for the household. The father or brothers of the woman, on the other hand, are concerned with organising the return of the brideprice. The acceptance of Girasia divorce, in contrast to the difficulty of divorce in upper- and middle-caste marriages, is enhanced by the easily repayable brideprice sums (in cash) and the wife's identification with her father's lineage rather than her husband's kin group.[18] There are, however, considerable negotiations between the wife-exchanging families before the brideprice is returned. The girl's father is interested in as much money as he can get and usually claims a *kayda* (compensation fee) from the husband for transgressing the social norm (see chapter 9, below). If, for example, the brideprice was Rs. 2,000/-, then a Rs. 200/- compensation fee may be deducted and Rs. 1,800/- would be returned by the girl's family to her husband. The amount of compensation is a marginal sum which depends upon the negotiation strengths of the parties, which in turn also depended on the level of guilt assigned to each party by the *panchayat* of the wife-exchanging lineages.

There are different kinds of compensation involved in the dissolution of marriage ties. For example, if a woman leaves her husband for another husband, the second husband pays a *dava* (literally, challenge; also close to the Hindi word *dhava*, attack) to the first husband. *Dava* is distinct from *dapa* (brideprice) both in amount and in mean-

---

18. According to Ortner (1981), difficulties in divorce in dowry societies are a result of the weakened relationship which the woman has, after marriage, with her natal group. Goody however asserts, 'one cannot interpret the rule against divorce as indicating a complete detachment from the natal family' (1990: 173).

ing. Although mainly to compensate the first husband for the brideprice he has paid, it also includes a sum in compensation to him by the second husband for 'cheating' another Girasia. Therefore the *dava* amount is more than the *dapa* by at least one-and-a-half times. The term *dava*, like *khichna* (marriage by 'capture'), implies force. But here the force used is not so much on the girl but rather against her husband's control of her, for which he had paid a brideprice. The second husband usually informs or connives with the girl's brother in a mutually beneficial arrangement. In other words, the girl's brother need not return his sister's brideprice if the second husband takes her and pays the *dava* amount. When the woman fails to return home, the first husband with his closest male lineage members go in search of her to demand either her return or an exorbitant *dava*. Both parties negotiate the compensation fee. Sometimes the fee is settled by intermediaries, usually the girl's brothers and the *patels* (headmen) of the villages to which the parties involved belong. In Girasia divorce, as in *hagai* (the engagement ceremony), the major concern centres on the settlement of the amount and the return of the brideprice respectively. Consequently, a considerable time is spent in negotiating money-related agreements between men of affinally related lineages.

The compensation aspect attached to brideprice payments is not unique to the Girasia. In Awan, in eastern Rajasthan, Gupta (1974) notes that a *jhagara* (in Hindi, literally 'fight') marriage payment is made for the *nata*, or second, non-ceremonial and less prestigious marriages held among castes other than the twice-born. According to Gupta, *jhagara* consists of the initial brideprice payment and an initial sum for minor expenses incurred by the first husband and paid by the second (ibid.: 146). Even though it is commonly believed that lower castes are able to practice easier divorce because there is a lesser concern with property, the Girasia material suggests the opposite may be true. The Girasia institution of divorce is used as a means of negotiating rights to money and labour and the more movable and consumable aspects of property, precisely because there is a concern with property.

Death

Money matters arising from death are seen to link widowhood with brideprice. On the death of either the husband or wife, there is no return of the brideprice. According to Palvi, *mitgyo, phir kun dapa aale?* (finished or wiped out, then who will give brideprice?). Ideally, after the death of the husband, the connection of his wife with his lineage becomes tenuous. This is particularly the case if the widow is young. During my stay, Jabli's husband Gona was murdered. Jabli was young, and it was believed that she was infertile. Palvi told me that soon after her husband's death, Jabli had begun to stay with Daga (her HFBS). Palvi predicted that Daga would discard her later, and; 'Her own brothers will not keep her because she does not listen to them, otherwise she would have gone back to them. In the end she will have to beg for *roti*'. Usually when a woman is widowed young, and whether or not she has children, she returns to her brother's household while her children remain with her late husband's brothers. Other men are interested in young widows, primarily because they will have to give a smaller brideprice to her father or brothers.

It is common for older widows to stay with their sons who have already established a separate household. No brideprice amount is returned for older widows, and they frequently do not go back to their brothers. Older widows are less welcome in their natal households as they have weaker ties with their brother's sons and their wives. However, the duty of the husband's lineage towards a widow is symbolically terminated on the twelfth day of the *nyath* (funeral). So the older widow who continues to stay in the household of her son is dependent on the attitude of his father's brothers towards her as well as her continued contributions to the domestic chores in the household. All older widows whom I met were continually busy with small but time-consuming jobs. Nathi Bai, who died in the year following my fieldwork, said, 'if I do not watch the field which is at some distance from our house, and which often involves sleeping out in the open, they will throw me out'. Nathi was in a particularly vulnerable social position as her son had died soon after her husband. Although she lived with her grandsons, they lived next to her husband's brothers who were averse to her presence.

Girasia widowhood is in contrast to the ideal-type Hindu case, where the widow remains attached to the husband's kin who are duty bound to look after her. The widow in turn has a duty to her husband's kin. She must bring up her husband's children and manage the property for them until they are adults (Tambiah, 1973). In practice, the upper- and middle-caste Hindu widows are subject to social restrictions such as wearing white, shaving the head and a prohibition on remarriage. It has been argued that because Hindu widows remain attached to the husband's agnatic group and remain the caretakers of his children's property, it becomes necessary to impose restrictions on widows as a means of containing property within the husband's lineage (Tambiah 1973, Parry 1979). In contrast Girasia widows who have no links with the property of the husband's lineage are less socially restricted but more economically vulerable.

Marriage Payments and Gender Inequalities

So far I have described Girasia brideprice more in terms of the strategies adopted by men in the lineage and family. The centrality of the brideprice payments to the monetary relationships among Girasia men has significant implications for Girasia women, as is implicit in the previous discussion. In this section, I look more closely at the meaning of brideprice in terms of the structural inequalities within the Girasia community and compare these with gender relations in other communities.

Girasia wives, like upper-caste Hindu women for whom dowry has been paid, are markers of the transfer of wealth. However, the difference between the Girasia and the upper-caste Hindu women lies in the increasing control of the latter over the amount and distribution of the marriage payments in the next generation. Girasia women, who may or may not remain as wives to one man, in contrast to the stricter monogamous tendencies among upper-caste Hindus, continue to be affiliated to their father's lineage and do not obtain a substantially greater control over the brideprice proceedings in their role as mothers-in-law. On the other hand, an initial lack of control over marriage payments, the image of the dependence of wives, and an ideological devaluation of women's labour are the significant similarities between Girasia and upper-caste Hindu women. Although valued in practical terms, the labour of Girasia women is devalued in ideological, prestige-related terms, and brideprice is not regarded as reflecting the important contribution which women make to production or reproduction. In a sense, women are 'dead investments [as] they give away their maintenance expenditure by working on the fields of another lineage'. In other words, the Girasia do not recognise the work of women on the fields of their natal household during the period they stay there. The image of the dependence of women, among both the Girasia and the other castes, is given ideological expression in the image of women as burdens on the resources of their husbands. Among the Taivars, although labour is objectively valued, no amount of work done by a woman is considered to be a compensation for her food and maintenance, products of a sublineage's property, which have been spent on her. The image of the dependence of Girasia women largely stems from their very real lack of ownership of property, legitimised by the Girasia as a consequence of the movement of women from their natal to their affinal villages (chapter 5).

Hindu wife-givers 'buy' the maintenance rights of their daughters through dowry. Among the Girasia a woman's labour buys her rights to maintenance, but only as long as she is seen to be working. (Her low work performance can be one of the major reasons for her husband to divorce her; see previous section). Girasia brideprice payments, in contrast to dowries, involve a transfer from father to husband of the rights to a woman's production and reproduction. In practice, dowry payments usually represent a greater transfer in the rights over the woman than do Girasia brideprice payments. This transfer of only partial rights is reflected in the absence of institutions which link the Girasia wife to her husband's property. The ideology surrounding brideprice transactions stresses strongly that Taivar women remain members of their natal group after marriage, as distinct from the upper- and middle-castes, where the wife becomes more 'incorporated'.[19] Yet the degree of autonomy in both cases is almost the same. In the Taivar case, a woman's autonomy is restricted by stressing the insecure attachment to the husband's group without a strong position in the natal group. In the upper-caste case, a woman's autonomy is restricted by a greater dependence on the husband's group.

The Taivar women are as 'controlled', in terms of their access to the productive resources, as upper-caste women but not as restricted in decisions regarding their sexual partners. Upper- and middle-caste fathers exercise a strict control on their daughter's sexual life in order to be able to perform *kanyadan*, or the ceremony whereby they 'gift' the virgin daughter to her husband. Thereby the upper-caste marriage becomes practically irrevocable.[20] Girasia women were

19. Goody (1990) has argued that the incorporation of the Hindu wife in her affinal household is more in appearance than in fact. The presents at, during and after a woman's wedding, as well as her continuing intimate relationships with her brothers and mother's brother, belie her complete detachment from her natal family. If this is in fact the case, then it would support my general argument, which states that there is in practice very little to distinguish between the structural positions of the Girasia women and other caste women.
20. Tambiah (1989), for example, differentiates Hindu dowry-society from African bridewealth society, as constituting a greater patriarchal subordination of women within the patrilineal context, reflected in the greater control of women's sexuality. In Africa, on the contrary, where within the patrilineal system there is a division between the sexual versus the reproductive control over women, the

freeer than upper- and middle-caste women to break the bonds set up by the marriage payment. While Girasia women can improve their existence by looking for a second husband, this alternative action is not open to upper-caste Hindu women. The choice of Girasia women is however restricted by the consideration of men of other lineages. The extent to which Girasia women are 'in control' of their decisions and can leave their husbands is therefore conditional upon other other men; for example, a second suitor being 'interested' in them and the approval of their father or brothers (see chapters 4 and 5). In this sense, the Girasia brideprice payments remain a symbol of the power of men in the gender hierarchy.

Of theoretical interest in the light of what has been said, is the debate within anthropology regarding the relation of women to the productive resources (especially the work of Sacks 1974, based on Engels' conception of the relations of men and women to private property). Sacks stresses that a low position is universally accorded to women in terms of their relation to the productive means, rather than by the cultural valuation given to the role of motherhood (1974: 207-22).[21] In addition to Sacks' argument, Moore (1985: 35) points out that cultural representations may also affect the relations of women to property. Moore argues that although women may seem economically subordinate, they actually possess political power, and thereby a high status. Girasia production is central to the household and heavily dependent on the productive and reproductive contributions of their women. The centrality of female labour is reflected in the importance given to the role of wives as reproducers, rather than as mothers or nurturers. The ease of divorce and the social acceptability regarding the bringing up of children by women other than their mothers, reinforces the centrality of labour and production in the definition of Girasia womanhood. Girasia women, unlike upper-caste Hindu women, have neither politically nor religiously defined structural status (see chapter 8, following). However, at the

---

former is seen to be less restrictive with regard to the freedom of decision-making which women have.

21. Sacks supports Engels historical position, which is that the subordination of women was a direct correlate of the movement of societies towards a male domination of private property. Before the existence of this notion of private property, the work of men and women, even though sexually divided, was accorded equal status. With the emergence of a category of enduring productive means ('private property') a hierarchy of producers came into existence. The importance of the household in production declined, and with it the position of women as the major domestic labourers.

level of the individual households, power was negotiated in both the cases (as suggested in chapter 4).[22]

In the upper and middle castes, women's domestic contribution is not seen as 'work' in the same sense as their husband's job which brings in an income. For Fruzzetti (1982), for example, because the bride is considered an economic liability to her in-laws, her father must continue to supply them gifts in order to share the burden (ibid.: 38). The flow of gifts from the wife's to the husband's side in the dowry case, supports the inferior position of the wife-givers (and the wife). Unlike middle- and upper-caste communities, there is no flow of gifts in Girasia marriage transactions. The brideprice amount is paid either in a single cash payment or in a few agreed instalments. Apart from the weak links with the natal and affinal property, I see both divorce and the marital mobility of Girasia women as facilitated by the exact monetary nature of the brideprice, which above all allows precise repayment. To take an example, when a Girasia woman contracts a second marriage, the closest male relatives of her first husband often haggle over the exact return of the brideprice as well as the precise sum of the *kayda* (compensation).

Whereas money sanctions Girasia marriage[23] it is religion, the notions of *dharma, kanyadan*, and the ideal state of wifehood for the woman which influences upper- and middle-caste marriages. The religious significance of the upper-caste conjugal relationship, reinforces dowry as a non-reversible, non-refundable relation between agnatic groups who exchanged wives.[24] Dowry is also returned with greater difficulty than Girasia brideprice, because of the type of goods that constitute it, usually a variety of consumables for the bride and her husband's family, distributed among the husband's collaterals. Such goods are especially difficult to account for, and regain control of, when the household is partitioned (Sharma 1984).

22. Rosaldo and Collier (1981: 275-321), for example point out, that the political nature of marriage is a personal strategy to access the means of production. In a similar vein, Moore (1988) sees the symbolic realm structuring conceptions about gender, which she does not necessarily believe reflects the social and economic positions of men and women (ibid.: 37).
23. A money income is the recognised advantage which the wife-givers have in the transaction. Once the payment is over, the marriage was socially, and ritually celebrated whenever the economic means permitted (chapter 4). The wife-giver was not thought to gain merit for his act, as in the upper castes.
24. For Goody (1990) dowry given as a 'gift' is only made to appear irreversible, in order to to resolve the tension between the inheritance by men of the lineage, and women through dowry, in the devolution of property. Presenting dowry as a 'gift' avoided a wife's future claims on the property of her male agnates.

A Girasia brideprice in money alone could be monitored specifically and precisely reimbursed on divorce. A brideprice in cash and a related accountability assist the Girasia in resisting obligations, anticipation, and the ambiguity involved in the gifting at other caste marriages.[25] As we saw in the previous chapter, the Taivars confined all the obligations arising from money, gifts and sharing to matters between agnates. Between affinal groups, on the other hand, transactions such as food and brideprice are matters of precise payment. As a consequence, wives mark the boundaries between kin groups which are similar (those who exchange wives) as well as those which are different (the wife-takers as opposed to the wife-givers). This is further reflected by the fact that as wives women are differentiated as 'better' or 'worse' according to the status of their lineage. At the level of the unstated are the intiatives taken by individual Girasia women.

The fact that individual Girasia women could attract the attentions of other suitors, or gain the assistance and cooperation of their brothers, reduces the possibility which men have in arranging the marriages of their natal women with a view to increasing their own status. It is in this light that one must regard the Girasia preoccupation with the maintenance of their lineage's status and the corresponding egalitarian ideal of the community. The Taivar Girasia marriages, in practice, reveals hierarchical tendencies at the boundaries of their prescribed affinal universe, but I suggest that their attempt to maintain rather than increase status represents the extent to which the initiative of women has compromised the consolidation of these hierarchical tendencies. In certain contexts, therefore, such as those that occur in their initiatives in forming marital alliances, Girasia women are viewed as 'out of control' by other Girasia men and women. To this extent, the Girasia and non-Girasia views of the 'freedom' of Girasia women from their men, are similar.

To summarise: the Girasia brideprice transactions must be seen in relation to their pattern of patrilineal descent where children belong to the father, their rule of marriage among 'equals', the absence of a female inheritance in movables, land or other immovables, the negotiated control over the sexuality of women and the opportunities for divorce. The Girasia transactions outwardly reflect certain similari-

---

25. It is the ambiguity in the expectations of both parties conducting the dowry payments that results in serious misunderstandings and sometimes in dowry-deaths. In spite of the direct correlation between the ambiguity of the nature and content of the gifts given in dowry and the dowry offences, Indian legislation (especially the 1984 Dowry Amendment Bill), has not been able to institute any preventive measures (EPW, Sept. 15, 1984).

ties among them and the dowry paying groups in the region. For example, they share a patrilineal descent pattern, lineage exogamy and the exclusion of women from an inheritance in land. On the other hand, certain outward differences between the ideal model of north Indian dowry and the Girasia brideprice are that a dowry is transacted in movable goods while a brideprice is only in money. Moreover, there is a strong accent on virginity in the dowry case which is accompanied by a rigorous control of female sexuality. Divorce is difficult in the instance of dowry payments but rather easier in the case of Girasia brideprice.

Marriage Payments, Shifting Economic Pressures and Identities

Recent studies of brideprice practising communities in India (Kishwar 1987, Bleie 1987) indicate that there is a decline in brideprice payments which is related to an increasing devaluation of women's labour. At the same time, recent studies and reports on dowry in the newspapers indicate rising levels of payments. Sharma (1984) relates rising dowry rates to the improved employment opportunities for men. She points out that, in contrast to the higher cash contribution of men to the household, the relative contribution of their wives in domestic chores has fallen. A rise in dowry, demanded due to the increase in cash income of the husband, has at the same time, according to Sharma, led to a devaluation of the contribution of women.[26]

The increasing levels of Girasia brideprice present a contrast to these contemporary studies of falling brideprice and rising dowry payments. I would argue that hitherto not enough has been said about who has the upper hand in the extraction of such payments. In this section I suggest that the two trends, of a rising Girasia brideprice on the one hand, and rising dowry rates on the other, may be seen as stemming from a common motivation of increasing the cash or other resource holdings of those who receive the payments, so long as this exercise does not threaten the existing gender hierarchy. Where brideprice has been equated with payments in kind, there the conversion to monetary payments in response to shifting demands in the wider economy may lead to a transformation in the nature of the

---

26. Similarly among Mukkuvar women, Ram (1988) observes far fewer benefits of the increased mechanisation of fishing (the major occupation of the community), proceeding to women. For Ram, the mechanisation of fishing has also resulted in a rising cash component of the dowry.

marriage payment itself. Bleie (1987) notes, that among the Oraon tribals of Bangladesh, there has been an increasing tendency to evaluate brideprice in money terms rather than in kind. Similarly the rising dowry demands among the Bengali Hindus in the region also show an increasing tendency to use marriage as a means to obtain money. Bleie notes that changes in the agricultural production system in Bangladesh have raised the demand for mobile, individual workers in the labour market. As a result, it profits women, who worked more in temporary daily wage jobs than did their men. As a consequence, the relative contribution of women to the household income increased. The changes in the agricultural system thus affect the Oraon household division of labour, where the man is regarded as the prime contributor to the household income. As a result, according to Bleie, the Oraon tribal men use traditional Bengali ('Hindu') conceptions to justify their own inactivity on the one hand, while they attach the Oraon ('tribal') meaning of work to traditional labour done by the women, on the other. In this manner ethnic symbols are differently genderised in an attempt to devalue the increased contribution to work which women make to the household. In the sphere of marriage payments this has broken down the previous equivalence of bride-donors and receivers, and led to the decline of brideprice in favour of dowry.

Bleie's example is an argument in favour of the idea that brideprice relates to the value of women's work. The potential rise in the cash component of the Oraon brideprice payments may be viewed as providing the wife-givers with motivation to increase their holdings. At the same time, it is also seen as a threat to the dominance of the husband (and the wife-takers) over the wife (and the wife-givers), fundamental to the Oraon patrilineal structure. Among the Ho tribals of Assam, Kishwar (1987) notes a more direct decline of the institution of brideprice, compared to the Oraon marriage payments. Rising land acquisitions within Ho society led to a hierarchisation and a simultaneous unwillingness on the part of better off families to pay brideprice for the incoming wives from the poorer families. The poorer families themselves were willing to forgo brideprice for the sake of better marital alliances with economically prosperous families. In both the Ho and Oraon societies, 'Hindu values' are used by the 'tribals' to rationalise their responses to economic change. These responses must be seen in the context of a rising poverty as a result of an increased dependence on external market factors.

Parry (1979) also points towards the role of external market factors in explaining changes in the brideprice amounts among the lower Kangra families. Unlike the Ho example, however, these changes led to an inflation rather than a decline in the institution of brideprice. Among the Rathi *biradari* in Kangra, British policies on land sales increased the saleability of land. Combined with an increase in employment opportunities this led to an inflationary trend in Rathi brideprice payments. The release of 'custom-locked' land and an increased income from better opportunities, 'allowed the market in women to find its true level' (ibid.: 244). The fact that fathers could explore the marriage market and, 'dispose their daughters to the highest bidders' (ibid.: 243) ensured a continuation of brideprice payments among the Rathis. The inflationary brideprice trend among the Rathis was also linked to the dowry payments of the upper *biradari* Rajputs. The latter paid dowry which was commensurate with their practice of prestigious hypergamous marriages which in turn left a shortage of women in the lower *biradaris*. In turn, the shortage of women in the lower *biradaris*, increased the money offered to the Rathis from members of their own *biradari*.

Among the Girasia there has been no possibility for an increasing land acquisition to hierarchise society (due to inequalities based on differential landholdings) and to establish the superiority of the wife-takers over the wife-givers as in the Ho case. Neither has there been a change in the agricultural production pattern with an accent on market wage dependence, as in the Oraon case. In the absence of external economic factors as an agency to hierarchise relations between households (true for the Ho tribals and Rathi Rajputs) or within the household (Oraon case), the Girasia response to a rising poverty has been to increase their brideprice payments. The inflationary trend of brideprice payments among the Girasia, who have not been affected by the marriage practices of the upper Rajput lineages, as was the case with the Rathis in Kangra, is I suggest, related to its payment only in the form of cash. Significantly, Girasia brideprice has always been paid only in money, usually converted from silver jewellery. The rising levels of brideprice over a period of twenty to thirty years from Rs. 80/- for the oldest wives to Rs. 3,000/- to 4,000/- for the recent brides is, I was told, linked to the fact that the prices of items which the Girasia buy from the market have risen. In other words, Girhaya brideprice inflation is not linked to an increasing 'value' of the labour of women but to rising prices, particularly of silver, in the market economy.

Incoming brideprice, because it is the largest amount of liquid money transacted at a given period, is most frequently converted into jewellery. There is a specified set of the items of jewellery which every

Girasia man aspires to possess. Jewellery items displayed by the wife, above all, reflect the prosperity of her husband's household (as an index of the income saved from present production) and his lineage (as jewellery is inherited). Besides the use of jewellery as a store of value, some items are pawned to pay off existing debts or as a means to collect money for further brideprice amounts. During one of my visits to the silversmith *(soni)* in Abu Road, a Girasia woman came to retrieve her pawned silver necklace *(hohri)*. Although women can collect pawned pieces of jewellery, it is the men who negotiate the exchange in the first place. According to Narayan Lal Soni, one of the main silversmiths in Abu Road: [27]

> In the past fifteen days approximately seventy-five Girasia *ne jewar girwi raakha* [have pawned their jewellery]. Of all my customers, ninety percent are Girasia. Most of the pawning takes place in the rainy season (for crop production), the *mela* season (for barter at the fairs), when they have to bring wives (most frequently in the summer) and periodically for the police cases. Most of my customers were those of my father's as well. Usually men come to pawn jewellery. The *byaaj* [interest] charged is Rs. 11/- *sekda* [per hundred] per year. At the most the jewellery is pawned for a year to a year and a half. Ten to twenty years ago, men used to wear jewellery as well. The three main items they would wear would be silver anklets, silver buttons on the shirt and a silver plated comb in the hair. Now none of these are worn. In comparison, women buy and wear more jewellery today than before. This is because they are getting their hands on more money. But still the pawning business is more than the actual sales. Personally we like the Girasia. Although they are uneducated they do not create *jhagda tanta* [problems and fights] and they are the largest of our customers. We weigh the jewellery they pawn and return it when they bring the actual sums and the interest.

I did not hear of any complaints amongst the Taivars against the unfairness or exploitation by the silversmith money lenders. Girasia money transactions are confined primarily to the buying and pawning of jewellery. Jewellery is bought strictly in cash, as are clothes. Most other small items of Girasia need could, on the other hand, be purchased with forest products or agricultural produce. As jewellery is an item considered to be the property of the male head of the household, the brideprice transaction and the related pawning of the items of jewellery, is strictly a matter between men. There is therefore no question of a woman's participation in the brideprice negotiations.

27. This interview was conducted in the month of May, which was in between the fair and marriage season for the Girhayas. It was also one of the few months of hardship and low food stocks, prior to the next sowing season.

In contrast to the Girasia pride in their brideprice transactions, a number of lower castes perceive their brideprice as shameful. Lower castes sharing spatial and socio-economic ties with all other castes are more likely to feel, and be made to feel, their inferior position. Subsequently, if the lower castes practice brideprice they are more likely to regard it as a 'lower' form. For example, Parry (1979) found that the Rathis were ashamed of their brideprice and Madan (1965) recorded concealed brideprice transactions among the Kashmiri Brahmins. I would suggest that the lower caste or lineages in Kangra and Kashmir practised brideprice payments because it was economically more remunerative although it was not consonant with their concerns with prestige. Among the numerically dominant Girasia, living in purely Girasia settlements and away from the multi-caste villages, the acceptance by the other castes is not a pressing concern. For the Girasia, therefore, there is less of a pressure to gain status in the outsider's eyes by an emulation of the dowry payments of the other castes.

In this chapter I have shown that despite the differences from upper- and middle-caste dowry practices, the Girasia brideprice system shares with other caste groups, a similar concern with a patrilineally-informed, prestige-related caste ideology. In the analysis of their marriage payments above I have argued that, when viewed in relation to their economic resources, prestige, and the cultural constructions of women, both the Girasia brideprice system and the ideal dowry system in India are fundamentally similar.

Chapter 8

RELIGION AND THE EXPERIENCE OF KINSHIP

*T*he focus of this chapter is on Girasia religious beliefs and practices and their relationship to the social context in which the Girasia live. I describe Girasia religion through the sacred spaces in which it is manifest (section 1). I do not analyse the rituals in detail, but focus instead on the social and economic implications of ritual occasions to comment on the gendered distribution of power in the Girasia community. Early social anthropological studies on Hindu religion have been concerned with the differences between the Sanskritic, or classical, philosophical and text-based aspects of religion on the one hand, and the popular, 'folk' religious practices, on the other hand (Srinivas 1952, Mandelbaum 1955). More contemporary studies (Berreman 1964, Babb 1975, Sharma 1970, Fuller 1979, 1988) have shown that the apparent disjunction between Sanskritic and popular Hinduism is one of 'differences of style or ritual dialect' (Babb, 1975: 27) and thus differences which are part of Hinduism rather than distinct from it. I discuss the role of the Girasia ritual experts as a means to understand the differences and similarities between the Girasia and non-Girasia and thereby the local, regional and supra regional aspects to Girasia religious experience (section 2). The Taivar Girasia have both shamanistic[1] and non-shamanistic ritual

---

1. I follow Seymour-Smith's basic definition of a shaman as, 'part-time religious specialist, whose abilities are based on direct personal experience' (1986: 256).

experts who are men from within the Girasia caste community. The neighbouring villages also have both kinds of ritual experts. However, in contrast to the Girasia pattern, the non-shamanistic ritual experts often belong to the higher, usually Brahmin caste, while the shamans are members of the lower castes. Girasia women are neither ritual experts nor major participants in the rituals. This was in contrast to the relatively intense religious participation of middle- and upper-caste women.

Locating the Sacred

During my stay, I was struck by the number of occasions when the Girasia got together (often more than once a week) to eat, sing, dance and seek blessings of the deities. Almost every Taivar gathering involved both the performance of a ritual and the distribution of some type of food. The gatherings were most frequently at night when all the Girasia could participate and were held especially when there was moonlight. The light of the moon and the light of the fires lit by the shrines played on the silver jewellery which the women wore and created a very different atmosphere from the day time. It was on these occasions that I felt far removed from life outside the village.

The meetings almost always commence with singing and dancing and it is only after several hours that the deities and spirits, generally referred to as *baosi* (a term of respect also used for elders who possessed supernatural knowledge) are invoked.[2] Usually only one deity is addressed at any one occasion. The deities are either male or female and are worshipped at specific places in the village. Only certain members of the community can act as ritual mediators *(bhopa)*. The occasions of communication with the supernatural are of two kinds : 1) those that are customary and consist of appointed days of worship according to the lunar calender. Such occasions usually consist of gatherings of more than one household and on some occasions bring together the whole village; 2) those that are spontaneous and brought about by circumstance, for example marriage, death or sickness. Sickness is the most common occasion for supernatural contact and involves the members of a single household, sometimes other members of the sublineage. Most deities have collective cere-

2. I use the word deity to mean divine beings represented in animal or human form. By spirits, I refer to the featureless supernatural beings. Spirits are also more mobile versions of the deities and manifest themselves in the possession of the shaman by 'his' deity.

monies at which a genealogically-specified number of people will attend, as well as instances where individuals approach the deities with a ritual mediator and a few family members. (This distinction between collective and individual worship is common to the popular practice of Hinduism in most of rural India; see Sharma, 1970).

This section describes briefly both individual and collective ritual occasions as they occur in Girasia sacred spaces (summarised in table 8.1, below). The description progresses from large collective gatherings, involving all the sublineages, to more individual areas of worship.

The Uncovered Shrines of the Lineage

The two major uncovered shrines in the village are those of the Mountain deity *(Bhakar baosi)* and the *Shitala Mata* (pox mother/goddess). Every Girasia village has one shrine to each of these deities. The Girasia shrine to the Mountain deity, situated on an open platform usually along a public path, was always the most visible and dramatic of the Girasia shrines. The Mountain deity, regarded as a benevolent and protective spirit, is physically represented by a small clay tablet of a man with a sword astride a horse (about six inches high). Large reddish-brown clay horses *(ghoda)*, each approximately four times the size of the tablet, dominate the platform and give the shrine a striking appearance. These horses, placed on a platform, were usually all facing in one direction, much like the battle position of an army cavalry division. The horses represent the offerings (sacrifice?) [3] made to the Mountain deity by individual Girasia whose special requests made in the form of an oath (*manauti*) had been fulfilled.[4] The collective worship of the Mountain deity takes place when all the eight Taivar sublineage participate in the annual *Baba-ki gair*, a festival of dance and drama on the second day of *holi purnima* (the full moon on the night before the Holi spring festival).[5] Holi is the

3. Possibly connected to the ancient Rajput custom of the horse sacrifice.
4. *Manauti* (the process of performing a penance of belief called *manyata*) is a voluntary invocation of the blessings of the deities, and a common feature at all the Taivar shrines. The *manauti* has to be made *baosi homo joije* (in front of the deity) either directly in front of the deity, or at home in a position facing the shrine of the deity. At least five men are required as witnesses. The hands and feet of the man who wishes to perform manauti are washed with water. He then pours water with both his hands in the direction of the *baosi*, promising a gift (payment ?) to the *baosi* if his penance is heard. *Manautis* are made by individual Taivar men in the presence of some of their male sublineage members.
5. At the *Baba-ki-gair*, the *bhopa* (ritual mediator) becomes possessed by the *Bhakar* spirit and blesses those of the congregation who come before him. The congre-

popular Hindu festival of colour, celebrated all over the north to welcome spring. It is mythologically related to the immolation of the evil Holika, sister of the corrupt Hindu King Hiranakush. Both conspired to kill the king's ascetically-orientated son Prahlad. Many Taivar daughters, married outside the lineage, return home for this occasion. The men and women (wives and unmarried daughters) who work away from the village, as wage labourers *(mazdoori)*, also return to the village.

Always placed close to the shrine of the Mountain deity is the shrine of *Shitala Mata* (literally, cool mother; referring to the pox goddess) because, according to the Taivars, the *Bhakar baosi* and *Shitala Mata* were, 'like brother and sister'. *Shitala Mata* is represented by a pockmarked stone set under a tree. She is worshipped to prevent afflictions of fevers and pockmarks. She is annually worshipped on the day following the *Baba-ki-gair* celebration for the Mountain deity. Compared to the annual ritual at the shrine of the Mountain deity, at the *Mata* (general term for female dieties and spirits in the region, 'mother' in Hindi) worship, most of the emphasis is on procuring her blessings, considered especially important for enhancing the fertility of women. At the blessing ceremony, the *bhopa* (mediums) of the Mountain deity and the *Mata* sit together although only the *Mata bhopa* (medium of the *Mata*) anoints the foreheads of the blessed. Songs and dances accompany the *Mata* worship, although on this occasion they had taken place the night before. They are more devotional in quality than the relatively abandoned celebration of the Bhakar *baba-ki-gair*.

The pox goddess, unlike the Mountain deity, is considered powerful because of her connection with illness, especially fevers. In one instance during my fieldwork, a child had become ill with chickenpox. When I visited her mother, she said *Mata baosi pomna aaya hai* (the revered goddess has come to stay as our guest). She believed that the disease had to be treated with care and reverence for fear that it would increase if the visiting deity was displeased. Thus the goddess is at the same time both feared and respected, and there is an ambiguity between illness and 'purity' (sacredness) in much the

---

gation only receive the blessing of the *bhopa*. The actual ceremony he performed for the *Bhakar* deity was marginalised by the collective celebration. The sublineages of the village put up short and humorous skits mocking positions of authority within the village and lineage, as well as the police or politicians of the district. In the process there was a lot of noise and dust with people talking, drums beating, singing and dancing. The frivolity of the celebration was in marked contrast to the more serious supernatural contact at the other Taivar shrines.

Table 8.1 Taivar Girasia Ritual Occasions

No.	Girasia Social Unit	Deity (sex, in order of importance)	Space of Deity	Ritual Mediator	Ritual Occasion (according to Hindu lunar calendar)
1.	The village (all the sublineages)	(i) *Bhakar Baosi* (M) (ii) *Shitala Mata* (F)	Open shrines placed close to each other under separate trees.	*Bhakar Bhopa* *Mata Bhopa*	(i) *Baba Ki Gair* (annual; every *dujam* after *holi purnima**) (ii) *Shitala Satam* (annual, *satam* after *holi purnima**) * usually in March
2.	2-3 sublineages	(i) *Bhairu Baosi* (M) (ii) *Amba Mata* (F) (iii) *Nag Devta* (N) (iv) *Dev Dhanni* (M) (v) *Gune/ Ganesh*	*Devra* (3 *devra* in Paoti, Malwa and Naal *phalli*).	*Bhairu Bhopa* with *Mata Bhopa* (one set for each *devra*)	*Rati Jaga* (every 3 months, held for *Bhairu Baosi*, during my fieldwork these were held on: (a) *Magh Satam* – beginning of Feb. (b) *Baisakh Purnima* – beginning of May (c) *Bhadho Sath* – beginning of August (d) *Kartik* – beginning of November
3.	Each sublineage	(i) *Path Baosi* (M) (ancestor spirit) (ii) *Phulera Mata* (F) (or *veer*)	– domestic shrine – domestic shrine	*Khoont* *Bhopa* of the *Hojvan*	(ia) *Beej* ceremony (annual, in September between sowing and harvesting the corn crop) (ib) funerals and marriages (ii) annual *Phulera Mata Manana* (after *beej* above)
4.	Each sublineage household	(i) *Bhooth* (ghost, M) (ii) *Malri* (evil magic)	Small objects placed in field near gates, boundary walls, house	Specialists, grain diviner (*devala*), exorcist (*jadhphook*)	Uncharted occasions, especially during sickness, disease, afflictions.
5.	'Believer' households (members of a low caste organisation)	Anop Das (human figure)	*Jhonpadi* (or hut)	none propagators	*Sangat Bhajan* (on occasions parallel to the customary rituals above)

same manner that Ram (1988) has described for smallpox afflictions among the Mukkuvar fishing community in south India. As Ram points out, serious bouts of illness are an affliction, but are also considered an 'opportunity to exercise the power of the divine in the form of surrender and faith' (ibid.: 99). Here, I find, the body can itself be treated as a ritual space.

The Covered Shrine of the Sublineage

The most important and elaborately decorated sacred space in the village is to be found in the *devra* shrine (literally, where the *dev* or deities stay; a common term in rural Rajasthan for a shrine to popular local deities, Kothari 1982, Gold 1987). The *devra* shrines are distinctive in that, unlike the Girasia huts of mud, clay and wood, they are constructed from cement and stone.[6] The durable quality of the shrine reflects, above all, its central place in Taivar life and, as I show in discussing the management, organisation and attendance of its deities, the *devra* symbolised the kinship divisions within the lineage. There are three *devra* in the Taivar village, which are associated with specific sublineages. The *devra* is usually located on a hill top and houses five deities, which are represented by painted clay tablets and supported by a mud platform inside the hut which runs along the wall facing the entrance.[7] The actual number of clay tablets varied from *devra* to *devra*, but are always copies of a similar set of five deities. The five deities in order of importance for the Girasia were: the *Bhairu* (male protector); the *Kuldevi* (clan mother); *Vasing Nag* (serpent deity); *Dharamraj* (pastoral hero) and *Ganesh* (elephant god of the Hindu pantheon).[8] Apart from the images of these deities,

6. The *devra* was also recognised as it flew a white flag in contrast to the red flag of the *Mata* (the Girasia associated the colour white with men).
7. The entrance of these *devra* was towards Molela, 'where the gods come from' (i.e., where they were literally made). The Taivars went to Molela in order to fulfil a vow made to a deity in the *devra*, in which the Taivar man would perform the service of bringing another representation (tablet) to the *devra* if the deity assisted him in a specific task. following the the deity's assistance and intervention in a particular manner. Among the vows made there was usually one which promised to *baosi lana* (literally, bring a clay tablet) from Molela.
8. *Dev dhanni* also known as *Dharamraj,* is a mythical hero and descendant of the Gujjars, a pastoral community in the region who are associated in folklore with Lord Rama and the creation of the universe. The *Kuldevi* or the clan goddess is considered responsible for the birth of the lineage. *Kala-Gora Bhairu,* the most potent and destructive of the deities, are the descendants of Shiva, the Hindu destroyer of the universe, and the protectors of his wife Parvati. The two *Bhairu*, one darker than the other, were represented on the halves of the same

there were also *veer* or formless protector spirits who were considered the 'soldiers' and slaves of the major deities. These spirits were represented by small featureless stones placed next to the deities, approximately four inches in height and covered in vermilion dots.

In the following lines, I look more closely at the ritual occasions surrounding the two main deities of the *devra*, the *Bhairu* and the *Mata*. These two deities are given prominence among the Girasia and the two ritual mediators associated with the *devra* shrine were for these two deities. *Bhairu*, regarded as the most important and powerful force among the dieties, was considered the 'head of the *devra* household'. The *devra* was, in fact, seen as a homage to his destructive powers. *Bhairu* was represented as a potent male force both in his western Indian regional manifestations (Kothari 1982, Gold 1987), as well as in Tamil Nadu in south India (Fuller 1988). The largest gatherings at the *devra* were for the quarterly *rati-jaga* (or night spent awake celebrating *Bhairu*). In practice, the *rati-jaga* was one night spent in *jagaran* (or waking the spirit)[9] and some hours of the following night in *samapti* (or in 'closure' of the celebration). The songs sung on this occasion remembered ancestors and the times of hardship faced by the sublineage. Most of the young adult Taivars remain outside the *devra* to sing and dance the *balar* (heroic, historic songs) until the early hours of the morning. All men and women outside the *devra* waited for the blessings and the distribution of the *prasad* (blessed and sacred food, among the Girasia usually a mixture of wheat flour, oil and molasses boiled in water) which takes place when the drums beat and the *bhopa dhunni* (or when *bhopa* is in trance). In the *jagaran* the congregation wait for the spirit of *Bhairu* to enter the mediator. In his possessed *(bhav)* state the *bhopa* is consulted by those Taivars who are in trouble. Their queries are put forward by the elder male members. The *bhopa* advises them and also blesses the rest of the congregation, who come forward one by one. The *samapti* on the next day is a shorter meeting and ends in the partaking of another round of *prasad*.

The *jagaran* for the *Bhairu* deity is also an occasion for the *velchhodna*, a ceremony at which certain male members of the commu-

---

tablet. *Kala bhairu* or the darker, more ferocious of the two is greatly revered by the Taivars. The *Bhairu* images are always found placed next to those of the *Mata*.

9. At the *jagaran*, or first night of the ritual for *Bhairu*, the *Bhairu bhopa* and *Mata bhopa* sit next to the *Bhairu* images. The *bhopas*, along with the *veliya*, prepare the ritual space and the food at dusk before the congregation arrive. First the offerings of *churma* and incense are made to the deities. By this time the night has progressed and the *devra* is filled with smoke and people. Outside in front of the *devra* the women sing songs and sway holding arms.

nity are promoted to a higher ritual status. These members are from among the *veliya* or the wearers of the white thread (around the neck) who perform tasks in the *devra* shrine which are associated with the preparation of the rituals and the sacred food. The v*eliya* are Taivar men who have been 'chosen' by *Bhairu,* often on the successful completion of a vow. They then feel compelled to become servants, *veliya,* to the *Bhairu* and perform all the chores for rituals in the shrine. The *Bhairu* ritual mediator also nominates some *veliya* to the next stage of service symbolised by giving them the brass ring or *veeti.* (All *bhopa* wear brass rings but all those who wear brass rings were not *bhopas.* The Bhairu *bhopa* is selected from among the wearers of the brass ring.) Although the Mata *bhopa* also takes part in blessing the congregation, only the Bhairu *bhopa* attains *bhav* (possession by a spirit) and advises 'patients'. For the Taivars there can be only one ritual mediator for Bhairu at a *devra* shrine because 'There is only one spirit of the *Bhairu* which resides in the *devra* like every Girasia household which has only one male head' (although there could be more than one clay tablet with the image of *Bhairu*). I also observed that there was a belief that if the *bhopa* was a closer kinsman, he would be more amenable to personal problems of members of the sublineage. However, members of all the sublineages attended the ritual ceremonies at all the *devra* because '*Bhairu* is one and the blessings are important'.

The *kuldevi* or *mata* is invoked on very different occasions from those of *Bhairu.* A major part of marriage ceremonies are constituted by the worship of the *Kuldevi/Mata.* For example, in a marriage the worship of the clan mother is a major part of the ceremonies. Separate drawings of the clan mother are made for the bride and groom which represent the different patrilineal lineages they come from. Like wives, the female deities also mark the differences between lineages. According to Phoola, the *kuldevi* (clan mother) of the Taivars is called *Amba Mata.* He said that the Khairadi and Dungaicha Girasia lineages (who were affinally related to the Taivars; see chapters 4 and 5), also have *Amba Mata* as *kuldevi.* This at once contests studies on clan organisation in India (Karve 1968, Deliege 1985, Meherda 1985, Dave 1960, Lal 1979, Sinha 1962, Navalkha 1959, Nath 1959) which claim that in all cases, the *kuldevi* or clan mother separates groups into those whom one may marry (of different clan mothers) and those whom one may not (of the same clan mother).[10] Moreover, I was told,

10. As if to reinforce this point, Phoola went on to say that only their village (not the Taivar households in the villages of Rada or Nichalagarh) did the Taivars

Religion and the Experience of Kinship

the earliest Taivar Girasia used to consider a different deity as their clan mother, pointing to the ambiguity of such classifications.[11]

Apart for the *Mata or Kuldevi* for the whole lineage, each sublineage also worships its own female deity, *phulera mata* (the specific names vary from sublineage to sublineage). The *phulera mata* has a distinct ritual space, usually in the oldest household of the sublineage. This space is also usually near that of the *path baosi* or ancestor of the sublineage and thus will be discussed in the subsection on household shrines, below.

I now turn briefly to some of the wider meanings of the *devra* in its role as a shrine of the sublineage. Each of the three *devra* in the Taivar village had a proprietorial group which consisted of the members of two to three sublineages.[12] There was a fourth *devra* in the village, the Bubariya *devra*. This *devra* catered to the affinally related, non-Taivar, Bubariya lineage households in the village. The Bubariya shrine had Bubariya ritual mediators. The *devra* arrangements reflected the Girasia boundaries within the lineage, both in terms of the spatial arrangements within a household, as well as symbolically in the relation between sublineages. They also reflected gender relations.

More than the shrine to the Mountain deity, that to Bhairu represents the sublineage's conquest of territory and symbolises the right to land procured by its earliest ancestors. According to one influential Taivar, 'When our fathers moved here, their gods also moved with them'. Prior to installing a *devra* shrine, the Bhairu *bhopa* in his possessed state finds a stone and is 'led to the space' where the *devra* should be built. The shrine as a concrete symbol of the ownership of

---

worship *Amba Mata*. The other Taivar households worshipped *Chamunda Mata*, as did the Bubariya affinal lineage, the Khejara Parmar Girasia with whom the Taivars had affinal connections and the Jambudi Parmar Girasia from whom the Taivars trace patrilineal descent (chapter 2). The other Girasia lineages worshipped clan mothers who had names such as *Dharu Mata, Kalhe Mata, Kheemraj Mata* and *Ashapuri Mata*. This last clan mother was worshipped by the Damar and Sawan Girasia lineages.

11. According to Phoola, the Taivars used to worship *Chamunda Mata* but since they had a fight with the other Parmar Girasia Rajputs, they had begun to worship *Amba Mata* instead. The oldest shrine to the Taivar clan mother was in Nichalagarh. It was a shrine to *Chamunda Mata* and had been established by Phoola's ancestors when they first came to Nichalagarh from Jambudi. Phoola said he went there very occasionally when he wanted to make a wish.

12. The three *devra* shrines are known by the names of the *phalli* sections in which they are located. The Naal *devra* 'belongs' to the Billath, Gokhlath, Rehmath and Raijjath sublineage; the Malwa *devra* belongs to the Vaijjath and Lailath sublineage; the Paoti *devra* belongs to the Khetrath and Devath sublineages. The distribution of the sacred and blessed food is done by specific members of these sublineages.

land by precedence is a common feature in this region of Rajasthan. Different castes in the nearby villages had their Bhairu shrines in their own sections of the village. The deep-seated belief in Bhairu is common to the region the Girasia inhabited. According to Kothari (1982) writing on popular shrines in Western Rajasthan: 'Bhairon appears as the guardian of the classical gods and goddesses and a small shrine to him can be seen facing or outside Hindu or Jain temples ... no habitation can be considered a village without a shrine to Bhairon, who is considered the protector' (ibid.: 22, 23). Kothari notes that Bhairu or Bhairon is a regional, protective male deity. The power attributed to Bhairu is so potent that all the communities revere him. Kothari also records that in folk belief Bhairon was regarded as one of the manifestations of the classical Hindu god Shiva. Singhi (1990), in his study of the upper-caste Jain merchant community of Sirohi comments, 'Each lane has a separate *than* [ritual place] for the deities Virji bawasi or Bhaironji, who are considered the protectors of those areas' (ibid.: 24).

Shrines in the House

The two main shrines in the house are to the ancestor spirit and the female protector spirit of the sublineage. The shrine to the ancestor spirit or *path baosi* is confined to a single sublineage in contrast to the open shrine for all sublineages and the covered *devra* shrine for selected sublineages. It is usually situated in the oldest house of the sublineage. The *path baosi* thus 'lived' with the members of the sublineage as part of the family, in contrast to the Bhairu *baosi* or *Kuldevi*, located in their own shrine. The sacred space of the *path* is demarcated by three vermilion marks on the lower side of the wall in the inner room of the hut. Here the annual *beej* celebrations are held after the annual sowing of corn in September for the 'spirits our forefathers believed in' and in turn celebrates the forefathers themselves.[13] The sacred space of the ancestors is also 'portable' in the sense that at the lifecycle rituals of marriage and death, a space is made sacred and the *path baosi* is 'invited'. The bride and the groom have separate *path* accompanied by a different design for the clan mother. The reason for two rather than one *path* for the bride and groom, I was told, is because, 'They are of different lineages and each lineage has its own ancestors and clan goddess'. The arrangement of a *path* requires a

13. Often the section of the hut which housed the shrine remained unused throughout the year. Songs were sung through the night at the hut of the *path baosi*.

combination of both sacred materials and special words *(mantra)* to be put together in a specified area. Consequently the ritual mediator has to have special instruction in its construction. It is the *khoont* rather than the *bhopa* who is the ritual mediator for the *path baosi*. While spirits 'used' the physical medium of the *bhopa*, the *khoont* himself does not become possessed (the section below details yet further differences between these two ritual offices).

The other shrine in the Girasia house is that of the female protector spirit, *phulera mata*. The shrine to the *phulera mata* is usually next to that of the *path baosi* inside the household of the sublineage elder. For example, Lala and his sons live in the oldest housesite of the Raijjath sublineage. The *path baosi* shrine is in the house of Lala's second youngest son Ramla. The *phulera mata* was in the adjacent house of Jhumla, his closest brother. The *phulera mata* was represented by a figure of a woman astride a tiger (a common regional representation of the clan mother among all castes).[14] The celebration of *phulera mata* was distinct from that of the *path baosi* and held after it. The *phulera mata* unlike the *path baosi* was a spirit *(veer)* of the *kuldevi* (see below on the *veer* or featureless spirits).

Individual Spirits and Jealousy, Illness and Witchcraft

The main male deity, Bhairu, and the two female deities, the clan mother and the pox goddess are considered strong and powerful deities who have *veer* or accompanying spirits. These spirits can be the souls of the dead as well as the living. They can be male or female spirits. They can be either harmful or helpful spirits. The Taivar Girasia often blame these spirits for illness and ailments in the community. During fieldwork I observed that most often it was the harmful or dissatisfied spirit *(malri)* which afflicted people. *Malri*s would inflict pain through spells called *mooth*. Palvi recounted her experience of *mooth* to me as follows

> Approximately four years ago my *anganwadi* [child-care centre] was not yet set up in a house and we used to meet under the peepal tree in front of Pema Patel's house. The first time the steel chairs arrived for our centre, Pema and the other elders sat on them. That Nichalagarh woman was also there. Kheema Patel insisted that I should also sit on a chair. I

14. The Brahmin *purohit* in the multicaste village of Ore have a similar image for their clan mother. The representation of the clan goddess is etched on a small (2 inch by 2 inch) silver plated plaque. The plaque is placed near the wall of the hut, with a *diya* (clay lamp), *kelu* (clay roof-tile used for the sacred embers) and *hankal* (the steel pronged instrument of every *mata*).

remember the Nichalagarh woman looked at me in a strange manner. When I got back that day I was cold and dizzy. I could only walk back until Hoja's well. From there I had to be helped home. At home I vomited blood and the *peelkhe-vala baosi* was called (Heva, the respected man of the *peelkha* tree). He did *jhadu* [literally, to sweep] with a date palm leaf and some *mantras*. It was the *mooth* of that woman that got me. One of my relatives had died of the same thing in Abu Road. He had passed blood also in his stool. It is all the burning (jealousy). When I wear the socks that you gave me, every one calls me *Moti-bai* (important woman) and they feel hot (jealous).

Palvi recounts reasons for jealousy or 'difference' as important factors which invite *mooth*.[15] The most dramatic affliction presented by the *veer* is its attack on a living soul, reflected in the accusation of witchcraft. Several times during fieldwork I heard the mention of *dakan* (literally 'witch' in Hindi). Twice women pointed out 'witches' to me, and said they could not give further details as they would fall sick. They said that they knew they were victims of witchcraft and tormented by these women from the slight fevers they had been getting recently. *Veer* could thus attack at the instigation of powerful deities or powerful humans and indicate the attacker's displeasure. While some women are regarded as *dakan*, to be in possession of a secret and evil power which could use malevolent *veer* to attack people, there is no similar sinister power attached to men. *Veer* are considered most powerful because they are highly mobile. I would suggest that it is because women are associated with both mobility and detachability (especially in their role as wives), that the *veer* are frequently seen to be women. Both men and women recounted a case from several years earlier, when a Taivar man had killed his mother with an axe to prevent her from exercising her evil powers. However, information on this subject was extremely difficult to obtain, mainly because of the danger it entailed for the person who conveyed the information. Various methods are used to appease the tormenting spirit, depending on which spirit has been identified as causing the problem.[16] For example, Heva's daughter and grand-

15. This was why she wore the socks I gave her only a few times and then gave them to her son to wear.
16. Jala, a Taivar member of the Naal phalli had been sick while I was in the Taivar village. The *Bhairu baosi* spoke through the ritual mediator who told him that he was affected by a *Dev* (deity) *veer* who was upset as he had not been given a place in the *devra*. The mediator predicted that unless the *veer* was installed, Jala would not get better. The two ritual mediators of the *devra* shrine in the Naal *phalli*, along with the sublineage elder and several others of the man's sublineage set out to find the spirit (*baosi kaadna*, to take out the spirit). They went in a single

child were both feeling sick and Heva decided it was the soul of his former wife that was tormenting them. He explained that 'she' was upset because she had not been given an elaborate funeral *(nyath)*. Now she demanded that she be made a *devi* (goddess). So Heva reenacted the process of burying her and deifying her *(devi-banana)* with his *haga bhai* (real brothers). They all ate together afterwards.

While all other deities are worshipped at appointed times and in specified places, the worship of the *veer* varies in place, time and numbers in the congregation. This is due to the fact that *veer* are identified with a variety of social tensions, illness, sickness and diseases which range from the awareness of jealousy to the more serious diseases of chickenpox and tuberculosis. More than other deities, the ritual space of the *veer* is the body of the victim rather than that of the ritual mediator.

In concluding this section, I would briefly like to highlight the major similarities and differences of Girasia religious processes as compared to other caste practices in the region. As mentioned earlier, belief in Bhairu is widespread in the region. Bhairu is considered the local manifestation of the Hindu god Shiva (some Girasia told me he was the protector of Shiva's wife). Like Shiva, Bhairu is considered powerful because of his association with destruction. The belief in *Mata* (the clan mother) is also common among the patrifocal caste groups in the region. A number of caste groups believe in the clan goddess Chamunda for example. Furthermore, the *path* is a common construction at all Hindu rites, especially of the household (Babb 1975, Gold 1987, Khare 1972). The belief in *veer,* spirits as causing fevers and illness, sometimes emanating from witches, has, moreover, been observed in multi-caste villages (Berreman 1964, Harper 1969, Babb 1975) and in rural Rajasthan (Carstairs 1988,

---

file, with the Mata *bhopa* in front holding a bunch of peacock feathers (which quivered to show that a spirit had entered the *bhopa*). The Mata *bhopa* was followed by the Bhairu *bhopa* (holding up the *guruj* or iron instrument of the *Bhairu* spirit), Shyama *patel* holding up a *halwani* (the iron part of the plough), a sublineage member blowing a conch, and finally men and boys beating two drums. They went from household to household. At each household they would light a fire in the hearth and hold the *halwani* upright in it. Depending on the kind of quiver it received, the *veer* was to be identified. Jala's *veer* was identified a day later, in the shape of a stone. It was washed with milk, anointed with vermilion paste, wrapped in a cloth to protect it from the 'winds', and then carried on a brass plate to the *devra* where it was ritualistically installed. Watching at some distance with a group of other women, I was told that we should not be in front of the procession as we could be struck by a *japta* (curse). No women were involved in the *baosi kaadna*. The hearth which played a central role in the identification of the *veer* implied a female role in Lala's suffering as did the fact that the *Mata bhopa* led the procession.

Lambert 1990). In terms of the specific rituals performed, there were also similarities between the Girasia and non-Girasia communities. For example, in the rituals of marriage and death (described in chapters 4 and 6 respectively) the Girasia use the 'pure' elements of turmeric, milk, clarified butter, cowdung, ash and water used in the Sanskritic (textual) Hindu rituals. Furthermore, all the Girasia rituals are accompanied by the distribution of *prasad.* The pan-regional element of these ritual observances is pointed out by Babb (1975). Babb highlights the similarities between popular and Sanskritic Hinduism on the basis of three crucial aspects. According to Babb (1975: 47) the elements common to the diverse rituals as practised by various communities in central India were firstly, a purity in approaching the divinity (in place, bodies, context and materials) which he called *puja.* Secondly, the rituals shared a common attitude of respect for the divinity or *pranam.* Finally, in each case, the congregation partook in the distribution of the sacred or blessed food *(prasad).*

Apart from the ritual practices within the village the Girasia like all other castes, also go on pilgrimages. The ostensible reasons are to ask for favours from other powerful deities in the region (see also Gold 1987). A number of Taivar Girasia made trips to Ambaji, a major shrine to the mother goddess Amba which was situated in Gujarat, close to the border with Abu Road. Ambaji is a popular place of worship in the region, where all castes congregate at certain times of the year. The Taivar Girasia went annually to Ambaji after Holi, especially if there had been a death in the family, or if a special vow was to be made. In this sense, the Girasia also share in the religious beliefs and practices of the region. It was in the Girasia celebration of *gaur* that I found the strongest affirmation of the Girasia sharing the traditions of the other communities in the region. The festival of *gangaur* is annually celebrated in most of rural and urban Rajasthan in the *tritiya shukla paksha* of the *chaitra* month (which falls in March or April depending on the position of the moon) of the Hindu lunar calendar. It is essentially a celebration of fertility. The mythological focus of the festival is the wedding of the celestial couple Shiva *(gan)* and Parvati *(gaur). Gangaur* is celebrated everywhere in Rajasthan as a festival of women wherein Parvati is worshipped as a symbol of conjugal bliss and marital faithfulness. On this occasion married women and unmarried girls worship Parvati to obtain her blessings for the long life of their husbands or for their good prospects of finding husbands.[17]

17. The *gaur mela* at Siawa lasted for two days and brought all the Girasia in the region together to witness the wedding of Shiva and Parvati, and the symbolic

While the story, myth and performance of the rite is the same as in other villages and cities, the idols of Shiva and Parvati are dressed in Girasia clothes and Girasia songs are sung accompanying the *balar* (Girasia historical ballads). In contrast to all other ritual occasions, Girasia women here are visible participants although not in authoritative roles (also see last section).

Here, I have described Girasia ritual spaces with reference to the genealogical and spatial ties among members of the village. Only very broad interpretations of the rituals have been put forward. I have also briefly compared Girasia and non-Girasia religious practices as a means of contextualising Girasia religious beliefs and processes. In the next section I discuss the role of the main ritual experts, the *bhopa*, *khoont* and *devala*, and their position within the lineage.

Religion and Power in the Lineage

The Shaman, Priest and Diviner

The *bhopa* (ritual mediator, shaman), *khoont* (priest) and *devala* (grain diviner) are the main authorities on Girasia religion in the village. Both the *khoont* and *devala* are 'religious technicians' (following Berreman 1964: 60) in the sense that they undergo specialised training, the *khoont* in the construction of ritual spaces and the *devala* in order to identify the afflicting spirit through the means of corn grains. The 'religious technicians' never become possessed by a spirit and are always paid for their services. The *bhopa*, on the other hand, is divinely selected in that he becomes possessed by the deity. The *bhopa*, unlike the *khoont* or *devala*, is attached to a deity and shrine without specific training or remuneration.

Bhopa are the most numerous and the most visible of the ritual experts in a Taivar village. I will first describe their position in the community. The Girasia *bhopa* is a medium in which the supernatural manifested itself. A *bhopa* is self-selected or 'chosen by the deity'.[18] Once the deity has specified the human medium it will frequent, the *bhopa* can himself entice the spirit to enter his body at times when communication is desired. The *bhopa* makes specific

---

vidaai or departure of Parvati to her in-laws. Parvati came as a bride from the care of one *bhopa* (her 'father'), who belonged to a section in Siawa village, and went to another *bhopa* (her 'in-laws') from another part of Siawa.

18. According to Kothari (1982) the phrase *bhopa pakarna*, (ibid.: 30), or catching the *bhopa*, was a common phrase especially among the lower-caste communities of western Rajasthan.

body movements and sounds when the spirit enters his body.[19] The *bhopa* is possessed ('visited') by the spirit of only one deity. The *bhopa* once visited by a particular spirit continues to be periodically possessed by the same spirit over time, especially at the occasions specified to celebrate the deity. More than one individual can be 'visited' by the same spirit. It is also not unusual to have more than one *bhopa* possessed by the same deity. At a particular shrine, however, there is only one *bhopa* of a particular deity. This was the *bhopa* who could demonstrate that he had more ritual strength *(pakar)* than others.

A *bhopa* need not be succeeded directly by his son.[20] According to Dopa Chela (son of an elderly *bhopa*), the son of a *bhopa* learned about possession by observing his father and could inherit the *bhav* (feeling/possesion) of a particular spirit. He can manifest *dhunni* vibrations/trance) sometimes, but he never assumes the role of *bhopa* in the *devra* as long as his father is alive. Thus if a *bhopa* is old and infirm it is more likely that the son of a previous *bhopa* will occupy his position. Depending on the circumstances which allowed the *bhopa* to establish themselves in the community, they have powers of varying strengths. Including the two *bhopa* for the open shrine, there were two *bhopa* at each of the three *devra*, making a total of eight official *bhopa* in the village for the shrines where more than one sublineage gathered. The three covered shrines each had two *bhopa* for the main deities *Bhairu* and *Mata*. In each case the *bhopa* came from the sublineages associated with the shrine, although the *bhopa* at the same shrine came from different sublineages.[21] I suggest that the distribution of *bhopa* positions between the sublineages indicates a diffusion rather than a concentration of ritual authority within the lineage.

The *bhopa* were observed to be given high regard at the time of possession only and are not necessarily respected outside their possessed state. Once the body is freed from the hold of the spirit and the *bhopa* returns to his 'normal' state, he is treated as an ordinary

19. The utterances and gestures told the audience when the *bhopa* was possessed. According to Laga *bhopa*, 'The Mountain deity makes a *killi-killi* noise, the *Bhairu baosi* a *ho-ho* sound, and the *Mata* an *ah-ah* utterance'.
20. At the Taivar *devra* in Malwa *phalli*, Chela, the senior Bhairu *bhopa* for many years began to go less frequently to the *devra* because of continuous sickness in his old age. Mada, his 'father's brother' had been *Bhairu bhopa* before him. As a result of Chela's sickness Mada's son, who manifested signs of *Bhairu* possession, took on the role of the *bhopa* of the *devra*.
21. In the Malwa *devra* the Vaijjath Taivars were successively the *Bhairu bhopas* while the Mata *bhopas* were always from among the Lailaths. This reinforced the Taivar assertion that the *Bhairu bhopa* was the more powerful (head of the household) and went to the sublineage who 'claimed the land first' (according to Mana *patel*).

member of the community. In other words the body of the *bhopa* becomes a sacred space only during the time of his possession.[22] As it is the spirit who seeks the *bhopa* and not vice-versa, outside his possessed state no-one attempts to influence the *bhopa* with the aim of a more sympathetic hearing from the deity. On the other hand, the advice, suggestions or insights the *bhopa* provides in his 'performance' are critically evaluated in comparison to the performance of other *bhopa* and might or might not earn him respect in the community. For instance, Mada's son, Sadma was believed to be a weak *bhopa* compared to his father. In normal interactions in the village, Sadma's words were not given much importance. The powers of individual *bhopa*, however, vary. According to Kothari (1982) it is the *bhopa* who is the main source of the maintenance and propagation of faith and a powerful *bhopa* may be able to reactivate worship at a dormant shrine.

Sometimes the *bhopa* works together with the *devala* (grain diviner), especially if the diviner feels the spirit he might identify is one who belonged to the *devra*, as the following example ilustrates. The first child of a young Vaijjath adult had been sick 'since the rains' (approximately twelve months earlier) when he was born. The parents had tried all cures, including the expenditure of money on medicines from the government doctors at Abu Road, to no avail. Finally, a ceremony in the Malwa *devra* was arranged, with Chela the old Bhairu *bhopa* (in preference to Sadma) and Naga the *devala* who was a member of the Lailath sublineage. The *devala* continuously regrouped a handful of corn grains given to him by the *bhopa*, in a circle on the floor of the *devra*. The process continued until he was able to isolate two groups of five grains each. These he placed, in turn, in his palms accompanied by the murmuring of a *mantra*. He then tied them up in two knots in a small cloth and repeated the procedure. This cloth would later be immersed in water and given to the sick child. The *devala* got paid in cash while the few family members present including the *bhopa* ate some *churma* (sweet *prasad*).

While the *devala* and *bhopa* can act together, the *khoont* does not accompany or sit next to a *bhopa*. The *khoont* is a ritual expert who is of special importance during the funeral ceremony (in the construction of the *path* for the *hankaudar* ceremony, as described in chapter 6) and ancestor worship (see above).[23] The *khoont* acquires his ritual

22. Similarly the body became a sacred space when a person was sick. In the case of sickness however the spirit was angry and had to be appeased.
23. According to Laga, these two occasions were special because *gair me bhairuji hove, mitti ka. Isme khoont ka kam jyada hidai* (In the house there is *Bhairuji* of

knowledge through training and practice. To be a *khoont* involves a voluntary undertaking by the individual to learn the order and sequence of the material objects and verbal chants in order to communicate with the ancestor spirit.

Laga was a *bhopa* of the Bubariya lineage households in the Taivar village, the only affinal lineage in the village to have its own *devra*. His father was a *khoont* (who had officiated at the funeral ceremony of Pema's daughter-in-law; see chapter 6). According to Laga, it had taken his father a year and a half to learn the techniques of a *khoont*. He had been a student (*chela*) at the age of 13 to 14 years, of a Taivar man of the Devath sublineage. To become a *khoont* Laga's father went to his *gur* (teacher) late at night. There they would first sing *bhajan* (devotional songs) and then talk after everyone else in the household was asleep. In the Taivar village, Laga said, there had been six well known *khoont*, of whom two had died. Two were Vaijjaths, two were Lailaths, one was a Gokhlath, and the sixth was from an affinal lineage. At present his father had five *chela*. Two were Devath, two were Raijjath, and one was a lower Bubariya. The *chela* came after the sowing of the corn (July/August) and remained until the next ancestor worship *(beej)* in September. Laga said that he had also learnt to be a *khoont* but never practised it because he felt *sharam* (shame) to do so in front of his father. Sometimes when his father was sleepy or tired Laga said he would talk to the *chelas*. Laga's father would go to other villages as well as to the *haga-vale* (natal kin) and other Girasia lineages in Sirohi *tehsil*. According to Laga, *Baosi ke liye jaana pede* (one has to go for the *baosi*).

While *khoont* can be members of affinal categories, a *bhopa* is always from within the natal patrifocal group. In certain cases the *bhopa* is from within the sublineage. While *bhopa* are not paid for their services, the *khoont* and the *devala* are both paid. Laga *bhopa* often acts as a *devala* as well. This illustrates two points. Firstly, that *bhopa* can be *devala*, that their positions are not mutually exclusive (although Laga is the only *bhopa* with whom I was acquainted who was also a *devala*. Secondly, that the *khoont* and *devala* are both positions which are open to affinal groups, because unlike the position of the *bhopa*, they are not lineage specific. The fact that they are paid reinforces the point made in chapter 6, that payment defines relations between affinal groups.

I find the differences between the Girasia authorities in the lineage and village similar to the religious experts among the Pahari,

---

sand. This is why the *khoont* works more there.) Both the *Bhairu* and the *path* ancestor were considered important protectors.

the north Indian hill community studied by Berreman. According to Berreman (1964), the Pahari also have both priests or Brahmins and ritual mediators or shamans as their religious experts. The Pahari *purohits* are the priests from Rajput or Brahmin high castes who undergo training and whose services are called upon for the life-cycle or other periodic rituals. The Pahari Brahmin *purohits* have an assured and inherited clientele. The Pahari shamans, on the other hand, belong to the untouchable Dom caste and are more frequently approached for remedial advice regarding periodic ailments and afflictions. The Pahari shamans are self-selected and perform in individualistic ways. They have no fixed clientele, which varies in accordance with their accuracy in identifying spirits. Berreman saw the Pahari shaman's power as restricted in three ways. Firstly, there are many shamans competing for clients. Secondly, the advice they give is not necessarily accepted and sometimes another shaman is sought. Thirdly, the supernatural speaks through the worshippers rather than through the shaman. Berreman shows that Pahari *purohits* and shamans are equally integrated into Pahari society with different and complementary roles to play (similarly observed for the Brahmin and *Baiga* lower caste in Chattisgarh in Central India, documented by Babb 1975: 179). Furthermore he observes that both rituals and beliefs are very similar among all the Pahari castes (ibid.: 54). Pahari Hinduism as a whole is rejected by the plains Hindus on the basis that in its practice it is associated with the lower castes.[24]

In contrast to the Girasia ritual experts, the Pahari shamans are paid for each individual session while the Brahmins are considered attached to certain houses and receive an assured payment in kind. The Taivar Girasia *bhopa* is not paid although he partakes in the consumption of the food. Moreover, the *bhopa* also contributes his share of flour for the feast. The Taivar Girasia *khoont* and the *devala*, on the other hand, are paid for each session separately. I would suggest that these differences from the Pahari ritual experts stem from the different constructions of the us or them category. Girasia *bhopa* are always from amongst members of the lineage. The *khoont* or *devala* can also be from affinal lineages and are not attached to any shrine. Although some households engage only certain *khoont* or *devala*, they will also seek others in case their advice is proven to be unsatisfactory. Nei-

---

24. According to Berreman this had enabled a category of non-traditional Brahmins to press for change through their emulation of high-caste plains Hindu practices. The shamans reaction to the threat was to encourage the belief that Pahari marriage in the plains Sanskritic style, including the payment of dowry resulted in barren wives and were short-lived.

ther the *bhopa* nor the *khoont* or *devala* are able to form an elite group because while the latter are competing individual practitioners, sub-lineage differences separate the *bhopa*.

The Elected Village Leader

Below, I describe briefly the role of the *sarpanch* or elected village leader, to show how in the absence of a divine sanction or a central position in the kinship structure, positions of authority are considered relatively weak. In the next chapter, which is concerned with conflicts among kin, I shall discuss the office of the *patel* or powerful lineage elders responsible for settling disputes.

The office of *sarpanch* is a five-yearly term, decided on the basis of an election, held in the presence of all the village members and conducted by the state government authorities. In terms of the observed political power related to his office, I observed that the *sarpanch* has very little influence among the Taivars. The *sarpanch* for the Taivar village, at the time of my fieldwork, was the Bhairu *bhopa* of the Malwa *devra*. It seemed that he was more powerful as the Bhairu *bhopa* than as the village *sarpanch* in determining the course of action of members of the community. The Taivars themselves spoke of the *sarpanch* as being a man who was 'for show' *(dikhava)*, which meant someone who could speak Hindi, the language of the government officers, was presentable and not necessarily clever. In addition, the Girasia also believe that if the *sarpanch* is a *bhopa*, he can not be disloyal to the interests of the community, for fear that the spirit of the deity will afflict him. In this manner the *sarpanch* serves as a means to voice Taivar complaints to the government, but not one through whom the government can influence the Taivars. Hence, in their choice of a *sarpanch* the Taivars effectively prevent outside control. It is also one reason why no government development schemes have ever taken root effectively.

Women and Religious Exclusion

Girasia women are not active participants at any ritual. They partake of the blessings but do not propitiate the deity. When they do initiate an access to the deities, it is regarded as the practice of evil magic or witchcraft. Girasia women do not perform domestic rituals because of the more rigidly and genealogically defined Girasia deities. Each lineage had its own, yet similar, set of deities. At most rituals, Girasia women (D, Z, W, M) sit at the outer periphery. The fact that both the daughter or sister category as well as the mother or wife category are marginal to all rituals is related to the fact that, while the latter category are affinal women and can not propitiate the gods of their husband because only members of the husband's lineage may do so, the former become affinal women and therefore can not occupy permanent positions of religious authority. Yet affinal women also do not propitiate their own natal deities in the husband's village, as one would expect. Like Girasia individuals, the deities are considered as attached to specific localities; therefore, for a wife to worship the deities of her natal lineage in her husband's village is seen as dividing the loyalties of the spirits. Girasia deities are protectors of their land and territory represented by the lineage. Although never stated in this manner, it was implied that for other deities to be worshipped in the sacred space of the clan (or lineage) deities would question the territorial and supernatural authority of the lineage.

None of the Girasia women were *bhopa, khoont, devala* or *patel,* nor were any women publicly possessed during the time of my fieldwork. At individual rituals such as the *manautis* (vows), and particularly where the welfare of children is concerned, women are present, but the organisation and the administration of the ceremony is carried out by the male members only. At feasts held in public places, such as at the *devra* or at marriages and funerals, the men organise, prepare and distribute the food. Thus positions of ritual specialists and the public or prestigious domain of cooking is restricted to Girasia men, as is true for men of other castes. Only on occasions at the household shrines, such as the *beej* or *phulera,* are the women allowed to cook. If the wife is of a slightly lower Girasia lineage, a wife or sister of another sublineage family cooks. The stipulations with regard to cooking emphasise a ritual hierarchy between Girasia men and women, wherein men are considered more ritually pure than women. While Girasia women may not cook at rituals because they are 'less pure' than Girasia men, among the upper-caste and middle-class Hindu groups, women perform rituals and also cook, mainly to increase the level of purity of their men, rather than of themselves; this reflects a similar gendered ritual hierarchy as among the Girasia. Further, it is only due to their increasing structural attachment to the husband's household that upper-caste women are able to perform the rituals for their husbands. A young upper-caste bride is less likely to take the initiative of conducting rituals and is told what to do by her mother-in-law, thus reflecting the subordination of an 'outsider' to someone who is is more representative of the interests of the husband's kin. The preoccupation with religion increases for the middle- and upper-caste wives over a period of time.

Upper- and middle-caste and class women are essentially religious practitioners of the domestic domain, while men are specialists who perform at public ceremonies. For Wadley (1988) this religious division of labour reflects the sexual division of labour. She maintains that, except for the wives of Brahman men, women at all levels are like lower caste men in that their religious participation is not textually sanctioned. In this sense she finds women experts in the oral rather than the textual tradition and occupying non-authoritative religious positions (ibid.: 36). Ideal Hindu wives are those who are dutiful, self-sacrificing and religiously orientated (Srinivas 1977, Kakar 1986, Dube 1988, Jacobson 1974, Jeffrey 1979, Wadley 1988, Sharma 1980). For many women religious rituals provide an emotional release from unsatisfactory marriages (Jacobson, 1974: 141). I would suggest that the difficulty of recourse to divorce in ideal-type Hindu marriages enhances the role of religious expression as a means of emotional release. Marriage can be particularly stressful for a woman due to the the high level of expectation on her conforming to the ideal of the 'good' wife on the one hand, and the low level of support from affinal kin (often including the husband) on the other.

The religiosity of the upper- and middle-caste wives is regarded as vital to the well-being of the husband's family and is especially linked to the personal well-being of the husband. The *karva chauth*, for example, is one of the annual fasts undertaken by the wife especially for the welfare of the husband. Even when women pray for their own well-being, it is usually to ask for good marriage or the birth of a son (their 'contributions' to the husband's household). The point I am making is not that the women need seek any necessarily separate welfare, but that when they do, it needs to be tied in with the contexts of their men. A man, on the other hand, has the unconditional right to strive for his own individual welfare or for the social good of the community for which he earns merit. Men never perform rituals for the welfare of their wives but may perform rituals for good crops or against disease (Wadley, 1988: 40). Husbands also do not cook for domestic rituals although they do so for the public rituals.

The Girasia wife is never sufficiently attached to carry out a ritual for her husband's wellbeing. Girasia brides are economically subordinated but not expected to perform ritual services for the husband. In case of any maladjustments in her marriage, rather than resort to ritual means the Girasia wife has the restricted option of 'running away', as described in chapter 4. In spite of contrasting levels of religiosity amongst Girasia and other, especially upper- and middle-caste women, they remain equally separated from the authoritative dimensions of religious practice, while at the same time being equally structurally subordinated to the patrifocal ideology implicit in their respective kinship and domestic organisations. Because both the Girasia sacred spaces and gatherings are based on a gendered definition of the lineage, both natal and affinal women are absent.

Chapter 9

CLASS, RESISTANCE AND IDENTITY

Among the households in the Taivar village were members of the Anop Mandal, a semi-religious and political organisation in southern Rajasthan. The Mandal has its headquarters in Sirohi city. It is essentially an organisation of some low-income groups and low castes, united in their opposition to what they perceived as the exploitative nature of the *bania*, or merchant caste of the Jain community. During the course of my fieldwork and subsequently, I was unable to locate any previous research on the Mandal. Members of the Anop Mandal call themselves *bhavik* (literally, possessing belief, 'believers'). They worship Anop Das, the Mandal's founder, sing devotional songs in Hindi and follow prescribed rules regarding the consumption of food and the dress of women. In all these respects, the Taivar members of the Mandal (Taivar 'believers') are led to oppose Girasia customs, especially of dress and worship, which are among the key, visible symbols of Girasia identity. In spite of this opposition, the Taivar 'believers' remain an intrinsic part of the Taivar lineage. With regard to the Anop Mandal organisation in the Taivar village presented in this chapter, I make three observations which are relevant to the arguments put forward in this book. Firstly, in spite of what might at the outset have seemed an opposition to Girasia beliefs and practices, I found that the Taivar 'believers' continue to have access to both the natural resources and a sense of belonging to the lineage. The economic and social necessity of maintaining kin ties prevented a separation of the Taivar members of the Anop Mandal from their Girasia lineage. I suggest that this is primarily possible due to the fact that the Taivar 'believers' have been able to recast the Mandal philosophy as extensions of Girasia religious beliefs. Secondly, there were a number of conflicts between kin of different Taivar sublineages regarding matters relating to property and concerning the sexual relationships of women. Taivar members of the Anop Mandal maintained their own identity but at the same time were divided amongst themselves according to their sublineage identities. The contest and solidarities within the kin group reinforces the central theme of this book, which is to show that differences are constructed to maintain distinct identities even though more fundamental similarities persist, and that women are used as major symbols in the portrayal of difference. Thirdly, the Taivar Girasia links with the lower castes in the region as represented in the Mandal, allow me to question the hierarchical structure of caste and the divisions between caste and tribe. What may seem superficially an attempt by a section of lower-income and caste groups to emulate higher caste values (through dress, food and language), is, I suggest, more a means of consciously constructing an identity separated from, rather than identical to, the upper castes. This move towards a lower-class solidarity and identity challenges the assumptions made by studies on social change in India, especially the assertion that among lower groups, social mobility and movement is always in the upward direction.

The present chapter is divided into two sections. Section one looks at a brief history and background of the Anop Mandal. The second section examines the nature of the Mandal organisation in the Taivar village and considers the implications of Mandal membership for Girasia women.

The Anop Mandal and Peasant Resistance in Southern Rajasthan

Economic and Political Context

The Anop Mandal is named after Anop Das, a Brahmin of the Sirohi district.[1] Anop Das rose to prominence as a redeemer in the

---

1. There were conflicting reports about whether Anop Das was a Brahmin or a Rajput. A majority of the informants believed he was a Brahmin.

early 1930s. The crux of his ideological position was to relate peasant poverty to the exploitation practised by one section of the regional community, the Jain *bania* (or trader and money-lender). A major reason for the popularity of Anop Das lay in his ability to explain at a popular level how economic hardships were a product of the political realities of the time. The 1920s had been a period of peasant and tribal revolts in the region.[2] Most of these agitations were protests against the imposition of land taxes, land ownership rights and forced labour *(begar)* exacted by the state (court and colonial officials). These measures were particularly punitive given the severity with which drought and famine had occurred in the region. The Girasia, along with the other poor farming communities, are known to have participated in the widespread protests which took place in response to the state's economic imposition. Although the protests were led by charismatic leaders such as Govind Guru and Motilal Tejawat, who were often lower- and middle-caste locals, there is little evidence to suggest that the regional agitations had any Girasia leadership.[3]

2. For example, see Mann (1983) on the Mavji and Govindgiri movements in south Rajasthan, especially in Dungarpur, Banswara and Udaipur to the southeast and northeast of Sirohi; Lal (1983) on the socio-religious movements of the tribals in southern Gujarat; Hardiman (1987) on the Devi movement in 1921-22 among the tribals in South Gujarat; Pande (1984), Singh (1983) and Ram (1986) on the Motilal Tejawat Bhil movement in Udaipur in the 1920s.
3. Ram (1986) in his book on the agrarian movement in Rajasthan (1913-47), devotes one chapter to the 'Bhil and Girassia Agitations' in southern Mewar (the eastern neighbour of Sirohi). He notes that in 1881 the Bhils protested against the census classification, prohibition on alcohol manufacture, establishment of police and customs, and the ban on the killing of witches (ibid.: 75). The agitations gained greater force and meaning under Govind Guru, a political and social leader from the Banjara caste in Dungarpur. Govind Guru had, by the force of his long standing work among the Bhils, been able to influence them to abstain from meat and alcohol, and to press the state for the removal of *begar* (forced labour) and for the establishment of selfgoverning *panchayat* (village councils). The Bhils were said to have been joined by the Girassias of Mewar in 1917 to press against *begar*, for the reduction of *bhog* (land revenue) and the removal of the petty taxes or *lag bag* (ibid.: 76). These protests were addressed to the *jagirdars* within whose principalities the hilly *bhumat* region of Mewar lay. The *jagirdars* in turn sought assistance from the British political agent to put down the revolts. (Ram records that in 1908 1,500 Bhils were shot: ibid., 76). In 1921 the peasants joined with the tribals and the protests were led by Motilal Tejawat, a trader from the Oswal caste in Udaipur. Essentially Tejawat's movement focused on a few demands (against forced labour, petty taxes, the disparity in taxes, high taxes and the tyrannical ways of the *jagirdars*; ibid.: 77). Motilal Tejawat became a notorious offender against the state. His views found followers among the Bhils and Girassias in Sirohi, Idar, Danta and Palanpur in Gujarat.

The participation of the Girasia in the incidences of peasant resistance in the region can be seen, for example, in Sirohi in 1922, when they are known to have stolen standing crops without payment of the state's share, showed a negligence in patrolling the Abu Road-Ambaji route, looted the corn granary of the *thana* (tax, customs and police outpost) and prevented other castes from performing *begar* (Ram 1986: 101). Ram notes that although the administration asked for discussions with the Girasia, their calls were ignored. And despite the offer of large-scale concessions in taxation from the ruler of Sirohi, their subsequent non-implementation led the Girasia to continue their agitations. The Girasia protests in Sirohi surfaced time and again between 1921 to 1929, as I see it, for two reasons: firstly, only partial concessions were offered by the government and secondly, lax implementation of these concessions by officials allowed a return to the previous situation. To add to the consternation of the impoverished farmers, in the 1930s and 1940s the land settlement (classification for purposes of revenue) machinery was put into operation. The revenue exercise instilled great fear in communities such as the Girasia who saw it as an extension of state control on their lives and perceived the classification of land as further evidencing their increasing lack of control over their surroundings and themselves.

There were at the same time wide ranging political changes taking place at the national level where leaders were preparing for Indian Independence. The protests of the 1920s in Rajasthan were also affected by the political climate at the national level. It was a time when the national movement for Indian independence became set on a direction of non cooperation with the British Government, under the leadership of Mahatma Gandhi.[4] The Praja Mandal (or peoples' organisations) were units of the Congress working in the states to raise the political conciousness of the citizens towards self-rule *(swaraj)*.[5] While most of the movements in the 1920s were inspired by, or supported, Gandhi's calls for the nationalist struggle, the Anop Mandal did not support the nationalist movement for Indian independence. Thus the Anop Mandal was probably quite isolated in its position as it went against the more popular sentiment of the time. The opposition of the Anop Mandal to the rising Congress popularity was, as I see it, related to the social

4. The decision for a non-cooperation movement meant that the goals of the national movement changed from participation in the government to the idea of *swaraj*, or an independent nation (Chandra 1989: 186).
5. In Rajasthan the Praja Mandal was first established in 1939 by Gokul Bhai Bhatt, a Brahmin of Sirohi and close associate of Mahatma Gandhi.

context of the members of the Anop Mandal and its origin within a princely state whose rulers were sympathetic to the British and were thus opposed to joining the nationalist struggle. There were, however, sections of the population in the princely states, particularly the middle and educated classes who actively supported the Congress. But the Congress supporters, who were organised into the Praja Mandal units in the different princely states of Rajasthan, were opposed by the Rajput rulers.[6]

The Congress-led Praja Mandal claimed to be on the side of the impoverished peasants and the landless tribals, and against what it perceived as a lack of democracy in the princely states. However, the Girasia and the other lower castes in the Anop Mandal associated the Praja Mandal with the Jains, who were among its main financiers. Anop Das's opposition to the Jains in the Praja Mandal was consistent with the attitude of the Rajput rulers. The upper-caste Rajputs also opposed the Praja Mandal and in this found the support of the British rulers. It suited the British to encourage the Rajputs in what they saw as every effort to thwart the wider aim of the Congress, which was for freedom through self rule.[7] In spite of pleas from influential Jains to ban the Anop Mandal, the British were not in favour of this. The Anop Mandal, buffered by the Rajput rulers' sentiments and British support, was able to survive as an organisation in the face of the immense mobilisation of the Congress in the non-princely states. This resulted in an unconventional alignment of the establishment, the British and the Rajput rulers, with the so-called 'subversive forces', the Anop Mandal.

The support that the Anop Mandal received from the state contrasts with the previous attitude of the state towards agitations in the region. I suggest this came about because both the British and the Rajput rulers were seen to be relinquishing power at a time when the Praja Mandal was gaining it (through its association with Gandhi and the national movement) and were seen to be ineffective in the *jagir* areas (Ram, ibid.: 119). The Devi movement in Surat in the 1920s, documented by Lal (1983) and Hardiman (1987), was similarly a movement of tribal protest. Among other issues it was opposed to oppression by the Parsi money-lending community which also dis-

6. According to Pande (1984), 'The Prime Minister of Udaipur (working for the rulers of the state of Udaipur) tried to strangle the organisation, and declared the organisation illegal .... everyone in a white cap was watched in suspicion'.
7. The Anop Mandal was inconvenient for the Jains as it not only opposed them ideologically but also actively opposed their election to government positions (Singhi 1990)

tilled and distributed alcohol. In contrast to the Mandal organisation, the opposition presented by the Devi movement was suppressed by the British and the Gaikwad rulers of the princely states in Gujarat, both of whom had revenue interests in the continuation of the Parsi trade. Hence, although the Devi movement was comparable to the Anop Mandal in its social basis, it differed in the structure of its support. I would suggest that this was one of the reasons for the demise of the Devi movement in the very decade in which it arose. Some historians, such as Ram (1986), suggest that the tribal Girasia protests ceased and the agitations in southern Rajasthan from 1929 onwards become more of a peasant undertaking championed by the Praja Mandal or socialist wing of the Congress. Contrary to Ram's suggestion that the Girasia protests were contained from the 1930s onwards, in this chapter I suggest that the Girasia discontent went underground in the form of the Anop Mandal organisation for various reasons outlined below. In fact the ineffectiveness of the earlier peasant leaders against the state's authority was, I suggest, among the reasons for Anop Das's caution in his relations with the state officials and, once their support declined, for the movement to become less visible.[8]

The Bania as Exploiter

During my association with the Anop Mandal members in the Taivar village, they always expressed strong, negative views on members of the Jain community, whom they called *bania*. Anop Das himself identified the Jain *bania* as the main economic exploiter in the region. The Anop Mandal must be seen in the context of the Jain relation to Hinduism. The Jains are a large and prosperous section of the Rajasthani population. Mainly traders by occupation, they represent the indigenous financial and money lending community. In Rajasthan the Jains are especially concentrated in the south as well as in Gujarat, where considerable ancient trade took place.[9] The origin of the Jain commu-

8. For Singh (1985) the 1920s mark a change from the previous spontaneous and isolated tribal revolts in India, to more organised movements which, 'could only be sustained ... through external stimuli' (ibid.: 157-8). The theorists like Singh who attribute the political organisation and action of marginal communities to external agency deny the possibility of indigenous political expression. A large-scale attempt to rethink this issue is that of the subaltern school of Indian history, which reinstates the initiative of organised political protest in the hands of the peasants (Sarkar 1985, Guha 1982). The Anop Mandal has been able to survive as an organisation largely due to the efforts of the members themselves.
9. Bayly (1983) emphasises the role of the Banias in providing the indigenous capital crucial for the expansion of the British empire in India.

nity is traced to the movement for reform of orthodox Hinduism which arose around the sixth century BC.[10] Both Jainism and Buddhism, which arose in the same period, opposed the restrictive practices of Hinduism. Confined to India, in contrast to the subsequent migration of Buddhism outside India, Jainism has had to constantly re-define itself in relation to Hinduism. This is reflected especially in the similar intra-caste structuring and the related concerns of purity and pollution which Hindus and Jains share (Jaini 1979, Humphrey 1985, Reynell 1985). Anop Das built on the separation of Jain culture from Hinduism to create an image of the Jains as outsiders and evil exploiters. Thus, for example, according to Anop Das the Hindu god Brahma created the Brahmans, the Rajputs descended from the god Vishnu and the Muslims from the god Mahesh. The fourth category of people were the Jain *bania* who were foreigners to the land as they came from Lanka (the southern island from where the evil king Ravana tried to destroy the Hindu kingdom of Rama, the son of the ruler of Ayodhya).[11]

The 'believer' image of Jain culture is grounded partially in fact. While the Hindus regard Ravana as an evil figure, in the Jain version of history he appears as a good figure and becomes a *tirthankar* (revered holy man). Anop Das used this fact to further the 'believer' notion that the Jains 'are descended from evil'. For example, in a publication entitled *Jagat Hitkarni* (literally 'welfare of the world'),[12] Anop Das stated:

> *Banie beimaan Lanka ke chamar hai ... Lanka ke dhed; usi tarah ka paap Ravana Hiranakush ke muvafik in banio ne bhi chalaya hai jiska naam kalukaal kaya hai. Meh ke naam ka Ravana jaadu kaa paap hom karta tho meh bund ho jaata aur kaal pad jaata, aur kaal pad kar sab sansar Lakshmi aur dhan kaboo mein kar liya tha aur Lanka mein le gaya*
>
> (1960: 17).

In other words, the wicked *bania* are the untouchables of Lanka who have spread their net of sin (*paap*, Jagat Hitkarni, 1960: 2)[13] over

---

10. According to Thapar (1986), 'In the later centuries Jainism moved to western India (where there are to this day some two million practising Jainas), parts of North India and to the South in the region of Mysore' (ibid.: 64). Perhaps because of their idiosyncratic interpretation of the doctrine of non-violence, the Jains developed into a trading community especially around the west coast (South Gujarat) area where they became moneylenders (ibid: 65).
11. As recounted by a gathering of 'believers' in the Taivar village on the occasion of a visit of one of their religious preachers (1987).
12. The book is a collection of printed speeches of Anop Das published after his death in 1960.
13. In other places in the text, *paap* or sin is replaced by the terms *jaadu, rakshasi vidya, Indrajaal*, meaning magic, demon power and illusion, the net of the God Indra.

the land in the same evil manner as Ravana and Hiranakush, the two evil rulers in Hindu mythology. The name of the sin is *kalukaal*. Ravana knew of the magic to stop the rain clouds and when famine fell, Ravana would capture all the wealth of the world and take it to Lanka. The *bania* practice the same kind of magic which they cleverly disguise from the world through falsification in their account books.[14]

The *Jagat Hitkarni* is Anop Das's plea to the administrators, especially the Rajput rulers, and also his 'brothers', 'the Hindu, Muslim, the English and the Sadhus, Sants and the five *parameshwar* [gods]' (ibid.: 1), to understand the invidious and sinister nature of the money-lenders who, by telling the authorities that he was a trouble maker, had prevented Anop Das from spreading his message to the people. It is important to remember the hardship caused by recent famine and drought at the time that Anop Das was writing. Periods of scarcity are also times when moneylenders are known to encroach into otherwise inaccessible, kin-locked property and savings (Stokes, 1978). In turn, the money-lenders themselves become targets of intense dislike among the poorer communities. It was especially in the years of drought that the animosity towards the Jains was strong, because the 'believers' felt that Jain moneylenders, 'tie up the rain clouds to take revenge over their debtors'.[15] Anop Das, for example, holds the *bania* responsible for disease and death in the region, in contrast to the foreign countries where there are no *bania*, where it rains well and people are not vulnerable to disease. Anop Das was not alone in his views of the *bania*. Other publications of the 1930s and the 1940s also tell of exploitation by the *bania*. Song number thirteen of the pamphlet *Bekason ki Awaz* (in Hindi this literally means 'the voice of the innocent') was written by Ganesh Lal Vyas, an activist of the Rajasthan Sevak Sangh (RSS; Pande 1984). The RSS was an organisation which represented the extreme nationalists in the Congress and was not as dominated by the Jains as the Praja Mandal. In a poem titled 'Mother Marwar', Vyas outlines the inviduous nature of the *bania* who on the one hand supplied the rulers with the capital to wage wars while destroying village self-sufficiency through bonded labour on the other. The RSS opposed the *bania* in as far as they could be identified with the ruling class.

It was Gandhi's association with Jainism which was central to Anop Das's rejection of his ideas. Gandhi was perceived first and foremost as a member of the *bania* caste from Porbander in Gujarat.

14. The account book of the *bania* is the popular symbol which represents the moneylenders to the other castes.
15. Also published in the form of a letter which had been sent to the government authorities by Mandal members.

The popularity of Gandhi which was responsible for the widespread diffusion of the national movement, was again used by Anop Das to justify his claim that the *bania* were rising to power and taking over the government as a result of their sinister 'magic'. The Anop Mandal was not alone in using Gandhi as a symbol. Gandhi had become a very powerful political image for protesting urban and rural groups alike. But most of these groups saw him as a 'good' rather than 'bad' force. In the same period as Anop Das, we find that in the Devi movement the Gandhian nationalists could only enlist the support of the tribals in southern Gujarat by representing Gandhi in the same image as that of the powerful and protective tribal deities, *Shiliya Dev* and *Simadiya Dev* (Hardiman 1987: 168-9). The tribals in Gujarat were won over by the assimilation of miraculous powers to Gandhi. This was in contrast to Gandhi's renunciatory actions which had more of an impact on the higher caste peasants and urban classes. The socialist wing of Gandhi's followers also used the association of Gandhi with the tribal gods to widen their support structure. Jitu Santal's tribal protest movement (1924 to 1932) in northwest Bengal, indicates a similar relation between Gandhi's image and subaltern protest. Jitu Santal appropriated Gandhi's authority with regard to reform among the lower castes to call for the same among the Santal community (Sarkar 1985: 157). Using Gandhi's idea of the *desh* (own country) against British domination, he was able to address the reduced economic and political control felt by the Santals to be a result of the tenancy legislation of the British and the competition from the Muslim peasants. Jitu expressed a need for a distinctive Santal identity through a reform of customary ways. The formation of the new 'Santal *desh*' and the related Santal identity was essentially an attempt to separate the Santals from the lower castes and peasants (ibid.: 157).

Both the Devi movement and Jitu Santal's movement differed significantly from the Anop Mandal in their use of the nationalist symbols of the time. Anop Das was quite unique in his portrayal of Gandhi as an evil *bania*. Although the Devi movement which Hardiman describes died down in the decade in which it arose, and Jitu Santal's movement ended with his death at the hands of the police in 1932 (ibid.: 138), the Anop Mandal is an ongoing organisation. Its capacity for organisation and the intensity of feelings it evokes is apparent from the attacks on Jain *sadhus* (ascetics) by the tribals, the most recent of which was reported to have occurred in Sirohi in 1985.[16] The negative

---

16. Personal communication of an incident in 1985 from the Deputy Inspector of police for Sirohi district (Sirohi city, 1986).

reference to Gandhi was also made by the Taivar 'believers'. According to Reeva, the head of the Anop Mandal in the Taivar village,

> It was Gandhi Matma who started the raj of the *bania* in the form of the Congress. He told Nehru that he would initiate him into politics provided he did what Gandhi Matma told him ... the government has since been under the *jadoo* [spell] of the *bania* ... When the state government came into contact with us they said they would take only one-seventh of our produce; now the situation has changed. There has been famine, drought and hardship, all due to these *bania*.

Reeva made an explicit connection between the economic decline experienced by the Girasia and the rise of the *bania* in national politics. In fact, explaining the increase in hardships as caused by *bania* strategies was among the most powerful and persuasive of the Anop Mandal arguments especially as there was little in local religious beliefs which addressed the increasing economic disparity between the rich and the poor in the region, as we shall see for the Taivars below.[17]

The Girasia 'Believers'

In 1986-87, there were nineteen Taivar households who followed the teachings of Anop Das. The Taivar 'believers' subscribed to the main teachings of Anop Das as laid down in the *Jagat Hitkarni*. These were to abstain from the consumption of meat and alcohol, to sing *bhajans* (devotional songs) in Hindi, and to understand and propa-

17. Prakash (1986) gives us an example of how some 'spirit believing' low-caste communities were able to articulate economic differences within their rituals. Prakash studied the Bhuinya (a community which was the major constituent of the category of labourers called the *kamia*) in colonial Bihar from the 1850s to the 1930s. He shows how the unequal relations between the *kamia* (labourer) and the *malik* (landlord) were reproduced in the *kamia* relations to their spirit *(preta)* world of ancestors and ghosts (dak, bhut). Over and above the reproduction of social and economic relations, the spirit-cult practices also allowed an interaction between the upper and lower castes, denied in other areas of *kamia-malik* existence. Among the *kamia*, the *malik* was also represented as a *devta* who could be benign (in matters relating to production), and malign (in the distribution of resources). In both these cases the *devta* was, 'identified with the power of the landlord' (ibid.: 225). Prakash observes that the *kamia* were able to explain the effect of the landlords' appropriation of their land, resulting from the colonial policy of revenue reorganisation, in terms of the contextually dependent nature of the *malik devta*. The relations centring around spirit rituals addressed the larger framework of social and economic imbalances, in which the *maliks* were both the upper castes as well as the landlords (ibid.: 209-30).

gate his views relating to the 'evil *bania*' who were responsible for drought, disease and death. The *bhajan* gatherings were usually in front of a xeroxed photograph of Anop Das in the verandah of the house of a 'believer'. The *bhajans* were held at regular intervals in the *jhonpadi*, the official hut of the the Taivar Anop Mandal. The *jhonpadi* was next to the house of Reeva, the head 'believer'. The three main figures in the 'believer' group in the Taivar village wore the *janeyu* (sacred thread worn by the twice-born Hindus). Women were members only if their fathers or husbands were members of the Anop Mandal (see final section, below).

Of the nineteen 'believer' households in the Taivar village, a majority (thirteen) of them belonged to the dominant sublineage. Seven of these households, which included the most fervent 'believers', were the sons of Mada. The other six households were distributed between the sons of Bava (two households), the son of Chela (one household), the sons of Kehra (one household) and Danda (two households). The remaining six households were distributed between two other sublineages (five, between Lailath and Raijjath), and an affinal Girasia lineage (one household).[18] The household-wise distribution of the 'believers' in the Taivar village indicates that they were more or less restricted to one sublineage (see also Fig 9.1). Considering the small number of 'believer' households, their existence depended to a large extent on what the other Taivars thought of them. The majority of the Taivars expressed concern to me over what they regarded as the divisive nature of the 'believer' beliefs. For example, according to Duda,[19]

18. Eleven out of these twenty-one households are in the *phalli* where the majority of the Vaijjath sublineage lives. There are four households of Taivar 'believers' who live outside the village, all of whom are directly related to the Vaijjath sublineage.

19. Duda was one of the three Taivar members who had left the Anop Mandal. He explained to me that he had become a *kabir panthi* (member of another regional religious organisation), which enabled him to sing devotional *bhajans,* believe in all Taivar *baosis* as well as have commensal relations with other Girasia. (Duda was the only Girasia *kabir panthi* whom I knew. He had been directly influenced by the low-caste veterinary compounder who worked in the village). Two other members left the Mandal during the period of my fieldwork. They were Pheva of the Lailath sublineage and Batha of the Vaijjath sublineage. The former left because of a fight over the payment of compensation which the Vaijjaths sought for the molestation of Lunda's daughter (see chapter 4). Batha was no longer a 'believer' because he had resumed eating meat and was always present at the ritual distribution of food. According to Palvi, the rest of the households thought Batha was a *khau* (or 'eater', greedy) and weak man. Yet Batha could not be taken to task as his hut housed the sacred shrine to the *raktiyo veer* (see chapter 8) of the Vaijjath sublineage.

'The 'believers' do not respect [*mante*] the *Bhakar* or Bhairu *baosi*, they refuse to drink water from others and they do not want our women to wear *baliyas*.

The Taivar Girasia did not, however, completely deride the Anop Mandal beliefs. As explained in Hindi by Gumla, a Girasia of Rada village, *bhavik ke paas kucchh mantra hain, ki dev ko naa maane tou bhi unko kucchh nahi hota hai. Hum naa maane tou hum bimaar ho jaate hain* (The 'believers' have some sacred chants so that, even if they do not believe in the deities, nothing happens to them. If we do not believe in the deities then we become sick). In other words, Gumla implied that although the 'believers' had changed their allegiance to the gods, the gods had not shown their displeasure. Hence the 'believers' must possess some exceptional qualities. Personally, Ramla felt; 'These are bad times, as the belief in the forces of good have decreased, and indiscipline has increased. If the "believers" can bring discipline and rigour to their lives then it is a good thing.' The respect accorded to the 'believers' by the Girasia was linked to the 'believer' experiences gained outside their communities. The 'believers' were regarded as more experienced in dealing with other castes than the average Girasia. This was especially evident in the 'believer' control over Hindi. The other Taivars could also not deny the power of literacy which the 'believers' had over them. Thus while the other Tiavars criticised the 'believers' for promoting internal differences, they appreciated their worldly wisdom and knowledge based on the interaction with other communities, as outlined below.

In the early 1950s a few Taivars were attracted to Anop Das's movement as it was a time when the Taivars experienced the most forcible state control in taxation. As discussed in chapter 2, Sirohi was one of the last areas to be surveyed under the land settlement for taxation and within its district, the *Bhakar* was the last area to be taxed in the late 1940s. The Taivar Girasia viewed the taxation as a loss of control over their own land. Conveying the sense of alienation the Girasia felt from their land, Heva, a Taivar 'believer' spoke of the 'capture' of the fertility of the Taivar land at the time of the survey when *jameen ke oopar hankal ghumai* (the government came and rotated their steel instruments over our land and sapped its strength).[20] The Girasia perceived their oppression as linked to the Indian National Congress rather than to colonial British or Rajput rule.[21] In Girasia collective

20. The Girasia used the *hankal*, an instrument made of steel, in the rituals of the clan mother. The *hankal* was used to absorb the spiritual afflictions of the Girasia victim.
21. When questioned about the pre-independence period, elder Taivars referred to, 'the better days of the *durbar* which entailed only a very occasional visit from a white man whose cheeks were very red from riding on the horse. Those were the

Identity, Gender and Poverty

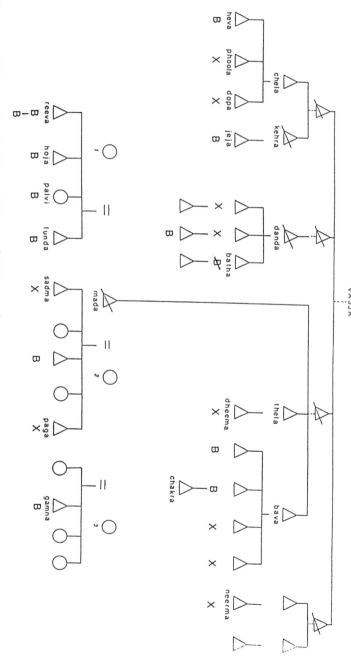

Figure 9.1 'Believers' in the Vaijjath Hojyan (Sublineage)

memory, the days of the *durbar* (the Rajput rule) and the British rule were indistinguishable in so far as both represented little interference with regard to land revenue, which was in the form of a low and flexible land tax. According to Heva 'believer', *Congress ne hame kangla kar diya* (the Congress has made us bankrupt). For him, the lions with open mouths on the Indian coins issued as a symbol of sovereignity represented the government's intention to 'eat' the Girasia.[22] While Girasia customary beliefs were more inwardly orientated and unable to account for deprivation on a wider scale, the Anop Mandal seems to have filled the gap between the perceived economic reality and Girasia religious beliefs. The Anop Mandal provided a political and spiritual explanation by linking the very real loss of control over land (through rigid taxation) to the 'magic' practised by the government. Although it was unsuccessful in the agitation against the imposition of taxes, continuing pressures of drought and famine and rising dependence on a market ridden by inflation contributed to visible economic disparities and provided a strong economic basis for the Mandal's continued existence. It was the economic basis of the Mandal protest which united the lowest income sections of castes in the region to form a class-type of association.

According to the Taivar 'believers', the Dholis (Hindu drum beaters) and Kumhars (Hindu potters) were the two main castes who were members of the Mandal. Anop Mandal members interacted with other lower castes, especially at the annual *bhajan* gatherings held at the various Mandal centres and at the headquarters in Sirohi city. 'Believer' *melas* (meetings) were held annually in villages where there was a significant Mandal membership. Palvi was aware of eight such places[23] stretching from Sirohi to Palanpur in northern Gujarat. If the *bhajan* locations were some distance away and members passed a village where there were other 'believers' they could expect to be entertained at the Mandal hut in that village. The Taivar 'believers' said that they respected members of the lower caste of Dholi, such as

---

days when we had to deposit only one-seventh of what we produced at the *thana* in Nichalagarh.'

22. Here Heva was referring to the Indian coins which have three lions back to back on one side of the coin. The lions are part of the national symbol adopted by the independent government. They stand on a platform which, in Hindi, says *satya mev jayati* (truth alone triumphs).

23. These villages were in Rohida, Santpur, Koteshwar, Sirohi city, Mount Abu, Vasa, Palanpur and Khapa (see map 1.1). Palvi had attended the three *melas* closest to the Taivar village and held in the villages of Rohida, Santpur and Koteshwar. The two more recent ones had been hosted by the Kumhar caste.

Ramlal Dholi for his dedication to their cause.[24] In socialising with the non-Girasia castes, the Taivar 'believers' broke with Girasia practice of keeping their distance from other communities, thereby setting themselves apart from the other Taivars. The Taivar 'believers' not only interacted with other lower castes, they also refused to partake in the meals cooked by the Girasia who ate meat. They further claimed to refuse water from non-'believer' households (although this was not observed in practice). In their abstinence from meat and alcohol, the 'believers' placed themselves in direct opposition to Girasia values, for example of the brotherhood, which were above all represented in the collective consumption of food. The hosting and provisioning of feasts was always an occasion to reveal the solidarity of sublineage members. The 'believer' abstention from such meetings was considered by the rest of the Taivars as a questioning of their ideal of the equality of lineage members.

The 'believers' also apparently disregarded the divine sanction of their lineage by refusing to participate in the collective gatherings where meat and alcohol were consumed. Taivar 'believers', in their abstention from meat, implicitly challenged the position of the Girasia deities and ritual experts associated with them. The type of food distributed on ritual occasions was considered by the Girasia to be according to the preferences of the deities themselves. For example, the *mata* was known to prefer offerings of blood and meat.[25] The 'believers' were opposed to the *bhopa* because they believed that to be possessed exhibited a weakness, like the consumption of alcohol and meat. Both possession and the habits of consuming alcohol and meat were signs of weakness because they exhibited situations where men were 'out of control'.

Although the Taivar 'believers' claimed to abstain from ritual occasions and feasts where meat and alcohol were consumed, I found that in practice the 'believers' were present, if not active participants, at the Taivar feasts or shamanistic activities. They would, however, not normally partake of the *prasad* or other food distributed. For example, Gamna a 'believer' continued to attend the *rati-jaga* (ritual of Bhairu). At the *rati-jaga* before Holi, he performed

---

24. Ramlal Dholi joined the Mandal after taking early retirement from the position of flag-master in the railway services. Unlike other 'believers' he wore a saffron robe and cap. During my fieldwork, Ramlal Dholi came to the Taivar village on his way to the *mela* ('fair' in Hindi, but for the 'believers' also refers to a 'believer' congregation) in Santpur (adjoining Abu Road).
25. The *mata* is symbolised by the colour red, associated with blood by the Taivars. Red is also a sign of marriage, and married women have their first skirt of red cloth.

some of the ceremonies which took place at the Malwa *devra* shrine. According to Gamna, these were some of the duties he was required to perform for his ancestors who were not 'believers'. Similarly Heva, a 'believer', also known as the *peelkhe vala baosi* (respected man of the *peelkha* tree), had recently been unwell. When his granddaughter also fell sick, he suspected that it was the ghost of his previous wife who was making her displeasure clear (chapter 8). In his dream she told him that he had not organised a proper funeral for her. Deva then decided to bury her, a Girasia custom reserved only for *bhopa*, respected persons, or small children. In doing so he would make her a *devi* (goddess). In this he obtained the help of his two non-'believer' brothers. However, although food was distributed after the ritual Heva did not kill a goat as an offering to the female deity. This incident illustrates how the 'believers' use both the Mandal as well as the customary Girasia rituals. Moreover Heva also practised the *jhadoo* or sweeping away of an afflicting spirit (as recounted by Palvi in the previous chapter).

The above observations of the actions of specific 'believers' suggest two points central to this discussion. Firstly, they show that despite the claims of a distinction based on separate religious beliefs and practices, the Taivar 'believers' also participate in the customary rituals of their community. Secondly, the examples above indicate that the symbolism associated with the consumption of meat is the most contested area of customary Girasia beliefs. Given the complexities of Girasia religious beliefs as outlined in chapter 8, it is easy to understand that the simpler Anop Mandal beliefs are less substantive. Although 'believers' are particularly coercive regarding the teachings of Anop Das, they are unable to 'convert' the rest of the Taivars who have an equally entrenched belief in their own deities, a belief periodically reinforced by fulfilled vows and successful *manyatas* (ceremonies showing faith). It is the nature of the customary Girasia beliefs, I suggest, which also allow them to understand the 'believer' position. For example, the individualistic part of the Taivar belief, reflected in individual afflictions by *veers*, in turn allows the non-'believer' Taivars to regard Anop Das as another *dev* or *veer* and the 'believer' religious beliefs as an extension of their own religious views.

Turning to the issue of the association of specific foods with religion and purity, we find that Anop Das himself had attempted to create a distinct 'believer' community in his call for abstinence from the consumption of meat and alcohol. The restrictions on the consumption of both substances are usually adhered to more rigidly by members of the upper- and upper-middle castes than among the lower castes, although the Rajputs are an exception in that the members of the higher lineages also consume meat and alcohol. The restriction on meat consumption, an item distributed at Taivar collective, ritual occasions, is the strongest 'believer' principle to affect the daily lives of the Taivar 'believers'. Taivar 'believers' explained to me that the consumption of meat represents violence and greed. As proof of this they point to the frequent thieving of goats amongst the Girasia, which is at the root of many a Girasia *panchayati*. The overriding concern with the prohibition of meat and alcohol has brought the Mandal closer, in academic terms, to other socio-religious *(bhagat)* movements in the region. Both the Devi movement and Jitu Santal's movement had equally strong and restrictive views on consumption. The Devi movement advocated an abstinence from the consumption of fish and alcohol; Jitu Santal insisted on the proscription of pigs and fowls.[26]

The relation of food to ritual is central in both Brahmanic textual religion and its popular versions. The Brahmanic image is popularly associated with groups who practice vegetarianism. By abstaining from meat and alcohol which have impure connotations, lower status groups are perceived as attempting to gain a Brahman-like superior status. It is in this sense that the abstinence from meat or fish may superficially be regarded as an attempt at upward mobility, as most theorists on *bhagat* or reform movements hasten to conclude. Reform movements of the *bhagat* kind have reinforced the popular notion among Indian anthropologists, at least up to the early 1970s, of the disjunction between the larger universe of Hindu religion, comprised of the Sanskritic pantheon of the major gods such as Brahma, Vishnu, Shiva etc., from the lower, local variations of the clan mother and the *Bhairu*.[27] The *bhagat* movements were seen to reinforce this divide, as in their strictures on consumption they were seen as moving away from these 'lower' forms of belief associated with meat and alcohol-consuming deities to a more pure and high form of worship. Whereas social scientists such as Mann (1983), who writes on the *bhagat* movement among the Bhils, emphasise the

26. Abstinence from meat and alcohol is also one of the main principles which informs the Jain religion. Yet in spite of a shared marginality in relation to the dominant Hindu culture and similar symbols of community, the Anop Mandal, representing the lower castes, remained vehemently opposed to the Jains.
27. But Fuller (1988) shows that the non-vegetarian/vegetarian distinction between the deities is not a sufficient marker of the two supposedly separate levels of Hindu belief and religious practice.

emergence of a hierarchy, I would suggest that existing differences are articulated and thereby maintained rather than hierarchised, as the example of the Girasia will show.[28]

In both the Girasia and the Santal case discussed above, and unaccompanied by changes in the marriage customs or spoken language, abstinence from meat takes on a meaning different from that which has generally been assumed to be a concern for 'purity' in the processes of emulation (often called 'hinduisation' for the tribals). The Anop Mandal, like the Santal movement, did not completely separate 'believers' from the rest of the community and this was reflected in the continuing strong bonds of kinship. Thus I would argue against the outsider position which sets up a simplistic connection between the calls to change lifestyles and the attempts at emulation, and would propose instead that the Anop Mandal allowed the expression of a different level of Girasia identity. Furthermore, despite the similarities with many of the *bhagat* practices and protest movements, the Anop Mandal differed from them in as much as its basis lay in linking poverty to Jain exploitation. In other words, the Mandal proposed that the deteriorating Girasia economic conditions were a result of the systematic practice of a specific religious and economic community. The shared antipathy towards the Jains has itself provided a platform to bring together more than one community of the immediate region of Sirohi, thus differing from the *bhagat* reform movements which have largely been contained within their respective communities.

Below I discuss the relationship between what appear to be contrasting Girasia identities based on kinship and class, in the context of the disagreements and disputes in the Taivar village. I outline the kinds of conflict and resolution mechanisms operational among the Girasia in order to evaluate the extent of 'believer' dissent in the Taivar lineage. This will also enable me to describe the important position of the *patel* who arbitrate disputes.

The Anop Mandal and Conflicts Among the Taivar Girasia

None of the Taivar 'believers' are particularly influential people in their village. In fact a number of 'believers' come from socially or economically marginal households, such as Heva, whose wife had

---

28. Mann (1983) claims that the existing egalitarian differences between the *mele* (literally, 'dirty' in Hindi), and the *ujale* (literally, 'enlightened') Bhils became hierarchised by the *bhagat* movement (ibid.: 312). The former maintained the traditional form of culture, which they saw as superior, while the latter became *bhagats* and maintained their superiority by deriding the former for their unclean habits.

died, or Jama, who is a resident son-in-law. Nevertheless, the ties of male kinship, especially for those men who were members of the Taivar lineage, link them to the men who have authority, such as the *bhopa* or religious expert and *patel* or dispute settler. For example, Sadma's 'true' brothers are 'believers' although he is not. Sadma, son of Mada, was the *sarpanch* (elected government village leader) and *Bhairu bhopa* at the time of my fieldwork. He had derived these positions of authority as a result of the prominence of his father Mada, although Sadma himself is regarded as a weak person. Sadma continues to consume meat and alcohol. The relations between the brothers remained cordial and respectful.[29] The fact that the 'believers' were enfolded within the *kaka-baba* relations is reflected in their involvement with conflicts within and between sublineages.

As I got to know the members of the different Girasia sublineages in the Taivar village, I became aware of a number of long standing disputes between the sublineages. These disputes surfaced in the frequent village *panchayati* (village councils) organised to settle the day-to-day quarrels, disputes and disagreements which arose among the Taivars. The main figure in the village councils is the *patel* of the sublineage.[30] The *patel* has legislative authority in the Taivar village. The office of the *patel*, like that of the *bhopa* is not necessarily inherited. However, it usually lies with the closest genealogical members of the family of the first-settled, or within the eldest household of the sublineage. Each sublineage has its own *patel*. Sometimes sublineages which have spread to more than one section of the village have more than one *patel*. To be *patel* required a tutelage under other *patels* and an attendance at village councils. According to Bhima, a *patel*, whose father has also been a *patel*:

> After my father's death, I accompanied Pheva Data and Dheema Thela (who were the *patel* in the Lailath and Vaijjath sublineages) to the *panchayati* and learnt from them. No, it is not necessary that a son should become a *patel* if his father has been one. Look at Mana who is the *patel* of Malwa *(phalli)*. He got his position from his father's brother who did

29. Similarly, Phoola was not a 'believer' but his eldest brother was. Phoola was influential as the Girasia school teacher of the village. Although neither a *bhopa* nor a *patel* he was well regarded for his ability to speak Hindi as well as his dealings with the government. He had gained his authority through the ability to mediate in the cases of conflict between the largely illiterate Girasia (although other adult Taivars could speak Hindi, very few could write it).
30. Apart from the *patel*, the Girasia *panchayati* consists of the members in conflict and usually the *bhopa* and other interested lineage members who may be asked to attend at the request of the aggrieved party.

not have any sons worth the title. The oldest *patel* is Pema in Nichali *phalli*. Because he comes from a senior family, he is regarded as the first *patel* of the village.

Materially, the office of *patel* is more remunerative than that of the *bhopa*. *Patels* receive food for each sitting of a *panchayati* and also obtain a share of any payments made between the disputing parties at the end of the *panchayati*. This distribution of food and money is a primary incentive for a man to become a *patel*. A *patel* is sometimes regarded by other Girasia as '*woh khaata hai*,' or one who 'eats', signifying greed. The office of *patel* also carries increased reverence and acclaim for the individual, in terms of his capability as a dispute settler. The offices of *bhopa* and *patel* are not necessarily mutually exclusive offices. For example Pheva Data is the Mata *bhopa* of the *devra* shrine in the Malwa section of the village as well as the *patel* of the Raijjath sublineage.

The *patel* (more than one are present if the conflict is between members of two sublineages) are important figures who decide the gravity of the offence committed and, in turn, the nature of compensation to be made by the guilty party to the victims. In as much as the *patel* are concerned with judging what was right or wrong according to Girasia rules, they made the boundaries of the community more tangible, as the following quotation reveals. According to Shyama:

> If a girl runs away with a non-tribal then the *kayda* [compensation] is Rs. 2,000/- and the girl is taken back. In the case of physical assault where no death occurs, the accused has to pay *vair* [indemnity] of Rs. 1,200/-, of which Rs. 200/- is distributed among the *panch* [members of the village council]. In the case of death, the accused has to pay *vair* of Rs. 25,000/. If a man runs away with an unmarried girl, he has to pay Rs. 500/- *kayda* to her parents of which Rs. 200/- is for the *panch*, and a Rs. 4,000/- *dapa*. The *dapa* [brideprice] varies from Rs. 4,000/- if the girl is of a lower lineage, to Rs. 5,000/- if she is of a higher lineage. If a man runs away with a married woman, he pays Rs. 1,000/- *dava* [brideprice compensation] to the first husband and spends money for a feast as *dan* [gift] which must include a goat, 4 kilos *ghee* [clarified butter], 4 kilos *atta* [wheat flour], and, 20 kilos of *gur* [molasses]. Besides, he has to give Rs. 500/- to the *panch*. In the case of the theft of a goat, the offender has to return 2 goats, as well as give Rs. 200/- to the owner and Rs. 200/- to the *panch*. If a buffalo is stolen, the offender will return 2 buffalos, cash up to Rs. 2,000/- to the owner and from Rs. 200/- to 400/- to the *panch* as well as Rs. 500/- to the informer. In the case of a quarrel over land, the *panch*s are present as well as the *patwari* [government land revenue agent], who measure the disputed portion with a rope and usually divide it exactly between the two parties. Each party also gives Rs. 100/- to the *panch*. In the case of fights, especially after drinking, *gur* is to be distributed and to be consumed

together. In the case of the theft of silver jewellery, the offender pays double the weight in silver. For a small piece of plastic or other jewellery, the payment of 1 coconut may be made.

During my fieldwork there were constant village councils to bargain about compensation fees.[31] Shyama's description quoted above shows the fees are graded according to the level of the crime, with murder at the highest end and petty theft at the lower. The fees also reflect the division between the status and non-status concerns in the lineage. Status is attached particularly to matters relating to women and livestock, and therefore the payments are highest for these. Moreover, Shyama's discussion of fees reinforces the point made previously in chapter 7, that even though women take the decision to leave their present husband for another man, the next husband makes the final decision and is held ultimately responsible, as reflected by the *dava* fee.

These disputes affect the ways in which the Taivar 'believers' interact with each other, especially in terms of the relationships between the 'believer' members of different sublineages or different sections within the same sublineage. For example, among the Vaijjath 'believer' households, the 'believer' sons of two brothers had

31. The most dramatic *panchayati*, with regard to the scale of participation, followed the death of Gona. Gona was guilty of adultery and was badly beaten by his lover's husband, a non-Taivar Parmar Girasia from Khejara living in the Taivar village as a *ghar jamai* (resident son-in-law). The man's wife, a Taivarni, was not subject to any collective sanction by the Taivars. The Taivars also blamed Gona for his irresponsible behaviour. However, Gona died two days after the altercation. The murderer fled the village with his family, and the Taivars were unanimous in their decision (following the direction of the *patel*) to take a life from the Parmar's sublineage in Khejara village. When they reached the village they found it deserted, all the village members had fled into the hills. (The tactic of flight to evade outsider government control was also used as a solution to internal aggression.) The Taivars then retreated to await either a retaliatory measure, which would mean an open armed battle, or the conciliatory measure of a *panchayati* to discuss the murder compensation fees *(vair)*. There was a scare approximately twelve hours later that the Khejara-*vale* (or people from Khejara) were approaching. Adult Taivar men and women carried their axes, bows and arrows, guns and sticks to the hilltops surrounding the Taivar village. Elder Taivar men and women hid their valuables in the fields and let their livestock loose in the fields and forest. After four days of waiting the vigil ceased, and there were rumours that the Parmar Girasia from other villages had restrained the Khejara Parmars. So the *panchayati* started, with both of the villages sending those few men of other lineages residing in their villages *(ghar jamais)* as emissaries, to communicate the decisions regarding the compensation payments. Two months later, when my fieldwork period ended, the *panchayati* still continued. When asked how long it would take, some Taivars said it could take a year or even longer.

parallel and separate *bhajan* sessions, whereas previously they used to sit and sing together. The reason for the split was due to a dispute over land. According to Chakra, brother of Bava:

> On the occasion of *Diwali* in 1985, just after the death of Mada, there was a fight over the land distribution between the sons of Mada and the sons of Bava, his brother. The *panch* of the village decided to distribute the disputed land into three equal portions between the descendants of the three brothers Mada, Thela and Bava. When it came to dividing the grazing and rain-fed land there was further disagreement. Lunda, Mada's youngest son, then brought a stick to beat his brothers and there was a big fight. Since then the sons of Mada and the sons of Bava have not been on speaking terms. Although we share the same well, we use different methods to extract water.

The fight between the brothers in the Vaijjath sublineage over land affected the 'believer' organisation, and the 'believers' who were sons of Mada held separate devotional song sessions from the 'believers' who were sons of Bava. But Chakra, Bava's grandson, would sometimes attend the devotional meetings held at certain households of the other 'believers'. The two houses where all the 'believers' would attend the devotional meetings were those of Heva, the *peelkhe vale baosi* (the spirit of the *peelkha* tree) and Palvi's household. Heva's house was an acceptable place to meet as he was not a son of either Mada, Thela or Bava. Palvi's household was acceptable (although less so than Heva's house), because Jama, her husband, was also not a son of Mada, Thela or Hawa. Yet the meetings were held less frequently at Jama's place because he was a *gharjamai* (resident son-in-law, not a member of the Taivar lineage) and Palvi showed a strong loyalty to her brothers, who were Mada's sons. The above example illustrates how divisions *within* the sublineage affect the Taivar 'believers'. In their interactions, the 'believers' also reflect the discord *between* sublineages. For example, only one household of the Lailath sublineage was a member of the Mandal. But when another dispute in a line of disputes arose, the Lailath household withdrew from the 'believer' group altogether. The decisive dispute involved the Lailath 'believer' household. The Vaijjaths had accused the son of the household of molesting their daughter (Pemli, daughter of Lunda, a Vaijjath 'believer'; see chapter 4). This accusation led to a *panchayati* between the two sublineages.[32]

The two examples above show that the 'believers' reproduce sublineage differences and even split along sublineage lines. Both the

---

32. The *panchayati* had not been resolved before I left, but the Lailath household did not come to the 'believer' *bhajans*.

transmission of 'believer' membership and the withdrawal from membership followed sublineage lines. In aligning with their sublineage's loyalties, the 'believers' followed the politics of the lineage in their own relations. Thus the Mandal is another channel through which inter-sublineage conflicts are broadcast. It is of course difficult to say whether these inter- and intra-sublineage divisions are accelerated owing to the Mandal membership or are natural progressions of family divisions in Girasia life. The result of all the conflicts mentioned above was that there was a drop in Mandal members from all the sublineages except the Vaijjath. This may be viewed negatively as well as positively. A dominant number of Vaijjaths in the Mandal would be detrimental to the 'believers' in terms of the egalitarian ideal of the lineage. Confining 'believer' belief to a single sublineage also made it more prone to effective opposition. On the other hand, the fact that the 'believers' are placed firmly within the numerically dominant sublineage in the lineage can be seen as a means of their survival, as the loyalty towards the sublineage is seen to override mere 'believer' concerns. The importance of the sublineage to the 'believers' is illustrated in their needs for marriage partners.

Marriage and 'Believer' Women

According to Heva, Reeva (his eldest step-brother), another (now deceased) Taivar and himself were the first Taivars to be initiated into the Mandal, approximately thirty-five years ago by, 'the Rajputs who came from Gaddu. We knew the people from that village as we had given our daughters there'. Hoja emphasised that the Anop Mandal ideas were legitimised for him because they came via the affinal relatives of the Taivars. I regard the continuing possibilities for the 'believers' to maintain affinal ties with other prescribed Girasia lineages as one of the main factors in their continued survival within the Girasia community, although the 'believers' themselves have the ideal of marrying into other Girasia 'believer' households'. If the 'believers' had not been able to give their daughters in marriage, they would have been unable to participate in the household, sublineage and lineage related activities with the other Taivars. The sublineage remains central in the definition of the Taivars as well as for the 'believers'.

It is the 'believer' abstinence from alcohol which assures them Girasia wives. All Girasia ideally believe that the habit of drinking alcohol is not good, although most Taivar men do drink alcohol. I was often told how this consumption leads to frequent disturbances in the village and could see this for myself, reflected in the numerous small-scale councils to settle fights ensuing from drunken behaviour. It is generally believed that by abstaining from alcohol, a man has greater control over his life and resources. Fathers of brides are consequently more willing to give their daughters to men who do not drink. I was told that by doing so they expected less trouble in affinal matters and better treatment of their daughters. It is the 'believer' ideal to give their daughters as wives to other 'believer' households.[33] In reality, however, this is not the case and often daughters marry non-'believers' and give up their 'believer' practices. Outgoing brides thus either contribute to reinforcing the 'believer' connections with 'believer' households in other lineages or revert to the more customary Girasia beliefs. The 'believers' do not conceive of their daughters' reconversion as a loss to their cause, and in this they followed the wider lineage marriage rules, wherein the status of the Taivar Girasia father within his lineage is not affected by his daughter's marriage (see chapter 5). On the other hand, Girasia brides who marry 'believer' grooms also become 'believers'. It is rarer to find a man joining the Mandal if his wife originates in a 'believer' household, although in the Taivar village I found that the two resident sons-in-law had done so. Palvi was a 'believer' because her brothers were and Jama her husband also became a 'believer'. The 'believer' position gave him some status with the 'believer' section of his wife's kin in comparison to his low position as a mere resident son-in-law among the rest of the Taivars.

So far, I have discussed 'believer' women only as vehicles in their husband's or father's desire for acceptance and recognition within the lineage and sublineage. In terms of the women themselves, I found that there is little difference in their roles and relations whether they were 'believers' or not. Within the Mandal organisation 'believer' women continue to be marginal. They never initiate the devotional meetings. At the meetings they occupy the outer space of the gatherings, as do Girasia women at other rituals described in the previous chapter. In other words, Taivar 'believer' women show a low degree of religious preoccupation, similar to that of the non-'believer' Taivar women. Although 'believer' ceremonies minimise the need for cooking and distribute only molasses after the devotional gatherings, distribution remains in the hands of men. 'Believer' women also cannot

---

33. Palvi said she had married her daughter into a village where there were other 'believers' and that her son-in-law was becoming one too. However, when I met the daughter on one of her visits to her natal village, she was wearing the *baliya* (white bangles) signifying her non-'believer' status.

speak Hindi. Thus 'believers' do not present a change in the customary Girasia relations between genders. In fact 'believers' use similar means to the non-Girasia to construct differences amongst themselves. For example, 'believer' men are not differentiated by clothing from other Taivar men, while their women are.

'Believer' women substitute the *baliya* (white bangle signifying marriage) and the traditional *odhani* (wrap) for plastic bangles and a thinner muslin wrap which other middle- and upper-class women in the region wear (see chapter 3). Yet 'believer' women continue to wear the *rebar puliyo* (choker; table 3.2) which every Girasia woman wears. 'Believer' wives maintain the *laaj kaadna* (veil) for certain categories of affinal men. The dress and attitudes of 'believer' women reinforce my own impression that 'believer' women, like other Girasia women, are not only the symbols of the belief of their men, but also reflect the extent to which the 'believer' and non-'believer' actions, though based on different beliefs, are similar rather than opposed.

I would argue, therefore, that while the 'believer' or other spiritual groups redefine their religious identities in different ways, it is much more difficult for them to question the patriarchal basis of their social organisations, and therefore less possible to effect a change in the structural relationship between genders. A similar observation is made by Wadley (1988) for women in the *bhakti* movement. The religious role of Hindu women is said to have been altered by the *bhakti* movement, traced to AD 700, which arose against the orthodoxy of the Brahmanic and Vedic rituals. In the *bhakti* tradition, unlike in orthodox Hinduism, women were allowed direct access to the pantheonic Hindu deities in temples; this may be compared to the contact women had previously had with the agnatic or household gods (Wadley 1988). However, Wadley notes, even in the *bhakti* rituals it was men who continued to be recognised as religious specialists (1988: 36). In contrast, in Jain religious practice, also founded on the basis of a rejection of the orthodox nature of the textual Hindu rituals, there is a high degree of religiosity amongst Jain wives. As Reynell (1985) suggests, this is because among the Jains the religiosity and penance of women is related directly to the prosperity achieved by their men in economic enterprises. So, once again, the determinant of women's religiosity lies in the motivations of men.

In conclusion, the three major points which emerge from the above discussion are: 1) that the 'believers' are not a hierarchically superior section of the Taivar Girasia community because of the restraining nature of the relationships in the lineage and sublineage. The 'believers', with regard to the egalitarian ideal of the Girasia lineage, may be seen instead as a means of further diffusing power in the Girasia brotherhood; 2) the 'believers' are not emulating the upper castes. Instead, in the Mandal organisation, apart from marriage, there is a high degree of interaction between some lower castes to the exclusion of the upper castes; 3) 'believer' women have the same structural position within the 'believer' category as they do within the Taivar lineage as a whole. The existence of the 'believers' as a distinct group among the Taivar Girasia shows, above all, that different constructions of identity may co-exist within a common collective identity. Furthermore, the 'believers' are another example of the extent to which women are indicators of the boundaries of identities. These have been the central concerns of this book, as I discuss in the final chapter.

Chapter 10

CONCLUSIONS

The Girasia have a distinct identity which cannot be suitably described in 'tribal' terms. The tribal nature of the Girasia is largely an ideological response by outsiders to the Girasia's own ideological position, which is opposed to their assimilation into mainstream political and socio-economic caste interactions. The Girasia case is not unique, and I suggest that their experiences may hold true for other groups seen to be 'outside' conventionally operating communities. Examples are provided not only in India, as in the case of the Bhils, but also elsewhere.[1] The tribalisation of the Girasia is connected to the images which non-Girasia project on them. Such images are informed by what is most negatively sanctioned in orthodox caste practices, such as the defiance of ritual and political authority, sexual freedom with women 'out of male control' and, to a lesser extent, with textually prescribed social rankings or ritual purity. These outsider images are reflected in the manner in which the Girasia have been presented by both the British and the Indian administrative and academic communities.[2]

The outsider perception of the Girasia is also rooted in economic inequalities, and the political and economic policies of successive governments which were insensitive to the impact of this legislation

---

1. The traveller-gypsies in England, as documented by Okely (1983) are in a very similar position to the *gorgio*-outsiders as the Girasia are to the non-Girasia.
2. What Said (1985) sees as a particularly 'western' and 'colonial' style of representing the Orient, I see present to a certain extent in the work of native authors.

on marginal groups.[3] The Girasia were petty landholders and amongst the weak, marginal and lower lineages of the Rajput state. History indicates there has been a change in their collective status vis-à-vis non-Girasia, largely as a result of the allocation to them of forest land and the subsequent restriction on their territorial and economic expansion. As a result the Girasia were impoverished and in outsider eyes have become more tribal in nature. Even if the Girasia were petty Rajputs in the past, this does not imply that they were regarded as such or treated any better by the non-Girasia.

It is a misrepresentation to suggest that the Girasia have become like a caste group, as is implied by those authors who favour the process of emulation, reflected in terms such as 'hinduisation' or 'rajputisation', to explain the changes in the collective status of specific communities. Such a view implicitly assumes a previously tribal (or non-caste) condition, which is not substantiated by the archival material on the Girasia presented in this book. Moreover, the emulation theorists assume that lower-caste and tribal groups have fewer concerns in maintaining the boundaries of their communities, considered to be manifested in the easy exchange of wives among the lower castes. Such beliefs are not well founded in the region of south Rajasthan. For the Girasia, as I have shown, the lineage sanctions on improper, or unprescribed, marriages, and the constant *panchayati* to settle disputes arising therefrom, reflect their concern in maintaining a social distance, or difference, from other non-Girasia groups. One of the conclusions of this book, therefore, is that it is not the case that higher castes have stricter boundaries than lower ones ('tribes'). On the contrary, the Girasia material shows that tribes may be equally conscious of status boundaries. What was common to the groups in the region was that they all considered those lower than them to have less strict status rules than they did themselves. However, what does seem to be true for the Girasia and other lower-class groups in the region is the context of poverty in which they operate which often compromises their concerns with status, making room for a more negotiated social order.

In spite of the pressures of economic hardship, and a social and political marginalisation from the other groups in the region, the Girasia have been able to maintain a distinct identity. This has been possible through the rules relating residence and access to resources

3. If there has been a concentration of tribal people in the hilly and unproductive pockets of various Indian states, rather than calling them tribal because they are marginal, there is perhaps the need to reframe the question, to ask why people in these areas are called 'tribal' in the first place.

to both patrilineal descent and rules prescribing marriage to equal-status affines. By such kinship rules, Girasia make their boundaries fairly impermeable. Furthermore, Girasia identity is reflected in their dress, jewellery, language, songs, and protective deities. The distinctiveness of the Girasia identity must, however, not be taken as an indication of their absolute separation from other caste groups, as both the Girasia and non-Girasia may make out. For the very institutions and practices which embody a Girasia identity also contain similarities whereby the Girasia are akin to other caste groups.[4] The simultaneous presence of similarities and differences within social organisations lies at the heart of questions of identity. For the Girasia, like the Rajputs, patrilineal kinship and territory play a central role in their sense of caste identity.

In each chapter of this book, I have described the interconnections between Girasia and non-Girasia styles of life. Everyone in the region stresses difference between communities but I, as an anthropologist, also perceived similarities in, for example, dress, rituals, fairs, marriage ceremonies and transactions. These can be linked to the common regional patrifocal concern with prestige, mirrored above all in the similar structural position of Girasia and non-Girasia women. Not only are there similarities between groups in the region, but the Girasia material indicates that the differences between north and south India are not necessarily that absolute. For example, in the Girasia marriage rules (chapter 5) and religious worship (of *Bhairu* or *Shiva* as against the *Vaishnavite* tradition of the north), we see elements of both the north and south Indian patterns. The distinction commonly drawn between north and south is perhaps a primarily text-based one, but when we look at popular practices it is not so clear.

The egalitarian nature of the Girasia lineage implied in the *kakababa* brother relations is reflected in the diffusion rather than the concentration of authority between religious, political and economic positions. Even in this tendency, the Girasia exhibit a common casteist trait. According to Thapar (1986), for example, the hallmark of early caste society has been precisely the manner in which absolute authority could not be invested in any single community or individual. Thus there were those with divine power, others with secular, legislative power and yet others with economic power. Ziegler (1978) has shown that the foremost concerns of the Rajputs

---

4. Leach (1964) has shown that it is mainly through political organisation that the Burmese Kachin and Shan groups are linked despite their contrasting socio-economic features

was in the egalitarian and corporate nature of their brotherhoods, even though these were often in conflict with the strategies of social mobility based on the cross-clan relationships of loyalty. The common, collective and egalitarian identity presented by the Girasia to the outside separates out as we move in towards the lineage. The same kinship mechanisms which are used at the all-Girasia level to distinguish themselves from the non-Girasia, are used inside the group to distinguish between lineages. One of the major levels of difference within the Girasia community lies in the distinctions between lineages, which is marked by the movement of wives. Kinship and affinity, defined by Fortes (1964) as a means to describe all other relationships, are used at this level to define the relationships between Girasia lineages. However, within the Girasia lineage, kinship is more related to the economy, in the manner in which Leach (1968) and Godelier (1974) define it. Inside the lineage the nature of resource ownership, codes of sharing, commensal and ritual occasions allow the Girasia to experience the common aspects of a lineage-defined identity. And Girasia kinship becomes, as Leach had noted for the Sinhala *variga*, an idiom to express the economic relations within the microcommunity. It is here that the sublineage and the person become significant entities of identity.

Again, in relations within the lineage, women are used as markers of difference. For example, in chapters 4 and 6, I show how differences between sublineages are articulated in controversies surrounding the control over the access of men to women's sexuality. I took the example of the Naal sublineage where the whole sublineage was collectively discriminated against, and the dispute between two families within the Lailath and Vaijjath sublineages. Moreover, within a sublineage, the economic differences between men are often mirrored in the amount of brideprice paid for wives, such as, for example, the *ghar-jamai* or resident son-in-law, for whom no brideprice is received, or Hoja's deaf and dumb wife for whom less brideprice was paid. In contrast to men, who have differentiated positions with regard to resources, women have the same, universal and much weaker access which is always mediated through men. Thus the relation of Taivar kinship to the economy of the lineage has different implications for the structural positions of Taivar men and women. Until recently structural differences based on gender have been largely ignored. The present example shows that men are embedded in a patrilineal structure which to a great extent organises the economy, whereas women, excluded from authoritative positions in these structures, are subject to the economic vagaries of particular contexts.

The insider levels of Girasia existence show a concern with prestige, economic resources and purity, preoccupations which require them to regulate the boundaries of, and within their community. These concerns are similarly manifested among other caste, subcaste or *jati* groups in the region. I suggest that it is because the Girasia institutions satisfy their needs of identity maintenance, lineage and gender hierarchies that there is little reason to expect change to take the form of an emulation of other caste practises. This view is reinforced by the nature of the Girasia membership in the Anop Mandal. What is significant in the Anop Mandal is the exclusion of the upper castes as a reference model. As I have shown in chapter 9, the Taivar 'believers' are neither emulating the upper castes nor becoming hierarchically superior to the other Taivar Girasia. The absence of fundamental change resulting from Mandal membership is seen particularly in the similar structural positions of 'believer' and non-'believer' Girasia women. Membership of the Mandal cannot be regarded as a move towards hinduisation among the Taivar Girasia, despite the resemblances to some lower-caste movements of reform. Instead, the 'believer' category may be seen as adding another, class-type dimension to the Girasia lower-caste identity.

In short, this book has argued for a nuanced approach to the study of identities in India which takes into account the ways in which people perceive and represent themselves and others in relation to the shifting historical, political, social and economic contexts of their lives.

APPENDIX 1

List of Scheduled Tribes: Rajasthan

1. Bhil, Bhil Garasia, Dholi Bhil, Dungri Bhil, Dungri Garasia, Mewari Bhil, Tadvi Bhil, Bhagalia, Bhilala, Pawra, Vasowa, Vasave
2. Bhil Mina
3. Damor, Damaria
4. Dhanka, Tadvi, Tetaria, Valvi
5. Garasia (excluding Rajput Garasia)
6. Kathodi, Katkari, Dhor Kathodi, Dhor Katkari, Son Kathodi, Son Katkari
7. Kokna, Kokni, Kukna
8. Koli Dhor, Tokre Koli, Kolcha, Kolgha
9. Mina
10. Naikda, Nayaka, Chotivala Nayaka, Kapadia Nayaka, Mota Nayaka, Nana Nayaka
11. Patelia
12. Seharia, Sehria, Sahariya

Source: Census of India 1981, Series 18-Rajasthan; Part IX: Special Tables for Scheduled Tribes, Appendix: 3

Note on Scheduled Castes and Scheduled Tribes

A person is identified as a member of a Scheduled Caste or Scheduled Tribe on the basis of the prescribed lists of the Scheduled Castes and Scheduled Tribes Lists (Amendment) order, 1976, issued by the President of India. Scheduled Castes can be among Hindus or Sikhs only, while a member of a Scheduled Tribe can profess any religion. If the person belonging to a Scheduled Caste or Scheduled Tribe has returned his or her caste or tribe, it is reckoned as a Scheduled Caste or Scheduled Tribe only if that name finds a place in the prescribed list.

Source: Census Concepts no. 22, xliv, Census of India 1981, Series 18-Rajasthan District Census Handbook, Sirohi, XIII-A, B

APPENDIX 2

Rural Population of Garasias and Bhils in Rajasthan by District

No.	District	Garasia population	Bhil population
1.	Ganganagar	22	292
2.	Bikaner	23	240
3.	Churu	0	76
4.	Jhunjunu	0	28
5.	Alwar	2	265
6.	Bharatpur	0	456
7.	Sawai Madhopur	22	959
8.	Jaipur	3	1,337
9.	Sikar	14	9
10.	Ajmer	0	15,944
11.	Tonk	1	7,563
12.	Jaiselmer	8	9,748
13.	Jodhpur	7	28,765
14.	Nagaur	1	165
15.	Pali	20,198	12,633
16.	Barmer	1	53,957
17.	Jalore	70	54,001
18.	Sirohi	58,191	46,823
19.	Bhilwara	103	65,909
20.	Udaipur	38,257	381,768
21.	Chittaurgarh	248	78,563
22.	Dungarpur	180	326,060
23.	Banswara	769	572,624
24.	Bundi	0	22,991
25.	Kota	25	43,806
26.	Jhalawar	0	50,671

Source: ST-6 Part B: Educational Levels of Scheduled Tribes in Rural Areas. 1038-1093, part IX, Special tables for Scheduled Tribes, Census of India 1981, Series 18–Rajasthan.

GLOSSARY

anganwadi	child-care centre
ashram	Hindi term for shelter; local term given to the tribal boys' residential school
aurat	popular Hindi or Muslim term used to refer to woman; Girasia term used for wife
baba	father's elder brother
bai	term of address for woman
baosi	term of respect for all deities and some men
beej	occasion of ancestor worship
beeja	other, different
bhagidar	shareholder
bhai	brother
bhajan	devotional song
bhakar	popular term for mountainous terrain east of Abu Road town
bhavik	members of the Anop Mandal
bhopa	ritual mediator; shaman
bigha	measure of land
bori	jute sack for storing and transporting grain; popular measure for grain
chori	'stealing', particularly of wives
chula	hearth
churma	sweet preparation for ritual feasts
dan	prestation
dapa	brideprice
dava	payment for wife-stealing
dussehra	Hindu festival
devala	grain diviner
donga	hill
gaaba	cloth; also symbol of menstruation
gainhu	wheat
gair	house

Glossary

ghagra	woman's skirt
ghar jamai	resident son-in-law
ghee	clarified butter
gugri	boiled corn
haga	'true', term referring to physical kinship
hagavale	blood relations
hagai	marriage by engagement
hahu	mother-in-law
hankaudar	first ritual of the funeral ceremonies
halmo	collective labour
hau	good; appropriate
hemo	me; we
hojvan	localised sublineage; section of the jath
holi	Hindu festival celebrating spring
homo-hata	restricted exchange; from *homo* or, in front of
jagirdar	pre-independence landholding title
jath	localised patrilineage
jeev	soul
jhulki	woman's blouse
kadna	to take out; to do
kaka	father's younger brother
kandiya	first feast, and second ritual performed at the funeral ceremony
khat	rope bed
khave or *khau*	to eat; be greedy in consumption
khichna	marriage by 'capture'
khichri	any salted mixture of boiled cereal
khoont	ritual expert
khoti	bad; not proper
kshatriya	warrior community by occupation
kuamathe	on, off the well
kuldevi	clan mother, goddess
laaj	shame felt by women
mahi	mother's sister; step-mother
meri	construction to store grain and house goats
makki	corn; maize
manyata	occasion to show belief
mata	female deity
matar	same as *churma* above, but salty rather than sweet
moma	mother's brother
moti	female superior in age or attitude
neenchu	low; inferior
nonki	small; young
nyath	funeral
odhani	woman's wrap

Glossary

paada	buffalo
patta	section of land
panchayati	local legislative council
patel	person with primary legislative authority
peethi	turmeric paste
phalli	spatial subsection of the village
pher	difference; social distance
piyar	natal village
prasad	sacred and blessed food
rati-jaga	night spent for worship of male deity Bhairu
roti	baked and unleavened bread
shadi	ceremonial marriage
shant	peaceful
sharm	shame
tehsil	smallest state administrative unit comprising a number of villages
vadku	metal dish of bride
vahu	term of address for bride
vanda	foliage of the corn crop

BIBLIOGRAPHY

Afshar, H., and Agarwal, B., eds. *Women, Poverty and Ideology in Asia: Contradictory Pressures, Uneasy Resolutions*. London: Macmillan, 1993.
Agarwal, B. *A Field of One's Own: Gender and Land Rights in South Asia*. Cambridge: Cambridge University Press, 1994.
Allen, M., and Mukherjee, S.N., eds. *Women in India and Nepal*. ANU Monograph on South Asia, No.8. Canberra: Australian National University Printing, 1982
Anderson, B. *Imagined Communities*. London: Verso, 1983.
Appadurai, A. 'Is Homo Hierarchicus?', *American Ethnologist,* vol.13, no.4 (1986): 745-61.
Appadurai, A., Korom, F., and Mills, M.A., eds. *Gender, Genre and Power in South Asian Expressive Traditions*. Philadelphia: University of Pennsylvania Press, 1991.
Ardener, S. *Defining Females: The Nature of Women in Society*. London: Croom Helm, in association with the Oxford University Women's Studies Committee, 1978.
Ardener, S., ed. *Perceiving Women*. London: Malaby Press, 1975.
Atal, Y., ed. *Sociology and Social Anthropology in Asia and the Pacific*. London: Wiley Eastern Limited and Paris: UNESCO, 1985.
Babb, L. *The Divine Hierarchy: Popular Hinduism in Central India*. New York: Columbia University Press, 1975.
Baden-Powell, B.H. *Land Systems of British India*. Oxford: Clarendon Press, 1892.
Baden-Powell, B.H. *A Short Account of the Land Revenue and Its Administration in British India; With a Sketch of the Land Tenures*. Oxford: Clarendon Press, 1913.
Bailey, F. *Tribe, Caste and Nation*. Manchester: Manchester University Press, 1960.
Banerjee, A.C. *Rajput States and British Paramountcy*. New Delhi: Rajesh Publications, 1980.
Barnard, A., and Good, A. *Research Practices in the Study of Kinship*. ASA: Research Methods in Social Anthropology, vol. 2. London: Academic Press, 1984.
Barnes, J. 'Social Science in India: Colonial Import, Indigenous Product or Universal Truth?', in Fahim, H., ed. *Indigenous Anthropology in Non-Western Countries*. Durham, NC: Carolina Academic Press, 1982.
Barnett, S. 'Identity Choice and Caste Ideology in Contemporary South India.', in David, K., ed. *The New Wind: Changing Identities in South Asia,* 1977.
Barth, F. 'Ethnic Processes on the Pathan-Baluch Boundary', in Gumperz, J., and Hymes, D., ed. *Directions in Sociolinguistics: The Ethnography of Communication*. New York: Holt, Reinhart and Winston, Inc., 1972.
_____ . 'Features of Person and Society in Swat.' [Collected Essays on Pathans], in *Selected Essays of Frederic Barth, vol. II*. London: Routledge and Kegan Paul, 1978.
Barth, F., ed. *Ethnic Groups and Boundaries: The Social Organisation of Culture Difference*. London: George Allen and Unwin, 1969.

Bates, C. 'Congress and the Tribals.' 231-53, in *The Indian National Congress and the Political Economy of India 1885-1985:* Sheppardson, M., and Simmons, C., eds. Aldershot, Brookfield, USA: Avebury, 1988.

Bayly, C. *Rulers, Townsmen and Bazaars: North Indian Society in the Age of British Expansion, 1770-1870.* Cambridge: Cambridge University Press, 1983.

Bell, D., Caplan, P., and Karim, W.J. *Gendered Fields: Women, Men and Ethnography.* London: Routledge, 1993.

Bennett, L. *Dangerous Wives and Sacred Sisters: Social and Symbolic Roles of High-Caste Women in Nepal.* New York: Columbia University Press, 1983.

Berreman, G. *Hindus of the Himalayas.* Berkeley: University of California Press, 1963.

———. 'Brahmans and Shamans in Pahari Religion.' in Harper, E., ed. *Religion in South Asia,* 53-71. Seattle: University of Washington Press, 1964.

———. 'Social Categories and Social Interaction in Urban India.' *American Anthropologist,* vol. 74: 567-86. Washington: American Anthropological Association, 1972.

Beteille, A. *Six Essays in Comparative Sociology.* Delhi: Oxford University Press, 1974.

———. *Studies in Agrarian Social Structure.* Delhi: Oxford University Press, 1974.

———. *The Backward Classes and the New Social Order.* Ambedkar Memorial Lecture. Delhi: Oxford University Press, 1981.

———. 'Individualism and the Persistence of Collective Identities'. Colchester, University of Essex, 1984.

———. 'The Concept of Tribe with Special Reference to India.' *Arch. Europ. Sociol.,* vol. XXVII, 297-318. Paper prepared for seminar in the Dept. of Anthropology, London School of Economics, 1986.

Bhowmik, K.L. *Tribal India: A Profile in Indian Ethnology.* The World Press Pvt. Ltd., 1971.

Bird, N. 'Conjugal Units and Single Persons: an Analysis of the Social System of the Naiken of the Nilgiris (South India)', unpublished Ph.D. thesis, University of Cambridge, 1982.

———. 'Wage Gathering: Socio-Economic Changes and the Case of the Food Gatherer Naikens of South India', in Robb, P., ed. *Rural South Asia: Linkages, Change and Development.* Collected Papers on South Asia no.5. London and Dublin: Curzon Press, 1983.

———. 'The Kurumbas of the Nilgiris: An Ethnographic Myth?' *Modern Asian Studies,* Vol. 21: 1. Cambridge: Cambridge University Press, 1987.

Bleie, T. 'Gender Relations among Oraons in Bangladesh; Continuity and Change.' *EPW,* vol. XXII, no. 17, Review of Women's Studies, 25 April, 1987.

Bose, N.K. *Tribal Life in India.* Delhi: National Book Trust, 1971.

———. *The Structure of Hindu Society.* (Translated from the Bengali with an introduction by A. Beteille.). New York: Orient Longman, 1975.

Boserup, E. *Women's Role in Economic Development.* London: George Allen and Unwin, 1971.

Bourdieu, P. *Outline of a Theory of Practice.* Cambridge: Cambridge University Press, 1977.

Brookes, J.C. *The History of Meywar.* Calcutta: Baptist Mission Press, 1859.

Caplan, P. 'Engendering Knowledge: the Politics of Ethnography'. *Anthropology Today,* vol. 4, no. 6, December 1988.

Caplan, P., ed. *The Cultural Construction of Sexuality.* London and New York: Routledge, 1987.

Caplan, P., and Bujra, J., eds. *Women United, Women Divided: Cross Cultural Perpectives on Female Solidarity.* London: Tavistock, 1978.

Carrithers, M., Collins, S., and Lukes, S. *The Category of the Person: Anthropology, Philosophy, History.* Cambridge: Cambridge University Press, 1985.

Carstairs, G.M. 'Bhil Villages of Western Udaipur: A Study in Resistance to Social Change', in Srinivas, M.N., ed. *India's Villages.* Bombay: Asia Publishing House, 1955.

_____. *The Twice Born: A Study of a Community of High Caste Hindus.* London: The Hogarth Press, 1957.

_____. 'Bhils of Kotra Bhomat', in Mathur, K.S. and Agrawal, B.C. eds. *Tribe, Caste and Peasantry.* Lucknow: Ethnographhic and Folk Culture Soc. U.P., 1974.

_____. *Death of a Witch: A Village in North India 1950-1981.* London: Hutchinson, 1983.

Chambers, R., Saxena, N.C., and Shah, T. *To the Hands of the Poor: Water and Trees.* London: Intermediate Technology Publications, 1989.

Chandra, B., Mukherjee, M., Mukherjee, A., Pannikar, K.N., and Mahajan, S. *India's Struggle for Independence.* Delhi: Penguin, 1989.

Chauhan, B.R. *A Rajasthan Village.* New Delhi: Vir Publishing House, 1967.

_____. 'Tribalisation.', in Vyas, N.N., Mann, R.B. and Chaudhry, N.D., eds., *Rajasthan Bhils.* Udaipur, India: MLV Tribal Research Institute, Social Welfare Dept., Govt. of Rajasthan, 1978.

Clifford, J., and Marcus, G. *Writing Culture: The Poetics and Politics of Ethnography.* Berkeley: University of California Press, 1986.

Cohen, A. *The Symbolic Construction of Community.* London: Tavistock, 1985.

Cohn, B.S. *An Anthropologist among the Historians and Other Essays.* Delhi: Oxford University Press, 1987.

Collier, J.F. *Marriage and Inequality in a Classless Society.* Stanford: Stanford University Press, 1988.

Collier, J.F., and Rosaldo, M.Z. 'Politics and Gender in Simple Societies', in Ortner, S., and Whitehead, H., eds. *Sexual Meanings.* Cambridge: Cambridge University Press, 1981.

Collier, J.F., and Yanagiasko, S.J., eds. *Gender and Kinship: Essays toward a Unified Analysis.* Stanford: Stanford University Press, 1987.

Comaroff, J.L., ed. *The Meaning of Marriage Payments.* London: Academic Press, 1980.

Copland, I. *The British Raj and the Indian Princes: Paramountcy in Western India, 1857-1930.* Bombay: Orient Longman, 1982.

Corbridge, S. 'The Ideology of Tribal Economy and Society: Politics in the Jharkand Land', 1950-1980. *Modern Asian Studies, vol.* 22: 1, 1988.

Crooke, W. *An Ethnographical Handbook for the N.W. Provinces.* Allahabad: N.W. Provinces and Oudh Govt. Press, 1890.

_____. *The Tribes and Castes of the N.W. Provinces and Oudh.* 4 vols. Calcutta, 1896.

_____. *The North-Western Provinces of India, their History, Ethnology and Administration* [with a new introduction by Mason, P.]. Karachi: Oxford University Press, Repr. Ed. of the 1892 volume, 1972.

Daniel, V. *Fluid Signs: Being a Person the Tamil Way.* Berkeley: University of California Press, 1984.

Das, Anop. *Jagat Hitkarni.* Sirohi, 1960.

Das, V. *Structure and Cognition: Aspects of Hindu Caste and Ritual.* Delhi: Oxford University Press, 1982.

_____. 'Subaltern as Perspective', in Guha, R., ed. *Subaltern Studies.* Delhi: Oxford University Press, 1987.

_____. 'Feminity and the Orientation to the Body', in Chanana, K., ed. *Socialisation, Education and Women: Explorations in gender identity:* 193-208. Bombay: Orient Longman, 1988.

Das, V., ed. *Mirrors of Violence: Communities, Riots and Survivors in South Asia*. Delhi: Oxford University Press, 1990.

Dave, P.C. *The Grasias*. Delhi: Bharatiya Adimjati Sevak Sangh, 1960.

David, K., ed. *The New Wind: Changing Identities in South Asia*. The Hague: Mouton Publishers, 1977.

Deliege, R. *Bhils of Western India: Some empirical and theoretical issues in Anthropology in India*. New Delhi: National Publishers, 1985.

_____. 'Replication and Consensus: untouchability, caste and ideology in India'. *Man (n.s.)*, vol. 27, (1992):155-73.

Dhanagre, D.N. 'Sociology and Social Anthropology in India', in Atal, Y., ed. *Sociology and Social Anthropology in Asia and the Pacific*. London: Wiley Eastern Ltd. and Paris: UNESCO, 1985.

Doshi, J.K. *Social Structure and Cultural Change in a Bhil Village*. Delhi: New Heights Publishers, 1974.

Doshi, S.L. *Bhils: Between Societal Self-Awareness and Cultural Synthesis*. New Delhi: Sterling Publishers, 1971.

_____. *Processes of Tribal Unification and Integration*. [A Case Study of the Bhils] Delhi: Concept Publishing Company, 1978.

Douglas, M. *Purity and Danger. An analysis of Concepts of Pollution and Taboo*. London: Routledge and Kegan Paul, 1966.

Dube, L. 'On the Construction of Gender: Hindu Girls in Patrilineal India', in Chanana, K., ed., *Socialisation, Education and Women: Explorations in gender identity*. Bombay: Orient Longman, 1988.

Dube, L., Leacock, E., and Ardener, S., eds. *Visibility and Power: Essays on Women in society and development*. Delhi: Oxford University Press, 1986.

Dube, S.C., ed. *Tribal Heritage of India. Vol.1: Ethnicity, Identity and Interaction*. New Delhi: Vikas Publishing House, 1977.

Dumont, L. 'Marriage in India: The Present State of the Question III. North India in relation to South India'. *Contributions to Indian Sociology, Old Series*, vol. 9 (1966): 90-114.

_____. *Homo-Hierarchicus: The Caste System and Its Implications*. Complete Revised Edition translated by Sainsbury, M., et al. Chicago: The University of Chicago Press, 1980.

Engineer, A.A. *Communalism and Communal Violence in India. An Analytical Approach to Hindu-Muslim Conflict*. Delhi: Ajanta Publications (India), 1989.

Enthoven, R.E. 'The Garasia', in *The Tribes and Castes of Bombay*. vol.I, Bombay 1920; Vol.II, Bombay 1922. Reprinted, Delhi: Cosmo Publications, 1975.

Epstein, A.L. *Ethos and Identity: Three Studies in Ethnicity*. London: Tavistock, 1978.

Fahim, H., ed. *Indigenous Anthropology in Non-Western Countries*. Durham, NC: Carolina Academic Press, 1982.

Forbes, A.K. *Rasmala: Hindoo Annals of the Province of Goozerat in Western India*. Edited with historical notes and appendices by H.G. Rawlinson. London: Oxford University Press, 1924.

Fortes, M. ' The Structure of Unilineal Descent Systems'. *American Anthropologist*, vol. 55: 25-39. Washington: American Anthropological Association, 1953.

_____. *Kinship and the Social Order*. Chicago: Aldine Publishing Company, 1969.

Fox, R.G. 'Professional Primitives: Hunters and Gatherers of Nuclear South Asia'. *Man In India*, vol.49 (1967): 139-60.

Fox, R. *Kin, Clan, Raja and Rule: State Hinterland Relations in Pre-Industrial India*. Berkeley: University of California Press, 1971.

Fried, M.H. *The Notion of Tribe*. Menlo Park, CA: Cummings Publishing Co., 1975.

Friedl, E. *Women and Men: An Anthropologist's View.* New York: Holt, Reinhart and Wilson, 1975.
Fruzetti, L. *The Gift of a Virgin: Women, Marriage and Ritual in Bengali Society.* New Brunswick: Rutgers University Press, 1982.
Fruzetti, L., and Ostor, A. *Kinship and Ritual in Bengal: Anthropological Essays.* New Delhi: South Asian Publishers Pvt. Ltd., 1984.
Fuchs, S. *The Aboriginal Tribes of India.* Delhi: Macmillan India, 1974.
Fuller, C.J. 'British India, or Traditional India? An Anthropological Problem'. *Ethnos,* vol. 28 (1977): 95-121.
_____ . 'Gods, Priests and Purity: On the Relation between Hinduism and the Caste System.' *Man,* vol.14, n.s. Published by the Royal Anthropological Institute of Great Britain and Ireland (1979): 459-76.
_____ . 'The Hindu Pantheon and the Legitimation of Hierarchy'. *Man,* vol.23, Published by the Royal Anthropological Institute of Great Britain and Ireland, (1988):19-39.
_____ . *The Camphor Flame: Popular Hinduism and Society in India.* Princeton, NJ: Princeton University Press, 1992.
Fuller, C.J., and Spencer, J. 'South Asia Anthropology in the 1980s'. *South Asia Research,* vol.10, no.2, November 1990.
Furer-Haimendorf, C.V. *A Himalayan Tribe: From Cattle to Cash.* Berkeley: University of California Press, 1980 .
_____ . *Highlanders of Arunachal Pradesh: Anthropological Research in North-East India.* London: Garland Fold Ltd. and New Delhi: Vikas Publishing House, 1982.
_____ . *Modern Development and Traditional Ideology among Tribal Societies.* Fourth D.N. Majumdar Lectures. Lucknow: Ethnographic and Folk Culture Society, 1983.
Ganguly, K.K. *Cultural History of Rajasthan.* Delhi: Sundeep Prakashan, 1983.
Gardner, P.M. 'Symmetric Respect and Memorate Knowledge: The Structure and Ecology of Individualistic Culture'. *South Western Journal of Anthropology,* vol. 22, (1966): 389-415.
_____ . 'Ascribed Austerity: A Tribal Path to Purity'. *Man,* vol.17, no. 3. Published by the Royal Anthropological Institute of Great Britain and Ireland, 1982.
Gautam, M.K. 'Santalization of the Santals', in David, K., ed. *The New Wind: Changing Identities in South Asia.* The Hague and Paris: Mouton Publishers, 1977.
Geertz, C. *Local Knowledge: Further Essays in Interpretative Anthropology.* New York: Basic Books, 1983.
Gell, A. 'The Market Wheel: Symbolic Aspects of an Indian Tribal Market.' *Man,* vol. 17, no. 5, (1982): 470-91.
_____ . 'Newcomers to the World of Goods: Consumption among the Muria Gonds', in Appadurai, A., ed., *The Social Life of Things.* Cambridge: Cambridge University Press, 1986.
Gellner, E. *Nations and Nationalism.* Oxford: Blackwell, 1983.
_____ . *The Concept of Kinship and Other Essays on Anthropological Method and Explanation.* Oxford: Blackwell, 1987.
Ghurye, G.S. *The Scheduled Tribes of India.* Second Edition. Bombay: Popular Book Depot., 1959.
Gledhill, J. *Power and Its Disguises: Anthropological Perspectives on Politics.* London: Pluto Press, 1994.
Goddard, V. 'Honour and Shame: the Control of Women's Sexuality and Group Identity in Naples', in Caplan, P., ed. *Cultural Constructions of Sexuality.* London: Routledge, 1987.

Godelier, M. 'Anthropology and Biology: Towards a New Form of Co-Operation'. *International Social Science Journal,* vol. XXVI, no. 4, (1974): 611-35.
_____. *Perspectives in Marxist Anthropology.* Cambridge Studies in Social Anthropology. Cambridge: Cambridge University Press, 1977.
_____. *The Making of Great Men: Male Domination and Power among the New Guinea Baruya.* Cambridge and Paris: Cambridge University Press and Editions de la Maison des Sciences de L'homme, 1986.
Gold, A.G. *Fruitful Journeys: The Ways of Rajasthani Pilgrims.* Delhi: Oxford University Press, 1989.
Goody, J. *Production and Reproduction: A Comparative Study of the Domestic Domain.* Cambridge University Press, 1976.
_____. *The Oriental, the Ancient and the Primitive: Systems of Marriage and the Family in Pre-Industrial Societies of Eurasia.* Cambridge: Cambridge University Press, 1990.
Goody, J., and Goody, E. 'Marriage and the Family in Gujarat', in Goody, J., ed. *The Oriental, the Ancient and the Primitive: Systems of Marriage and the Family in Pre-Industrial Societies in Eurasia.* Cambridge: Cambridge University Press, 1990.
Goody, J., and Tambiah, S.J. *Bride-Wealth and Dowry.* Cambridge: Cambridge University Press, 1973.
(Government of India Publication) *The Adivasis.* The Publications Division, Ministry of Information and Broadcasting, GOI, 1955.
Government Reports. *1889-1890: Summary of the Events of the Administration of the Sirohi State, Western Rajputana. For the Biennial Year Sumvat 1946-1947.* (By M.C. Dewan of Sadar Office.) Bombay: Education Society Press, 1892.
_____. *Report on the Administration of the Sirohi State.* Bombay: Education Society Press, 1900-1901.
_____. *Summary of Events of the Administration of the Sirohi State.* Bombay: Education Society Press, 1902,1903,1904-05.
_____. *The Imperial Gazetteer of India,* vol XV, *Karachi to Kottayam..* New edition: Oxford: Clarendon Press, 1908.
_____. *The Imperial Gazetteer of India,* Provincial Series, *Rajputana.* (Compiled by Major K.D. Erskine.) Calcutta/Oxford: Government Printing Press, 1908.
_____. *The Palanpur Agency Directory,* vol. I. (Compiled by F.S. Master.) Ahmedabad: Praja Bandhu Printing Works, 1908.
_____. *The Imperial Gazetteer of India,* Provincial Series, vol.I, *Bombay.* Calcutta: Government Printing Press, 1909.
_____. *Mahikantha Agency Directory.* (Compiled by F.S. Master.) Rajkot: Liberal Laxmi Printing Press, 1922.
_____. *Report on the Administration of the Sirohi State.* Jaipur: Government Printing Press, 1943-44.
_____. *Rajasthan District Gazetteers: Sirohi.* (By B.N. Doundhiyal.) Jaipur: Govt. Central Press, 1967.
_____. *Census of India 1981.* Series 18 *Rajasthan.* Part IX. *Special Tables for Scheduled Tribes.* Delhi: Controller of Publications, 1983.
_____. *Census of India 1981.* Series 18 *Rajasthan. District Census Handbook-Sirohi.* Parts XIII A and B. Ajmer: Fine Art Printing Press, 1983.

Other Reports

Report on Sati, *The Illustrated Weekly of India,* 4 October, 1987.
Report on the Anti-Reservation Protests and the Mandal Commission, *India Today,* 15 September, 1990.
Report on the Project of the Anthropological Survey of India, *Times of India,* September-October, 1990.

Grierson, G.A. *Linguistic Survey of India,* vol. IX, part III, *Bhil Dialects and Khandeshi*: 5-7, 26-9. Calcutta: Supdt. Government Printing, 1907.
_____ . *Linguistic Survey of India,* vol. IX, part II, *Rajasthani and Gujarati.* Calcutta: Supdt. Government Printing, 1908.
Guha, R. 'On some aspects of the Historiography of Colonial India', in *Subaltern Studies,* vol.I: *Writings on South Asian History and Society.* Delhi: Oxford University Press, 1982.
_____ . *Elementary Aspects of Peasant Insurgency in Colonial India.* Delhi: Oxford University Press, 1983.
Guha, R., ed. *Subaltern Studies,* vol.I. Delhi: Oxford University Press, 1982.
_____ . *Subaltern Studies,* vol. IV. Delhi: Oxford University Press, 1985.
_____ . *Subaltern Studies,* vol. VI. Delhi: Oxford University Press, 1987.
Gupta, C.S. *Village Survey Monograph 'Goriya'.* Census of India 1961: XIV, Rajasthan, Part VI-C. Delhi: Manager of Publications, 1966.
Gupta, G.R. *Marriage, Religion and Society: Pattern of Change in an Indian Village.* Delhi: Vikas Publishing House, 1974.
Hall, S. 'The Question of Cultural Identity', in Hall, S., Held, D., and McGrew, T., eds, *Modernity and Its Futures.* Oxford: Polity, in assoc.with the Open University, 1992.
Hardiman, D. *The Coming of the Devi: Adivasi Assertion in Western India.* Delhi: Oxford University Press, 1987.
Harper, E.B. 'Fear and the Status of Women'. *South Western Journal of Anthropology,* vol. 25 (1969): 81-95.
Harper, E.B., ed. *Religion in South Asia.* Seattle: University of Washington Press, 1964.
Harris, O., and Young, K. 'Engendered Structures: Some Problems in the Analysis of Reproduction', in Kahn, J., and Llobera, J., eds. *The Anthropology of Pre-Capitalist Societies.* London: Macmillan, 1981.
Haynes, E.S. 'Alwar: Bureaucracy versus Traditional Rulership: Raja, Jagirdars and New Administrators 1892-1910', in Jeffrey, R., ed. *People, Princes and Paramount Power.* Delhi: Oxford University Press, 1978.
_____ . 'Lineage-based Resource Management on the North Indian Arid Zone Frontier 1860-1980'. Paper given at Forests, Habitats and Resources: A Conference in World Environmental History. N. Carolina: Duke University, 1987.
Hershman, P. 'Virgin and Mother', in Lewis, I.M., ed. *Symbols and Sentiments.* London and New York: Academic Press, 1977.
Hirschon, R., ed. *Women and Property - Women as Property.* London: Croom Helm, and New York: St. Martin's Press, 1984.
Hocart, A.M. *Caste: A Comparative Study.* London: Methuen and Co, 1950.
Hockings, P., ed. *Dimensions of Social Life. Essays in Honour of David G. Mandelbaum.* Berlin: Mouton de Gruyer, 1987.
Hodson, T.C. *Indian Census Ethnography 1901-1931.* New Delhi: Govt. of India Press, 1937.
Humphrey, C.H. 'Taboo and Supression of Attention', in *Defining Females: The Nature of Women in Society,* Ardener, S., ed.. London: Croom Helm, 1978.
_____ . *Karl Marx Collective: Economy, Society and Religion in a Siberian Collective Farm.* Cambridge: Cambridge University Press, 1983.
_____ . Barbara Ward Lecture, Oxford. Unpublished, 1985.
_____ . 'Some Aspects of the Jain Prayer: The Idea of "God" and the Symbolism of Offerings'. *Cambridge Anthropology,* vol. 9, no. 3, 1-9. Cambridge: Department of Anthropology, 1985.
Hutton, J.H. *Caste in India: Its Nature, Functions, Origins.* Cambridge: Cambridge University Press, 1946.

Inden, R.B. 'Orientalist Constructions of India'. *Modern Asian Studies,* vol. 20, no. 3, 401-46. Cambridge: Cambridge University Press, 1986.
Inden, R.B., and Nicholas, R.W. *Kinship in Bengali Culture.* Chicago and London: The University of Chicago Press, 1977.
Indian Anthropological Society Publication *Tribal Women in India.* Calcutta: Indian Anthropological Society, 1978.
Jacobs, S. *Women in Perspective: A Guide for Cross-Cultural Studies.* London: University of Illinois Press, 1974.
Jacobson, D. 'The Chaste Wife: Cultural Norm and Indian Experience', in Vatuk, S., ed. *American Studies in the Anthropology of India.* New Delhi: Manohar and American Institute of Indian Studies, 1978.
Jacobson, D., and Wadley, S. *Women in India: Two Perspectives.* Columbia: South Asia Books, 1977.
Jaini, P.S. *The Jaina Path of Purification.* London: University of California Press, 1979.
Jeffrey, P. *Frogs in a Well: Indian Women in Purdah.* London: Second Press, 1979.
Jeffrey, R., ed. *People, Princes and Paramount Power. Society and Politics in the Indian Princely States.* Delhi: Oxford University Press, 1978.
Jodha, N.S. 'Drought and Scarcity in the Rajasthan Desert'. *EPW,* vol. IV, no.16, April 1969.
_____. 'Famine and Famine Policies: Some Empirical Policies, Some Empirical Evidence'. *EPW,* vol. X, no.41, Review of Agriculture, October, 1975.
_____. 'Effectiveness of Farmer's Adjustment to Risk'. *EPW,* vol. XIII, Review of Agriculture, June 1978.
Kakar, S. *Shamans, Mystics and Doctors: A Psychological Inquiry into India and its Healing Traditions.* Boston: Beacon Press, 1982.
_____. *Inner World: A Psychoanalytic Study of Childhood and Society in India.* Second Edition. Delhi: Oxford University Press, 1986.
Kandiyoti, D. *Women, Islam and the State.* Basingstoke: Macmillan, 1991.
Kapadia, K.M. *Marriage and Family in India.* Third Edition. Oxford: Oxford University Press, 1966.
Karve, I. *Hindu Society - An Interpretation.* Second Edition. Poona: Deshmukh Prakashan, 1968.
_____. *Kinship Organisation in India.* Third Edition. Bombay, London, New York: Asia Publishing House, 1968.
Keesing, R.M. *Cultural Anthropology, A Contemporary Perspective.* Second Edition. Japan: CBS, 1981.
_____. 'Ta'ageni: Women's Perspectives on Kwaio Society', in Strathern, M., ed., *Dealing with Inequality: Analysing Gender Relations in Melanesia and Beyond.* Cambridge: Cambridge University Press, 1987.
Khare, R.S. 'Hierarchy and Hypergamy: Some Interrelated Aspects among the Kanya-Kubja Brahmans'. *American Anthropology,* 74, 1972.
_____. *Culture and Reality: Essays on the Hindu System of Managing Foods.* Simla: Institute for Advanced Studies, 1976.
_____. *The Hindu Hearth and Home.* New Delhi: Vikas Publishing House, 1976.
_____. *Normative Culture and Kinship: Essays on Hindu Categories, Processes and Perspectives.* New Delhi: Vikas Publishing House, 1983.
Kishwar, M. 'Toiling Without Rights: Ho Women of Singhbhum'. *Economic and Political Weekly,* vol. XXII, no. 3, 1987.
Kishwar, M., and Vanita, R., ed. *In Search of Answers: Women's Voices.* London: Zed, 1984.
Kolenda, P. *Caste in Contemporary India: Beyond Organic Solidarity.* Menlo Park, California: The Benjamin/ Cummings Publishing Co., Inc., 1978.

———. *Regional Differences in Family Structures in India.* Jaipur: Rawat Publications, 1987.

Koppers, W. *Die Bhil in Zentral-Indien.* Horn-Wien: Verlag Ferdinand Berger, 1948.

Kosambi, D.D. *An Introduction to the Study of Indian History.* Bombay: Popular Prakashan, 1956.

Kothari, K. 'The Shrine: An Expression of Social Needs', in, Elliott, J., and Elliott, D., eds., *Gods of the Byways: Wayside Shrines of Rajasthan, Madhya Pradesh and Gujarat.* Oxford: Museum of Modern Art, 1982.

Kothari, R. *Caste in Indian Politics.* New York: Orient Longman and New York: Gordon and Breach, 1970.

Kuper, A. *Anthropology and Anthropologists: The Modern British School.* London, Boston and Melbourne: Routledge and Kegan Paul, 1983.

Lal, R.B. *Sons of the Aravallis: The Garasia.* Ahmedabad: Gujarat Vidyapith Tribal Research and Training Institute, 1979.

Lala, S.R. *History of the Sirohi Raj - From the Earliest Times to the Present Day.* Allahabad: Allahabad Prioneer Press, 1920.

Lambert, H. 'Healing the Body: Dimensions of Ethno-Medicine in Rural Rajasthan'. Paper for the meeting of the UK South-Asian Anthropology Group, Sept. 1990.

Leach, E.R. *Political Systems of Highland Burma.* London: The Athlone Press, 1964.

———. 'Caste, Class and Slavery: The Taxonomic Problem', in DeRevck, A., and Knight, J., ed., *Caste and Race: Comparative Approaches.* London: J.A. Churchill , 1967.

———. *Pul Eliya: A Village in Ceylon. A Study of Land Tenure and Kinship.* Cambridge: Cambridge University Press, 1968.

———. *Rethinking Anthropology.* Second Edition. London School of Economics Monographs on Social Anthropology, no. 22. London: The Athlone Press, 1971.

Lee-Warner, W. *The Protected Princes of India.* London and New York: Macmillan and Co., 1894.

Levi-Strauss, C. *The Savage Mind.* London: Weidenfeld and Nicholson, 1966.

———. *The Elementary Structures of Kinship.* Boston: Beacon Press, 1969.

Lewis, I.M., ed. *Symbols and Sentiments.* London and New York: Academic Press, 1977.

———. *Ecstatic Religion: An Anthropological Study of Spirit Possession and Shamanism.* Harmondsworth: Penguin, 1978.

Liddle, J., and Joshi, R. *Daughters of Independence: Gender, Caste and Class in India.* London: Zed Press, 1986.

Lyall, A.C. *Asiatic Studies: Religous and Social.* First Series. London: John Murray, 1907.

MacCormack, C., and Strathern, M., eds. *Nature, Culture and Gender.* Cambridge: Cambridge University Press, 1980.

Madan, T.N. *Family and Kinship: A Study of the Pandits of Rural Kashmir.* London: Asia Publishing House, 1965.

———. 'The Hindu Woman at Home', in Nanda, B.R., ed., *Indian Women from Purdah to Modernity.* New Delhi: Vikas Publishing House, 1976.

———. 'Anthropology as the Mutual Interpretation of Cultures: Indian Perspective', in Fahim, H., ed., *Indigenous Anthropology of Non-Western Countries.* Durham, NC: Carolina Academic Press, 1982.

Madan, T.N., and Sarana, G., eds. *Indian Anthropology: Essays in Memory of D.N. Majumdar.* London: Asia Publishing House, 1962.

Majumdar, D.N. *A Tribe in Transition: A Study in Culture Pattern.* Calcutta: Longmans, 1937.

———. *Races and Cultures of India.* London: Asia Publishing House, 1961.

Malcolm, J. *Memoirs of Central India, Including Malwa and Adjoining Provinces,* vol.I., 1823. Irish University Press, Shannon, Ireland, 1972.

Mandelbaum, D.G. *Society in India*. Berkeley: University of California Press, 1970.
_____ . 'The Todas in Time Perspective'. *Reviews in Anthropology*, vol. 7, no. 3, 1980.
Mani, L. 'Production of an Official Discourse on Sati in Early Nineteenth Century Bengal'. *Economic and Political Weekly*, vol. XXI, no. 17, 1986.
Marriot, M. 'Hindu Transactions: Diversity without Dualism', in Kapferer, B., ed., *Transactions and Meaning: Directions in the Anthropology of Exchange and Symbolic Behaviour*. Philadelphia: Institute for the Study of Human Issues, 1976.
_____ . and Inden, R.B. 'Social Stratification: Caste', in *Encylopaedia Britannica*, Fifteenth Edition. vol. 27: 348-56. Chicago: The University of Chicago Press, 1985.
Marx, K. *Pre-Capitalist Economic Formations*. Hobsbawm, E.J., ed. London: Lawrence and Wishart, 1964.
Mathur, K.S., and Agrawal, B.C., eds. *Tribe, Caste and Peasantry*. Lucknow: Ethnographic and Folk Culture Society, 1974.
Mathur, U.B. *Ethnographic Atlas of Rajasthan (with reference to Scheduled Castes and Scheduled Tribes)*. Census of India 1961, vol. XIV. *Rajasthan*. Delhi: Manager of Publications, Govt of India, 1969.
_____ . *Folkways in Rajasthan*. Jaipur: The Folklorists, 1986.
Matthiasson, C.J., ed. *Many Sisters: Women in Cross-Cultural Perspective*. London: The Free Press and Collier Macmillan Publishers, 1974.
Mayer, A.C. *Caste and Kinship in Central India - A Village and Its Region*. Berkeley: University of California Press, 1966.
Mazumdar, V. *Symbols of Power: Studies on the Political Status of Women in India*. Bombay: Allied Publishers, 1979.
McGilvray, D.B., ed. *Caste Ideology and Interaction*. Cambridge Papers in Social Anthropology, no. 9. Cambridge: Cambridge University Press, 1982.
Meharda, B.L. *History and Culture of the Girasias*. Jaipur: Adi Prakashan, 1985.
Mehta, B.S. *Garasias. Tribes of India*. New Delhi: Bhartiya Adimjati Sewak Sangh, 1950.
Mehta, R. 'From Purdah to Modernity', in Nanda, B.R., ed. *Indian Women: From Purdah to Modernity*. New Delhi: Vikas Publishing House, 1976.
Meillasoux, C. *Maidens, Meal and Money: Capitalism and the Domestic Community*. London, Cambridge, New York: Cambridge University Press, 1981.
Minturn, L., and Hitchcock, J.T. 'The Rajputs of Khalapur, India', in Whiting, B.B., ed., *Six Cultures: Studies of Child Rearing*, 1963.
Mohanty, C. 'Under Western Eyes: Feminist Scholarship and Colonial Discourses'. *Feminist Review*, vol. 30: 61-88. Cambridge: Cambridge University Press, 1988.
Moore, H. *Space, Text and Gender*. Cambridge: Cambridge University Press, 1985.
_____ . *Feminism and Anthropology*. London: Polity Press, 1988.
_____ . 'When is a Famine not a Famine?' *Anthropology Today*, 1990.
_____ . *A Passion for Difference: Essays in Anthropology and Gender*. Oxford: Polity Press, 1994.
Naik, T.B. *The Bhils: A Study*. Delhi: Bhartiya Adimjati Sevak Sangh, 1956.
Nanda, B.R. *Indian Women, From Purdah to Modernity*. New Delhi: Vikas Publishing House, 1976.
Nandy, A. *The Intimate Enemy: Loss and Recovery of Self under Colonialism*. Delhi: Oxford University Press, 1983.
Nath, Y.V.S. 'Bhils of Ratanmal: Lineage and Local Community'. *The Economic Weekly*, VI, 49, (1954): 1355-60.
Navalkha, S.K. 'The Authority Structure among the Bhumij and Bhil: A Study of Historical Connections'. *The Eastern Anthropologist*, vol. 13, no. 1: 27-40. Lucknow: Ethnographic and Folk Culture Society, 1959.

Needham, R., ed. *Rethinking Kinship and Marriage*. London: Tavistock, 1971.
O'Flaherty, W.D. *Women, Androgynes and Other Mythical Beasts*. Chicago and London: The University of Chicago Press, 1980.
O'Hanlon, R. 'Recovering the subject: Subaltern studies and Histories of Resistance in Colonial South Asia'. *Modern Asian Studies,* vol. 22, no. 1: 189-224. Cambridge: Cambridge University Press, 1988.
Okely, J. *The Traveller-Gypsies*. Cambridge: Cambridge University Press, 1983.
Omvedt, G. *We will Smash this Prison! Indian Women in Struggle*. London: Zed Press, 1980.
Orans, M. *The Santal: A Tribe in Search of a Great Tradition*. Wayne State University Press, 1965.
Ortner, S. 'Is Female to Male as Nature is to Culture?', in Rosaldo, M., and Lamphere, L., ed., *Women, Culture and Society*. Stanford: Stanford University Press, 1974.
_____ . 'Theory in Anthropology since the Sixties'. *Compararative Studies in Sociology and History* , vol. 26, no. 1: 126-66 (1984).
Ortner, S.B., and Whitehead, H. *Sexual Meanings: The Cultural Construction of Gender and Sexuality*. Cambridge: Cambridge University Press, 1981.
Ostor, A., Fruzzetti, L., and Barnett, S., ed. *Concepts of Person: Kinship, Caste and Marriage in India*. Cambridge, Mass.: Harvard University Press, 1981.
Padel, F. 'Anthropologists of Tribal India: Merchants of Knowledge?' Paper presented at the South Asian Social Anthropologists meeting on Orientalism and the History of Anthropology of South Asia, 1988.
Pallat, R. *Rajasthan Ki Vanvihari Janjatiyan*. Udaipur: Hiran Magri, 1987.
Pande, R. *People's Movement in Rajasthan. Selection from Originals*. Vol. 1. Jaipur: Shodhak, 1984.
Papanek, H., and Minault, G., ed. *Separate Worlds: Studies of Purdah in South Asia*. Delhi: Chanakya Publications, 1982.
Parry, J.P. 'Egalitarian Values in a Hierarchical Society'. *South Asian Review,* vol. 7, no. 2, January, 1974.
_____ . *Caste and Kinship in Kangra*. London: Routledge and Kegan Paul, 1979.
_____ . On the Moral Perils of Exchange', in Parry, J. and Bloch, M., ed. *Money and the Morality of Exchange*. Cambridge: Cambridge University Press, 1989.
Pathy, J. *Tribal Peasantry Dynamics of Development*. New Delhi: Inter-India Publications, 1984.
Pathy, J., Paul, S., Bhaskar, M., and Panda, J. 'Tribal Studies in India: An Appraisal'. *The Eastern Anthropologist,* vol. 29, no. 4: 399-417 (1976).
Plunkett, F.T. 'Royal Marriages in Rajasthan'. *Indian Sociology,* n.s., no. VII, 1973.
Prakash, G. 'Reproducing Inequality: Spirit Cults and Labour Relations in Colonial Eastern India'. *Modern Asian Studies,* vol. 20: 209-320 (1986).
Quigley, D. 'Is Caste a Pure Figment, the Invention of Orientalists for their own Glorification?' *Cambridge Anthropology,* vol. 13, no. 1: 20-37 (1988).
_____ . 'Kings and Priests: Hocart's Theory of Caste'. *Pacific Viewpoint,* New Zealand, 1988.
_____ . *The Interpretation of Caste*. Oxford: Clarendon Press, 1993.
Raheja, G.G. *Ritual, Prestation and the Dominant Caste in a North Indian Village*. Chicago: The University of Chicago Press, 1988.
Raheja, G.G., and Gold, A.G. *Listen to the Heron's Words: Reimagining Gender and Kinship in North India*. Berkeley: University of California Press, 1994.
Ram, K.' Mukkuvar Women: The Sexual Contradictions of Capitalist Development in a South Indian Fishing Community.' Ph.D. thesis, Australian National University, Canberra, 1988.

Ram, P. *Agrarian Movement in Rajasthan, 1913-1947 A.D.* Jaipur, India: Panchsheel Prakashan, 1986.
Rao, M.S.A. 'Rewari Kingdom and the Mughal Empire', in Fox, R.G., ed. *Realm and Region in Traditional India.* New Delhi: Vikas Publishing House, 1977.
Ray, R. 'Mewar: The Breakdown of the Princely Order', in Jeffrey, R., ed. *People, Princes and Paramount Power: Society and Politics in the Indian Princely States.* Delhi: Oxford University Press, 1978.
Redfield, R. *Peasant Society and Culture: An Anthropological Approach to Civilization.* Chicago: Chicago University Press, 1956.
Reynell, J. 'Honour, Nurture and Festivity: Aspects of Female Religiosity amongst Jain Women in Jaipur.' Unpublished Ph.D. Thesis, University of Cambridge, 1985.
Rosaldo, M., and Lamphere, L. *Women, Culture and Society.* Stanford: Stanford University Press, 1974.
Rosin, T.R. *Land Reform and Agrarian Change: Study of a Marwar Village from Raj to Swaraj.* Jaipur: Rawat Publication, 1987.
_____. 'Quarry and Field: Sources of Continuity and Change in a Rajasthani Village', in Hockings, P., ed. *Dimensions of Social Life: Essays in the Honour of David G. Mandelbaum.* Berlin: Mouton de Gruyter, 1987.
Roy-Burman, B.K. 'Dynamics of Persistence of Tribal Community in India'. *The Eastern Anthropologist,* vol. 31, no. 1, (1978): 93-99.
_____. 'Tribal India: New Frontiers in the Study of Population and Society'. *Indian Anthropologist,* vol. 8, no. 2 , (1978): 73-88.
_____. 'The Post Primitives of Chhota Nagpur'. *Trends in Ethnic Group Relations in Asia and Oceania.* Paris: UNESCO, 1979.
_____. 'Transformation of Tribes and Analogous Social Formations'. *Economic and Political Weekly,* vol. XVIII, no. 27, (1983): 1172-74.
Rudolph, S.H., and Rudolph, L.I. *Essays on Rajputana: Reflections on History, Culture and Administration.* New Delhi: Concept Publishing Company, 1984.
Russell, R.V., and Hiralal, R.B. *The Tribes and Castes of the Central Provinces of India.* vol. IV. London: Macmillan and Co., 1916.
Sacks, K. 'Engels Revisited: Women, the Organisation of Production and Private Property', in Rosaldo, M., and Lamphere, L., ed. *Women, Culture and Society.* Stanford: Stanford University Press, 1974.
_____. *Sisters and Wives: the Past and Future of Sexual Equality.* Westport, Connecticut: Greenwood Press, 1979.
Saha, S. 'The Territorial Dimension of India's Tribal Problem', in Sheppardson, M. and Simmons, C., eds. *The Indian National Congress and the Political Economy of India, 1885-1985.* Aldershot and Brookfield: Avebury, 1988.
Sahlins, M.D. 'The Segmentary Lineage: An Organisation of Predatory Expansion.' *American Anthropologist,* vol. LXIII, (1961): 322-45.
_____. 'Culture and Environment, The Study of Cultural Ecology', in *Horizons of Anthropology,* Sol Tax, ed.:132-48. Chicago: Aldine Publishing Company, 1964.
_____. *Tribesmen.* Englewood Cliffs: Prentice Hall, 1968.
_____. *Stone Age Economics.* London: Tavistock, 1974.
_____. *Culture and Practical Reason.* Chicago and London: The University of Chicago Press, 1976.
_____. *Islands of History.* London and New York: Tavistock, 1985.
_____. 'Economic Anthropology and Anthropological Economics'. *Social Science Information,* vol. 8, no. 5, (1990): 13-33.
Said, E.W. *Orientalism.* London: Penguin Books, 1987.

Sakala, C. *Women of South Asia: A Guide to Resources*. New York: Kraus International Publications, 1980.
Sanday, P. *Female Power and Male Dominance on the Origins of Sexual Inequality*. Cambridge: Cambridge University Press, 1981.
Sarkar, T. 'Jitu Santal's Movements in Malda, 1924-1932; A Study in Tribal Protest', in Guha, R., ed. *Subaltern Studies*, Vol. IV. Writings in South Asian History and Society. Oxford: Oxford University Press, 1985.
_____ . 'The Woman as Communal Subject: Rashtrasevika Samiti and Ram Janmabhoomi Movement'. *EPW*, vol. XXXII, 31August 1991.
_____ . *Khaki Shorts, Saffron Flags: A Critique of the Hindu Right*. Delhi: Orient Longman, 1993.
Schneider, D. *A Critique of the Study of Kinship*. Ann Arbor: University of Michigan Press, 1984.
Scott, J.C. *Weapons of the Weak: Everyday Forms of Peasant Resistance*. New Haven: Yale University Press, 1985.
Searle-Chatterjee, M., and Sharma, U., eds. *Contextualising Caste: Post Dumontian Approaches*. Sociological Review Monograph Series. Oxford: Blackwell, 1994.
Selwyn, T. 'The Order of Men and the Order of Things: an Examination of Food Transactions in an Indian Village'. *International Journal of the Sociology of Law*, vol. 8, London: Academic Press, (1980): 297-317.
Sen, A. *Poverty and Famine*. Oxford: Oxford University Press, 1981.
Seymour-Smith, C. *Macmillan Dictionary of Anthropology*. London: Macmillan, 1986.
Shah, A.M. *The Household Dimension of the Family in India*, 1974.
_____ . 'Division and Hierarchy: An Overview of Caste in Gujarat'. *Contributions to Indian Sociology,* vol. 16, (1982): 1-33.
Shah, G. 'Tribal Identity and Class Differentiation: a Case Study of the Chaudhari Tribe'. *Economic and Political Weekly,* Annual Number, February 1979.
Shah, V. *Gujarat ke Adivasi*. Ahmedabad: Gujarat Vidyapeeth, 1968.
Sharma, G.D. *Rajput Polity - a Study of Politics and Administration of the State of Marwar 1638-1749*. New Delhi: Manohar Book Service, 1977.
Sharma, G.N. *Social Life in Medieval Rajasthan (1500-1800 A.D), with Special Reference to the Impact of Mughal Influence*. Agra: Lakshmi Narain Agarwal, 1968.
_____ . *Rajasthan Studies*. Agra: Lakshmi Narain Agarwal, 1970.
Sharma, U. 'The Problem of Village Hinduism'. *Contributions to Indian Sociology,* vol. 4, (1970): 1-21.
_____ . 'Women and their Affines: the Veil as a Symbol of Separation'. *Man,* n.s., vol. 13. London: The Royal Anthropological Institute of Great Britain and Ireland, (1978): 218-33.
_____ . *Women, Work and Property in North West India*. London and New York: Tavistock, 1980.
_____ . 'Dowry in North India', in Hirschon, R., ed. *Women and Property - Women as Property*. London: Croom Helm, 1984.
Sherring, M.A. *Hindu Tribes and Castes as Represented in Benares*. Calcutta, 1872.
_____ . *The Tribes and Castes of Rajasthan*. Offprint from *Hindu Tribes and Castes,* vol. III, first published in London in l88l, reprint. Delhi: Cosmo Publications, 1987.
Singer, M., ed. *Traditional India: Structure and Change*. Philadelphia: American Folklore Society, 1959.
Singh, B. 'The Bhil are not a Single Tribal Whole'. *Man in India,* vol. 61, no. 1, (1981): 89-96.
Singh, C. *Common Property and Common Poverty: India's Forests, Forest Dwellers and the Law*. Delhi: Oxford University Press, 1986.

Singh, K.S. *Tribal Society in India: An Anthropo-Historical Perspective*. New Delhi: Manohar Publications, 1985.
Singh, K.S., ed. *Economies of the Tribe and their Transformation*. New Delhi: Concept Publishing Company, 1982.
_____ . *Tribal Movements in India*. vol. 2. New Delhi: Manohar Publications, 1983.
Singh, R. 'The Role of the Bhagat Movement in the inception of Caste features in the Bhil Tribe'. *The Eastern Anthropologist*, vol. 23, no. 2, (1970): 161-70.
_____ . 'Labels and Identity in South Rajasthan'. *The Eastern Anthropologist*, vol. XXVII, no. 4, (1974): 325-35.
_____ . 'Gauri Rituals of the Bhils'. *Folklore* (Calcutta), vol. 17, no. 1, (1975): 13-16.
Singhi, N.K. 'A Study of the Jains in a Rajasthan Town', in Humphrey, C., and Carrithers, M., ed. *The Assembly of Listeners: Jainism in Society*. Cambridge: Cambridge University Press, 1990.
Sinha, S. 'State Formation and Rajput Myth in Tribal Central India'. *Man in India*, vol. 42, (1962): 1.
Srinivas, M.N. *Social Change in Modern India*. Bombay: Orient Longman, 1972.
_____ . The Changing Position of Women in India. *Man*, vol. 12, no. 2, (1977): 221-38.
Srinivas, M.N., ed. *India's Villages*. Bombay: Asia Publishing House, 1955.
Standing, H. *Dependence and Autonomy: Women's Employment and the Family in Calcutta*. London: Routledge, 1991.
Stern, H. 'Power in Traditional India: Territory, Caste and Kinship in Rajasthan', in Fox, R.G., ed. *Realm and Region in Traditional India*. New Delhi: Vikas Publishing House, 1977.
Stokes, E. *The Peasant and the Raj. Studies in Agrarian Society and Peasant Rebellion in Colonial India*. Cambridge: Cambridge University Press, 1978.
Strathern, M. 'Self-Interest and the Social Good: Some Implications of Hagen Gender Imagery', in Ortner, S., and Whitehead, H., eds. *Sexual Meanings*. Cambridge: Cambridge University Press, 1981.
_____ . 'Subject or Object? Women and the Circulation of Valuables in Highlands New Guinea', in Hirschon, R., ed. *Women and Property - Women as Property*. London: Croom Helm and NewYork: St. Martin's Press, 1984.
_____ . 'An Awkward Relationship: the Case of Feminism and Anthropology'. *Signs*, vol. 12, 1987.
Stutchbury, E. 'Blood, Fire and Mediation: Human Sacrifice and Widow Burning in Nineteenth Century India', in Allen, M., and Mukherjee, S.N., ed. *Women in India and Nepal*. Canberra: Australian National University Printing, 1982.
Tambiah, S.J. 'From Varna to Caste through Mixed Unions', in Goody, J. ed. *The Character of Kinship*. Cambridge, London, New York: Cambridge University Press.
_____ . 'Bridewealth and Dowry Revisited: the Position of Women in Sub-Saharan Africa and North India'. *Current Anthropology*, vol. 30, no. 4, Aug-Oct., Wrenner Gren Foundation for Anthropological Research, 1989.
Tapper, R., 'Ethnic Identities and Social Categories in Iran and Afganistan', in Tonkin, E., MacDonald, M., and Chapman, M., ed. *History and Ethnicity*. London: Routledge, 1989.
Thapar, R., *A History of India, Volume I. From the discovery of India to 1526*. London: Penguin Books, 1986.
Tod, J., *Annals and Antiquities of Rajasthan, or the Central and Western Rajput States of India*. edited by William Crooke. Oxford: Oxford University Press. (First published 1832), 1920.
Trautman, T. *Dravidian Kinship*. Cambridge: Cambridge University Press, 1981.

Unnithan, M. 'Caste, Tribe and Gender in South Rajasthan'. *Cambridge Anthropology*, vol. 15, no. 1 (1991): 27-45.

_____. 'Constructing Difference: Social Categories and Girahya Women, Kinship and Resources in South Rajasthan.' Ph.D Dissertation, Department of Social Anthropology, University of Cambridge, 1991.

_____. 'The Politics of Marriage Payments in Southern Rajasthan'. *South Asia Research*, vol. 12, no. 1 (1992): 60-73.

_____. 'Girasias and the Politics of Difference in Rajasthan: "Caste", Kinship and Gender in a Marginalised Society', in Searle-Chatterjee, M., and Sharma, U., eds. *Contextualising Caste*.Sociological Review Monograph Series: 92-121. Oxford: Blackwell, 1994.

Unnithan-Kumar, M. 'Gender and 'Tribal' Identity in Western India'. *EPW*, vol. XXVI, no. 17 (1991): 36-9.

_____. 'The State, Rajput Patriarchy and Women's Agency in 19th and 20th Century Rajasthan.' Unpublished paper presented at 'Gendering History' conference, York, 1996.

Unnithan, M., and Srivastava, K. 'Gender Politics, Development and Women's Agency in Rajasthan', in Grillo, R., and Stirrat, R., eds. *The Anthropology of Development* Oxford: Berg, 1997.

Van der Veen, K.W. *I give Thee My Daughter: A Study of Marriage and Hierarchy among the Anavil Brahamins of South Gujarat*. Assen: Van Gocum and Company NV, 1972.

Vanaik, A. *The Painful Transition: Bourgeois Democracy in India*. London: Verso, 1990.

Vidyarthi, L.P. *Rise of Anthropology in India: A Social Science Orientation*. vol. I.: *The Tribal Dimensions*. Delhi: Concept Publishing Company, 1978.

_____. 'Research on Tribal Culture in India', in *Sociology in India: Retrospect and Prospect*, Nayar, P.K.B., ed. Delhi: BR Publishing Corporation, 1986.

Vyas, N.N. *Bondage and Exploitation in Tribal India*. Jaipur and Delhi: Rawat Publications, 1980.

Vyas, N.N., and Mann, R.S., eds. *Indian Tribes in Transition*. Jaipur and Delhi: Rawat Publications, 1980.

Vyas, N.N., Mann, R.S., and Chaudhry, N.D., eds. *Rajasthan Bhils*. Udaipur: MLV Tribal Research and Training Institute, 1978.

Wadley, S.S. 'Brothers, Husbands and Sometimes Sons: Kinsmen in North Indian Ritual'. *The Eastern Anthropologist*, vol. 29, no. 2, (1976): 149-70.

_____. 'Sitala: The Cool One'. *Asian Folklore Studies*, vol. XXXIX, (1980): 33-63.

_____. 'Women and the Hindu Tradition', in Ghadially, R., ed. *Women in Indian Society*. New Delhi and London: Sage Publications, 1988.

Whitehead, A. 'Women and Men: Kinship and Property, Some General Issues', in Hirschon, R., ed. *Women and Property - Women as Property*. Croom Helm, London, and St. Martin's Press, New York, 1984.

Wilberforce-Bell, M. *History of Kathiawad from the Earliest Times*. London: William Heinemann, 1988.

Wolf, M. *A Thrice Told Tale: Feminism, Modernism and Ethnographic Responsibility*. Stanford: Stanford University Press, 1992.

Yalman, N. 'On the Purity of Women in the Castes of Ceylon and Malabar'. *Journal of Royal Anthropological Institute of Great Britain and Ireland*, 1963, pp. 25-58

Young, K., Wolkowitz, C., and McCullagh, R., eds. *Of Marriage and the Market*. London: CSE Books 1981.

Ziegler, N.P. 'Some Notes on Rajput Loyalties during the Mughal Period', in Richards, J.F., ed. *Kingship and Authority in South Asia*. Madison: University of Wisconsin Publication Series, 1978.

INDEX

Abortion, 119
Abu Road Tehsil, 32-36, 57, 66, 87, 213
Adoption, 172, 200, 201
Affinity, south and north Indian, 138
Affinity/Affinal Village, 23, 110-120, 141
Agency, women's, 24, 118, 119, 187, 201, 207, 209
Anop Mandal, 238-264
Appadurai, A., 6n
Apparel (Dress), women's, 20, 21, 23, 24, 73, 74-75, 108, 109, 262, 266

Babb, L., 215, 227, 228, 233
Baden-Powell, B.H., 54, 59, 160n
Barnett, Steve, 10
Bell, D., et. al., 39n
Berreman, G., 5n, 215, 227, 233
Beteille, Andre, 14, 82/83
Bhaiachara, 160
Bhairu, 174, 219-225, 227, 254, 266
Bhakar, 34, 35, 37, 53-58, 66, 86-88, 92, 159, 161, 174, 249
Bhavik, 247-264
Bhil dialect, 41
Bhil Girasia, 83
Bhil lineage, 153
Bhil Marriage, 19, 153-155
Bhil population, 32-34
Bhil status, 19, 87, 88, 144, 153, 264
Bleie, T., 210, 211
Body, male, 63
Bombay, 54
Boserup, E., 191
Boundaries (symbolic), 1, 5, 6, 20, 170, 209, 265, 268
British colonialism, (administration, paramountcy), 45-47, 51, 5263, 81, 82, 85-87, 249
British colonialism (classification), 9, 81, 82, 85, 87, 92, 241

Caplan, P., 20n, 49n
Carstairs, M., 87, 88, 154, 227

Caste substance, 'substantialisation', 9, 10
Census, 16, 17, 47, 82-84
Chamber, R et al., 28, 29
Chandra, B., 71n, 241n
Chhachhi, A., 71n, 72
Class, lower, 12
Class solidarity, 3, 239
Cohen, A., 4, 6
Collective Occasions, 173, 175-182, 252
Collier, J., 20n, 172, 192, 208n
Collier, J and Yanagisako, S., 20n
Common Property, 85, 88
Communal Politics, Communalism, 70-73
Conflict, Dispute, 166, 167, 239, 255-260
Congress Party, movement, 80, 81, 241-243, 249, 251
Consecutive partners, 139
Copland, I, 47n, 50, 52n, 56, 57

Das, Veena, 12, 65, 71, 72, 95
Dave, P.C., 18, 33, 68n, 83
Deities, village, 217, 220
Deliege, R., 85, 87, 88, 153, 154
Descent, 21, 59
Differences, economic, 30, 31, 186, 187, womens', 31, Social, 79
Divorce, Widowhood, 22, 201, 204
Douglas, M., 20n
Dumont, L., 7-9, 11n, 15, 144, 145, 150n, 151n, 152, 169

Education, 41, 249
Equality/Inequality, Egalitarianism, 8, 15, 31, 39, 40, 41, 205
Ethnicity, 5, 12

Fieldwork, 38
Folklore, 142
Food Distribution/transaction, 168-170, 173, 216, 221, 228, 252, 254
Forest Products/Production, 30, 84, 85, 88-90, 167, 183-186
Fox, R., 3, 59-61

Index

Fuller, Chris, 8n, 9n, 15, 47n, 51, 215, 221
Funeral, 175-182
Furer-Haimendorf, 89, 92, 154

Gandhi, M.K., 80, 241, 245-247
Gathering, 30
Gell, A., 187
Gellner, Ernest,
Ghar Jamai, 31, 106, 117, 148, 149, 161, 199, 259, 267
Gift, 43, 109, 147n, 169n, 193, 194, 206, 208
Giras, 54-56
Girasia dialect, 41
Girasia landrights, 53-59
Goddard, V., 20n, 23
Gold, A.G., 221, 227
Goody, J., (and Goody, E.,) 189-194, 199, 202, 206n, 208n
Gossip, Joke, 22
Government, 41, 43, 80, 81, 83
Grierson, G., 41,42
Guha, Ranajit, 12, 67
Gujarat, 19, 32, 33n, 42, 55-57
Gypsies, 23, 264n

Hall, Stuart, 5
Hardiman, 240n, 242, 243, 246
Haynes, E., 85n, 87n
Hierarchy, gender, 193, 207, 210
Hierarchy, occupational, 16
Hierarchy (caste, lineage, family), 6, 7, 14, 32, 40, 49, 79, 145, 150-154, 192, 209, 211, 254, 255
Hinduism, popular, 215, 221, 224, 227-229, 233, 254, 255, 266
Hocart, A.M., 7-9, 15
Hospitality, 41, 169, 188
Household, 100-103, 176
Humphrey, C., 26, 244

Ideological classification, 8
Ideological context, 4
Ideological devaluation, women's, 21, 24, 31, 205
Ideological similarity, 16
Individual, Individualistic, 15
Inside/outside, 5, 6, 22
Irrigation, 157, 161, 162, 166
Isogamy, 138, 150, 151

Jain Community, 66, 224, 238, 242, 243-247, 248, 262
Jati, 8, 95
Jewellery, 23, 24, 74, 76-78, 183, 212-214
Jodha, N.S., 29, 30
Jungali, 87

Khare, R., 227
Khat, 40
Khoont, 177, 179, 231-234
Kinship, lineal, 3-5, 20-21, 31, 60, 62, 94-134, 135, 140, 144-148, 159

Kinship, symbolic, 11, 62, 73, 267
Kinship, physical, 73
Kinship, classificatory, 96
Kinship, territorial, 3, 97, 100
Kinship, social, 110
Kinship solidarity, 60, 61
Kishwar, M., 189, 190n, 210, 211
Kothari, R., 71
Kothari, K., 221, 224

Labour, women's, 20, 21, 31, 42, 112, 113, 171, 184, 185, 196, 197, 205, 207, 210
Lal, R.B., 33, 57, 240n, 242
Landholding Title, 46, 48-50, 51, 55, 161,162, 198, 199
Leach, E., 266, 267
Levi-Strauss, Claude, 15-16
Lineage sanctions, 145, 146
Livelihood, 29
Lower Girasia, 136, 142, 146
Loyalty, 59, 60, 153
Lyall, A.C.,48, 50, 59, 60, 84-85

Madan, T., 14n, 214
Mandelbaum, D., 215
Mani, L., 64
Market, 24, 39, 90, 107, 108, 159, 167-168, 182-188, 212-213
Market, women, 22
Marriage, capture, 122-128
Marriage payment, (brideprice) rates, 197, 212, 267
Marriage payment (brideprice) inflation, 212
Marriage payment (brideprice) negotiation, 202, 203
Marriage Payments, (brideprice/bridewealth/dowry), 21, 32, 172, 189, 194-214
Marriage Rules/ Practices, 120-155, 260
Marriott, McKim, 9
Martial Qualities, 9n, 45, 62, 72
Mata, 218-225, 227, 252
Meherda, B.I., 18, 33, 68n
Mehta, R., 66
Meillasoux, C., 192n
Menstruation, 114
Methodology, 38
Methodology, reflexivity, 38-41
Methodology, questionnaire, 42
Mina, 32, 69
Moneylending, mortagage, 161, 213, 245
Moore, H., 26, 207
Mughal, Muslim, 45, 48, 50, 51, 55, 56, 79, 183, 184n, 245

National identities, politics, 72, 247
National movement, 12

Okely, A., 23, 264n
Oral history, 53, 63, 90, 91

Index

Pandey, G., 71n
Papanek, H., 65, 66
Parry, J., 64, 144, 145, 147, 148, 150-152, 189n, 211, 212, 214
Patel, 179, 256, 257
Pattidari/patta, 50, 55, 57, 156, 160
Plunkett, F.T., 152, 153
Polygyny, 121, 152, 191
Population, 33-36
Poverty, 28-31, 211, 212, 251, 255-256, 265
Prakash, G., 247n
Prestational interaction, 11
Prestige, Honour, 16, 27, 47, 192
Property, women's, 198-200, 206
Protest, General, 12, 13, 240, 241, 246, Flight, 13, 92 Classification, 17
Purdah, *laaj kaadna*, 22,23, 26, 65, 66, 73, 111, 117, 262
Purity/Pollution, 7, 10, 25, 31, 83, 218, 264, 268

Raheja, Gloria, 10n, 11, 169, 181
Railways, 35, 36
Rajput (lineage/clan,/brotherhood), 3, 10, 45, 46, 49, 59, 60, 63-65, 69, 135, 136
Rajput Chauhan, 52, 53n, 58, 59
Rajput Ethic, honour, 46, 63, 64
Rajput Girasia, 33, 150
Rajput identity, 46-48, 69
Rajput landholding 48-59
Rajput lineage cycle, 60
Rajput marriage, 49
Rajput Parmar, 52, 59
Rajput state, 49, 51, 60, 85, 265
Rajput women, 63-67, 70, 73
Rajputisation, 18, 19, 265
Ram, K., 191n, 210, 220
Rasput community, 67
Ray, R, 47n, 49n, 50, 51
Rebari, 35
Reciprocity, 42, 143
Representation/Writing 38, 39, 59
Reproduction, women's biological, 104, 105, 171-173
Restricted exchange, 147, 149
Ritual exclusion, women, 234-236
Ritual experts, 215, 216, 229-233
Roles, Girasia wives, 110-112
Rosaldo, M., 172, 208n
Rudolph, Rudolph, S., 47n, 52-53n

Sacred spaces, 215-220, 223, 231
Sahlins, Marshall, 9n, 61
Said, E., 38n, 264
Sanskritisation, 18, 47
Sarpanch, 234
Sati, 47, 64, 65, 70-73
Scarcity (drought, famine), 29, 30, 37, 88-92, 183, 245, 251
Scheduled Caste, 17, 35, 82, 83
Scheduled Tribe, 17, 28, 34-36, 82, 83, 84n

Searle-Chatterjee and Sharma, U., 7n
Self respect, 28
Sexuality, women's, 21-23, 39, 73n, 206, 209, 210, 267
Shaman *(Bhopa)*, 179, 216, 218, 229-234, 252, 253, 256
Sharedholdings, Collective Labour, 166, 167, 174
Sharma, G.N., 47n, 50n
Sharma, U., 21, 194, 208, 215, 217, 236
Sherring, M., 46n, 48n, 49n, 57, 59
Shifting cultivation, 86, 87
Shifting identities, 5
Shifting land titles, 55-58
Shrine, 65, 217-225
Siblingship, 108, 109
Sickness, 216, 218, 225-227, 231, 249
Singh, S., 240n
Sirohi State, 52, 53
Sociology, 14, 15n, 16
Spirits, Spirit possession, 180n, 217, 221, 225-227, 230, 231, 247n, 253
Srinivas, 18, 47, 236
State policies, 47
Stern, H., 46n, 61, 152
Stokes, Eric, 52, 160n
Strategy, individual, 26
Strategy, lineage, 63
Strathern M., 38n
Structural Change, 7
Subaltern, 12, 13
Sublineage, Girasia, 140-144
Subordination, women's, patriarchy, 24, 25
Subsistence, 20
Symbolic roles, women, 20, 119, 170, 262, 263, 267

Tambiah, S.J., 152, 191, 192, 199, 200n
Tax, land, 54, 55, 58, 85, 86, 89, 240, 241, 249, 251
Thapar, R., 45n, 244, 266
Tod, James, 18, 50, 52n, 53, 54, 55, 59, 87, 88
Training, 40
Transactions, Caste, 11, 183
Tribal Research Institute, 17n, 32
Tribalised, Tribalisation, 4, 17-20, 47, 80, 81

Vanaik, A., 71n
Varna, 8
Varna, Kshyatriya, 9, 45
Varna, Brahmin, 8
Virginity, women's, 206, 210
Voices, women's, 26
Vulnerability, economic, 28
Vyas, V., 68n

Wadley, S., 22, 236, 262
Watershares, Wells, 162, 163
Wedding, 129-134
Work value, women's, 20, 31, 189, 191, 211

Ziegler, P., 46n, 48-50, 51, 63, 84, 266-267